Email Discourse Among Chinese Using English as a Lingua Franca

Yuan-shan Chen · Der-Hwa Victoria Rau
Gerald Rau
Editors

Email Discourse Among Chinese Using English as a Lingua Franca

Springer

Editors
Yuan-shan Chen
Department of Applied English
National Chin-Yi University of Technology
Taichung
Taiwan

Gerald Rau
Chiayi
Taiwan

Der-Hwa Victoria Rau
Institute of Linguistics
National Chung Cheng University
Chiayi
Taiwan

ISBN 978-981-10-0676-0 ISBN 978-981-287-888-5 (eBook)
DOI 10.1007/978-981-287-888-5

Springer Singapore Heidelberg New York Dordrecht London

Softcover re-print of the Hardcover 1st edition 2016

Printed on acid-free paper

Springer Science+Business Media Singapore Pte Ltd. is part of Springer Science+Business Media (www.springer.com)

Acknowledgments

Producing a book is always a team effort. We are grateful for the tremendous support we have received from the many contributors. Their dedication, patience, and understanding during the production of this book have been highly appreciated. We also wish to thank the reviewers for providing their valuable comments, which have immeasurably strengthened the individual chapters, and thus the whole book. Our appreciation also goes to our assistants, Mr. Hsuan-Yu Tai and Ms. Tzu-Wei Hsiang, for their work in helping with the preparation of the manuscript. Special thanks also go to the Ministry of Science and Technology (formerly National Science Council) in Taiwan for their financial support (grant numbers: NSC-101-2628-H-167-001, MOST 103-2410-H-167-009). Finally, we want to express our appreciation to the staff at Springer Publishing for giving us the opportunity to publish this volume and for their support throughout.

Yuan-shan Chen
Der-Hwa Victoria Rau
Gerald Rau

Contents

Contributors

Miao-Hsia Chang Department of English, National Taiwan Normal University, Taipei, Taiwan

Hsuan-Yu Tai Institute of Linguistics, National Chung Cheng University, Chiayi, Taiwan

Xinren Chen Department of English, School of Foreign Studies, Nanjing University, Nanjing, China

Yuan-shan Chen Department of Applied English, National Chin-Yi University of Technology, Taichung, Taiwan

Jean Curran Department of English, National Taiwan Normal University, Taipei, Taiwan

Yihong Gao Research Institute of Linguistics and Applied Linguistics, Peking University, Beijing, China

Tzu-Wei Hsiang Institute of Linguistics, National Chung Cheng University, Chiayi, Taiwan

Chih-Chun Hsu Center for Teaching and Learning Development, National Taiwan Normal University, Taipei, Taiwan

Yueh-Kuei Hsu Department of English, National Taiwan Normal University, Taipei, Taiwan

Hsin-chou Huang Institute of Applied English, National Taiwan Ocean University, Keelung, Taiwan

Li-Jung Huang Department of English Language, Literature and Linguistics, Providence University, Taichung, Taiwan

Wan-jing Li Institute of Linguistics, National Chung Cheng University, Chiayi, Taiwan

Jianda Liu National Key Research Center for Linguistics and Applied Linguistics, Guangdong University of Foreign Studies, Guangzhou, China

Pi-Hsia Lü Department of English Language, Literature and Linguistics, Providence University, Taichung, Taiwan

Der-Hwa Victoria Rau Institute of Linguistics, National Chung Cheng University, Chiayi, Taiwan

Gerald Rau Chiayi, Taiwan

Wei Ren National Key Research Center for Linguistics and Applied Linguistics, Guangdong University of Foreign Studies, Guangzhou, China

Lin Xiao Research Institute of Linguistics and Applied Linguistics, Peking University, Beijing, China

Chapter 1
Introduction

Yuan-shan Chen, Der-Hwa Victoria Rau and Gerald Rau

During the past few decades, English has become the dominant global lingua franca. In a broader sense, English as a lingua franca (ELF) includes not only speakers from the Expanding Circle (e.g., Taiwan, China), but also speakers from the Inner (e.g., the U.S., Britain) and Outer Circles (e.g., India, Singapore). ELF is not the practice "of orientation to the norms of a particular group of English speakers, but of mutual negotiation involving efforts and adjustments from all parties" (Jenkins 2009, p. 201). Since the millennium, there has been a steady growth of empirical studies targeting English as a lingua franca in oral academic discourse, which have focused on the specific linguistic features and the communicative strategies used to achieve mutual understanding. However, little attention has been paid to English in written texts, a gap identified by Jenkins et al. (2011) in their recent review of ELF research.

This book thus aims to fill this gap by investigating Chinese speakers' email discourse in an English-as-a-lingua-franca context. Thanks to computer technology, cyber communications have become more and more popular in the global village. Unlike formal academic writing, email discourse does not have well-established conventions, and email writers need to have high linguistic and pragmatic competence to compose appropriate emails. The chapters in this collection address a wide range of email discourse by Chinese speakers of English. To our knowledge, this is the first edited volume devoted solely to Chinese speakers' email discourse in English. We target Chinese speakers of English because they constitute the largest population from the Expanding Circle who use English in a lingua franca context. It is our sincere hope that the studies reported in this volume will inspire others to further explore this issue.

Y. Chen (✉)
Department of Applied English, National Chin-Yi University of Technology, Taichung, Taiwan
e-mail: yuanshan@ncut.edu.tw

D.-H.V. Rau
Institute of Linguistics, National Chung Cheng University, Chiayi, Taiwan

G. Rau
Chiayi, Taiwan

Y. Chen et al. (eds.), *Email Discourse Among Chinese Using English as a Lingua Franca*, DOI 10.1007/978-981-287-888-5_1

1.1 Organization of the Book

This volume is divided into four large sections, based on the relationship between the sender and the recipient. The first section includes four chapters on aspects of student email to their professors, including terms of address, discourse organization, apologies, and requests. The second section comprises three chapters on student email to the international academic community, including identity construction, relationship building, and prevention of misunderstanding. The two chapters in the third section examine openings/closings and apologies in the context of student emails to international peers. Finally, the last section is devoted to email in the workplace, an underrepresented genre in the literature, including email communication within an academic office, in publication of an edited volume, and in detection of email fraud in a business context.

1.1.1 Section 1: Emails from Students to Professors

In Chap. 2, Rau and Rau examine how address forms were used by a group of graduate students in science and technology when emailing an American writing instructor, and whether instruction played a role in enhancing students' email literacy. They found that most students tended to use the same address terms throughout the course without any changes, while four demonstrate evidence of negotiation of personal relationship with the instructor using various terms of address over time. Similarly, most of the students used rather formulaic closings, with very few indicating any personal relationship with the instructor. In the middle of the course, the instructor took one class period to model how various forms of address terms and closing would have an impact on power/solidarity and distance/closeness relationships, but the findings showed that only five students manifested development in email writing. The authors explained that the students might have viewed email as simply a platform to submit homework assignments, so there was no need to negotiate relationship. Furthermore, there was limited exposure of the students to email guidelines because the focus of the course was writing academic papers, not email. From this study, it seems that for students to advance in email literacy, they need to be aware of the importance of negotiating relationship with the addressee, and more time needs to be devoted to email instruction.

In Chap. 3, Huang examines 76 emails Taiwanese students sent to their professor. Of these emails, half were written by graduate students, while the other half were written by undergraduate students. The two groups of data were analyzed in terms of language choice, function, patterns of the main messages, and spoken and written features. English was the dominant language for both groups of students when writing emails to their professor, perhaps because they were English majors. However, the study also found that the students would sometimes code-switch between English and Chinese. Eight different email functions were identified, including request, inquiry, thanking, providing information, apologizing, asking for leave of absence, confirmation of appointment/information, and wishing. Regarding patterns of email messages, the graduate students tended to adopt a more formal style of writing, while the undergraduate students tended to adopt a less formal style of writing. Finally, both graduate and undergraduate emails consisted of written and spoken features.

Chang, Curran, Hsu, and Hsu in Chap. 4 studied the waffle phenomenon, or excessive use of linguistic forms to achieve a communicative goal, in apology emails by a group of L2 learners. A total of 60 students participated in this study, with 20 native proficient speakers of English, 20 Chinese EFL learners, and 20 proficient speakers of Chinese in Taiwan. The findings showed that the learners did waffle, that is, being over-informative in their messages, especially in the account they provided. In terms of pragmalinguistic differences, they tended to use "Direct apology," but the forms they used for this strategy were limited compared to those used by native speakers of English and native speakers of Chinese. In addition, the learners tended to use an informal tone of voice when addressing their professors, which was regarded as inappropriate in a student–professor relationship. Finally, one striking finding is that the Chinese email messages tended to be clear and succinct. Such brevity in Chinese emails, according to Chang et al., needs to be further explored in future studies.

Chapter 5, by Li and Chen, investigates how a student's email is perceived by professors in Taiwan. In this study, an email request written by a student studying at a university of technology was used as a prompt. They interviewed 13 professors from the Department of Foreign Languages and Literature and from the Teacher Education Center at a university in southern Taiwan about their evaluation of student responses to the email prompt in terms of politeness and effectiveness. The findings suggest that in terms of politeness, most professors regarded setting the tone of an email to be important since tone can denote the student–professor relationship. In addition, the professors also thought that following a standard letter format in the order of subject, greeting, message, and closing is essential for a polite email. As for effectiveness, the authors concluded from the interview protocols that a clear subject line, an attainable requestive goal, and provision of possible solutions to faculty are the most important. The study closes with pedagogical implications and suggestions for future studies.

1.1.2 Section 2: Emails from Students to the International Academic Community

Section 2 discusses email discourse from students to the international academic community. In Chap. 6, Chen investigated how Chinese graduate students formulate requests to international researchers through emails and how they constructed identity for themselves and the requestees when they made requests. By collecting data from written emails and interviews, Chen found that the students exhibited a high degree of formality when making requests using more formal words and long complex sentences but fewer contractions and elliptical sentences. In addition, Chinese students also showed deference in terms of relational identity in which they used an address term such as *Professor + first/last name* to show high esteem for the requestees. Other email components such as complimentary closings and signature all indicated that Chinese students tended to keep a distance from the requestees in revealing their respects, which was considered typical in Chinese culture. Based on the contents of the emails, it was also evident that the participants positioned themselves as graduate students by mentioning their status, expressing grounds for their requests, and so on. They also identified the unfamiliar and invisible researchers as academic people of excellence. Therefore, Chen concluded that successfully constructing self- and other identity was of significance in making academic requests.

Along the same line of student emails to international academic community members, Xiao and Gao selected a particular type of emails and provided us with a different perspective on English as a lingua franca in Chap. 7. They attempted to look at how Chinese students formulate their "*Taoci*," or networking emails, when communicating with overseas potential supervisors. Xiao and Gao's study revealed that the Chinese students employed two major strategies, *guanxi* (*relationship*) *Taoci* and *academic Taoci*, to create more opportunities for themselves to be admitted to the universities they wished to enter. In terms of *guanxi Taoci*, power-oriented strategies and solidarity-oriented strategies were special characteristics used by the Chinese students. With respect to *academic Taoci*, the findings revealed that the Chinese students employed strategies such as creating shared academic interests and referring to personal academic strengths. Although two types of Taoci were identified in this study, it was found that *academic Taoci* was more prominent than *guanxi Taoci*. Based on the findings, Xiao and Gao modeled the supervisor–applicant relationship into Taoci types and concluded that in *Taoci* emails, the strategies the Chinese applicants employed not only showed traditional Chinese collectivism, but also revealed individualism by presenting self-qualifications, giving these emails a particular flavor with a discourse structure mixing eastern and western cultures.

In Chap. 8, Ren collected authentic email data and explored how Chinese university students used remedial and preemptive pragmatic strategies to resolve misunderstanding and non-understanding to achieve successful intercultural communication in ELF email discourse. It was found that the Chinese students employed three remedial strategies. For instance, they would either make explicit metalinguistic comments to signify the misunderstanding or provide elaborations of the situation when a receiver misunderstood them or they would use focused questions and metalinguistic comments to remedy non-understanding. In terms of preemptive strategies, Ren found that when English was used as a lingua franca, the Chinese students did not assume that there was a homogeneous norm and thus attempted to create shared knowledge and common ground or employ confirmation checks to maintain communicative effectiveness and understanding.

1.1.3 Section 3: Emails from Peer to Peer

Section 3 concerns email discourse between peers. In Chap. 9, Huang investigated intercultural communication in emails by looking at openings and closings in emails constructed as Taiwanese students corresponded with Japanese or Italian keypals. The study showed that the majority of the emails had an opening. However, a closer look at the differences in openings among Japanese, Taiwanese, and Italians showed that Japanese and Taiwanese students used a more formal opening than Italian students. These differences could be viewed as cultural differences, as Asians tended to show deference, whereas Italians showed solidarity. With regard to closings, ethnic differences were also found to be a factor in the use of closings. Huang found that Taiwanese students used *farewell/ending salutation* least frequently and used more *no closing* than the other groups. These differences might be attributed to the difficulties of applying appropriate closings in email writing or less focus on the closings. On the other hand, Japanese used closing strategies most frequently, indicating influences from their language in which politeness strategies are emphasized.

In addition to differences between ethnic groups, differences between higher and lower proficiency Chinese students of English are explored by Liu and Ren in Chap. 10, particularly their perceptions of sociopragmatic variables when making apologies to foreign students in emails. To elicit data, the participants were asked to respond to discourse production tasks and a questionnaire. While the two groups differed in their English proficiency, it was found that proficiency did not affect their perceptions of sociopragmatic factors. In addition to sociopragmatic factors, this study also found that, unlike previous research on spoken language, lower proficiency students used longer apologies than higher proficiency ones when they wrote emails. They postulated that lack of pragmatic competence and influence by Chinese culture might be the reasons why lower proficiency students wrote longer apologies. In other words, lower proficiency students felt that they needed to write more to show they have apologized enough, since repetition of apologies is considered to be a sign of sincerity in Chinese culture. Finally, the results revealed that the higher proficiency group was more capable of using their pragmatic competence in the sense that they employed more upgraders to formulate a more appropriate apology.

1.1.4 Section 4: Emails in the Workplace

Section 4 addresses email discourse in the workplace. In Chap. 11, Lü investigated how professional secretaries in a private university departmental office in Taiwan made requests to their faculty in email communication. By investigating institutional discourse, the researcher could observe the process as novice participants became experts and observe how institutional talk and institutional rules were taught and learned. The study first explored the degree of directness and internal and external modifications used in their discourse, and then examined the politeness standards of 'cultural insiders.' Such professionals are often faced with uncertainties regarding style and politeness strategies in email interaction especially in hierarchical relationships where the power asymmetry needs to be maintained. The results showed that the senior secretaries tended to use more direct strategies and more internal and external modification devices, showing that they failed to follow the principle of deference politeness or 'negative politeness' held in Western society. The strategies that the senior secretaries employed thus gave the faculty the impression of having no choice in the matters. On the other hand, the findings revealed that the novice secretary used more conventionally indirect strategies and fewer modifiers. Moreover, it was found that she lacked assurance in her identity as a practicing professional in the asymmetrical academic context.

Chen, in Chap. 12, attempts to investigate how ELF communication is maintained through email interactions. Unlike much of the previous research on email, which has examined how students wrote emails to make requests of faculty, this paper investigated how an editor demonstrated her symbolic competence and negotiated face with contributors through email communication in a context where English was used as a lingua franca. The major data were collected from the editor's email exchange during a two-year editorial process. An interview was also conducted to elicit her understanding of her relationship with the contributors, changes of relationship, and particular events during the editorial process. The data were analyzed based on symbolic competence and Face Constituting Theory. The findings showed that, in terms of symbolic competence, the editor displayed subjectivity by positioning herself in different roles, historicity by referring to her past experience, performativity to create a reality, and reframing by reestablishing the situation. In terms of face, the findings showed that face was not only realized as co-constituted interactional processes but also realized as individual wants. There is also a suggestion that the findings could lead to future ELF research, with particular emphasis to how symbolic competence and facework are manifested in interactional and relational EFL email communication.

In Chap. 13, Hsiang investigated hacking and fraud emails by doing an elaborate analysis of differences between emails sent by the hacker and an employee. Through the use of the Intercultural communication model developed by Scollon and Scollon (1995), with its focus on involvement and independence as well as inductive and deductive patterning, the paper examines the differing writing styles employed by a Taiwanese employee and an email scam artist in order to better understand sociolinguistic differences between their correspondences. After comparing a total of 31 emails exchanged between the two of them and a foreign customer, it can be seen that the Taiwanese employee used a number of approaches to communicate with the customer, such as inductive and involvement strategies. These may be employed due to a perceived power imbalance between the two and cultural factors leading the employee to think more of the team as a whole. Conversely, the hacker used a more deductive, challenging and independent style of discourse, demonstrating lack of company loyalty and interest in individual gain.

While the dataset may not be expansive enough to draw detailed conclusions, there is plenty of evidence of Scollon and Scollon (1995) strategies being employed in the email exchanges to warrant further exploration in this field.

References

Jenkins, Jennifer. 2009. English as a lingua franca: Interpretations and attitudes. *World Englishes* 28(2): 200–207.

Jenkins, Jennifer, Alessia Cogo, and Martin Dewey. 2011. Review of developments in research into English as a lingua franca. *Language Teaching* 44(3): 281–315.

Scollon, Ron, and Suzanne Wong Scollon. 1995. *Intercultural Communication*. Oxford: Blackwell Publisher Ltd.

Part I
Emails from Students to Professors

Chapter 2
Negotiating Personal Relationship Through Email Terms of Address

Der-Hwa Victoria Rau and Gerald Rau

Abstract This study investigated whether and how English L2 students use terms of address to negotiate personal relationship when writing email to an English-speaking addressee and how instruction affected email writing in an English as a lingua franca (ELF) setting. The email data were collected naturally in two classroom settings where the second author was the instructor of an ESP class in scientific writing and recipient of the letters. The data, comprising various speech acts, were analyzed and interpreted qualitatively within the framework of interactive sociolinguistics and ethnography. Email writing is not a monolithic genre but varies from informal texting style to formal letters depending on the purpose of the communication. The results suggest that the desire to negotiate relationships by the use of terms of address in email writing can play a role in enhancing second-language acquisition, whereas the perceived lack of need to negotiate personal relationship might impede acquisition. Modeling of appropriate email communication was insufficient, in part due to the asymmetrical relationship between students and teachers, but specific instruction in principles of email writing was beneficial in helping students acquire the necessary skills.

Keywords Pragmatics instruction · Terms of address · Salutation · Signature · Negotiation of relationship

2.1 Introduction

Terms of address are a delicate point of departure in negotiating personal relationship in spoken and written communication (including electronic-mediated communication). Terms of address have been a particular topic of interest in intercultural

D.-H.V. Rau (✉)
Institute of Linguistics, National Chung Cheng University, Chiayi, Taiwan
e-mail: lngrau@ccu.edu.tw

G. Rau
Ching Jiang Learning Center, National Chung Cheng University, Chiayi, Taiwan
e-mail: gerryrau@hotmail.com

Y. Chen et al. (eds.), *Email Discourse Among Chinese Using English as a Lingua Franca*, DOI 10.1007/978-981-287-888-5_2

communication (Scollon and Scollon 2001, p. 45) as they are related to negotiation of "face," an important aspect of politeness theory (Brown and Levinson 1987; Gu 1990). The decision of how to address the interlocutor reflects the perceived power and solidarity relationship between the addressor and the addressee. Brown and Gilman (1972) pointed out that solidarity dominates power as the most important semantic in selecting address forms in contemporary European pronouns. This symmetrical solidarity is interpreted as a reflection of the dominant utilitarian discourse system, its practices of socialization, its assumptions about face politeness, and its forms of discourse (Scollon and Scollon 2001, p. 175). Whereas symmetrical solidarity in some American business contexts leads to the practice of using first names reciprocally as an involvement strategy of politeness, symmetrical deference is preferred in some Asian business contexts using Title+last name as an independent strategy of politeness (Scollon and Scollon 2001, pp. 136–137). In academic settings, the use of address forms often assumes an asymmetrical power and solidarity relationship (Formentelli 2009). Tannen (1993) considered the linguistic strategy of power and solidarity to be ambiguous and doubly binding. Power binds two individuals in a hierarchical interdependence by which both have rights and obligations to each other. Solidarity also binds two individuals in a closeness interdependence in which both are empowering and empowered.

According to Scollon and Scollon (2001, pp. 272–273), the choice of terms of address in intercultural communication is a social action, which is not totally free but follows a restricted range of shared social norms. The norms are positioned within multiple discourses (interdiscursivity), borrow from other discourses and texts (intertextuality), and respond to prior and following communications (dialogicity) based on their proposed principle of communication; therefore, the choice of terms of address in an academic setting is by no means prefigured and unchanging but can vary depending on the particular mode of communication, the degree of familiarity between the instructor and student, the personality of the instructor, and the type of course being taught (Wright 2009). In addition, the terms of address may even vary according to the dynamics of the relationship of the same dyad as illustrated in dramas or novels (Friedrich 1972; Lin 1996).

In email communication, terms of address have been identified as a move of politeness in the script of request (Li et al. 2011). Certain terms of address in an English email sent to a Taiwanese professor can be perceived as rude in an English as a lingua franca (ELF) setting (Li 2013, p. 50). Although over half of the Taiwanese students in a sample of university students writing English email requests to their professors used "Dear teacher"[1]" (Li et al. 2011), a form of address also preferred at English cram schools in Taiwan (Huang 2009), Taiwanese professors viewed this usage negatively, as "better than nothing," a direct translation of Chinese politeness rather than a standard format in English (Li 2013, p. 51).

[1]Teacher is a direct translation of the Chinese equivalent *laoshi* (老師). It is used in Chinese to address educators of all levels, including college professors.

Previous studies on terms of address have used survey methods or grouped members of the same ethnicity together for the purpose of comparison in a quantitative design (Fasold 1990, pp. 1–38). However, this practice may prevent us from noticing the variation in terms of address used in natural communication as the personal relationship is negotiated and developed in the choice of address forms. In addition, as natural data from sociolinguistic interviews are not easy to obtain due to the observer's paradox (Labov 1972; Wolfram 2011), it has become necessary to use a qualitative approach (Mackey and Gass 2005, pp. 162–184) to gather empirical data longitudinally (e.g., Lu 2012). To trace the negotiation of relationship, a discourse analysis based on the framework of interactive sociolinguistics (Schiffrin 1994) is ideal. In a classroom setting, email communication between the instructor and the students forms a natural set of data that can be collected and used anonymously (e.g., Hartford and Bardovi-Harlig 1996). Each student's email interactions with the instructor throughout the whole semester can also form a natural case study (Duff 2008) to trace pragmatic development as instruction in email politeness is introduced during the class.

In this study, development of an English email literacy is explored by focusing on the modeling and instruction that the instructor provided and the choices the students made to use not only more intelligible (e.g., Seidlhofer 2001, 2004) but also more pragmatics-oriented email communication in an ELF setting where English is used for academic purposes. The study aimed to investigate how terms of address demonstrate development of personal relationship in email communication in a classroom setting and how instruction in email writing might have a positive effect on students' development of pragmatic competence in English. The research questions are as follows:

1. What forms of address and closing do students use when emailing their English-speaking instructor? Do the students vary each to negotiate their interpersonal relationship with the instructor?
2. What role do modeling and instruction play in learning how to write socially acceptable email? What implications does this have for the importance of direct teaching of email writing as a component of ESP in an ELF setting?

2.2 Methods

This study followed a qualitative[2] ethnographic research design combined with action research to identify best practices in teaching and learning email writing. The methodology of ethnography follows Scollon and Scollon's (2001, p. 17)

[2]An anonymous reviewer suggested that a statistical analysis in the quantitative research norm might be more appropriate to address the effect of direct instruction, but as the available data from the small sample did not meet the requirements for meaningful statistical analysis, we believe that a discourse analysis of individual cases is the best choice given the circumstances.

"interdiscourse communication," which is based on "fieldwork, participant observation, 'strange making,[3] and contrastive observation." Action research is defined by Wallace (1998, p. 1) as "the systematic collection and analysis of data relating to the improvement of some aspect of professional practice."

2.2.1 Research Site

The research site is a university in central Taiwan where graduate students in science and technology are required to publish scientific papers in English before graduation. To assist students with limited English proficiency, the extension program at the university offered a course on English scientific writing, taught by the second author, a native speaker of English with extensive academic background in biology, science education, and English editing. Each section of the course met for 24 h, covering genre analysis (Swales 1990; Swales and Feak 1994, 2000) and writing tips.

The course was offered twice during 2012–2013. The spring section, from March 2012 to May 2012, consisted of 22 students, all of whom were graduate students at the university. The fall section, from October 2012 to January 2013, consisted of 9 students, of whom five were graduate students at the university while four were working. Of these, two had recently obtained their Ph.D.s and were seeking to publish research related to their Ph.D. while working in the same field, and two were teachers, one simultaneously working on a second master's degree. A distribution by major and gender is shown in Table 2.1. Some of students were

Table 2.1 Participants: Spring and Fall

Position	Field	Male	Female
Graduate student	Electrical Engineering	7	1
Graduate student	Chemical Engineering	3	0
Graduate student	Mechanical Engineering	1	0
Graduate student	Physics	1	0
Graduate student	Chemistry/Biochemistry	3	1
Graduate student	Life Science	1	2
Graduate student	Seismology	1	0
Graduate student	Finance	0	1
Total Spring		17	5
Graduate student	Electrical Engineering	4	0
Graduate student	Communication Engineering	1	0
Employed	Neuroimaging	1	0
Employed	Psychology	0	1
Employed	Teacher (Special Education)	1	0
Employed	Teacher (English)	0	1
Total Fall		7	2

signed up by their advisors to take this course, but the majority took it based on their own perceived needs.

Lacking access to the electronic course pages at the university, the instructor used email to send copies of the course materials to students. Students were likewise asked to submit their homework electronically to the instructor via email, making email the natural means of communication outside class. Nevertheless, since the course was ungraded and did not count for credit toward graduation, many students attending the class did not submit homework on a regular basis. Although the degree of their previous experience emailing to instructors was unknown, it is assumed that graduate students in Taiwan are quite familiar with receiving English emails from instructors who were trained in English-speaking countries.

Based on the importance of email in current academic communication and previous studies that have shown the importance of direct instruction in pragmatics (Cohen 1996), one class period in the middle of the course was devoted to email pragmatics. Data were collected before and after instruction to compare how students improved due to instruction.[3] To ensure ethical practices while ensuring natural communication (Rossman and Rallis 2003, pp. 61–87), the study was explained to students during the last class meeting and they were given the opportunity to opt out of having their emails used, which none did. Pseudonyms have been assigned to each to ensure anonymity.

2.2.2 *Email Instruction*

Email instruction was conducted in the seventh week of each 12-week course. In both sections, the instructor began with general principles of email etiquette. The instructor then introduced three factors affecting relationships (power, distance, and imposition) and discussed how these affect the degree of formality expected in communication, with higher levels of each leading to greater formality. In the first section, this was followed by instruction in what salutations, closings, and signatures were considered more or less formal. Specific suggestions were also given for communicating politeness in the body of request and apology emails. In the second section, this was placed within the framework of five principles of communicative success (Appendix 1, modified from Chen 2011):

1. Terms of Address (Relationship);
2. Amount of Information (Clarity);
3. Recognition of Imposition (Cooperation);

[3]We agree with an anonymous reviewer's comment that it is difficult to draw the conclusion that the development of students' pragmatic skill in email writing during the whole semester is purely the result of direct instruction, as the email instruction only took one class period. In fact, as our method is a qualitative discourse analysis, we tried to avoid jumping to such a reductionist conclusion.

4. Manner of Asking (Politeness); and
5. Correctness of Form (Comprehension).

2.2.3 Data Analysis

The data constitute email correspondence between the instructor and 22 students (5 females and 17 males) in the spring section and 9 students (2 females and 7 males) in the fall section. An initial coding of speech acts was done by the first author, on an intuitive basis, revealing the main email functions to be homework submission, request, apology, gratitude, question, and response to the instructor's email. The data were then recoded by the second author, noting the occurrence of all possible combinations of these categories. The correlation between the two codings was greater than 90 %.

Table 2.2 displays the distribution of email functions found in our students' data in descending order. The number of students' emails to the instructor ranged from minimally one to maximally 33. It is clear that homework submission (with request expressed or implied) is the most frequent email function. Eight students emailed the instructor only once, that email being homework submission. Although acknowledgement of receiving email had the second highest frequency, all of the occurrences came from one student, who acknowledged receipt of every email from the instructor. The most frequently occurring speech acts in our student email data are request (30) and apology (25), with far fewer occurrences of gratitude (13) and question (11). It is interesting to note that most of the requests and apologies accompanied homework submission, either a request for comments or an apology that it was submitted late, whereas most of the occurrences of gratitude and question did not accompany homework submission, but were in response to the feedback provided by the instructor when returning homework.

As shown in Table 2.3, the instructor used email primarily to return students' homework with attached comments, to send class materials to the whole class, and to respond to students' emails. Among teachable speech acts, request (14), apology (6), and gratitude (3) stand out as the most common. In addition to comments within the returned homework, the instructor always wrote something in the text of the email, as illustrated in Appendix 3. Typically, if many students submitted something the same week, the instructor would write a very brief comment in the email, but if there were fewer student submissions, he would take the time to write more. Many students submitted homework early in the semester, when they were asked to submit a model article from the journal they intended to submit to, or a prewrite of their own article, but progressively fewer submitted later in the course as later stages of the writing process were discussed, because they had not reached that point in their own research and writing. Samples of emails sent with class materials as attachments can be seen in Appendix 4. Examples of request, apology, and gratitude expressed to the whole class can be found in Appendices 5, 6, and 7, respectively.

Table 2.2 Students' email functions

Function	With homework	No homework
Homework submission with brief text	26	
Homework submission with no text	25	
Acknowledgement of receiving email		20
Homework submission with request	18	
Homework submission with comment	16	
Homework submission with apology	11	
Gratitude		7
Response		6
Homework submission with request and apology	7	
Apology		4
Question		4
Homework submission with question	3	
Request		2
Apology and question		2
Request and gratitude		2
Homework submission with gratitude	1	
Homework submission with request and gratitude	1	
Question and gratitude		1
Apology and gratitude		1
Response with question		1
Total	108	50
Total with request	26	4
Total with apology	18	7
Total with gratitude	2	11
Total with question	3	8

The fact that students' use of email functions mirrored the instructor's use indicates an important emergent pattern, called a Zipfian type of organization of language (Goldberg 2006), which has been demonstrated to facilitate language development. According to Ziph's law, as cited in Larsen-Freeman and Cameron (2008, p. 120), "the more common words in a language account for geometrically more word tokens in a language than do the less common ones." In other words, as the same words and patterns are used on a smaller scale, they are repeated on a larger scale. As a result, the pattern of email writing is not prefigured by rules but emerges as frequent usages accumulate in the interactions. This is why Larsen-Freeman and Cameron posited that language use is a fractal, a geometric shape that is self-similar at different levels. This pattern not only emerges in phonological (Rau et al. 2009) and morphosyntactic acquisition (Rau et al. 2012), but also in development of pragmatics, as evidenced in our data. Our finding provides support for exemplar-based theories of second/foreign language acquisition in

Table 2.3 Instructor's email functions

Function	To class	To student
Return of homework with brief comment		29
Return of homework with comments		22
Response		19
Sending class materials	19	
Sending class materials with request	7	
Request	5	1
Return of homework with apology		3
Gratitude	1	1
Sending class materials with apology	1	
Question		1
Response and question		1
Response with apology		1
Return of homework with request		1
Return of homework with apology and gratitude		1
Totals	33	80
Total with request	12	2
Total with apology	1	5
Total with gratitude	1	2
Total with question		1

which "frequency of exposure to, and use of, constructions play a vital role..." (Gries and Wulff 2005, p. 196).

Negotiation of relationship can be most clearly observed in the terms of address, including salutation, closing, and signature. Our research thus focused on whether these three loci of discourse changed and if so how that might mark politeness, hierarchy, and distance.

Finally, we explored whether email teaching can facilitate students' communication in academic settings. For the spring section, the students were specifically requested to submit an email to the instructor before the instruction on email was delivered on April 26, 2012. Appendix 2 contains the letter of request from the instructor to elicit email samples from the students. At the end of that class, students were asked to "write an email in the form of a request and ask for feedback on your homework."[4] Differences in email writing before and after instruction were compared. The email instruction was delivered on November 28, 2012 for the fall class, so comparisons of data were made before and after this date.

[4]An anonymous reviewer questioned whether this could have influenced the relative frequency of email types, but few students responded to the request (Spring: 1 request before instruction, 3 requests and 2 apologies after; Fall: 1 apology after = total 4 requests and 3 apologies). All of the others were at the initiative of the students, so the pattern still holds.

2.3 Negotiation of Relationship

The first research question investigated what terms of address the students used in addressing their English-speaking instructor and whether the students varied these to negotiate their interpersonal relationship with the instructor. We will first look at the email sent from the instructor, to see what model the students had for English email, then at the forms used by students, and finally whether there was any indication of negotiation of personal relationships.

As shown in the appendices, when the instructor emailed the whole class he regularly addressed the letter, “Dear class.” Materials for the first class in the first section were sent from the extension program, so students had already met the instructor when he sent them email in that section. In the first email sent to the second section, sent before the beginning of the course, the instructor addressed the class as “Dear Students in English Scientific Writing” to make sure they understood the purpose of the email, but reverted back to “Dear class” in the rest of the correspondences. In his first email to the first section, he used “Dr. Rau” as his signature, a habit carried over from his previous high school teaching indicating a hierarchical relationship. However, in the rest of the emails, he consistently used “Gerry Rau” as his signature to maintain an egalitarian but distant relationship.

When the instructor emailed homework back to students with comments, he usually addressed them by first name only without endearment. When responding to individual questions, however, he would use “Hi” or “Dear” before the name of the student. Also, in returning homework the week of instruction he used a more formal style, with “Dear XX,” and “Sincerely,” to model that for the students.

The instructor is a middle-aged white male who frequently uses an analyzer’s reporting style (Tannen 1995) for professional email correspondences. In his email to the students in this class, the contents were mostly informational (Biber et al. 1994) as they served mostly the functions of sending course materials and making comments on the students’ homework (see Table 2.3). As the instructor’s email rarely included examples of gratitude and questions (see Table 2.3), the students must have learned those two speech acts elsewhere.

Tables 2.4 and 2.5 present the student data from the two sections, showing the various terms of address used by students before and after instruction, listed in order with the earliest first. A“*” indicates the first email for that student after instruction in email. The symbol “–” indicates that there is no address form, no closing, or no signature. Data are not shown for students whose data were consistent throughout the course or for whom we have insufficient data.

The majority of the students in the class, those whose data are not shown, showed no evidence of feeling a need to negotiate a relationship with the instructor. Twelve students (nine in section 1, three in section 2) wrote only one email to the instructor, usually the first or second week, or used email only as a means of homework submission two or three times without any personalization. Their purpose apparently was to learn what they could by attending the class without written interaction with the instructor. Seven other students (four in section 1, three in section 2) used

Table 2.4 Terms of address in spring section

Email function[a]	Salutation	Closing	Signature
Bob			
HB	Dear Dr. Rau,	–	Bob (I Hong Tsai)[b]
HB	Dr. Rua	Thanks!	Bob(I Hong Tsai)[b]
HC	Dear Rau,	–	Bob (I Hong Tsai)[b]
HR#	Dear Rau,	Sincerely,	Bob (I Hong Tsai)[b]
HAR#*	Dear Gerry,	Sincerely,	I Hong Tsai (Bob)
Oscar			
Q	Dr. Rau		student Oscar
HC	Dr. Rau,	Sincerely yours,	Lai, Da-Nian
HC	Prof. Rau:	Sincerely yours	Oscar
G*	Dear Dr.Rau	Sincerely Yours,	Oscar Lai
Nancy			
HB	–	Best regards,	Nancy
H	–	–	–
HR#*	Dear Dr. Rau,	Sincerely,	Nancy Lin
HB	Dear Dr. Rau,	Sincerely,	Nancy Lin
G	Dear Dr. Rau,	–	Nancy Lin
Lisa			
HB	Dear Teacher Gerry,	Best Regards,	Shu-Fen Yao (Lisa)
AQ	Dear Teacher Gerry,	Best Regards,	Shu-Fen Yao (Lisa)
HR	Hi Teacher Gerry,	Best Regards,	Shu-Fen Yao (Lisa)
Q	Dear Teacher Gerry,	Best Regards,	Shu-Fen Yao (Lisa)
GA*	Dear Prof. Rau	Sincerely,	Shu-Fen Yao (Lisa)
Janet			
HB	Dear Teacher:	–	Janet Lai
HA	Dear Professor:	–	Janet
HB	Dear Teacher:	Thank you.	Janet
HR#*	Dear Prof. Rau:	Sincerely yours,	Janet
HG	Dear Prof. Rau:	–	Janet
G	Dear Prof.Rau	Sincerely yours,	Janet
Harold			
HC	Dear Mr. Rau	Sincerely,	Harold Chen
HB	Dear Mr. Rau:	–	–
HA	Dear Mr. Rau:	Sincerely,	Harold Chen
HB	Dear Mr. Rau	Sincerely,	Harold
H	–	–	–
HR#	Dear Mr. Rau:	Sincerely,	Harold Chen
HAR#*	Dear Prof. Rau:	Respectfully yours	Ph. D Harold Chen

(continued)

Table 2.4 (continued)

Albert			
H	–	–	–
HQ	Dear Prof. Rau:	best regard	Albert Chia-Min Kuo
H	–	–	–
HB	–	–	–
H	–	–	–
H	–	–	–
H	–	–	–
A#*	Dear Prof. Rau:	Sincerely,	Albert Chia-Min Kuo
Scott			
HR	Hi Pro. Rau,	BRs,	Scott, Yi-Ming Wang
HRA	Hi Pro.Rau,	–	Scott
HB	Hi Dr. Rau,	BRs,	Scott
R	Hi Dr.Rau,	Thank you very much!	Scott
HR	Hi Dr.Rau	–	EMing
HR	Hi Dr. Rau	–	Scott
HR#	Hi Dr. Rau	BRs,	Scott

[a]*H* homework sent as attachment with no text; *HB* homework sent/returned with brief note; *HC* homework sent/returned with comment; *R* request; *A* apology; *G* gratitude; *Q* question; *K* acknowledgement of receipt; *S* response to questions or comments. # Response to instructor's letter requesting special email submission.
[b]Date included on line with signature
*First email after email instruction in class

essentially the same terms of address throughout the class. Four of these students consistently used a formal letter style, apparently drawn from former instruction for writing letters. While it was unclear whether they had had any formal instruction in email writing before, they certainly came with a general schema of letter writing in English. Two wrote something the first time and copied it each successive time, changing only the information regarding the particular assignment, as evidenced by identical spacing and typographical errors in the unchanged sections. One who knew the instructor outside of class used an informal style consistent with their personal relationship.

We next examined the eleven students showing evidence of change in their terms of address to see if any of that change could be attributed to negotiation of relationship. At least four cases demonstrate evidence of negotiation of personal relationship with the instructor by choosing various terms of address in the emails.

Table 2.5 Terms of address in fall section

Name Email function[a]	Salutation	Closing	Signature
Allan			
H	–	–	–
Q	Hi Gerry	–	Allan
S	Dearf Gerry	–	Allan
H	–	–	–
S	Dear Gerry	–	Allan
H	–	–	–
SQ	Dear Professor	–	Allan
S	Dear Professor	–	Allan
H	–	–	–
A	Dear Professor	–	Allan
HGR	Dear Gerry	–	Allan
HQ	Dear Gerry	Thank you	Allan
HQ	Dear Gerry	Thank you	Allan
A	Dear Gerry	–	Allan
G	Dear Gerry	Thank you every much	Allan
Edgar			
HC	Dear Dr. Rau:	Many thanks	Edgar Ho
HC	Dear Mr. Rau :	Best regards	Edgar [Chinese]
HC	Dear Mr. Rau:	Best regards	Edgar [Chinese]
HA	Dear Mr. Rau:	Best regards	Edgar
HA	Hello Mr. Rau:	Thanks! Have a nice day!	Edgar
Doug			
HB	Dear Professor Rau	Best regards	[Signature line]
HA	Dear Sir	–	Doug
HB	Dear Sir	cheers	Doug
HB	Dear Rau	Best regards	Doug Chen
G	Dear sir	Take care!	[Signature line]
H	–	–	–
H	–	–	–
A*	Dear Dr. Rau	Sincerely	Doug

[a]*H* homework sent as attachment with no text; *HB* homework sent/returned with brief note; *HC* homework sent/returned with comment; *R* request; *A* apology; *G* gratitude; *Q* question; *K* acknowledgement of receipt; *S* response to questions or comments.
*First email after email instruction in class

2.3.1 Four Cases of Negotiating Personal Relationships with the Instructor

Bob used various forms (e.g., "Dear Dr. Rau," "Dr. Rua" (sic) and "Dear Rau") when his purpose was homework submission. As there is no need to negotiate relationship when submitting homework, he did not even pay attention to typos in the address forms (Excerpt 1). But after instruction, he sent a letter of apology to the instructor (Excerpt 2), not only using the expressions that had been taught but also apparently expressing a feeling of growing closer to the instructor, as expressed in the choice of greeting, "Dear Gerry." At the same time, he used his Chinese name first and dropped the date in closing. This seems to indicate a move from relating to the instructor in a hierarchical relationship with his English name preceding his Chinese name to a solidary relationship but with his Chinese identity preceding his English identity. After the class was over, he has seen the instructor on campus several times and has waved and sometimes talked briefly.

(1) From Bob, 2012/3/20

Dr. Rua

The attached files are my prewriting and the model article.
Thanks!

Bob(I Hong Tsai) 2012.03.20

(2) From Bob, 2012/5/2

Dear Gerry,
I am sorry for inconvenience that I handed in the assignment late. The attached file is my evaluation about the model article. I wonder if you could give me advice or feedback on my evaluation.

Sincerely,
I Hong Tsai (Bob)

Oscar also seems to give evidence of negotiating relationship through terms of address. He began using "Dr. Rau" and "Prof. Rau" without endearment. After instruction, he decided to add the endearment "Dear Dr. Rau." What is more interesting is that his signature varied from "student Oscar" to "Lai, Da-Nian," then to "Oscar," and finally to "Oscar Lai," a progression from Chinese solidarity, Chinese distance, English solidarity, to English distance, the last in a voluntary expression of gratitude sent after the class was over.

Allan, who is older than most of the other students and teaching while working on a second masters degree, moved from "Hi Gerry" or "Dear Gerry" to "Dear Professor," and back to "Dear Gerry" at the end. The reason he used "Dear Professor" in the middle of the class can perhaps be attributed to an interlude when he asked for special help with his MA thesis writing. At that point, both authors of this paper were involved in responding to his questions on research design. The instructor took an advisor's role and thus was addressed accordingly. Allan's continued use of "Dear Gerry" was not affected by the instruction because he took a sick leave on the day of instruction, but rather was a reflection of his personal relationship with the instructor who shared his background working with mentally retarded children.

Edgar also seemed to move toward a solidarity relationship as the course progressed. His greeting changed from Dear Dr. Rau to Dear Mr. Rau and then to Hello Mr. Rau. At the same time, his signature changed from Edgar Huang to Edgar, followed by his full name in Chinese characters, to Edgar. He was also the only one who used "have a nice day" in the closing of his email, showing concern for the addressee's life and desire to construct a relationship with him. This also was independent of instruction, as he did not email the instructor after the instruction in email writing.

2.3.2 *Salutation, Closing, and Signature*

The connection between the choice of specific terms of address and the desire to negotiate personal relationships is mediated by the purpose of the email. For example, in an email which intends to perform the speech act of apology, the addresser tends to use a more friendly and polite salutation, a kind and sincere closing, and a formal signature to express the desire to build a close and solid interpersonal relationship with the addressee. It is also hard to decide whether the choice of specific terms of address is due to earlier formulaic instruction the addresser has had or due to heartfelt consideration of solidarity relationships. Therefore, the specific communication context is important when asserting a direct link between terms of address and negotiation of relationship. We will discuss specific examples in Sect. 2.4.

In the 11 students' emails, most closings were formulaic with no regard to the addressee's personal life. This is probably a reflection of the fact that the major function of email in this class was sending homework. The only examples we found of personal closings were Edgar's "have a nice day" in his email sending homework with an apology and Doug's "Take care" in his email expressing gratitude. This indicates that although salutations and signatures have provided evidence of negotiation of personal relationships, closings appear to be an underrepresented politeness strategy, at least in our limited data.

2.4 Role of Instruction

The second research question explores how modeling and instruction assisted students in recognizing the need to negotiate relationship by the use of terms of address in email writing. We discuss several cases to illustrate how explicit instruction in email writing plays a role in second-language acquisition, especially when there is a need to negotiate personal relationship in a speech act.

During the email instruction, the second author as the instructor specifically addressed degree of formality, parts of an email, and essential components in request and apology (Li et al. 2011; Yang et al. 2011), as shown in Appendix 1. In particular, the instructor emphasized how the different address forms to the instructor in the salutation and the various forms of closing and signature reflect power/solidarity and distance/closeness relationships. There is evidence from the data that this instruction in how to express various degrees of politeness and establish interpersonal relationships (Lantolf and Thorne 2006) encouraged students to choose to assert their own identity and their relationship with the instructor.

When the class was asked to send an email of request or apology to the instructor before instruction, Harold showed his proficiency in email writing using good structure and many frozen expressions (Excerpt 3), using Dr. Rau as a term of address as he had consistently up to that point. After instruction, during which the instructor talked about how Mr., Dr. or Prof. might all be appropriate in different social settings, he decided to use Prof. Rau as the address form (Excerpt 4). At the same time, he changed his signature to "Ph. D Harold Chen," apparently to assert his academic identity, although he was a Ph.D. student not a Ph.D. at that time.

(3) From Harold, 2012/4/25

Dear Mr. Rau:

As requested in your email, I am writing to inform that I have submitted my file.
With regard to figure 2 in my file, I would like to put five curves in a figure.
However, I am uncertain whether this formation is clear or not for you.
I would appreciate it if you give me any suggestion.

I look forward to hearing from you.
Thank you

Sincerely,
Harold Chen

(4) From Harold, 2012/5/3

Dear Prof. Rau:
I am sorry that I submit it to you late.
The attachment is the word file about the evaluation of my model paper
I would appreciate it if you could recept it.

Respectfully yours
Ph. D. Harold Chen

Albert also benefited from instruction. Although he used a formal address "Dear Prof. Rau" in his first email (Excerpt 5), he did not use a consistent style, following a formal greeting with use of exclamation and small letters at the beginning of sentence, similar to a texting style. After instruction, he submitted a letter of apology to fulfill the instructor's request (Excerpt 6), demonstrating a consistent formal style. All of his other emails, however, were mere homework submission, attachments with no text in the email. This evidences that only when there is a perceived need to negotiate interpersonal relationship will there be an opportunity for second-language acquisition. Scott also showed a mix of formal and informal use in his email. Unfortunately, he did not send an email after instruction, so we have no way to judge whether the instruction was effective in his case.

(5) From Albert, 2012/3/20

Dear Prof. Rau:
Hello professor! I have no idea about the file "[name] article.pdf". what do I have to sent about this assignment ? thanks!!
The attachment file is my "pre-writing" assignment.

best regard
Albert Chia-Min Kuo

(6) From Albert, 2012/5/3

Dear Prof. Rau:
I apologize that I cannot finish the homework on time because I was preparing my mid-term exams this week.

Sincerely
Albert Chia-Min Kuo

Three of the female students in the class also provided evidence of the importance of instruction in learning how to negotiate relationships in email. Nancy started with no address form in her emails, with a signature of "Nancy." After instruction, she used "Dear Dr. Rau" to address the instructor and signed her name as "Nancy Lai." Two other female students transformed their relationship with the instructor from Chinese politeness to English academic hierarchy as a result of instruction. Lisa began with "Dear Teacher Gerry" or "Hi Teacher Gerry." After instruction, she used "Dear Prof. Rau." Similarly, Janet began with "Dear Teacher" or "Dear Professor" and ended with "Dear Prof. Rau." All of these illustrate how specific instruction on email writing made a difference in socializing the students into English academic culture.

Doug, who has a Ph.D. and is working at a nearby hospital, moved from "Dear Professor Rau" to "Dear Sir" and "Dear Rau," and finally to "Dear Dr. Rau" after instruction. His signature also moved from a fixed email signature to "Doug" and "Doug Cheng" and finally back to "Doug." His variation in terms of address and signature indicates a process of negotiation of relationship, and that the instruction helped him position himself appropriately in the academic hierarchy.

Although comprehensible output is necessary for second-language acquisition (Swain and Lapkin 1995), it is not sufficient in itself, as it ignores the difference in forms appropriate for different interpersonal relationships. Modeling by the instructor alone was insufficient to help students choose appropriate forms, in part due to the asymmetrical relationship. When the instructor wrote a request, as illustrated in Appendix 5, he would normally use 'please,' followed by the request. This is considered appropriate in an asymmetric power relationship, from high to low, but considered socially inappropriate when students copied the same form, as in (7). Instruction helped students understand the nature of interpersonal relationships and choose appropriate forms of making requests, as shown in Excerpt 8.

(7) From Jack, 2012/4/25

Dear Dr. Rau,
I am writing in response for the homework this week. I have attached the document to this email.
Could you please send me some feedbacks about the figure?

Best regards,
Jack Liu

(8) From Jack, 2012/5/3

Dear Dr. Rau,
The attached file is my analysis of the model paper. I would appreciate it if you could look over the analysis and give some comments.

Best regards,
Jack Liu

Finally, there was one case in which the student manifested development in email writing due to instruction through the content of the email, rather than the terms of address. Henry, whose data are not shown in the table, had the most frequent email interactions with the instructor. He always wanted to talk to the instructor before class and during the break. He also always acknowledged receipt of email from the instructor and asked where the PowerPoint was if the instructor was late sending materials. Although he demonstrated no change in forms of address, closing, or signature, apparently being comfortable with the formal style he used consistently, there was evidence of the importance of instruction in other areas. In (9), written before instruction, he uses the phrase "Would you please give me some comments on my assignment about figure?" After instruction (Excerpt 10), he applied the principles taught in class by modifying the request to the more polite form, "I would appreciate it if you could look over my assignment and give me comments on it." Even after the course was over,[5] he continued to apply the principles and frozen expression of email politeness in his writing, expressing various speech acts (Excerpt 11).

[5]An anonymous reviewer suggested that retrospective interviews could be conducted with the research subjects to figure out the real reason for their choices. While we agree that this would have strengthened the research, most of the students have graduated and moved elsewhere in the 2 years since the data were collected. Even if the subjects were successfully located, their ability to recall and accurately analyze their motivation 2 years prior is far from certain.

(9) From Henry, 2012/4/24

Dear Dr. Rau,
The attachment is the assignment for this week.
Would you please give me some comments on my assignment about figure?
Thank you.

Yours sincerely,
Henry Hsu

(10) From Henry, 2012/5/3

Dear Dr. Rau,

Attached is the assignment for the discussion section.
I am sorry that I miss the deadline of my assignment this week.
I apologize for the inconvenience my mistake may cause.
I would appreciate it if you could look over my assignment and give me comments on it.
Thank you.

Yours sincerely,

Henry Hsu

(11) From Henry, 2012/6/8

Dear Dr. Rau,

Thank you for giving me good guideline for scientific writing.
I also learn a lot from the class.
In addition, I appreciate it very much that you give me comments on my weekly assignment.
Finally, I could not find the attachment from the email.
I would appreciate it if you could give me the new syllabus that I could take a look on it.
Thank you very much.

Yours sincerely,
Henry Hsu

2.5 Conclusion

In summary, email is not a monolithic genre but is inherently fluid, varying according to the demand and the function of the speech events. As a mode of electronic communication, it can take the place of an e-course platform for homework submission, overlap with the functions of informal texting, or exhibit a more formal style. In two of most frequently occurring speech acts in academic email, i.e., requests and apologies, the negotiation of personal relationship can be observed most clearly in the use of terms of address to position the addressor and the addressee. It is also clear from the data that email politeness is both teachable and learnable because those who continued to email the instructor after email writing was taught indicated an informed decision to choose socially appropriate and consistent address forms and signatures, as well as using models to lessen the imposition of a request.

There is also evidence that in ESP instruction in an ELF setting, as in biliteracy, both instructor and student actions are essential. While the instructor was able to both model and provide instruction in principles of email writing, if students viewed email as simply a platform to submit homework rather than a place to negotiate relationship, there was no evidence of learning. Perhaps, the goal in ELF email instruction should not only simply be mutual intelligibility but should also include the importance of negotiation of relationship.

Although negotiation of interpersonal relationship is a key notion in the research, the major part of the discussion was restricted to a description of students' changing terms of address. Due to the limitation of the available data, we have not been able to provide a full account of how the change in terms of address reflected or lead to negotiation of interpersonal relationship, what kinds of negotiation were made in terms of email terms of address, what specific changes of interpersonal relationship occurred as a result of negotiation, or why the students chose to make those negotiations in email terms of address. Since the focus of the class was scientific writing rather than email writing or writing in general, and since the instructor wanted to ensure that the email communication was as authentic as possible, students were never asked to practice email writing skills, nor were they asked to consider what their relationship was with the professor and how that should be reflected in their email correspondence.

We do not claim that students' change of use of terms of address or the negotiation of interpersonal relationship in terms of address is solely caused by explicit instruction. Changing personal relationships over time undoubtedly plays a role in choice of terms of as well. We also acknowledge that the changes of terms of address in the students' emails may not be solely caused by the need to negotiate interpersonal relationship, but may be motivated by their desire to try out what they learned in class about email pragmatics. However, this study has provided some evidence from a few limited cases that students benefit from email instruction, and that since terms of address are important in negotiating personal relationships, this component should be actively incorporated into email instruction.

Appendix 1: Instruction on Principles of Communicative Success in Email

1. Terms of Address (Relationship)

   A. Salutations

      Dear Prof. Rau/Dear Dr. Rau (Formal, academic)

Dear Mr. Rau (Formal, non-academic)
Dear Gerry (Formal, close)
Dear Professor (Particular individual unknown and unimportant)
Dear Sir (Particular individual unknown and unimportant)
Hello Dr. Rau (Less formal, academic)
Hello Mr. Rau (Less formal, non-academic)
Hi Gerry (Informal, close)
Hi (Informal, close, frequent contact)
No salutation (Very informal, text/chat style)

B. Closings

Respectfully yours, Truly yours (Very formal)
Sincerely (Formal, general business)
Cordially, Best regards/wishes (Less formal)
Thank you (Informal)
No closing (Very informal)

C. Signature

Dr. Gerald A. Rau (Very formal)
Dr. Rau (Formal, distant)
Gerald Rau (Formal)
Gerry (Informal)

D. Salutations to avoid

Dear Teacher (Translation from Chinese)
Dear Dr. Gerald Rau (Do not use first name with title/last)
Dear Prof. Gerry (Titles attached to last name, not first)
Dear Rau (Last name should have title)

E. Closings to avoid

Your student (Avoid, Chinese use)

2. Amount of Information (Clarity)
Example from apology email: I cannot come to class tomorrow:

For personal reasons (too little information)
Because I need to take my mother to the doctor (appropriate)
Because my mother has chronic arthritis, and can't get around by herself, but my brother has a meeting in Taipei, so I have to go up to Miaoli to take my mother to see the doctor, and won't be able to get a bus back in time to make it to class (too much information)

3. Recognition of Imposition (Cooperation)
Example from request email: Can justify by emphasizing

Their ability: 'Since this is your area of specialty …' (best)
Relationship: [Often implied by talk of shared work] (typical)
Your need: 'Since the deadline is tomorrow …' (worst)
Leave decision in their hands, with reasonable time frame

'If you could' (expressed or implied)

4. Manner of Asking (Politeness)
   Example from request email: (most to least polite)

   I wonder if you could help me
   Could you please help me
   Could you help me
   Can you please help me
   Can you help me
   I hope you can help me
   I want/need you to help me
   Help me

5. Correctness of Form (Comprehension)

   Simple better than complex, less likely to be misstated or misinterpreted

Appendix 2: Letter Requesting Email Before Instruction

2012/4/24

Dear Class,

Tomorrow evening we will talk about writing email (requests and apologies) in addition to the discussion section. In order for me to see what you already know, I have a request: I would like each of you to write me an email this week.

If you are submitting a Figure, please write the email as a request—ask me to give you feedback on the Figure. If you are not submitting a Figure, please write the email as an apology—that you are not submitting a Figure.

Thank you.
I will send you the ppt handout tomorrow.
See you Thursday.

Sincerely,
Gerry Rau

Appendix 3: Letters Sent to Individual Students: Returned Homework, Showing Examples Coded as Brief Note (HB) and Comment (HC)

2012/3/25 Gerry Rau

XX,
Attached is a copy of your prewrite, with comments.
Gerry Rau

2012/4/12 Gerry Rau
Dear XX,

Here is your methods section, with comments. Please feel free to ask in class if there is anything you do not understand. Take the time to go through the corrections (using the track changes, move to the next change feature) to see what types of mistakes you tend to make, then pay attention to that issue in future sections. I have not made every necessary correction, perhaps, but have tried to call attention to common mistakes, and correct some of the occasional ones.
Gerry Rau

Appendix 4: Letters Sent to the Whole Spring Class: Sending Attachment

2012/5/24
Dear Class,

As last week, I will provide copies of the handout on the results/discussion section, which you will need to do the work in class, but if you want to make copies of the ppt or other pdf files, that is up to you. Sorry this is getting to you so late this week.

Please bring your Model Article to class (printed or electronic form).

See you tonight.
Gerry Rau

Appendix 5: Letters Sent to the Whole Spring Class: Request

2012/3/20
Dear Class,

Please remember to send me your assignments today. As I said, please send me whatever you have, even if you do not feel it is complete. Everything you submit for this class is part of a work in progress, not a final product. If you are having problems, tell me about it and send me what you have and I can help you take the next step.

See you Thursday.
Gerry Rau

Appendix 6: Letters Sent to the Whole Spring Class: Apology

2012/4/19
Dear Class,

Attached you will find a copy of the handout for tonight. It is larger than usual due to the number of figures included, so give it time to download.

I am sorry to be sending it to you later this week than usual, and hope it does not cause too much inconvenience. It has been a busy week for me, as I am sure it has been for some of you. I should be able to get it to you earlier again next week.
I look forward to seeing you this evening.
Gerry Rau

Appendix 7: Letter Sent to the Whole Spring Class: Gratitude

2012/6/7
Dear class,

Thank you for the learning experience. Teachers always learn as much as students, if not more. I have learned a lot about the writing process in helping you through it, and hope you have as well. I have modified the syllabus based on my experience, to make it more useful to future classes (see attached). There will be another session in August/September, if you know anyone else who would benefit from it.
I think I have returned all of your work with comments, but if you sent something and did not get a response let me know and I will take a look. Otherwise, best wishes for your future careers.
Gerry Rau

References

Biber, Douglas, Susan Conrad, and Randi Reppen. 1994. Corpus-based approaches to issues in applied linguistics. Reprinted in Li Wei (Ed.), 2011. *The Routledge applied linguistics reader*. 185–201. London: Routledge.

Brown, Roger, and Albert Gilman. 1972. The pronouns of power and solidarity. In *Language and social context*, ed. Pier Paolo Giglioli, 252–282. Harmondsworth: Penguin.

Brown, Penelope, and Stephen C. Levinson. 1987. *Politeness: Some universals in language usage*. New York: Cambridge University Press.

Chen, Yuan-shan. 2011. The development of a speech act profile. Paper presented at the 16th congress of applied linguistics (AILA): Harmony in diversity: Language, culture and society. August 23–28, Beijing Foreign Studies University.

Cohen, Andrew D. 1996. Developing the ability to perform speech acts. *Studies in Second Language Acquisition* 18(2): 253–267.

Duff, Patricia. 2008. *Case study research in applied linguistics*. New York: Lawrence Erlbaum Associates.

Friedrich, Paul. 1972. Social context and semantic feature: The Russian pronominal usage. In *Directions in sociolinguistics,* eds. John Gumperz and Dell Hymes, 270–300. New York: Holt, Rinehart and Winston.

Fasold, Ralph. 1990. *The sociolinguistics of language*. Cambridge, MA: Blackwell.

Formentelli, Maicol. 2009. Address strategies in a British academic setting. *Pragmatics* 19(2): 179–196.

Goldberg, Adele. 2006. *Construction at work: The nature of generalization in language*. Oxford: Oxford University Press.

Gu, Yueguo. 1990. Politeness phenomena in modern Chinese. *Journal of Pragmatics* 14: 237–257.

Gries, Stefan Th, and Stefanie Wulff. 2005. Do foreign language learners also have constructions? *Annual Review of Cognitive Linguistics* 3: 182–200.

Hartford, Beverly S. and Kathleen Bardovi-Harlig. 1996. "At your earliest convenience": A study of written student requests to faculty. In *Pragmatics and Language Learning*, ed. Lawrence F. Bouton, 55–69, vol. 7. Urbana-Campaign: Division of English as an International Language. University of Illinois.

Huang, Chao-Li. 2009. *Politeness in children's language use in EFL language classroom in Taiwan*. Unpublished Master's thesis, Providence University, Taichung, Taiwan.

Labov, William. 1972. *Sociolinguistic patterns*. Philadelphia: University of Pennsylvania Press.

Lantolf, James P., and Steven L. Thorne. 2006. *Sociocultural theory and the genesis of second language development*. New York, NY: Oxford University Press.

Larsen-Freeman, Diane, and Lynne Cameron. 2008. *Complex systems and applied linguistics*. Oxford: Oxford University Press.

Li, Wan-Jing, Yuan-shan Chen, and Der-Hwa Victoria Rau. 2011. What constitutes an appropriate email request? In *Multimedia-Based Multicultural Instruction and Research: Innovative 21st-Century Approaches via Literature and Language*, ed. Ying-hsiung Chou, 151–166. Taipei: Crane.

Li, Wan-Jing. 2013. Politeness and effectiveness of English request emails: Taiwanese professors' perspectives. Unpublished Master's thesis. National Chung Cheng University, Chiayi, Taiwan.

Lin, You-Rong. 1996. *An analysis of the use of "nin" and "ni" in the mundane world*. Unpublished Master's thesis, Providence University. Taichung, Taiwan.

Lu, Pi-Hsia. 2012. A nexus analysis approach toward Taiwanese secretaries' ESP needs and communicative strategies. Unpublished doctoral dissertation. National Kaohsiung Normal University, Taiwan.

Mackey, Alison, and Susan M. Gass. 2005. *Second language research: Methodology and design*. Mahwah, NJ: Lawrence Erlbaum Associates.

Rau, Der-Hwa Victoria, Hui-Huan A. Chang, and Elaine Tarone. 2009. Think or sink: Chinese learners' acquisition of the voiceless interdental fricative. *Language Learning* 59(3): 581–621.

Rau, Der-Hwa Victoria, Lan-Hsin Chang, Yung-Hui Chien, and Lu Hsiao-Yun. 2012. From corpus to classroom: Investigating dative alternation of "give". In *Investigating language at the interface*, ed. Ming-Yu. Tseng, 27–76. Kaohsiung: Center for the Humanities and the College of Liberal Arts. National Sun Yat-sen University.

Rossman, Gretchen B., and Sharon F. Rallis. 2003. *Learning in the field: An introduction to qualitative research*, 2nd ed. Thousand Oaks, CA: Sage Publications.

Schiffrin, Deborah. 1994. *Approaches to discourse: Language as social interaction*. Oxford: Blackwell.

Scollon Ron and Suzannie Wong Scollon. 2001. *Intercultural communication*, 2nd ed. Malden, MA: Blackwell.

Seidlhofer, Barbara. 2001. Closing a conceptual gap: The case for a description of English as a lingua franca. *International Journal of Applied Linguistics* 11: 133–158.

Seidlhofer, Barbara. 2004. Research perspectives on teaching English as a lingua franca. *Annual Review of Applied Linguistics* 24: 209–239.

Swain, Merrill, and Sharon Lapkin. 1995. Problems in output and the cognitive processes they generate: A step towards second language learning. *Applied Linguistics* 16: 371–391.

Swales, John. 1990. *Genre analysis: English in academic and research settings*. New York: Cambridge University Press.

Swales, John M., and Christine B. Feak. 1994. *Academic writing for graduate students: Essential tasks and skills*, 2nd ed. Ann Arbor, MI: The University of Michigan Press.

Swales, John. M. and Christine B. Feak. 2000. *English in today's research world: A writing guide*. Ann Arbor, MI: The University of Michigan Press.

Tannen, Deborah. 1993. The relativity of linguistic strategies: Rethinking power and solidarity in gender and dominance. In *Gender and conversational interaction*, ed. Deborah Tannen, 165–188. Oxford: Oxford University Press.

Tannen, Deborah. 1995. The power of talk: Who gets heard and why. Reprinted in Dallin D. Oaks (Ed.), 2001. *Linguistics at work: A reader of applications*. 242–259. Cambridge, MA: Heinle & Heinle.

Wallace, Michael J. 1998. *Action research for language teachers*. New York: Cambridge University Press.

Wolfram, Walt. 2011. Fieldwork methods in language variation. In *The SAGE handbook of sociolinguistics*, ed. Ruth Wodak, Barbara Johnstone, and Paul Kerswill, 296–311. Thousand Oaks, CA: Sage Publications.

Wright, Saundra K. 2009. Forms of address in the college classroom. In *Proceedings of the 23rd International Congress of Onomastic Sciences*. York University, Canada. http://yorkspace.library.yorku.ca/xmlui/handle/10315/4053?show=full.

Yang, Suya, Yuanshan Chen, and Victoria Rau. 2011. Evaluation of American and Taiwanese English speakers' apologies. In *Multimedia-based multicultural instruction and research: Innovative 21st-century approaches via literature and language*, ed. Ying-hsiung Chou, 106–124. Taipei: Crane.

Author Biographies

Der-Hwa Victoria Rau (何德華) is professor of linguistics at National Chung Cheng University in Taiwan. Her research interests include sociolinguistics, applied linguistics, and Austronesian linguistics. In addition to her major works on Yami (Austronesian language) grammar, dictionary, and textbooks, she has also produced a textbook on Research methodology in teaching Chinese as a second language.

Gerald Rau teaches English Scientific and Engineering Writing at National Chung Cheng University Ching Jiang Learning Center in Taiwan. A semi-retired science teacher, he has taught ESL students for many years, has edited numerous papers in the natural sciences, medicine, applied mathematics, engineering, and linguistics, and is the author of *Mapping the Origins Debate*.

Chapter 3
Discourse Organization and Features of Email Writing Among EFL Students in Taiwan

Li-Jung Huang

Abstract This study investigates how Taiwanese EFL learners use their linguistic repertoire to communicate with their teachers in emails. A corpus of 76 emails were collected and analyzed according to (1) language choice; (2) function; (3) patterns of the main messages; and (4) spoken and written features. The results show that, first, both groups of students prefer English as the main language of communication in their emails. Moreover, the students were found to code-switch in the emails. Second, two main functions were identified in the emails: request and inquiry. Third, three main elements were found in students' email writing: a self-identification of the student, the main purpose of the email (e.g., request, inquiry, and apology), and an optional thanking formulaic expression. Comparing graduate and undergraduate students, the writing style of the graduate students is more formal than that of the undergraduate students. In terms of features of email writing, email is unique in the sense that it combines features from both speech and writing. Finally, the students were found to employ strategies of visualizing nonlinguistic characteristics in emails which are prominent in spoken interaction.

Keywords Email · Computer-mediated communication · Language choice · EFL learners

L.-J. Huang (✉)
Department of English Language, Literature and Linguistics,
Providence University, Taichung, Taiwan
e-mail: ljhuang@gm.pu.edu.tw

Y. Chen et al. (eds.), *Email Discourse Among Chinese Using English as a Lingua Franca*, DOI 10.1007/978-981-287-888-5_3

3.1 Introduction

3.1.1 Computer-Mediated Communication (CMC)

Since the early 1990s, the popularization of Internet use has inspired vigorous research in the area of language use in computer-mediated communication (CMC). Herring (1996, p. 1) defines CMC as 'communication that takes place between human beings via the instrumentality of computers.' Due to the constraint of technology, most media in CMC still require the use of text in writing; hence, the focus of CMC research has been on the use of languages. Specifically, the term CMD was proposed (Herring 2001) to capture the uniqueness of the discourse structure of various media in CMC. According to Herring (2001, 2007), the study of CMD is a specialization within the study of CMC, with an emphasis on language and language use in computer-networked environments, and by its use of methods of discourse analysis to address the emphasis.

There are different types of CMC. A common distinction made in CMC is based on synchronicity of participation (Kiesler et al. 1984). According to this criterion, there are two types of CMC: synchronous and asynchronous. Synchronous communication refers to interaction that takes place in real time via delay chats, chat rooms, or instant message. Asynchronous communication allows the CMC users to access the media at a different time. Email is an example of this type (Herring 2001). Email is a basic form of asynchronous Internet communication, which allows text messages to be sent to a specific address(es) (Hine 2000). While other forms have faded over the time (e.g., BBS and MSN), email remains the most used and reliable CMC medium. Its users cover a wide range of people. A survey conducted by Rogen International (2001) indicates that the use of email has grown by more than 600 % in 6 years from 1995 to 2001. Two features of email account for the use and preference of email as a communication means. First, email is asynchronous in which it does not require the real-time coexistence of sender and receiver for communication to occur. Second, email can address multiple recipients in a single action and senders can distribute messages quickly and easily, as it is convenient and low cost (Gains 1999).

3.1.2 Email

Earlier research on emails has mainly discussed the use of English in relation to the dichotomy of spoken/written styles (e.g., Baron 2000; Crystal 2001; Gruber 1997). However, more recent studies have examined how multilinguals use their linguistic resources online generally and in email communication specifically (e.g., Danet and Herring 2007; Paolillo 1996; Su 2003; Warschauer et al. 2002). Similar to face-to-face interaction, language choice has become a tool for bilinguals and multilinguals to exploit in emails. In terms of functions of emails, previous research (e.g., Harrison 1998; Huang 2004) suggests that most emails serve a referential function, as opposed to an affective function (Holmes 2013). Huang's (2004) study of a social network of Chinese–English bilinguals in Taiwan found that emails were mainly used for organizing meetings, exchanging information, and delivering announcements. Similarly, Chen's (2006) study found students mainly wrote to their supervisors for referential function. This suggests that unlike face-to-face interaction, emails are mainly used for transactional purposes.

The dichotomy of spoken/written features of emails has been much discussed in previous research. For example, Murray (1995) identified several such features: the use of deletion of subject pronouns (also known as ellipsis), determiners, and auxiliaries; use of abbreviations; lack of correction of typos; and lack of mixed case. More recently, Cho (2010) compared linguistic features of emails and written memoranda in an academic workplace and found the email sample differed from the memoranda in containing more features common in spoken interaction such as structural reductions, expressive features, greeting and leave-taking formulas, and instances of linguistic innovation. Emails also exhibit written features commonly found in letter writing such as openings and closings. Crystal concluded that the language of emails is "in the middle" (2001, p. 41) containing both spoken and written features. In sum, email is an intermediate form of discourse which shares features with both written and spoken language. It is written and asynchronous, but it is also interactive and informal. Although early research characterized the language of email as either an oral- or writing-based standard of communication, 'almost all contemporary studies seem to agree that electronic language is equally influenced by both' (Vurdien 2011, p. 62).

To address the uniqueness of email writing, this study aims to demonstrate how Taiwanese students use their linguistic repertoire, including Chinese and English, to communicate with their teachers in email writing.

3.1.3 Internet Use and Language Use in Taiwan

Taiwan is well known for its well-constructed network and development in computer technology. As early as 2005, an investigation of the International Telecommunication Union (ITU) on the prevalence of computer and Internet use ranked Taiwan as the fifth highest country in prevalence of computer use and fourth in prevalence of Internet use. More generally, according to Internet World Stats (2013), the number of Internet users in Taiwan has been increasing since 2000, with the percentage of Internet users growing from 28.1 % in 2000 to 70.1 % in 2010, more than doubling over the period of 10 years. The most recent survey conducted by ITU indicated the percentage of Taiwan's population who are Internet users reached 76 % in 2012 (ITU 2013). Similarly, a recent survey conducted by TWNIC on Internet usage of the sample population (over 12 years old) during a period of 3 months in 2013 found that 79.18 % of the sample population had used Internet before and 76.58 % of the sample population had used the Internet within 6 months.

In terms of the age of the Internet users, according to the same survey, 100 % of those ranging in age from 20 to 24 were Internet users, while in the age groups of 15–19 and 25–34, Internet use reached over 90 %. This shows that the largest population using the Internet comprises teenagers and young adults. The increasing online population in Taiwan indicates the significance of the medium in people's daily life, thus highlighting the importance of understanding the nature of the Internet usage, including language practice.

Taiwan is a multilingual community where several Chinese languages and aboriginal languages are spoken on the island. The majority languages in Taiwan include Mandarin and Taiwanese, with Mandarin being the lingua franca. In addition, the Ministry of Education (MOE) of Taiwan has stipulated English as the only mandatory foreign language taught in schools, with obligatory instruction starting in primary school. This emphasis on English may be attributed to the status of English as a global language (Crystal 1997), leading to the majority of people learning English as a foreign language (EFL) in Taiwan. Because of the advantage of Taiwan being a multilingual speech community and a society where Internet use is widespread, Taiwan provides an ideal site for studying language use phenomena in the CMC setting.

3.1.4 Research Questions

Focusing on two groups of EFL learners, this study addresses four research questions:

1. What language do EFL learners of Chinese background use in emails when corresponding with their teacher?
2. What are the main functions of the emails?
3. What are the common patterns of the main messages in the emails?
4. What are the spoken and written features of emails?

3.2 Methods

3.2.1 Email Corpus

The email corpus includes 76 emails written by Chinese-speaking students majoring in English to a Chinese/English bilingual teacher (also the researcher). Out of the 76 emails, 38 were written by undergraduate students and 38 were written by graduate students. The researcher collected the emails over a span of 3 months from 2012 to 2013. The email correspondence was observed by the researcher first and then collected. All the emails from the students to the teacher over the span of time were collected, accounting for the corpus of the study.

Table 3.1 Information of the participants

	Male	Female	Total
Undergraduate	6	13	19
Graduate	5	7	12
Total	11	20	31

3.2.2 *Participants*

In total, there are 31 student participants contributing to the email corpus. The participants include 19 undergraduate students majoring in English and 12 graduate students majoring in linguistics at a university situated in central Taiwan. Both groups of students were recruited from the Department of English. The students were all Chinese/English bilinguals speaking Mandarin and/or Taiwanese as their first language(s). Since English or linguistics is their major, the students are in an environment where English is used at least in the classroom context. In terms of age, the age range of the undergraduate students is from 19 to 22 and that of the graduate students is from 24 to 26. Most of undergraduate students who contributed the emails were sophomore, junior, and senior students, while most of the graduate students who contributed the emails were in the process of writing up their MA theses. As mentioned earlier, the largest group of Internet users in Taiwan is the age group of 12–25. This corresponds roughly to the age of the participants, thus enabling the understanding of how this group of youngsters uses languages in email writing. In terms of gender, the graduate group includes seven female students and five male students; and the undergraduate group includes 13 female students and six male students (see Table 3.1). The teacher is female, in her 30 s at the time of data collection. She teaches mainly linguistics courses in the Department of English and is the instructor and supervisor of the undergraduate and graduate students. The teacher is also the researcher, offering an emic view (Androutsopoulos 2006) in approaching the data.

3.2.3 *Procedures*

The procedures for collecting and analyzing the data include three stages: (1) observation, (2) data collection, and (3) data analysis. First, the observation provides the researcher information about the participants as well as frequency of email correspondence. Second, emails between the period of November 2011 and January 2012 were collected and compiled together for the two groups of the students—undergraduate and graduate—and the data collection was completed by January 2012. Finally, four analyses were conducted: (1) language choice of the EFL students in emails; (2) function of the emails; (3) patterns of the main message in the emails; and (4) spoken and written features in emails. The analyses included three stages. First, a second rater was invited to participate in the data analysis procedure in order to avoid subjective judgment of a single rater (i.e., the researcher). Second, a list of coding categories was generated from the data and from previous studies (e.g., Huang 2004; Lin 2008 for language choice; Harrison 1998; Huang 2004 for functions; Guffey 2010 for discourse structure of emails; and Murray1995; Herring 2007 for spoken and written features) by the two raters. Finally, the analyses were conducted. Since there were minimal differences in the analyses by the two raters, an inter-rater reliability test was not conducted. The only difference identified by the two raters was regarding the analysis of function of emails in the category of request where two instances of request were identified as inquiry/request by the second rater. These two cases were discussed by the two raters and were both classified as requests based on the main function of the emails.

3.3 Findings and Discussion

This section is divided into three sections. Section 3.3.1 describes the general pattern of language choice and function of the email corpus. This offers a general understanding of how languages and emails are used by EFL learners in their email writing. The email structure is decomposed into four main parts including opening, main message, closing, and signature. Section 3.3.2 analyses the patterns of the main messages in the emails. Section 3.3.3 describes written (opening, closing, and signature) and spoken features of the language used in email. The relationship between language choice and written features such as openings and closings is also discussed. In addition, the use of visualization of nonlinguistic features is described.

3.3.1 Language Choice and Function of Emails

3.3.1.1 General Pattern of Language Choice of Emails

Table 3.2 shows the language choice of the emails by the two groups of the students: undergraduate and graduate. A chi-square test was performed in order to provide evidence for the relationship between the two groups of the students and the language choice of emails. The result shows that there is a significant difference between the two groups of the students in relation to their language choice in emails, X^2 (2, $N = 76$) = 13.033, $p < 0.05$. Out of the 76 emails, more than 50 % of the emails were written in English, followed by a mix of Chinese and English (24 %), and Chinese (18 %). In the emails by the undergraduate students, 42.1 % of the emails were in English, 34.2 % were in Chinese, and 23.7 % were in a mix of Chinese and English. In the emails by the graduate students, most of the emails were written in English accounting for over 70 % (73.7 %), followed by a mix of Chinese and English (23.7 %). There is only one email written in Chinese. This indicates that both groups of students preferred English as the main language of

Table 3.2 Number of emails in relation to language choice

	Undergraduate	Graduate	Total	Percentage (%)
English	16	28	44	58
Chinese	13	1	14	18
Chinese/English	9	9	18	24
Total	38	38	76	100

communication in their emails. The students were also found to use both Chinese and English; that is, code-switching occurred in their email writing. Chinese did not seem to be the preferred language in emails by the graduate students. As opposed to the graduate students, undergraduate students also used Chinese in their emails.

Several factors can account for the predominant use of English in the corpus. First, the recipient of these emails is a linguistics teacher who uses mainly English in her classes. Second, the students are English majors. Furthermore, the context is an institutional one where English is taught as the students' major or where most of the content subjects are taught in English. This means that the context facilitates the use of English. According to Clyne (1991), sociolinguistic factors determine the choice of language. These factors include interlocutor, domain, and channel of communication, just to name a few. Although his discussion is restricted to face-to-face interaction, the same can be applied to CMC. Since the recipient (i.e., the teacher) and the context (i.e., the Department of English) as well as the background of the students are all related to English, the students may feel compelled to use English instead of Chinese; that is, English is considered the *unmarked* language for communication (Myers-Scotton 1993), accounting for the use of English in emails in a non-English-dominant context (see also Danet and Herring 2007).

Previous literature has emphasized the role of English as an international language, thus facilitating the use of English in CMC (see e.g., Warschauer et al. 2002). However, since both the students and the teacher are Chinese native speakers and the participants are located in a Chinese speech community, the status of English as an international language does not seem to be a concern here. The influence of contextual factors seems more relevant in discussing the participants' language choice. As mentioned by Herring (2001), language use in CMC reflects the influence on the linguistic choices of computer-mediated discourse (CMD) users of social factors such as participant demographics and situational context.

3.3.1.2 Functions of Emails

Table 3.3 lists the functions of emails identified in the email corpus by the two groups of students. A list of functions was derived based on the data. They comprise request, inquiry, providing information, thanking, apologizing, asking for leave of absence, confirmation of appointment or information, and wishing, in that order. A chi-square test was also performed to determine the relationship between the two

Table 3.3 Number of emails according to their function

Function	Undergraduate	Graduate	Total
Request	9	19	28
Inquiry	7	9	16
Thanking	8	2	10
Providing information	5	5	10
Apologizing	2	2	4
Asking for leave of absence	4	–	4
Confirmation of appointment/information	3	–	3
Wishing	–	1	1
Total	38	38	76

groups of the students and the functions of the emails. The result shows that there is a significant difference between the two groups of the students in the functions of the emails, X^2 (7, $N = 76$) = 14.716, $p < 0.05$.

As has been found in previous studies (e.g., Harrison 1998; Huang 2004), the data in this study indicate that most emails serve a referential function. In general, most of the emails served the functions of request and inquiry. Request is an act of asking for something to be done while inquiry refers to questions intended to get information. These two functions accounted for more than 50 % of the email corpus. The data found that students mainly wrote to the teacher to ask for help, for writing a recommendation letter, for the possibility of having a make-up exam, and for uploading course information on the university website. Following request, students wrote to their teacher for the purpose of inquiry; that is, asking for information about various matters; for example, asking for their grades or clarifying some concepts discussed in the course. Other functions which occurred relatively frequently were to provide information (e.g., the time and location of an oral exam on the part of the graduate students), and to thank the teacher for something the teacher had done for them earlier (e.g., writing a recommendation letter). Other functions were to apologize for imposing on her for a request made earlier, to ask for a leave of absence, and finally to confirm the time and location for an appointment or to confirm information mentioned in earlier emails. Comparing the two groups of students, undergraduate students wrote to their teacher for a slightly wider variety of functions and they wrote for these functions with relatively similar frequency. The top three functions for undergraduate students were request, thanking, and inquiry. On the other hand, the top three functions for graduate students were request, inquiry, and providing information. Providing information refers mainly to information regarding the graduate students' oral exams details such as location and time, so it is not surprising that this category is less common in undergraduate emails.

Examples of emails serving these functions are as follows:

(1) Would you please put the third take-home exercise on e-learning?
(2) I have enclosed the final project in this email, please check it.
(3) I am Kim. I want to ask for my score for final exam. [sic][1]
(4) Just wanna ask if we could know our grade of final exam.
(5) I will present my proposal at 12.10 on Wednesday, January 4th. The presentation will take place in room 400.
(6) I am Holly. Although I didn't get the scholarship, still thank you to help me to write the recommend letter!
(7) Thank you. The exercise is online now.
(8) I'm sorry. I'll upload the record later after my class.
(9) I am Ruth… Because the graduation photos will be taken on 11/20 Fri., I will not be able to attend the class that morning.
(10) I am E4X Tom, taking Language and Culture. I'd like to ask for a leave of the class this week for my Mother has been in hospital several days and she gets very sick now… I am sorry I fail to present the class this week.
(11) I will be at room 300 on time and bring my medical certificate…
(12) I forgot to tell you, Merry X'mas.

Examples (1) and (2) are examples of requests, where students ask the teacher to upload an exercise online (1) or revise writing done by the student (2). These examples also illustrate that the requests can be realized differently; that is, using the interrogative form as in (1) or the imperative form with a politeness marker 'please' as in (2) (see also Sect. 3.3.2). The choice of vocabulary in example (2) is also of a more formal nature, as indicated by the choice of the verb 'enclose.' Examples (3) and (4) inquire about the student's score for the final exam. They are both inquiries, with (3) using a direct 'I want' statement (see also Chen 2006) and (4) using the more indirect 'if clause.' Example (5) provides information about the presentation of a proposal. Examples (2) and (5) are particularly common in the emails of the graduate students, as they are mainly writing to ask the teacher to revise their writings or to provide information about their presentations or oral exams. Examples (6) and (7) serve the function of thanking, with (6) of a more elaborate style than (7). Example (8) shows a case of apologizing for forgetting to upload a piece of information online with the conventional expression 'I'm sorry' followed by a statement of future action. Examples (9) and (10) are asking for leave of absence. They illustrate that when the students ask for leave of absence, self-identification and explanations are given. Example (11) is to confirm an appointment with the teacher and, finally, example (12) is to wish the teacher a happy holiday.

Harrison (1998) and Huang (2004) observe two major functions of emails: interactional and transactional. In particular, Huang (2004) finds that the majority of her emails have an interactional function with only a few serving a purely transactional purpose. As opposed to Huang's (2004) study, which examined email

[1]In the following examples, details about the students are changed and pseudonyms are used. All the examples are excerpts from the email corpus. All the typos and formats follow the original texts in the emails.

correspondence among a social network of friends, the data in the present study show that the emails serve mainly a transactional function, with the exception of one email wishing the teacher Merry Christmas (example (12)). This can be attributed to the nature of the corpus being situated in the academic context where the email correspondence is between students and a teacher and where requests are frequently performed through email. This finding is similar to Chen's (2006) where she discusses the request strategies in English used by a Taiwanese student to the professors in email writing, in which the function of request appears to be common in institutional contexts.

Finally, it should be noted that the functions identified in the corpus refer to the main function of the emails. The identification of the functions in the emails is based on the main function. However, there are cases where more than one function is included in a single email. Example (10) shows that after the main message, asking for a leave of absence, the student includes an apology. The following section describes the structure of the main messages in the emails which will also illustrate the multi-functions included in the same email.

3.3.2 Discourse Organization of Email Message

Guffey (2010) identified four elements in email message components: (a) an informative subject line, (b) an opening, (c) a body, and (d) a closing. The subject line is built into the email system, while opening, body, and closing are elements that the email users include in their actual writing. This section will discuss different components and stylistic features of emails in the corpus. As this study examined EFL students' use of languages in email, the focus of this section is on their use of English in order to see how they organized their email messages in the target language. Section 3.3.1.2 describes the use of emails for different functions. Following this, we discuss the patterns of the main messages in terms of these functions. The focus is on request, inquiry, thanking, apologizing, and asking for leave of absence, since providing information and confirmation of appointment/information mainly make use of the structure of declaratives. Generally speaking, the overall pattern of the emails includes (a) a self-identification of the student, (b) the main message of the email (e.g., request, inquiry, and apology), and a thanking formulaic expression regardless the function of the message. Thanking is optional and these elements occur in both Chinese and English. However, the discussion here is restricted to English.

In terms of request, the most common pattern is 'request + reason' or the other way around for both groups of students. Other elements such as self-identification, thanking, apology, and promise for future action are optional. Self-identification is often included at the beginning of email correspondence and it is more common among undergraduate students. In the undergraduate student corpus, fifteen include self-identification. The initial contact always includes self-identification. However, later correspondence does not require this on the part of the student. The difference between the two groups of students may be due to the fact that the graduate students tend to correspond with the teacher more frequently than the undergraduate students.

The following lists a few examples:

(13) Please have a look.
(14) Just hope you can give me a opportunity, because I have a risk for…
(15) I am your Introduction to X student of Thursday morning. My name is Adam. I think my score is not ideal. Hope professor could gives me a chance to improve. I promise I will do better in next semester. Thank you professor.

Example (13) illustrates a simple direct request in imperative form with a politeness marker 'please.' In contrast, example (14) illustrates a request in interrogative form provided with a reason. Example (15) shows a case of a request with the pattern of 'self-identification + reason + request + promise for future action + thanking.' As can be seen from these examples, the request strategies range from a simple short request in imperative form to a more elaborate one. Chen (2006) finds that the pattern of email writing by a Taiwanese student using English in the academic context is of an inductive approach. That is, the request strategy follows the order of (a) self-identification, (b) abstract or pre-request without giving a specific purpose, (c) lengthy personal details/contextual information for performing the request, and (d) request act or purpose statement. In her research of request strategies in emails among native and nonnative speakers of English, Biesenbach-Lucas (2006) also suggests that email requests are realized through predominantly indirect forms. In contrast to these studies, this study shows that students used a relatively simple request strategy without too many personal/contextual details.

In terms of inquiry, the basic forms used by the two groups of students vary slightly. The most common pattern by the graduate students is 'reason + inquiry.' The optional elements include self-identification, thanking, and apology. To ask a question, graduate students almost always include a reason explaining the inquiry. However, the most common pattern by the undergraduate students is a simple 'inquiry.' The optional elements are self-identification, thanking, and reason. The following two examples illustrate the difference of inquiry strategies between the two groups of students. Example (16) shows the pattern of 'reason + inquiry,' a common strategy used by graduate students. Example (17) shows the 'I want' statement commonly used by undergraduate students.

(16) I would like to discuss the data analysis with you this week. Do you have free time this week?
(17) I want to ask for my score for final exam.

In terms of thanking, the common pattern for the graduate students is 'thanking + promise for future action + wishing,' while the pattern for the undergraduate students is 'reason + thanking.' The graduate students tend to use a more elaborate style for thanking than undergraduate students. Moreover, there are more variations of usage among the undergraduate students, ranging from a simple formulaic expression 'thank you' to a more elaborate pattern 'thanking + reason + promise for future action + thanking.' Example (18) shows the pattern by a graduate student 'thanking + promise for future action + thanking + wishing.' Examples (19) and (20) are both produced by undergraduate students where (19) includes a formulaic expression and (20) a more elaborate pattern.

(18) Thank you so much. I will work on it right away. I appreciate all your help! Merry Christmas to you and your family.
(19) Thank you very much for your help.
(20) Thank you for sending the information of my score. I know I did not do my best this semester. The result is all my fault. I promise I will study harder on next time. Thank you professor. Hope you have a good winter break.

Whereas graduate students tend to be more elaborate when thanking, undergraduate students tend to be more elaborate than graduate students when performing apologies. The common patterns by the undergraduate students are 'apology + promise of future action' (21) and 'reason + apology + more details about the reason' (22). The apology strategies for the graduate students can range from a simple pattern of 'reason + apology' (23) to 'reason + apology + more details about the reason + thanking' (24). Examples are as follows:

(21) OK!! I'm sorry. I'll upload the record later after my class. I'll send you letter after I finish it.
(22) I seldom check my e-mail, so didn't notice this email about now and i'm truly sorry. If I did check my mailbox earlier, I would have come to you because I have some problems about my school work.
(23) I forgot to merge the table! Sorry!
(24) I can't finish 6 all in the deadline. I'll hand in the other 2 during winter vacation. Sorry for this, I tried, but really can't do them all, but I wanna finish my job after the deadline. Thank you, professor.

Finally, asking for a leave of absence only appears in the emails of the undergraduate students. The basic pattern of asking for a leave of absence is 'self-identification + leave of absence + reason' with the order of leave of absence and reason being reversible. The optional elements are apology and thanking. Example (10) illustrates the pattern with an apology at the end of the message.

(10) I am E4X Tom, taking Language and Media. I'd like to ask for a leave of the class this week for my Mother has been in hospital several days and she gets very sick now… I am sorry I fail to present the class this week.

3.3.3 Spoken and Written Features

In terms of features of email writing, email is unique in the sense that it combines features from both speech and writing. In comparison with written features, two elements from letter writing were identified: openings (also known as greetings or salutations) and closings. Although both openings and closings are considered optional in email writing, openings occur far more frequently than closings. Closings are further divided into two elements: pre-closings and signatures. Generally speaking, pre-closings occur less frequently than signatures. Moreover, emails are found to exhibit spoken features such as subject pronoun deletion and use of abbreviations. In the following, these features will be described.

3.3.3.1 Written Features

In terms of written features, the analysis focuses on openings, pre-closings, and signatures. Table 3.4 shows that out of the 76 emails, openings occurred in 68 emails, signatures occurred in 50 emails, and pre-closings occurred in 32. Chi-square tests were performed on the three written features in order to determine whether the two groups of students differed significantly in use of these features. The results from the chi-square tests show that in terms of openings, the result is not significant ($p = 0.262$). However, in terms of pre-closings and signatures, the results are significant (pre-closings, $p = 0.020$ and signatures, $p = 0.004$). In almost 90 % of the emails, the students included an opening. This indicates that opening is a major element in emails. Signatures also constituted an important element in email writing accounting for about 66 % of the corpus. The slightly lower use of signatures in emails may be due to the function of a medium where the recipient automatically knows the identity of the sender based on the email address. In terms of pre-closings, the usage is still common although it is far less than that of openings.

Table 3.4 also illustrates the use of these written features in relation to the two groups of students. We see that graduate students tended to provide signatures, while in about half of the undergraduate corpus of emails, they tended not to provide a signature at the end of the email. A similar trend was found for pre-closings, where graduate students tended to provide pre-closings more than undergraduate students. In terms of openings, both groups of students provided an opening at the beginning of the email. The use of these features exhibited written features common in letter writing, suggesting the graduate students considering email a more formal medium of communication.

Tables 3.5 and 3.6 show the language choice for openings, pre-closings, and signatures for the undergraduates and graduates, respectively. Chi-square tests were performed in order to determine whether there was a difference between the two groups of the students in the choice of language used for the three features. The results from the chi-square tests show that in terms of openings, the result is

Table 3.4 Written features of emails in terms of openings, pre-closings, and signatures

	Undergraduate	Graduate	Total	Percentage (%)
Openings	32	36	68	89
Pre-closings	11	21	32	42
Signatures	19	31	50	66

Table 3.5 Language choice and written features among undergraduate students

	Openings	Pre-closings	Signatures
English	15	10	13
Chinese	13	1	5
Chinese/English	4	0	1
Total	32	11	19

significant ($p = 0.000$); however, in terms of pre-closings and signatures, the results are not significant, with p values both above 0.05 (pre-closings, $p = 1.000$ and signatures, $p = 0.053$). That is, undergraduate and graduate students use different language choices for openings, but not for pre-closings and signatures. It should be noted that the p value for signatures almost reached the significance level.

From Table 3.5, we see that English was predominantly used for all three features by undergraduate students. The use of English was more prominent in pre-closings and signatures. There was only one example of pre-closing in Chinese and 5 out of the 19 examples of signatures were in Chinese. As mentioned in Sect. 3.2.1, the students are English majors, which means that most of them have an English name, facilitating the use of English signatures.

Furthermore, the data show that about nine types of openings were used in the email corpus. The use of openings ranges from no opening to more formal opening, but most of the emails include a relatively formal opening. The following includes only examples of openings and pre-closings, as signatures entail use of names. The use of openings occurs in both languages as well as a mix of Chinese and English. Patterns of openings include the following:

(25) Dear + Professor/Teacher (+Last name)
(26) Dear + First name (+teacher)
(27) *Laoshi* (teacher)
(28) *Laoshi* (teacher) + *ninhao*/*nihao*
(29) (Dear +) *Huang Lijung* or *Lijung* + (laoshi) + *ninhao/nihao*

As can be seen from the examples, the more common English patterns are 'Dear + Title' with or without Last name and 'Dear + First name.' The Chinese examples include the use of Title (*laoshi*) with or without the formulaic expression of Chinese greeting, *ninhao* or *nihao*, the former *nin* referring to the formal you (V form) and the latter *ni* the informal you (T form). The distinction of the T/V form is peculiar in that it is mainly used in writing, that is, in formal style or between interlocutors where there is a marked difference in power relation (Holmes 2013). However, as can be seen in the email corpus, the use of *nin* (V form) was not always practiced by the students, indicating that the students may not consider the power difference as an important factor in the medium of email, leading to the more common usage of *ni*, the informal you. Furthermore, the use of the Chinese title can occur with the first name or the full name, as in example (29). What is interesting is that terms such as professor and teacher are not only used as a title but also as an address term. Such usage exhibits a pragmatic transfer from the Chinese language

Table 3.6 Language choice and written features among graduate students

	Openings	Pre-closings	Signatures
English	34	20	29
Chinese	2	1	2
Chinese/English	0	0	0
Total	36	21	31

as the title *laoshi* (teacher) and *jiaoshou* (professor) can be used as address terms. This is a feature unique to EFL learners of Chinese background. Example (29) further shows a case where both Chinese and English are used for an opening where 'dear' is used together with the first name and the title in Chinese.

In terms of pre-closings, the data reveal that less than half of the emails included a pre-closing. Moreover, the pre-closing displayed two extremes, either none or a more formal expression. Examples of pre-closings include the following:

(30) Sincerely
(31) Best regards
(32) Best wish
(33) Best
(34) *Zhu shen ti jian kang*

As illustrated in example (30), the most frequently used pre-closing in English is 'sincerely,' a formulaic choice. Examples (31) to (34) occur only once. The Chinese expression is also a formulaic one wishing the recipient good health, a common expression in Chinese in letter writing.

Table 3.6 shows the language choice of the selected written features among the graduate students. A preference for English is even more prominent among the graduate students. Over 90 % of openings, pre-closings, and signatures were in English. Only two openings, one pre-closing, and two signatures were in Chinese. Examples of openings produced by graduate students include the following:

(35) Dear Professor/Dr. + Last name
(36) To Professor + Last name
(37) Dear + First name
(38) Hello + Professor
(39) Last name + *laoshi* (teacher) + *nihao* (Greeting)
(40) Title + *ninhao* (Greeting)

Similar to the undergraduate students, the more common English patterns are 'Title + Last name' and 'First name.' The two Chinese examples include the use of Title (*laoshi*) and a formulaic expression of greeting, *ninhao* or *nihao*. The term 'professor' is also used as an address term. There was not as much variation in the use of openings as there was for the undergraduate students. Finally, the use of the more formal format of 'Dear + Title/Last name/First name' indicates that the students tend to apply the rule of letter writing when corresponding by email.

Examples of pre-closings produced by graduate students include the following:

(41) Best/Best regards
(42) Sincerely yours/Sincerely

These two examples are commonly found in the corpus, illustrating a transfer of formulaic expressions common in letter writing to email writing. This conforms to the claim of the pervasive influence of traditional writing on email text, in which it includes both an opening and a signature (e.g., Vurdien 2011). Both groups of students also used conventional pre-closings, again illustrating the transfer of linguistic features in letter writing to email writing. The findings indicate that students not only transferred their language practice to another language but also their language practice from one medium to another medium.

3.3.3.2 Spoken Features

The analysis of the spoken features of the emails found that most of these features were restricted to the use of English; thus, this section will mainly focus on describing spoken features in English. Similar to Murray (1995), we have found features such as use of deletion of subject pronouns and determiners, choice of colloquial vocabulary, multiple punctuations, lower case usage for upper case, typos, onomatopoetic words, and abbreviations. Onomatopoetic words refer to the textual representation of auditory information such as prosody, laughter, and other nonlanguage sounds (Herring 2001). Although previous studies (e.g., Danet 2001; Lin 2008; Shi 2010) found acronyms and abbreviations, multiple punctuations, and onomatopoetic words to be common in online writing, this study only found a few examples of acronyms and abbreviations (i.e., *BTW* for by the way, *ps* for post script, *FB* for facebook, *ASAP* for as soon as possible, and *Fri*. for Friday). There were also a few examples of multiple punctuations (e.g., ??? or !!!!!) and of onomatopoetic words (e.g., *haha*). The use of acronyms and abbreviations can be explained by the principle of economy (Clyne 1991), the use of multiple punctuations is for emphasis, and the use of onomatopoetic words is for expressiveness.

Spoken features that were found to be common in the corpus are deletion of subject pronouns and determiners, choice of colloquial vocabulary, lower case usage for upper case, and typos. Examples of deletion of subject pronouns and determiners, choice of colloquial vocabulary, lower case usage for upper case, and typos include the following:

(43) Just hope you can give a opportunity
(44) I seldom check my e-mail, so didn't notice this email…

(45) Although I didn't get the scholarship, still thank you to help me to write the recommend letter!
(46) Hope that everything write correctly…haha
(47) Sorry for this, I tried, but really can't do them all, but I wanna finish my job after the deadline.
(48) I am student in X class. yesterday I was sick, so I did not take final exam

Examples (43) to (47) illustrate cases where students delete the subject pronouns, a characteristic common in spoken interaction. According to Biesenbach-Lucas and Weasenbach (2001), ellipsis occurs infrequently in academic texts. This suggests that the students do not perceive email correspondence with the teacher as an academic context. Determiners are also deleted as in example (48). However, this usage could also be explained by the fact that these are EFL learners. That is, the lack of determiners may not be a deliberate act. Instead, it was due to students' proficiency level in English. We can also see the use of lower case for 'i' instead of the conventional use of upper case in example (47). The same applies for 'yesterday' in the same example. The choice of the colloquial vocabulary is also in the email writing such as the use of 'wanna' in example (47). Cases of typos can be seen in example (43) where 'an' is required instead of 'a' and in example (45) where the noun 'recommendation' is required instead of the verb 'recommend.' Again the issue of typos is an interesting one since it can be treated as a disregard for typos or it can be accounted for by errors transferred from the first language of the students, i.e., Chinese (see the following for further discussion).

Following this finding, a question that needs to be addressed is 'are such errors caused by inattention or lack of knowledge of the standard language forms?' As suggested by Herring (2001), the majority of these seemingly spoken features are deliberate choices made by users to economize on typing effort, mimic spoken language features, or express themselves creatively. If that is the case, the desire to reduce the amount of typing and the failure to edit the emails lead to a speech-like conversational style, resulting in the use of the above-listed spoken features. The principle of economy does seem to be an important reason accounting for the use of acronyms and abbreviations or failure to edit the text. This is indeed found to be common in CMD. However, it is also possible that the students failed to edit the errors due to their proficiency level in English. Examples of such include the following:

(49) Please have a look of the flowing changes below which is marked in the rec [sic] color.
(50) Actually, most of the moved-parts are repeted in Chap. 5.
(51) I am your Introduction to English Linguistics student of Thursday morning.
(52) I promise I will do better in next semester.
(53) I am student in Language and Culture class.
(54) I'll send you letter after I finish it.
(55) Here's the reminding mail for the scholarship.
(56) If I have any question, hope you would be my consulter.
(57) I was finished counting the number of words.

(58) Professors can still have your lunchbox…
(59) I know I have so much space to progress.
(60) If the revision is not correct. I'll revise again immediately.

Examples (49) and (50) show cases of disregard of typos as is claimed in previous work in CMD. As opposed to these typos, examples (51) to (60) illustrate errors resulting from L2 proficiency level or from L1 influence. Examples (51) and (52) demonstrate misuse of prepositions common in the production of EFL learners. Examples (53) and (54) show lack of articles also common in the production of ELF learners. Examples (55) to (56) illustrate the wrong use of vocabulary, 'reminding' for 'remaining' and 'advisor' for 'consulter.' Example (57) shows the misuse of passive structure. Examples (58) to (60) show influences from the students' first language, Chinese at various levels. Example (58) demonstrates again the use of title as an address term, a conventional practice in the Chinese language. The use of title as an address term is transferred from Chinese to English, a feature unique to students of Chinese background. Examples (59) to (60) demonstrate the influence of the Chinese at the sentential level. Example (59) is a direct translation from the Chinese structure, and example (60) transfers the 'if-clause' structure from Chinese to English, resulting in ungrammaticality in English. These examples suggest that although the principle of economy is of central concern to email writers, the linguistic background of the writers needs to be taken into consideration as illustrated in this study. It may be the case that EFL learners using English in their emails deliberately make use of spoken features due to the influence of the medium of email; however, it should be noted that EFL learners are also influenced by their language proficiency level in English and by their first language, resulting in various typos or errors in their writing in emails. As stated by Biesenbach-Lucas and Weasenforth (2001), students' use of English in more formal contexts may have been restricted by their level of proficiency and first-language background.

A final spoken feature analyzed is the use of emoticons. The students were found to employ strategies of visualizing nonlinguistic characteristics in emails which are prominent in spoken interaction. Emoticons are icons for the expression of emotion, or for marking one's intent as nonserious. These are combinations of keyboard characters designed to show the emotional facial expression. They are composed of clusters of typographic symbols, and are popularly known as 'smileys' (Godin 1993; Sanderson 1993). In total, there were 24 tokens of emoticons identified in the corpus of which 14 were produced by undergraduate students and 10 were produced by graduate students, indicating undergraduate students prefer such usage. This may also suggest that, similar to other findings in this study, compared to graduate students, undergraduate students considered the email medium to be more informal. Table 3.7 shows some of the emoticons found in the data.

This confirms earlier claims that email conventions are not restricted to written language usage (Biesenbach-Lucas and Weasenforth 2001), and that the students may not check the texts prior to posting them (Vurdien 2011), contrary to the finding by Sotillo (2000) that asynchronous CMC allows the users more time to edit the text.

Table 3.7 Emoticons

Icon	Meaning	Icon	Meaning
:-) :) : D	Smiley face or happy	:p	Tongue sticking out; playful
@@!	Confused	> <	Troubled
Q_Q	Crying	^^; ^_^	Smiley face or happy

Finally, it should be noted that although undergraduate students tended to treat email as a more informal medium of communication, a mix of both spoken and written features was often present in the same email. Examples (61) and (62) illustrate such usage:

(61) Dear Diana,
Just wanna ask if we could know our grade of final exam [emoticon]?
sincerely,
Anna

(62) Dear Professor Diana,
hahaha, I forgot the attachment. Please have a look!
Best regards,
Steven

In example (61), we see that all the written elements including opening, pre-closing, and signature are present. However, spoken features such as deletion of subject, use of unconventional case for 'sincerely,' and choice of colloquial vocabulary 'wanna' as well as emoticon are also used. Similarly, in example (62), opening, pre-closing, and signatures are all present. However, an onomatopoetic expression is also used. Considering the opening is of a formal nature with the opening of 'Title + first name,' it is interesting to see the use of an informal expression such as the onomatopoetic expression. Furthermore, the use of first name instead of last name after the title also illustrates influences from the Chinese practice of the younger generation where first names are commonly used together with titles.

3.3.4 Addressing the Research Questions

To answer research question 1, the EFL learners of Chinese background used both English and Chinese in their email communication to their teachers. Their preferred language, however, was not their first language; English was found to be more frequently used, by both undergraduate and graduate students. Furthermore, code-switching between Chinese and English was found in the emails. This preference for English is explained by the influence of the contextual factors including interlocutor (i.e., teacher), context, and background of the student as English majors. This suggests that language use is highly variable in CMC. This variation reflects the influence on the linguistic choices of CMD users of social factors such as participant demographics and situational context (Herring 2001).

Regarding research question 2, there were eight functions identified in the corpus, with request and inquiry being the most common functions. This suggests that students mainly correspond with the teacher for these functions in an institutional context. Other functions include thanking, providing information, apologizing, asking for leave of absence, confirmation of appointment/information, and wishing.

Regarding research question 3, the main messages of the email were analyzed in terms of their patterns. It was found that the EFL learners used various patterns to realize various types of messages including request, inquiry, thanking, apologizing, and asking for leave of absence. Generally speaking, the graduate students employed patterns that were more formal in nature than the undergraduate students. This indicates that graduate students considered the email medium a more formal context than undergraduate students.

Finally, regarding research question 4, the findings reveal that email draws on both written and spoken forms of communication. On one hand, written features such as openings and closings are common in email writing. On the other hand, spoken features such as deletion of subject pronouns, determiners, and abbreviations, just to name a few, are also present in the emails. The identified spoken features can be explained from two perspectives: from the principle of economy and from first language influence. To sum up, the findings indicate that email is of a hybrid nature which includes features from both written and spoken forms of communication. However, it should be borne in mind that the background of the email users as EFL learners exerts an influence on their use of a second language, i.e., English.

3.4 Conclusion

3.4.1 Contributions and Implications

There are three contributions from this study. First, this study provides insights into naturally occurring language in an email communication in teacher–student interaction in a multilingual community. Second, this study provides further understanding on the EFL learners' use of emails in terms of function and structure of the main messages. Given the crucial role of email in the twenty-first century, analyzing email messages may yield significant information as to the purpose for which people write emails (Kirkgoz 2010). Finally, the study identifies both spoken and written features in emails produced by EFL learners. Specifically, it provides further understanding of how EFL learners use English in email communication, suggesting that the style of language used is influenced by both the medium and their first language. As stated by Danet and Herring (2007), hundreds of millions of people are participating online today in languages other than English, in some form of nonnative English, or in a mixture of languages, and this trend is projected to continue in the years to come. Together, the discourse analysis of emails gives a comprehensive picture about the features and practices of language use in email communication in institutional context.

These findings have a number of implications. As noted by Crystal (2001), 'email had extended the language's stylistic range in interesting and motivating ways… it is an opportunity, not a threat, for language education' (p. 133). First, the study can inform language teachers' diagnostic assessment of language use with the focus on first language influence. This can further help understand how EFL learners transfer their first language into their second language at various levels including pragmatic transfer. Third, this study highlights the importance of email communication in teacher–student interaction, suggesting that email can be used in teaching. Finally, the findings may be useful for teachers in the teaching of written communication in English.

3.4.2 Limitations and Suggestions for Future Research

There are two major limitations in this study. First, the collection of the data included one-sided emails, from students to the teacher only. The correspondence from both sides may yield further insights into the nature of email communication. The findings shed light on the complexity of EFL learners' use of languages in email writing. However, to understand how interaction is carried out, analysis of emails from both sides is required. This brings us to the second limitation, where only a single corpus was under investigation. A more extensive corpus including correspondence between different role relationships would allow the possibility of seeing if role relationship affects language use in emails. This could expand the scope of EFL learners' email practices involving other kinds of power relations. Finally, students' proficiency level in English seems to be a factor worthy of investigation. Future research could examine how students of different proficiency levels use English in email communication. As Yates and Graddol (1996) rightly point out, CMC cannot be viewed as a single genre but has to be divided into several distinctive forms of communication. This suggests that further research is required in understanding email discourse.

References

Androutsopoulos, Jannis. 2006. Introduction: Sociolinguistics and computer-mediated communication. *Journal of Sociolinguistics* 10(4): 419–438.

Baron, Naomi. 2000. *Alphabet to email: How written English evolved and where it's heading*. London: Routledge.

Biesenbach-Lucas, Sigrun. 2006. Making requests in email: Do cyber-consultation entail directness? Toward conventions in a new medium. In *Pragmatics and language learning*, ed. Kathleen Bardovi-Harlig, César Félix-Brasdefer, and Alwiya S. Omar, 81–108. Honolulu, HI: Second Language Teaching and Curriculum Center, University of Hawai'i.

Biesenbach-Lucas, Sigrun, and Donald Weasenforth. 2001. E-mail and word processing in the ESL classroom: How the medium affects the message. *Language Learning & Technology* 5(1): 135–165.

Chen, Chi-Fen Emily. 2006. The development of e-mail literacy: From writing to peers to writing to authority figures. *Language Learning and Technology* 10(2): 35–55.

Cho, Thomas. 2010. Linguistic features of electronic mail in the workplace: A comparison with memoranda. *Language@Internet*, 7(3). http://www.languageatinternet.org/articles/2010/2728. Accessed 16 Dec 2012.

Clyne, Michael. 1991. *Community languages: The Australian experience*. Cambridge: Cambridge University Press.

Crystal, David. 1997. *English as a global language*. Cambridge: Cambridge University Press.

Crystal, David. 2001. *Language and the Internet*. Cambridge: Cambridge University Press.

Danet, Brenda. 2001. *Cyberpl@y: Communicating online*. Oxford: Berg.

Danet, Brenda, and Susan Herring. 2007. Introduction: Welcome to the multilingual Internet. In *The multilingual Internet: Language, culture, and communication online*, ed. Brenda Danet, and Susan Herring, 3–39. New York: Oxford University Press.

Gains, Jonathan. 1999. Electronic mail-a new style of communication or just a new medium? An investigation into the text features of e-mail. *English for Specific Purposes* 18(1): 81–101.

Godin, Seth. 1993. *The smiley dictionary: Cool things to do with your keyboard*. Berkeley: Peachpit Press.

Gruber, Helmut. 1997. Email discussion lists: A new genre of scholarly communication. *Wiener Linguistische Gazett* 60(61): 24–42.

Guffey, Mary. 2010. *Essentials of business communication*, 8th ed. Mason: South-Western Cengage Learning.

Harrison, Sandra. 1998. Email discussions as conversation: Moves and acts in a sample from a listserv discussion. *Linguistik Online* 1. www.linguistickonline.de/harrison.thm. Accessed 28 Nov 2012.

Herring, Susan., ed. 1996. Computer-mediated communication: Linguistic, social and crosscultural perspectives. Amsterdam/Philadelphia: John Benjamins.

Herring, Susan. 2001. Computer-mediated discourse. In *Handbook of discourse analysis*, ed. Deborah Schiffrin, Deborah Tannen, and Heidi Hamilton, 612–634. Oxford: Blackwell.

Herring, Susan. 2007. A faceted classification scheme for computer-mediated discourse. *Language@Internet,* 4(1). http://languageatinternet.org/articles/2007/761. Accessed 14 Oct 2012.

Hine, Christine. 2000. *Virtual ethnography*. London: Sage.

Holmes, Janet. 2013. *An introduction sociolinguistics*, 4th ed. Harlow: Pearson.

Huang, Daphne Li-jung. 2004. *Code-switching and language use in emails: A case study of a network of Chinese-English bilinguals in Taiwan*. Unpublished doctoral dissertation, University of Melbourne, Melbourne, Australia.

Internet World Stats. 2013. Internet users in the world. http://www.internetworldstats.com/stats.htm. Accessed 12 Sep 2012.

ITU. 2013. Yearbook of statistics - Telecommencation/ICT indicators. http://www.itu.int/pub/D-IND-YB/2013. Accessed 12 Sep 2012.

Kiesler, Sara., Siegel, Jane, and McGuire Timothy. 1984. Social psychological aspects of computer-mediated communication. *American Psychologist* 39(10): 1123–1134.

Kirkgoz, Yasemin. 2010. Analyzing the discourse of e-mail communication. In *Handbook of research on discourse behavior and digital communication: Language structures and social interaction*, ed. Rotimi Taiwo, 335–348. Pennsylvania: IGI Global.

Lin, Yi-Lin. 2008. *Language use and code-switching on BBS in Taiwan*. Master's thesis, Providence University, Taichung, Taiwan.

Murray, Denise. 1995. *Knowledge machines: Language and information in a technological society*. London: Longman.

Myers-Scotton, Carol. 1993. *Social motivations for code-switching: Evidence from Africa*. Oxford: Claredon.

Paolillo, John. 1996. Language choice on soc.culture.punhab. *Electronic Journal of Communication* 6(3). http://www.cios.org/. Accessed 12 Apr 2012.

Sanderson, David. 1993. *Smileys*. New York: O'Reilly and Associates.

Shi, Kai-Yi. 2010. *Language use and code-switching in computer-mediated communication, focusing on MSN Messenger in Taiwan*. Master's thesis, Providence University, Taichung, Taiwan.

Sotillo, Susana. 2000. Discourse functions and syntactic complexity in synchronous and asynchronous communication. *Language Learning & Technology* 4: 82–119.

Su, Hsi-Yao. 2003. The multilingual and multi-orthographic Taiwan-based internet: Creative uses of writing system on college-affiliated BBSs. *Journal of Computer-Mediated Communication* 9 (1). http://jcmc.indiana.edu/vol9/issue1/su.html. Accessed 16 Jan 2011.

Vurdien, Ruby. 2011. Email discourse. *Modern English Teacher* 20(1): 62–68.

Warschauer, Mark, Ghada El Said, and Ayman, Zohry. 2002. Language choice online: Globalisation and identity in Egypt. *Journal of Computer-mediated Communication* 7(4). www.ascusc.org/jcmc/vol7/issue4. Accessed 16 Jan 2011.

Yates, Simeon, and David, Graddol. 1996. *'I read this chat is heavy': The discursive construction of identity in CMC*. Mexico: International Pragmatics Conference.

Author Biography

Li-Jung Huang (黃麗蓉) is currently teaching at the Department of English Language, Literature and Linguistics at Providence University in Taiwan. She obtained her doctoral degree in Applied Linguistics at University of Melbourne, Australia, in 2004, and has been teaching at Providence University since then. Her research interest is in the areas of bilingualism, cross-cultural communication, sociolinguistics, and computer-mediated communication.

Chapter 4
Do Chinese Students Waffle in Their Apologies?: An Exploration into EFL Learners' Emails

Miao-Hsia Chang, Jean Curran, Yueh-Kuei Hsu and Chih-Chun Hsu

Abstract This study aims to investigate whether the "waffle" phenomenon is revealed in EFL learners' apology emails in an academic context. A total of 60 students participated in this study. They comprised three groups of undergraduate students: 20 native proficient speakers of English (PSEs), 20 Chinese EFL learners (EFLCs), and 20 proficient speakers of Chinese (PSCs). The results demonstrate both generality and specificity in language users' apology realizations. The generality is indicated by all the participants' preference for "Direct Apology," "Account," "Taking on Responsibility," and "Offers of Repair." Specificity is noticeable in the waffling of the "Account" strategy by EFLCs. The findings shed light on the importance of explicit instruction of the pragmalinguistic features and the sociocultural values accepted in the target culture, and in the case of the current study, formality and conciseness of the language.

Keywords Apologies · Waffling · Chinese EFL learners · Pragmalinguistic features · Sociopragmatic features

---

M.-H. Chang (✉) · J. Curran · Y.-K. Hsu
Department of English, National Taiwan Normal University, Taipei, Taiwan
e-mail: mhchang@ntnu.edu.tw

J. Curran
e-mail: curran.jean@gmail.com

Y.-K. Hsu
e-mail: hsu.yuehkuei@gmail.com

C.-C. Hsu
Center for Teaching and Learning Development, National Taiwan Normal University, Taipei, Taiwan
e-mail: tomato400@gmail.com

Y. Chen et al. (eds.), *Email Discourse Among Chinese Using English as a Lingua Franca*, DOI 10.1007/978-981-287-888-5_4

4.1 Introduction

In the past few decades, there has been an increasing interest in the role of pragmatics in second/foreign language learning and teaching (e.g., Blum-Kulka et al. 1989; Olshtain and Cohen 1983; Bardovi-Harlig and Hartford 1993, 1996; Hinkel 1994; Scollon and Scollon 1995, to name just a few). These studies emerged as a response to Austin's (1962) and Searle's (1969, 1976) development of speech-act theory and Hymes' (1972) introduction of the notion of communicative competence. It is believed that effective communication involves speakers' appropriate use of their sociocultural knowledge in addition to their linguistic knowledge (Olshtain and Cohen 1983, p. 19). Inappropriate use of the language, i.e., "pragmatic failure" (Thomas 1983) has been noted to frequently occur in the semantic formulas or linguistic content of L2 learners' speech acts, e.g., apologies (House 1989; Blum-Kulka et al. 1989), compliments (Billmyer 1990), expressions of gratitude (Eisenstein and Bodman 1993), requests (Hassall 2001; Pan 2012; Blum-Kulka et al. 1989), complaints (Chen et al. 2010, 2011), and refusals (Felix-Brasdefer 2004). In particular, the "waffle phenomenon," defined as "excessive use of linguistic forms to fill a specific discourse 'slot' or 'move'" (Edmonson and House 1991, pp. 273–274), violates Grice's (1975) maxim of quantity, and has been shown to prevail in EFL learners' speech acts (Blum-Kulka and Olshtain 1986, p. 170). The lack of pragmatic appropriateness might result in a native speaker hearer's impatience and the judgment that the speaker is infringing upon the maxim of relevance (Grice 1975) and therefore "weaken[s] the force of the speech act" (Blum-Kulka and Olshtain 1986, p. 175).

Advances in technology have had a great impact on the ways that individuals communicate with one another. Among the different modes of interaction between learners of English and native speakers of English, email correspondence is a major means of computer-mediated communication (Hewings and Coffin 2004; Pan 2012). In line with the findings reported in previous L2 pragmatic research, it was noted that EFL learners demonstrate an overuse of the external modifications accompanying their head speech acts, e.g., "Excuse me, but I've had a bad quarrel with my girl-friend and this has influenced my driving condition" uttered by a nonnative speaker versus a brief apology "Sorry about that, mate" by a native speaker when a driver in the parking lot backs into someone's car (Edmondson and House 1991, p. 276; Blum-Kulka et al. 1989, p. 15). This study aims to investigate whether the "waffle" phenomenon is revealed in EFL learners' apology emails in an academic context. English and Chinese native speakers' emails serve as a baseline for us to see if nonnative speakers deviate from English native norms and if the learners perform transfer (Kasper 1992) from the Chinese language. Specifically, we address the following research questions:

1. Do the Chinese EFL learners (hereafter EFLCs) reveal the waffle phenomenon in their apology emails?
2. If waffling is observed in interlanguage apologies, what strategies are waffled?

3. Are there any pragmalinguistic and sociopragmatic differences between Chinese EFL learners and proficient English speakers (hereafter PSEs) in the linguistic content of the apology strategies? If yes, what are these differences?
4. Are there any differences between the EFL learners and proficient Chinese speakers (hereafter PSCs) and between proficient English speakers and proficient Chinese speakers in their email apologies?

4.2 Literature Review

4.2.1 Apologies in Interlanguage Pragmatics

Apologies are a type of speech act "about a state of affairs specified in the propositional content." Classified as "expressives," apologies presuppose the truth of the proposition expressed (Searle 1979, p. 15). They are a "negative ritual" (Goffman 1971, p. 90, cited in Trosborg 1995, p. 373) composed of "actions which are potentially difficult or "embarrassing" for the speaker" (House 1989, p. 303). The need for an apology arises when an interactant perceives an action as violating a certain social norm(s). That is, an apology is a "convivial speech act" (Leech 1983, pp. 104–105; Trosborg 1995, p. 373) that "provides remedial accounts and assurances" and makes up for the breaching of social norms or interference with the hearer's interests. In so doing, it maintains the harmony between the speaker and the hearer (Trosborg 1995, pp. 373–374). The act of apologizing, therefore, involves two participants. The first participant, the "apologizer," refers to one or more people who perceive themselves as being responsible for the offensive act, and the second participant, the "recipient," refers to those who were offended and who deserve an apology (Olshtain and Cohen 1983, pp. 20–22).

A number of interlanguage pragmatists have identified the semantic content and potential strategies employed by speakers to express apologies. Blum-Kulka et al. (1989) have conducted one of the most influential studies on the speech acts of apologies (and requests). Following Olshtain and Cohen (1983), Blum-Kulka et al. (1989, pp. 19–20) argued that the act of apology can be performed either by an explicit *illocutionary force indicating device* (IFID) (Searle 1969, p. 54ff), which comprises a routinized set of linguistic expressions of regret, or by an utterance whose semantic content relates to "(a) the cause for the act that the speaker did or abstained from doing, (b) the speaker's responsibility for the act that was perceived as a breach of social norms, (c) the speaker's willingness to offer repair for x, and (d) a promise of forbearance on the speaker's part" (Blum-Kulka et al. 1989, p. 20).

In their Cross-cultural Pragmatic Speech Act Realization project (CCSARP) based on results from Discourse Completion Tests (DCTs), following Olshtain and Cohen (1983), Blum-Kulka et al. (1989, p. 20) proposed five potential strategies of apology along with their respective linguistic realizations. In addition to these five strategies, "tactical moves" may be made by the speaker to "divert the hearer's attention from his or her own responsibility for the offense" (Blum-Kulka et al. 1989, pp. 293–294). Such moves are sometimes referred to as "Evasive Strategies" (Trosborg 1995, p. 379).

In the present study, the aforementioned six strategies are included for our analysis of the email messages. Below, we give a list of these six types of strategies followed by their definitions and examples:

1. IFID: an explicit illocutionary force indicating device
2. Taking on Responsibility
3. Explanation or Account
4. Offer of Repair
5. Promise of Forbearance
6. Evasive Strategy

An IFID (illocutionary force indicating device) is a device using a direct statement to perform a speech act. In the case of apology, an IFID contains expressions such as *(be) sorry, apologize, regret, excuse,* or *I'm afraid*, which enables the speaker to seek forgiveness from the hearer for a previous action by the speaker that violated a given norm or social etiquette. This may be considered as "sincere" or as a simple acknowledgement for the breaking of the social etiquette/norms (House 1989, p. 308). IFIDs may also be accompanied by modifiers for intensification of the force of the apology (Blum-Kulka et al. 1989, pp. 290–291):

- I'm *very/terribly/so/really/awfully* sorry.
- Emotional expressions/exclamations: *Oh/Oh no/Oh Lord/God!*
- Expressions marked for register: I *do* apologize.
- Double intensifier or repetition of intensifying adverbial: I'm *really dreadfully* sorry./I'm *very, very* sorry.
- Please: *Please* forgive me.
- Concern for the hearer: *I hope I didn't upset you.*

"Taking on Responsibility" refers to expressions whereby the speaker expresses responsibility for the offense which led to the need for an apology. It causes face threat (Brown and Levinson 1987) to the speaker but serves to appease the hearer. It contains substrategies that range from explicit self-blame to a strong denial of responsibility. Self-deficiency was included in House's (1989, p. 310) analysis, and six other strategies were proposed by Blum-Kulka et al. (1989, pp. 291–292):

- Self-deficiency: *I just cannot be on time.*
- Explicit self-blame: *My mistake.*
- Lack of intent: *I didn't mean to upset you.*
- Justify hearer: *You're right to be angry.*
- Expression of embarrassment: *I feel awful about it.*
- Admission of facts but not of responsibility: *I haven't read it.*
- Refusal to acknowledge guilt: *It wasn't my fault./It's your own fault./I'm the one who should be offended.*

An "Explanation" or "Account" contains expressions which provide the reasons for the offense "by pointing to the source of offense…over which the speaker has no control" (House 1989, p. 309), e.g., *I missed the bus* and *The traffic was terrible* (Blum-Kulka et al. 1989, p. 293).

An "Offer of Repair" is used when the speaker expresses the wish to compensate for the damage or inconvenience caused by the offense, e.g., *I'll pay for the damage*.

A "Promise of Forbearance" occurs when the speaker feels strong guilt and thus shows that the offense will never occur again, e.g., *This won't happen again.*

An "Evasive Strategy" emerges when the speaker "seeks to minimize the degree of offense, either by arguing that the supposed offense is of minor importance…or by querying the preconditions on which the complaint is grounded" (Trosborg 1995, p. 379). The first five substrategies below are from Blum-Kulka et al. (1989, pp. 293–294), and the sixth and seventh substrategies are from Trosborg (1995, p. 379):

- Query precondition: *Are you sure we were supposed to meet at 10?*
- To act innocently/to pretend not to notice the offense: *Am I late?*
- Future/task-oriented remark: *Let's get to work, then!*
- Humor: *If you think that is a mistake, you ought to see our fried chicken*!
- Appeaser: A compensatory offer which does not directly relate to the offense: *I'll buy you a cup of coffee.*
- Minimizer: *Oh what does that matter, that's nothing.*
- Blaming someone else: *Who bumped into me just now?* (Example from Shih 2006, p. 45).

To sum up, apologies comprise a set of substrategies employed by a speaker who perceives himself/herself as being responsible for an act that violates social norms or interferes with the hearer's interest. With apologies, the apologizer saves his/her face, makes up for the breaching of norms, and maintains a harmonious relationship with the recipient.

4.2.2 Waffling in Interlanguage Pragmatics

It has been argued that there is a tendency for EFL learners to use "too many words" (Blum-Kulka and Olshtain 1986; Edmonson and House 1991) to achieve a particular communicative goal. Such verbosity is a manifestation of the violation of the Maxim of Quantity in the Gricean Co-operative Principle, which requires that speakers not make their contribution more informative than is required (Grice 1975). Instead of being more explicit, the use of prolific expressions may result in "pragmatic failure" (Thomas 1983) or misunderstanding between speakers, and this is especially the case when an ESL or EFL student lacks pragmatic awareness (Blum-Kulka and Olshtain 1986, p. 166).

Studies which discuss the waffling phenomenon in interlanguage pragmatics have mainly focused on requests and apologies. House (1989) has been by far one of the most influential researchers on waffling in apologies. A questionnaire adapted from the CCSARP (See Sect. 4.2.1) was used to examine the choice of apology strategies ("IFIDs," "Intensifiers," "Responsibility," "Account," "Repair," "Promise," "Minimize and Concern for the Hearer") in seven situations (p. 310) by first-year university students who were German native speakers, German learners of English, and British English native speakers. The results showed that German learners used a wider range of strategies to realize their speech act of apology than the English native speakers; the latter group also exhibited an overriding inclination to use *sorry* across different situations. There was also a tendency for German EFL learners to be "more verbose and expansive" in their apologies (p. 322).

Other studies in waffling place their primary concern on the requestive behaviors by nonnative speakers (NNSs). Based also on the CCSARP data, Faerch and Kasper (1989) investigated the internal and external modifications of requests of native Danish, German, and English speakers and NNSs of Danish–German and Danish–English speakers. The analysis showed that compared to internal modifiers, external modifiers used by NNSs are "longer and more explicit" and "have their own propositional content and illocution" (p. 244). Such explicit and verbose language is in contrast to that of native speakers (NSs), who tend to use more implicit, conventional indirect means to perform the same speech act (e.g., *How about a glass of wine* by a NS vs. *Would you like to drink a glass of wine with me*? by a NNS).[1] This is motivated by the learners' affective purpose of avoiding a lack of mutual comprehensibility and achieving "clarity" and "self-assertion" given their limited language ability (p. 245). Instead of addressing the waffling of NNSs as a deficient performance, Faerch and Kasper suggest that a different set of criteria be invoked for evaluation of learners' success (p. 246). Similar findings are reported in Hassall (2001), who compared the requestive realizations of NSs and NNSs of Indonesian. Eliciting data from interactive role plays, Hassall (2001) found that there was a serious underuse and a lack of variety of internal modifications by NNSs. On the other hand, while the NSs and NNSs used similar types of supportive moves, the supportive moves by the NNSs contained excessive information, especially in the strategy of "grounder." A similar methodology was adopted by Economidou-Kogetsidis (2012, p. 172). The Greek advanced ESL learners in their study were also found to use a significantly higher number of disarmers and preparators to downplay the force of the imposition of the request. Pan (2012), in a volume on research related to interlanguage request modifications, reported the results of her study of the requests in email discourse by Chinese NNS university students. Her research showed that NNSs of Chinese rely heavily on supportive moves (e.g., promise of reward, sweetener, showing apologies) to soften the

[1]The contrast between these two utterances is also one of formality, with the former sounding more intimate, and the latter more distant. Language learners tend to use a more formal style when they speak to someone in an intercultural communication using the learner's second language. We thank one of the reviewers for pointing this out.

impositive force of their requests (p. 149). These external modifications could occur as syntactically simple sentences to lubricate the request. The use of sweeteners, for example, serves to enhance the positive face of the recipient so that there is a higher chance for the request to be successful. The lengthiness and over-informativeness of EFL students were also observed in Chen's (2006) two-and-a-half-year longitudinal study on emails written by an advanced nonnative speaker—a female PhD student studying in the US. This student's emails to her peers and professors were analyzed, and interviews were then conducted regarding the motivation and purpose of these emails. The student revealed that her emails were long and contained many details because she deemed short emails "cold, direct, and impersonal" (p. 41).

While the studies reviewed above found that advanced students are bound to interact in a more "content-oriented" way (House 1989, p. 312) to ensure that their speech acts are successfully conveyed, such a tendency was not confirmed in Trosborg (1995), Otcu and Zeyrek (2008) and Economidou-Kogetsidis (2012), all of whom used role plays to collect interlanguage requests. It is argued that this might have been due to the data elicitation instrument method and the proficiency level of the learners observed (Economidou-Kogetsidis 2012; Trosborg 1995). With role plays, speakers might have less time to monitor their output and therefore be more inclined to undersupport their requests.

In brief, waffling has been exhibited in interlanguage requests, especially in EFL learners' language use in DCTs. Although Chen (2006) analyzed the email language by an EFL learner, apologies in emails in academia have yet to be explored.

4.2.3 Apologies by Chinese EFL Learners

Tsai's (2002) study explored and analyzed the uses of apology by Mandarin Chinese speakers. Three social factors were examined: ranks of imposition, power, and social distance. It was found that more formal and elaborate expressions were used in situations when the offense was more severe, when the addressee had higher social power, or when the speakers' relationship was less intimate. A different variable—gender—was investigated in Liu's (2008) work on Chinese apologies. It was shown that females tended to use more apology strategies but less direct language. Tsai (2007) compared the DCT and the role-play method. The results showed that the subjects tended to use direct expressions of apology, acknowledge their responsibility, and offer repairs in apology situations both on DCTs and in role plays.

Apart from Chinese apologies used by Chinese NSs, Shih (2005) analyzed English apologies by Chinese junior high school EFL learners. It was found that native speakers used a wider variety of apologies than nonnative speakers across different social situations. The higher the NNSs' proficiency was, the richer the students' apologies were.

Shih (2006) conducted by far the most comprehensive study of English apologies used by Chinese EFL college learners in Taiwan in their responses to DCT questionnaires. It is most relevant to our study as it focuses on EFL college students. Following Blum-Kulka et al.'s (1989) and Trosborg's (1995) classification, H.Y. Shih noted all the participant groups preferred "Direct Apologies," "Offer of Repair," and "Acknowledging Responsibility," with "Direct Apologies" occurring most frequently, followed by "Acknowledging Responsibility" and "Offer of Repair" (p. 57) (for similar findings see also Bergman and Kasper 1993; Cohen and Olshtain 1981; and Holmes 1990). "Promises of Forbearance" were more frequent in these EFL students' apologies though no significant difference was found. As for "Explanation" and "Repair," they demonstrated a complementary distribution, namely, Chinese and English native speakers used more "Explanation" than "Repairs." In severe situations, however, native English speakers used more repairs than explanations in comparison to the learners. "Acknowledgement of Responsibility" exhibited similar patterns in the English apologies, whereas fewer tokens were found in the Chinese data. Four other social variables were also investigated: severity of offense, gender, social status, and social distance. It was found that the degree of severity, status, and distance were correlated with the use of "Repair," "Concern," and "Promise." The closer the interlocutors were, the more the speakers used evasive strategies and informal language. The use of apologies was also sensitive to gender, as men tended to use more "Evasive Strategies" than women did across different situations. On the whole, the EFL learners, especially those with lower levels of proficiency, exhibited negative transfer of the sociocultural value from the Chinese language in the use of "Promise of Forbearance" and "Evasion." In other words, the learners demonstrated sociopragmatic failure (Thomas 1983) in their speech acts. In addition, pragmalinguistic failure (Thomas 1983), i.e., deviation of the linguistic forms from the target language, was found in the learners' apologies, e.g., the use of "forgive(ness)," use of questions instead of a direct statement, use of the verb *try to*, etc.

The findings reported above reveal both cross-cultural similarities and differences in the use of apologies. First, most speakers use "Direct Apology," "Repairs," and "Responsibility" as the main strategies. Second, there is a positive correlation between learner's proficiency level and the complexity of the apology strategies. Third, a more severe offense would elicit more "Repairs" or "Explanations." Fourth, the closer the speakers' relationship is, the more informal the language is. However, all of these results are based on data elicited from DCT questionnaires or role plays. None of them analyzed authentic language use. In this study, we examine apologies from emails sent by students to their professors. In the following, we review studies of speech acts in email communication.

4.2.4 Features of Email Apologies

Email is considered to be one of the most widely used forms of communication in both academic and business settings. In the higher education context, email is a primary form of communication between instructors and students, and this is particularly true as more and more classes are offered online (Lightfoot 2006).

In her article on the linguistics of email, Baron (1998) applied a speech/writing framework to email and commented that in terms of social dynamics, email was more like writing, in lexicon and style, more like speech, and in format and syntax, one observes a mix of both writing and speech. In brief, email is a hybrid of writing and speech. Due to its multi-layered features, communication in email deserves a line of inquiry in its own right.

Since apologies serve an important social function as well as expressing regret for some offense, several authors have chosen to examine differences in email apologies as compared to those spoken or in writing, and to investigate if particular problems arise when using email to make an apology.

Using Cohen and Olshtain's (1981) categorization of the speech act of apology, Hatipoğlu (2004) analyzed email apologies and compared them with those in spoken and written language. The dataset consisted of 126 email messages collected in a university setting. For each email collected, the criterion was that it contained a remedial expression. The analysis yielded very few examples of a request for forgiveness. The results concur with Baron's research (1998), reviewed above, where email apologies have some features of spoken English, some features of written English, and some new forms that are distinct from spoken or written forms of communication.

In an effort to develop teaching methods and materials for Japanese students learning German as a foreign language (GFL), Harting (2006) conducted a study of email language. Participants in Harting's study were asked to write emails for four situations involving differing degrees of imposition and differing power relationships. These included the following: (1) An email to a friend to apologize for losing a dictionary that had been borrowed; (2) An email to a professor to apologize for losing a dictionary that had been borrowed; (3) An email to a friend to apologize because the sender would need to be absent from the last session of a study group; and (4) An email to a professor to apologize because the sender would need to be absent from the last session of a seminar. The emails were analyzed utilizing both the categories established by Olshtain and Cohen (1983) and additional categories created by the author. The emails were analyzed for the presence of one of the following 12 criteria: (1) greeting, (2) introductory sentence, (3) IFID either with or without an intensifier, (4) expression of responsibility, (5) account of the cause, (6) offer of repair, (7) promise of forbearance, (8) intensification, (9) downgrading, (10) concluding sentence, (11) farewell statement, and (12) name. Results of the analysis showed that overall, the German emails seemed more formal, as if they were almost like a letter. In contrast, Japanese emails were more likely to focus on the speech act of apologizing. The GFL students were more likely to use IFIDs and to use them with intensifiers. When the emails were examined by level of imposition and power relationships, a number of observations were made. In situations where the imposition was lower (apologizing for being absent from a study group or seminar), the German students were more likely to take responsibility for the absence and offer a promise of forbearance while the Japanese learners preferred to explain the reason for the absence. When the person receiving the email was an instructor, both groups tended to use more formal language. Japanese students were more likely to express responsibility for their absences in a very detailed manner, while German students did not.

Park et al. (2005) took a novel approach to an investigation of apologies in emails when they examined the cross-cultural differences in apologies that appeared in American and Korean email advertising. The emails were one of five different types: (1) no apology, (2) simple apology, (3) an apology plus a statement accepting responsibility for bothering the recipient, (4) an apology with an explanation which stated that it was hoped that the recipient would find the information useful even though it was unexpected, and (5) an apology that accepted responsibility and provided an explanation. The results showed that there were no significant differences between culture and the various types of apologies. However, it is interesting to find that 41.81 % of the Korean advertising messages contained an apology as compared to only 2.99 % of the American email advertisements.

In short, email is a hybrid form of communication, and the use of apologies varies from culture to culture. Compared to the studies of apologies in emails in other languages, less attention has been directed to the use of apologies in English emails written by Chinese EFL students in academic discourse. It is to this topic that the current study turns. Prior to presenting and discussing the results, the method employed in the present study is described.

4.3 Data, Coding, and Analysis

The focus of the current paper is on apologies in email discourse where students write to their instructors because their assignments will be submitted late or they need to be absent from meetings. We chose such scenarios as the target of the present investigation since they are the most common forms of apologetic interaction in academic encounters between students and professors. Two dimensions are involved in such email discourse: the severity of the offense and the status of the participants (Olshtain and Cohen 1983, p. 21). In academia, submissions of assignments/projects on time and regular class attendance have generally been regarded as two important academic responsibilities for students. Delayed submission of assignments or failure to attend a class/meeting is regarded as a violation of a student's responsibilities, and is thus discouraged or even disallowed. Such conduct is usually accompanied by a penalty from the class instructor as the instructor is the authorized party to determine the students' grades. This in turn affects the choice of semantic formulas in an apology (Olshtain and Cohen 1983, p. 21). As the teacher and the student are of an unequal status relationship, the student is perceived to be responsible for the offensive act and must offer an apology, while the teacher perceives him/herself as deserving an apology from the student for such acts. In other words, the relationship between the instructor and the student is a hierarchical one. The instructor has full authority to determine the students' grades. In the syllabuses of the courses involved in this study, it is clearly indicated that late assignments or absence from class would severely affect the students' grades.

A total of 60 students participated in this study. They comprised three groups of undergraduate students: 20 native proficient speakers of English (PSE) (10 females and 10 males), 20 Chinese EFL learners (EFLC) (14 females and six males), and 20 proficient speakers of Chinese (PSC) (17 females and three males). All of the PSEs were born in the US, are Caucasian, and are native speakers of American English. They majored in subjects in engineering or medical science. The EFLCs consisted of English majors from a national university in northern Taiwan, with their English proficiency at the high-intermediate level. The PSCs were undergraduates from the same Taiwanese university with their majors being English, humanities, or natural science. The average ages of the PSEs, EFLCs, and the PSCs were, respectively, 19.75, 21.25, and 21.6. The PSEs and EFLCs were asked to contribute their previous English email messages sent to their instructors in which they apologized for their absence from a class meeting or about a late assignment. The PSCs were asked to contribute their Chinese email apologies sent to their class instructors for the same purpose. All of the emails were written and sent between September 2011 and March 2014. Pseudonyms were used to protect the identities of the participants when their examples were cited for our discussion. The permission to take part in the follow-up interview via Facebook or face-to-face encounter from the participants was also granted in the consent form.

Apart from the apology strategies reviewed in Sect. 4.2.1, our initial observation showed that there are some strategies that seem to be unique to Chinese speakers: "Asking for Forgiveness" from the addressee and "Showing Intimacy" with the addressee. In addition, since the main purpose was to examine how the speakers deployed their messages in an apology email, the strategies "Greeting," "Self-identification" in the beginning, and "Thanking," "Polite Marker," and "Complimentary Close" at the end of the messages were also coded. Excluded from the coding were the salutation line, which contained the recipient's title and name, and the signature line, which sometimes included a short formulaic expression before the name line, e.g., *Best (regards), Sincerely (yours).* In total, fourteen strategies were analyzed, as listed below[2]:

Beginning:
Greeting (GR); Self-identification (ID)
Main message:
Direct Apology (DR); Account (AC); Taking on Responsibility (RS); Offer of Repair (RP); Promise of Forbearance (PM); Feeling of Remorse (RM); Evasion (EV); Showing Intimacy (IN); Asking for Forgiveness (FG)
Ending:

[2]In Blum-Kulka et al. (1989), House (1989) and Shih (2006), another strategy was identified and analyzed: Concern for the hearer. Although it has been noted that Chinese speakers are more likely to employ this strategy (Wallwork 2011, p. 230), it was not used by the participants of our study. Therefore, the strategy was excluded from our analysis.

Thanking (TH); Complimentary Close (CC); Polite Marker (PL)

The apology email messages elicited were then coded and analyzed mainly in terms of (a) the total length of the email message and (b) the length of each strategy. The length of each strategy used by EFLCs and PSEs was measured according to the number of words occurring in the strategy. A two-tailed *t*-test was used to compare the overall length of the EFLCs' and the PSEs' emails and the respective length of each strategy used by these two groups. As for the length of the Chinese emails, the sentences were segmented into words (*ci*, 詞) using the Chinese Word Segmentation System developed by Academic Sinica (http://ckipsvr.iis.sinica.edu.tw/). Since there has not been a conclusive determination of Chinese sentence length in written discourse (e.g., Tsai 2010; Zhou et al. 2011), the respective length of each strategy and the total length of the Chinese emails will only be used for raw frequency comparisons.[3]

4.4 Results and Discussion

4.4.1 Overall Distribution

Table 4.1 displays the means and standard deviations in the overall length of the PSE and EFLC email messages. An independent two-sample *t*-test was used to analyze the data. Because the homogeneity of variance assumption was violated, Welch's t was computed, $t\ (25.708) = 0.828$, $p = 0.415$, which revealed that there is no significant difference between the two groups' emails.

In general, the mean length of the PSE's emails was shorter than that of the EFLCs, although a significant difference was not observed. In (1), the sixth subject in PSE (S6) provides a brief account for why she could not make the meeting. The remainder of the message is primarily about how to repair the situation. In (2), however, the EFLC engages himself in an extremely long narrative to explain why he missed the meeting while only a brief statement of apology is made. The following discussion will reveal even more clearly that the two groups differ in the deployment of their strategies and their linguistic contents.[4]

[3]In Tsai's (2010) study on English translated patent abstracts compared with their original Chinese abstracts, the average sentence length was 62.37 in the Chinese abstracts, with a range of 11.5–229 words per sentence. The average number of words per sentence in the English text was 35.71, with a minimum of 13.14 and maximum of 125 words (standard deviation: 24.12). The great difference in the two languages indicated inconsistencies in sentence length. A similar inconsistency was also observed in Zhou et al. (2011) in their survey of the ratio of English sentence length to Chinese sentence length in a bilingual corpus which includes 2,840,000 sentence pairs.

[4]The lexical, pragmatic, punctuation, or other errors of the students' emails are kept intact in the examples cited.

Table 4.1 Overall length of the PSEs' and EFLCs' emails (PSCs' mean: 36.95)

	PSE	EFLC
N	20	20
Mean	68.10	78.45
SD	21.956	51.427

(1) PSE-S6 (Female) (71 words)
Hello, Professor!
I'm so sorry I missed the meeting with you yesterday. I had a meeting for another class that ran a little late and I couldn't leave early.
Is there any way I can reschedule a meeting with you? If you'd like to or if it's best for you, I could even just meet with you right before our class. Please let me know what I can do!
Thank you very much,
Lisa

(2) EFLC-S1 (Male) (110 words)
Dear Elena,
I'm really sorry for not attending the class for today, and this Monday. Since last week l'd been busy working for the drama competition. On Monday morning 7 a.m. I felt headache so terribly that I could't get up. Also, I kept running nose. I should have been aware that it's a sign of serious sick. But I still ignored it. Until this morning, I had a fever. So I missed freshmen English class for the whole week. But I have told Katherine to inform me if there is any assignment that I should do. And now I just finished consulting the doctor.
"sorry" again.
By the way, Happy new year!
Ian

It is worth noting that the standard deviation among EFLCs' emails (51.427) is much higher than that of the PSEs (21.956). In fact, a closer investigation shows that of the 20 EFLC email messages, five have a length of over 100 words, and five below 40 words. A post-hoc interview was conducted to see whether the participants differed in their perceptions about distance, power relation, or severity of the offense that could account for the variation in length. Regarding distance, the responses show that all PSEs felt that they were distant from their instructors, whereas most EFLCs and PSCs thought that they were familiar with their instructors. As for power relation and severity of the offense, all thought that the instructors were of higher social status and that the offense would have a serious effect on their grades. Despite the familiarity between the two Chinese participant groups and their instructors, only five EFLCs wrote messages of great length (over 100 words), whereas there were another five EFLCs whose message length was less than 40 words. The variation in email length, therefore, does not seem to be a result of perceived close relationship with the instructor but of individual style in writing.

On the other hand, the PSCs' emails contain concise and terse messages, with an average length of 36.95 words per message (see Table 4.1), as exemplified by (3) (with English translation enclosed in brackets []):

(3) PSC-S2 (29 words)
Professor Kathy老師您好:
我是Ariel張玉玲, 因爲明天早上我們學校有重要活動不便離開, 所以明天的英語教學研討可能無法出席, 先跟您請假,很抱歉～
Ariel
[Dear Professor Kathy,
I am Ariel Yu-ling Chang. I probably won't be able to attend the seminar on English Language Teaching tomorrow morning because there is an important event at our school tomorrow morning and it won't be convenient for me to leave. I hereby ask for a leave now. I'm sorry.
Ariel]

In addition to the brevity of the email message in PSC's emails, most of them employed fewer strategies. Table 4.2 presents the total number of students in each group who use a given strategy.

Several things can be seen from Table 4.2. First, EFLCs employ the greatest diversity of strategies in their apologies, followed by PSEs and PSCs. That is, of the 14 strategies, the EFLCs, PSEs, and PSCs used 12, 9, and 7 types of strategies, respectively. The pattern differs from H.Y. Shih's finding (2006) that PSEs used the most strategies. Second, concerning the frequency of each strategy in the emails, almost all students directly apologized (DR) or provided explanations (AC) for the offensive acts. However, overall, fewer students identified themselves (ID), took responsibility (RS), offered reparation (RP) for the offense, or expressed gratitude to their instructors (TH). Still fewer students used other strategies in the apology emails. The disparity between EFLCs' and PSCs' performance suggests that the rich strategy types shown in EFLCs' email messages may not be an effect of L1 transfer since PSCs' email messages are generally shorter and contain a brief message, while EFLCs' emails are comparatively longer.

The discussion that ensues focuses on the strategy types that occur in significant numbers. The strategies which were not frequently observed in the database are excluded from the discussion: GR, PM, RM, EV, IN, FG, CC, and PL.

Table 4.2 Distribution of strategy types of PSEs, EFLCs, and PSCs[a]

	GR	ID	DR	AC	RS	RP	PM	RM	EV	IN	FG	TH	CC	PL	OT[b]
PSE	2	4	18	16	6	18	0	0	4	0	0	10	4	0	1
EFLC	0	5	20	17	5	9	1	1	2	2	2	7	2	0	4
PSC	0	10	16	14	1	17	0	0	0	0	1	10	0	1	0

[a]*GR* Greeting, *ID* Self-identification, *DR* Direct Apology, *AC* Account, *RS* Taking on Responsibility, *RP* Offer of Repair, *PM* Promise of Forbearance, *RM* Feeling of Remorse, *EV* Evasion, *IN* Showing Intimacy, *FG* Asking for Forgiveness, *TH* Thanking, *CC* Complimentary Close, *PL* Polite Marker, and *OT* Other strategies
[b]*OT* Other strategies are excluded from the discussion

4.4.2 Self-identification

In the email apologies, students may begin the message with "Self-identification." As shown in Table 4.3, only five of the EFLCs' emails began by providing their names before the main message, and only four students from the PSE group identified themselves. Comparatively, ten PSCs began their email messages with their name and department. A *t*-test was used (t (7) = −2.016, p = 0.084), which showed no significant difference between the total number of words of "Self-identification" used by the EFLCs and the PSEs.

In spite of the similar pattern observed in the EFLCs' and PSEs' email beginnings, two general observations can be made about this use. First, degree of familiarity seems to account for the divergent occurrence between the English and Chinese email messages. Whereas the EFLC and PSE students' emails were mostly sent to instructors of smaller-size classes whose instructors remember the students' names more easily, some of the PSC emails were sent to instructors of larger classes where it is highly possible that the instructors did not know most students' names. This might have triggered the perceived need to give one's name even if the email is also closed with the sender's name. Second, among the 19 sentences of "Self-identification" by the three subject groups, 17 occurred in female students' emails. According to Lightfoot (2006), females "put more thought" than males into writing emails to their instructors or to their peers. Compared to males, women "tend to be more aware and concerned with the special nature and characteristics of e-communication" (p. 223). That is, by identifying oneself at the beginning of the email, the relationship between the offense and the participant involved is established so that the apology speech act is more effective. Extracts (4)–(6) are respective examples from the three subject groups:

(4) EFLC-S16 (Female)
Hi, teacher,
I am Lucy in pattern practice class. Sorry for handing in my draft of presentation so late. If you don't have time to read it before the class, that would be ok:") I just want to keep my promise to email it to you before the presentation although now is maybe the last minute……:-(
See you tomorrow, love you and thank you
Lucy

(5) PSE-S20 (Female)
Dear Professor Roff,

Table 4.3 Self-identification by EFLCs and PSEs (PSCs' mean length: 6.90)

Strategy		EFLC	PSE
Self-identification	N	5	4
	Mean	5.60	9.50
	SD	3.21	2.38

This is Iris Mitchell, from your Tuesday English 450A class. This past week has been very busy for me since I caught the flu and am behind on all my work, would it be okay if I turned in the up-coming assignment a couple of days late?
Thanks,
Iris Mitchell

(6) PSC-S6 (Female)
老師您好:
我是教育系*101*級的趙如玉, 下個星期四早上因爲要參加學校文學院的畢業生活動需和您請假一次, 謝謝
如玉敬上
[Dear Professor:
This is Ruyu Chao from the Education Department 101. I need to ask for a leave of absence from next Thursday morning's class because I will attend a graduation ceremony. Thanks.
Sincerely yours,
Ruyu]

4.4.3 IFID—Direct Apology

An IFID refers to a set of formulaic expressions which show the speaker's apology for a potentially offensive act, e.g., *(be) sorry, apologize* (Austin 1962), *regret*, etc. IFIDs may also be accompanied by modifiers for intensification. Table 4.4 provides the statistical results of the use of IFIDs by PSEs and EFLCs. As can be seen, EFLCs and PSEs are similar in terms of the mean length of the "Direct Apologies." No significant difference was found between the two groups (t (36) = −1.158, p = 0.255).

The nonnative and the native groups, however, do differ in the types of tokens they used to apologize to their instructors. First, EFLCs almost invariantly used *sorry* to express their apologies, whereas the PSEs employed a wide range of expressions for "Direct Apologies," including *sorry, apologize, apology*, and *regret*, with *apologize* being the most preferred verb in IFID (11/19, >50 %). This is different from House's (1989, p. 322) finding that German learners use a wider variety of tokens compared to PSEs' overriding frequency of *sorry*. Second, there is a lack of variety in the EFLCs' internal modifiers (Hassall 2001). That is, they always employed a degree adverb before the formulaic apology word *sorry*, e.g., *really, so, truly*, and *terribly*. Although PSEs also use *so* and *very*, they also use other adverbs, e.g., *humbly* and *sincerely*, and the IFID formulas are of a richer

Table 4.4 Distribution of IFIDs by EFLCs and PSEs (PSCs' mean length: 7.63)

Strategy		EFLC	PSE
Direct	N	20	18
	Mean	12.55	15.11
	SD	5.55	7.98

variety, e.g., *cannot…enough* and *regret to inform*. Third, there is a slightly larger standard deviation in the PSEs' IFIDs (7.98). This is mainly due to the lack of IFIDs in two students' messages and three longer IFIDs written by the PSEs. The latter three emails contain longer IFIDs in which the students use "Direct Apologies" both at the beginning and toward the end of the emails. Consider the following examples:

(7) PSE-S4 (Male)
Dear Dr. Tran,
I *regret to inform* you that I will be unable to attend our meeting scheduled on Monday July 25th at 9:30. I *sincerely apologize for* any inconvenience this might pose on your end…
Best,
William Dillon

(8) PSE-S5 (Male)
Dear Professor Einsberg,
I hope your day is going well. I am extremely sorry about this, but something urgent has come up, and I will not be able to attend our meeting tomorrow. I have tried my best, but there was no way I could get out of this other obligation. Is there any other date we can meet? Once again, *I am very sorry about this and cannot apologize enough*. Also, I hope the rest of your week goes well.
Your student,
Patrick Malcom

(9) EFLC-S19 (Female)
Dear teacher,
I am really, really sorry about delaying this homework! Although the rule has seriously warned us that there is no accept of the delaying homework, I think I still should hand in them to complete my duty. I will receive any punishment of this delaying! *Really sorry about* it.
Susan

As for the PSCs' email messages, it can be seen from the raw frequencies displayed in Table 4.4 that their "Direct Apologies" are generally shorter (7.63). The IFID usually takes the linguistic forms of *buhaoyisi*, *baoqian*, and *duibuqi*. Extract (10) typifies the conciseness in the PSCs' "Direct Apology":

(10) PSC-S7 (Female)
Dear 慧敏老師:
昨日的課程因身體不適而未能出席, 沒有上到的進度我會趕快跟上的, 老師不好意思了!:(
學生李淑芷 敬上
[Dear Professor Huimin:
I was absent from class yesterday because I didn't feel well. I will make up for what I have missed yesterday. *I'm sorry for this, teacher*! :(
Sincerely yours,

Student Shu-zhi Li]

In short, when expressing "Direct Apologies" to the instructors, EFLCs and PSEs exhibit linguistic realizations that are of similar length. However, the EFLCs lack variety in their forms, while the PSEs used various types of formulaic expressions and intensifiers to strengthen the apology. In contrast to the wordiness of the two English groups, "Direct Apologies" in the Chinese emails are generally shorter.

4.4.4 Account or Explanation

An "Account" or "Explanation" is one of the most common strategies used by the three groups of participants. It is used when the students provide a reason for their absence or late assignments. Table 4.5 shows that EFLCs are extremely verbose in the use of this strategy, with the average length of the sentence almost 2.5 times that of the PSE group. Statistical analysis also revealed a significant difference among the EFLCs and PSEs (t (16.750) = 2.932, p = 0.009).

Of the 20 EFLCs, 17 provided an account for the offense. A qualitative analysis of each student's email further indicates that seven among the 17 EFLCs display waffling in this strategy, including three accounts whose lengths range from 98 to 180 words. Comparatively, each PSE has similar length, with the longest account having only 26 words. In addition to differences in length, EFLCs also differ from the English native group in terms of the content of the account. That is, the English learners are more likely to share details of their personal lives, while the native speakers' email messages seem more formal and no personal information is implied (Faerch and Kasper 1989). (11)–(13) clearly manifest the divergence in these students' emails:

(11) EFLC-S17 (Female)
Dear teacher,
I am now preparing for my practicum. Tomorrow is my first class, and I am so nervous about it. Hope that I can send you the report before we meet on Wednesday
Thank you so much!
Best,
Betty

(12) EFLC-S3 (Male)
Dear Elena,
I would like to say thank you very much for your concern.
Besides, Elena, may I explain a little about the two missing occasions?

Table 4.5 Account by EFLCs and PSEs (PSCs' mean length: 17.50)

Strategy		EFLC	PSE
Account	N	17	16
	Mean	50.65	19.06
	SD	43.91	6.53

This year, I continue to serve as an advisor for my high school's service learning projects and I am responsible for the sophomore students and the affairs of the whole club. Last Thursday afternoon to yesterday night was the annual service camp held by my club. And since October, I have been preparing the documents to school, discussing with my partners, leading sophomores to train the freshmen school brothers for the preparation of the service camp. I did feel a lot of pressure and sometimes I skipped or asked for leave for some reasons, including last Thursday's Freshman English class and last Monday's AL class :(I should have informed you earlier this week about my situation. Not until I received your letter did I remember that I should write this letter to you asap. Last night I got back home at 22:30 and went to bed at 23:30. But this morning when I woke up, I felt uncomfortable and kept coughing, I may have to go to see a doctor this afternoon.[5]
I do want to apologize for missing class again. For the journal 5, I would *try my best* to send it to you :" (
I hope Elena can forgive my carelessness and irresponsibility.
Sincerely,
Roger

(13) PSE-S8 (Female)
Hi Professor!
This is Eva Miller, from your Anatomy class. I'm really sorry, but I can't make it to today's class. *There's something else that I have to do, so I won't be able to make it.* Is it okay if you send me any homework that you assign to us? I'll try to borrow notes from someone in class. Again, I'm really sorry!
Eva Miller

As shown in the extracts above, EFLC (S3) provides excessive and unnecessary details about his personal life to explain his absence. The extreme verbosity is a far cry from the PSEs' plain account. Furthermore, even if the EFLC's (Betty) "Account" in (11) is not long, it shows intimacy by disclosing her personal feeling. The PSEs, however, hedge about the exact reason for the absence, e.g., *There is something…* and *due to unforeseen circumstances*, making the emails sound more formal and impersonal (see also Chen 2006).

Analysis of how PSCs use the "Account" strategy shows that the waffling could be an interlanguage influence rather than transfer. As Table 4.5 shows, the average length of this strategy in the PSCs' emails is short (average: 17.5 words). Although personal affairs may be stated in the email, they are brief and to the point, with no elaboration of the details. Consider (14–15), which, respectively, contain 19 and 9 words of "Account" and each sounds more like a formal email in a business setting:

(14) PSC-S3 (Male)
老師,

[5]The "last Thursday's *Freshman English class*" in this email refers to the class in the week before last. It is not a typo but an error resulting from the student's direct translation of 上上週 'last-last-week' in Chinese.

我星期一晚上系上跟老師必須要共同討論, 所以我要跟老師請假一次真的很不好意思這麼晚才跟您說, 謝謝=)
[Professor, *I have a discussion meeting with a teacher in my department on Monday evening, so I need to ask for a leave*. I'm sorry for informing you of this so late.
Thank you.
Daniel]

(15) PSC-S8 (Female)
湘琴老師您好:
我是修習教學實習的學生劉秀美, 今早因身體不舒服, 有點發燒因而缺席, 真的十分抱歉!今天上課內容我已詢問過同學了, 請老師放心。謝謝!
學生劉秀美
[Dear Professor Xiangchin,
I'm Hsiumei Liu from your Teaching Practicum class. I was absent this morning because I didn't feel well and had a slight fever. I'm really sorry for this. I have asked a classmate about what we discussed in class today. Please do not worry.
Thank you.
Student Hsiumei Liu]

To sum up, all three participant groups employed the strategy of "Account" when apologizing to their instructors. The nonnative speakers of English, in particular, are disposed to waffling by being over-informative in their messages, whereas both native groups give precise and shorter messages. The prolixity of nonnative speakers' "Account" is also noted by Hassall (2001) among learners of Indonesian. Furthermore, an interlanguage feature is displayed in the English learners' language, characterized by the tendency to provide too much personal information with this strategy. In fact, as revealed by the instructors to whom the emails were addressed, such verbosity is inappropriate in that the students gave "too much background information" that is not addressing the offense. The instructors also thought it inappropriate for students to treat them as friends. That is, professional distance is deemed by the instructors to be important in the correspondence and should have been maintained in the academic emails at issue.[6] In contrast to the profuseness of personal information in the emails written by the EFLCs, the PSCs' accounts were relatively short, carried a formal and detached tone, and conveyed only necessary information for the communication.

4.4.5 Taking on Responsibility

"Taking on Responsibility" is a strategy to show that the apologizer is responsible for the offense made. The strategy serves to appease the hearer, and in this case functions to maintain the relationship between the student and the instructor. Table 4.6 shows that five students from the EFLC group and six from the PSE

[6]One instructor responded in the post-hoc interview with the comment: "I'm not their friend."

Table 4.6 Responsibility by EFLCs and PSEs (One PSC's length: 9.00)

Strategy		EFLC	PSE
Responsibility	N	5	6
	Mean	12.60	17.83
	SD	8.17	6.97

group express their responsibility for the offense, whereas only one PSC employs this strategy. No significant difference was found between the EFLCs' and the PSEs' email messages (t (9) = −1.148, p = 0.281).

Regarding the substrategies of "Responsibility," all writers in all three groups choose from among the following three substrategies: "Explicit self-blame," "Justify hearer," and "Admission of facts," as exemplified below:

(16) EFLC-S4 (Male)
Professor Elena,
This is Sean.
I might not be able to show up for the class this week (11/7) because something happened in my family in Taichung. My father is not home, and I'm the only boy in my family, so I need to be there to make some arrangements. *I know that I need to do my individual presentation this week, and I have uploaded my slides to moodle, but could I do it next week?* So sorry for any inconvenience caused.
Best,
Sean

(17) PSE-S12 (Male)
Dear Dr. Freud,
I extend my apologies for the tardiness of the last assignment due and am inquiring in whether or not an extension on the due date is possible. I have made some progress into the assignment, but was unable to finish due to unforeseen circumstances that made it very difficult to attend to my responsibilities.
Attached to this e-mail is the progress I've made into the assignment for your reference. *I am willing to accept partial credit for the assignment if you allow me to finish it to completion, but I will leave that to your judgement.*
Again, my apologies for my tardiness,
Sam
Student number 8610888
SamCummings@aol.om

(18) PSC-S18 (Female)
老師您好:
我是大一共同英文科的Debbie。
很抱歉, 應於5/17繳交的作業我延遲到今天才寄信詢問。
請問老師, 我在明天5/22中午前將紙本作業交至您的辦公室是否還來得及?
我願意接受遲交的扣分處置, 真的很不好意思造成老師困擾。
學生Debbie

[Dear Professor, This is Debbie from the Freshman English class. I'm sorry for not emailing you until now about the delayed assignment due on 5/17. Would it be too late if I submit the paper copy to your office by 5/22 noon? *I'm willing to accept any deducted points as a penalty for the late assignment*. I'm sorry to have caused any inconvenience to you.
Debbie]

The examples above manifest the differences between the PSEs and the EFLCs when they expressed their responsibility for the offense. The EFLCs are briefer and use more informal forms when they blame themselves for the offense, e.g., *I know that...* or *that was my mistake*. More elaborate, formal and academic language, however, is used by the PSEs, e.g., with the formula *I understand that...* and/or the responsibility explicitly expressed, e.g., *accept all responsibility*. The formality of PSEs' language reflects a similar trend to that shown in the previous discussion about "Accounts" or "Explanations."

Contrary to the PSE pattern, only one PSC email message includes a "Responsibility" statement. The use of this strategy by both groups of Chinese speakers shows that Chinese participants in our study are less inclined to attribute the cause of the offense to themselves when an example of inappropriate academic conduct is made. The avoidance of acknowledging one's responsibility may stem from their love of *mian-tzu* 'face,' the intention to show oneself as having better social character. In so doing, the speaker may be less vulnerable to receiving unfavorable comments and situate themselves in a better social position (Hu 1944) when inappropriate academic conduct is exhibited.

In short, EFLCs and PSEs display similar patterns in their "Responsibility" strategy and substrategies. By contrast, almost all PSCs choose to opt out. In Bataineh and Bataineh's (2006) study, students remained silent in their emails to be exonerated from blame. Whether the PSCs also opted out for similar reasons requires further research.

4.4.6 *Offer of Repair*

"Offer of Repair" refers to a strategy by which the writer expresses a wish to provide a remedial measure to compensate for the offense made. Table 4.7 shows that all three participant groups use this strategy, and there was no difference between the length of "Repair" between EFLCs and PSEs (t (25) = −1.711, $p = 0.100$).

In spite of the lack of significant difference in the length of the "Offer of Repair," the results given in Table 4.7 demonstrate a different trend from that of the "Account" strategy. That is, most of the native English speakers (18 PSEs) explicitly state their willingness to compensate in some way for the offense, and the steps they will take to make amends, whereas only nine EFLCs exhibit an intention to resolve the issue. In particular, recall that EFLC-S3 in (12) (see Sect. 4.4.4) gave

Table 4.7 Offer of repair by EFLCs and PSEs (cf. PSCs' mean length: 15.24)

Strategy		EFLC	PSE
Repair	N	9	18
	Mean	16.67	22.89
	SD	8.37	13.07

a lengthy explanation for the absence; however, the statement for a reparation to be made contained only 14 words and did not give a specific time for submission of the make-up assignment. The following extracts further illustrate the difference between EFLCs' and PSEs' "Repair" statements:

(19) EFLC-S19 (Female)
Dear teacher,
I am really, really sorry about delaying this homework! Although the rule has seriously warned us that there is no accept of the delaying homework, *I think I still should hand in them to complete my duty*. I will receive any punishment of this delaying! Really sorry about it.
Sandy

(20) PSE-S1 (Male)
Dr. Galton:
I want to apologize for missing our meeting this afternoon; I'm afraid that an unfortunate series of events threw a monkey wrench into my day's plans. *I understand that your schedule remains busy for quite some time, so I am completely flexible in either rescheduling our meeting, catching up on the discussion with others who were there, or stopping by your office during a few free minutes of your time. Please let me know which option is most convenient for you at your leisure.* I apologize again and hope that I have not caused you too much trouble.
Sincerely,
Ted

(21) PSE-S6 (Female)
Hello, Professor Ford!
I'm so sorry I missed the meeting with you yesterday. I had a meeting for another class that ran a little late and I couldn't leave early. *Is there any way I can reschedule a meeting with you? If you'd like to or if it's best for you, I could even just meet with you right before our class. Please let me know what I can do!*
Thank you very much,
Lisa

As clearly shown in the emails above, the PSEs directly address the issue by attaching a "Repair" statement to assure the instructor that the reparative work has indeed been completed, e.g., *had done the homework, flexible in rescheduling the meeting* and *would like to turn it in*. The PSEs' messages also sound more polite and less imposing with modal auxiliaries, e.g., *I was wondering if I could still get that turned in*, or by providing options for the remedial work. That is, PSEs show clear intent and a polite attitude as they address the remedies explicitly. This usually requires several sentences to get the message across. As for the EFLCs, among the nine "Repair" messages, only two directly state the time to submit the missed assignment. The other seven students convey only tentativeness and hypotheticality in the message regarding their ability to carry out the remedy, e.g., *I would try my best…, I think I still should.*

There are, however, individual variations in the PSEs' "Offers of Repair" as is shown in the larger standard deviation (13.07) than that of the EFLCs. This is due to the longer "Repairs" found in some of the PSEs' emails (58, 39, 37, and 33 words, respectively). The longest email is illustrated by (20), where the student wrote three consecutive clauses to inquire what can be done to make up for the missed appointment. This again shows the more serious attitude taken by the PSEs toward the offense they have made.

As for PSCs, they show a similar tendency in their use of "Repair" strategies. Of the 20 PSCs, 17 indicate the repairs that will be made following the email, including 15 who explicitly indicate that the absence or tardiness has been dealt with. Excerpt (22) is an example:

(22) PSC-S14 (Female)
老師抱歉又忘記了....非常感謝您還寄信提醒!
檔案已附件在信件中了, 謝謝老師!
教育103 張淑玲
[Professor I'm sorry that I forgot again. Thank you very much for sending me an email reminder. The file has been attached to this mail. Thank you, Professor.
Education 103 Shuling Chang]

One reason for the lack of the "Repair" strategy in the learners' emails might be their unfamiliarity with common vocabulary or prefabricated chunks that can be used to state a remedy in question. The PSCs' "Repairs," by contrast, contain commonly used terms such as official leave-of-absence form (假單) or about making sure to obtain the notes from the lecture they had missed (e.g., 上課內容已請教過同學, in (15)). Expressions like *to reschedule the meeting, I'm completely flexible in…, catching up on the discussion, to sort out another date/time* seem to be less accessible to the English language learners due to their limited language repertoire. Explicit teaching of relevant vocabulary or expressions, therefore, is necessary for students to express themselves more effectively.

In short, EFLCs differ from PSEs with respect to the length and the content of the strategy. Unlike the prolific language used in the EFLCs' "Accounts" for the offense (Sect. 4.4.4), elaboration is not exhibited in the EFLCs' "Repair" strategy. Instead, their "Repair" messages tend to be short and indirect. Slightly longer sentences (see Table 4.7) are used by PSEs to describe the remedial move they have taken, or will take, to compensate for the violation of the academic norm at issue. PSCs resemble PSEs in that most students clearly state the reparative work having been or to be fulfilled. This is against Shih's (2006) argument that PSCs, like EFLCs, tend to evade responsibility by giving indirect statements. Whether this is due to the different elicitation methods or to the change in students' attitudes toward their instructors in the last few years requires further study.

4.4.7 Thanking

As they bring their emails to a close, the students usually use polite markers to prepare for the closure, thank the instructor, and then end with a complimentary statement showing good wishes for the addressee's future. Among these strategies, "Thanking" appears in significant numbers (7 EFLCs, 10 PSEs, and 10 PSCs). That is, around half of each group expressed thanks toward their instructors to conclude the email. Table 4.8 shows that no significant difference is found in terms of the length of the Thanking message (t (15) = −0.556, p = 0.587). This strategy mainly contained typical expressions of gratitude, e.g., *xiexie* (謝謝) and *Thank you.*

(23) PSC-S4 (Female)
Dear Professor Thomas,
今天早上我要回南部一趟參加表姊的婚禮。
已請事假，下個禮拜會拿假單給老師:p
謝謝老師:)
Lori
[Dear Professor Thomas,
I have to go back to the south to attend my cousin's wedding. I have submitted my leave of absence. I will give you the leave form next week. *Thank you, Professor*:)
Lori]

(24) PSE-S15 (Female)
Dear Prof. White,
I apologize for submitting this assignment late. As my French midterm was unexpectedly moved to an earlier date, I was unable to finish the paper and submit it by the deadline. *Thank you for your understanding.*
Take care.
Sally Praad

4.4.8 Summary

So far, we have investigated apology emails written by EFLCs, PSEs and PSCs to their instructors about absence from meetings or late assignments. Four research questions are addressed:

Table 4.8 Thanking by EFLCs and PSEs (PSCs' mean length: 2.2)

Strategy		EFLC	PSE
Thanking	N	7	10
	Mean	6.86	5.10
	SD	8.11	4.98

1. Do the Chinese EFL learners reveal the waffle phenomenon in their apology emails?
2. If waffling is observed in interlanguage apologies, what strategies are waffled?
3. Are there any pragmalinguistic and sociopragmatic differences between Chinese EFL learners and proficient English speakers in the linguistic content of the apology strategies? If yes, what are these differences?
4. Are there any differences between the EFL learners and proficient Chinese speakers and between proficient English speakers and proficient Chinese speakers in their email apologies?

Regarding the first and the second questions, the answer only partially agrees with the literature that EFL students waffle in their speech acts (e.g., Edmonson and House 1991; House 1989). In other words, EFLCs give a significantly longer response as a grounder, i.e., "Account," for their deviant conduct. No significant difference in length is found in the other strategies. The difference in "Account" may be attributed to EFLCs' mistaken judgment about what an official email of apology should be like in academic correspondence. On the other hand, in both the "Account" and "Repair" expressions, the EFLC emails tended to carry an informal tone by dwelling on personal matters and/or minimize the repairs that should have been the focus of the emails. The instructors, however, felt that the students should maintain a professional instructor–student relationship, and the focus of the email should be on the repairs that will be made.

With respect to the third question, we find that there are pragmalinguistic and sociopragmatic differences in some of the EFLCs' apology strategies. In terms of pragmalinguistic differences, first, in the use of "Direct Apologies," compared to the richer language of PSEs, EFLCs were generally invariant in terms of the forms of their "Direct Apologies" and used a limited set of intensifiers. In addition, in the "Repair" strategies, EFLCs show tentativeness and evasiveness in the remedial work to be completed, whereas PSEs use more explicit language to detail the reparative measures taken, or that will be taken, by the writer. The less frequent occurrence of EFLCs' "Repairs" may be due to a lack of familiarity with the relevant vocabulary or expressions to state how a "Repair" was made or will be made.

Regarding sociopragmatic differences, as stated above, the EFLCs show intimacy with their instructors. A tone of informality is exhibited in their emails, e.g., in their statements of "Responsibility." However, this tone was deemed inappropriate by the instructors. Furthermore, the EFLCs do not state what remedial work will be made or are indirect in their "Offer of Repair." A stronger personal involvement is also imbued in the use of these strategies. These instances of sociopragmatic differences stem from the learners' inapt evaluation of the sociocultural norms of the target language. That is, in academic emails, directness, formality and conciseness are desired. Misunderstanding of the target language norms may result in breakdowns in communication.

As for the fourth research question, a striking characteristic of the PSC group is the simplicity of their language. Although no formal statistical comparison is made with PSCs' email messages, all of their messages are much shorter than the other two groups' messages. In addition, the messages are clear and succinct, directly addressing the offense without much elaboration. The motivation behind the brevity of the Chinese emails is worth further exploration.

4.5 Conclusion and Pedagogical Implications

This study investigated apology strategies in academic emails used by English native speakers, EFL learners, and Chinese native speakers. In general, the results demonstrate both generality and specificity (Faerch and Kasper 1989) in language users' apology realizations. The generality is indicated by preference of all participants for "Direct Apologies," "Accounts," "Taking on Responsibility," and "Offers of Repair." Specificity is noticeable in the total number of the strategies and the linguistic realizations of the apologies. The findings summarized above shed light on the importance of explicit instruction of the pragmalinguistic features and the sociocultural values accepted in the target culture, and in the case of the current study, formality and conciseness of the language. The EFL learners' performance reflects a misconception about the appropriate relationship between students and instructors. There is a lack of understanding that professional distance needs to be maintained in academic correspondence. Explicit teaching of email etiquette, therefore, is called for in the EFL language classroom with incorporation of related cultural knowledge and assumptions, and appropriate language use. One issue that the current research does not address, due to fewer email messages being written by male students, is how gender affects the use of apologies in academic email messages written by Chinese students. That is, gender differences might be a confounding factor in terms of length and the types of strategies employed. On the other hand, the attitudes and beliefs implicated in the PSCs' emails, which are different from previous inquiries (Shih 2006), may be suggestive of the changing sociocultural values of contemporary Chinese university students. It is suggested that future studies tackle these issues so that a fuller picture of apology behaviors by Chinese EFL/ESL students could be revealed.

References

Austin, John L. 1962. *How to do things with words*. Oxford: Oxford University Press.

Bardovi-Harlig, Kathleen, and Beverly S. Hartford. 1993. Learning the rules of academic talk: A longitudinal study of pragmatic change. *Studies in Second Language Acquisition* 15: 279–304.

Bardovi-Harlig, Kathleen, and Beverly S. Hartford. 1996. Input in an institutional setting. *Studies in Second Language Acquisition* 18: 171–188.

Baron, Naomi S. 1998. Letters by phone or speech by other means: The linguistics of email. *Language & Communication* 18: 133–170.

Bataineh, Ruba Fahmi, and Rula Fahmi Bataineh. 2006. Apology strategies of Jordanian EFL university students. *Journal of Pragmatics* 38: 1901–1927.

Bergman, Marc L., and Gabriele Kasper. 1993. Perception and performance in native and nonnative apology. In *Interlanguage pragmatics*, ed. Gabriele Kapser, and Shoshana Blum-Kulka, 82–107. Oxford: Oxford University Press.

Billmyer, Kristine. 1990. The effect of formal instruction on the development of sociolinguistic competence: The performance of compliments. Unpublished doctoral dissertation, University of Pennsylvania, Philadelphia.

Blum-Kulka, Shoshana, and Elite Olshtain. 1986. Too many words: Length of utterance and pragmatic failure. *Studies in Second Language Acquisition* 8: 165–180.

Blum-Kulka, Shoshana, Juliane House, and Gabriele Kasper. 1989. Investigating cross-cultural pragmatics: An introductory overview. In *Cross-cultural pragmatics: Requests and apologies*, ed. Shoshana Blum-Kulka, Juliane House and Gabriele Kasper, 1–34. *Norwood*, New Jersey: Ablex Publishing Co.

Brown, Penelope, and Stephen Levinson. 1987. *Politeness: Some universals in language usage*. Cambridge, UK: Cambridge University Press.

Chen, Chi-Fen Emily. 2006. The development of e-mail literacy: From writing to peers to writing to authority figures. *Language Learning and Technology* 10: 35–55.

Chen, Yuan-shan, Chun-Yin Doris Chen, and Miao-Hsia Chang. 2010. The effects of instruction on Chinese university students' productions of complaint behaviors in American English. *Taiwan Journal of TESOL* 7(1): 29–65.

Chen, Yuan-shan, Chun-Yin Doris Chen, and Miao-Hsia Chang. 2011. American and Chinese complaints: Strategy use from a cross-cultural perspective. *Intercultural Pragmatics* 8(2): 253–275.

Cohen, Andrew D., and Elite Olshtain. 1981. Developing a measure of sociocultural competence: The case of apology. *Language Learning* 31: 113–134.

Economidou-Kogetsidis, Maria. 2012. Modifying oral requests in a foreign language: The case of Greek Cypriot learners of English. In *Interlanguage request modification*, ed. Maria Economidou-Kogetsidis, and Helen Woodfield, 163–201. Amsterdam/Philadelphia: John Benjamins.

Edmondson, Willis, and Juliane House. 1991. Do learners talk too much? The waffle phenomenon in interlanguage pragmatics. In *Foreign/second language pedagogy research: A communicative volume for Claus Faerch*, ed. R. Phillipson, E. Kellerman, L. Selinker, M. Sharwood, and M. Swain, 273–287. Clevedon: Multilingual Matters Ltd.

Eisenstein, Miriam, and Jean Bodman. 1993. Expressing graditude in American English. In *Interlanguage pragmatics*, ed. Gabriele Kasper, and Shoshana Blum-Kulka, 64–81. New York: Oxford University Press.

Faerch, Claus, and Gabriele Kasper. 1989. Internal and external modification in interlanguage request realization. In *Cross-cultural pragmatics: Requests and apologies*, ed. Shoshana Blum-Kulka, Juliane House, and Gabriele Kasper, 221–247. Norwood, NJ: Ablex Publishing Corporation.

Felix-Brasdefer, J. César. 2004. Interlanguage refusals: Linguistic politeness and length of residence in the target community. *Language Learning* 54: 587–653.

Goffman, Erving. 1971. *Relations in public: Microstudies of the public order*. Harmondsworth: Penguin.

Grice, H. Paul. 1975. Logic and conversation. In *Syntax and semantics 3*, ed. Peter Cole, and Jerry L. Morgan, 41–58. New York: Academic Press.

Hatipoğlu, Çiler. 2004. Do apologies in e-mails follow spoken or written forms?: Some examples from British English. *Studies about Languages* 5: 21–29.

Harting, Axel. 2006. Investigating German and Japanese apologies in email writing. In *JALT2005 Conference Proceedings*, ed. K. Bradford-Watts, C. Ikeguchi, and M. Swanson. Tokyo: JALT.

Hassall, Tim. 2001. Modifying requests in a second language. *International Review of Applied Linguistics in Language Teaching* 39: 259–283.

Hewings, Ann, and Caroline Coffin. 2004. Grammar in the construction of online discussion messages. In *Applying English grammar: Functional and corpus approaches*, ed. Caroline Coffin, Ann Hewings, and Kieran O'Halloran, 134–154. London: Edward Arnold.

Hinkel, Eli. 1994. Native and nonnative speakers' pragmatic interpretations of English texts. *TESOL Quarterly* 28(2): 353–376.

Holmes, Janet. 1990. Apologies in New Zealand English. *Language in Society* 19: 155–199.

House, Juliane. 1989. Oh excuse me please: Apologizing in a foreign language. In *English als Zweitsprache* [English as a second language], ed. B. Ketteman, P. Bierbaumer, A. Fill, and A. Karpf, 303–327. Arbeiten aus Anglistik und Amerikanistik. Tübingen: Narr.

Hu, Hsien Chin. 1944. The Chinese concepts of face. *American Anthropologist* 46: 45–65.

Hymes, Dell. 1972. On communicative competence. In *Sociolinguistics: Selected readings*, ed. J. Pride, and J. Holmes, 269–293. Harmondsworth: Penguin.

Kasper, Gabriele. 1992. Pragmatic transfer. *Second Language Research* 8: 203–231.

Leech, Geoffery Neil. 1983. *Principles of pragmatics*. London: Longman.

Lightfoot, Jay M. 2006. A comparative analysis of e-mail and face-to-face communication in an educational environment. *Internet and Higher Education* 9: 217–227.

Liu, Zi-ying. 2008. A pragmatic study of sex differences in Mandarin apology strategies of Taiwanese undergraduate students. Unpublished MA thesis, National Hsinchu University of Education.

Olshtain, Elite, and Andrew D. Cohen. 1983. Apology: A speech act set. In *Sociolinguistics and language acquisition*, ed. Nessa Wolfson, and Elliot Judd, 18–35. New York: Newbury House.

Otcu, Bahar, and Deniz Zeyrek. 2008. Development of requests: A study of Turkish learners of English. In *Developing contrastive pragmatics: Interlanguage and cross-cultural perspectives*, ed. Martin Pütz, and JoAnne Neff-van Aertselaer, 265–300. Berlin/New York: Mouton de Gruyter.

Pan, Ping Cathy. 2012. Interlanguage requests in institutional e-mail discourse. In *Interlanguage request modification*, ed. Maria Economidou-Kogetsidis, and Helen Woodfield, 119–161. Amsterdam/Philadelphia: John Benjamins.

Park, Hee Sun, Hye Eun Lee, and Jeong An Song. 2005. I am sorry to send you SPAM: Cross-cultural differences in use of apologies in email advertising in Korea and the U.S. *Human Communication Research* 31: 365–398.

Scollon, Ron, and Suzanne Wong Scollon. 1995. (2nd ed.) *Intercultural communication: A discourse approach.* Oxford, UK: Blackwell.

Searle, John. 1969. *Speech acts: An essay in the philosophy of language*. Cambridge, UK: Cambridge University Press.

Searle, John. 1976. A classification of illocutionary acts. *Language in Society* 5: 1–23.

Searle, John. 1979. *Expression and meaning: Studies in the theory of speech acts*. Cambridge, UK: Cambridge University Press.

Shih, Hsi-chun. 2005. The effect of English proficiency and social variables on L2 apology strategies: A case study on Taiwanese EFL junior high school students of Taipei County. Unpublished MA thesis, National Taipei University of Education.

Shih, Hsiang-Yi. 2006. An interlanguage study of the speech act of apology made by EFL learners in Taiwan. Unpublished MA thesis, National Sun-Yat Sen University.

Thomas, Jenny. 1983. Cross-cultural pragmatic failure. *Applied Linguistics* 4: 91–112.

Trosborg, Anna. 1995. *Interlanguage pragmatics: Requests, complaints and apologies*. Berlin: Walter de Gruyter.

Tsai, Po-Chen. 2002. A study of the speech act of apology in Chinese. Unpublished MA thesis, Tsing Hua University.

Tsai, I-ting. 2007. Studying apologies: A comparison of DCT and role-play data. Unpublished MA thesis, National Sun-Yat Sen University.

Tsai, Yvonne. 2010. Text analysis of patent abstracts. *The Journal of Specialised Translation* 13: 61–80.

Wallwork, Adrian. 2011. *English for academic correspondence and socializing*. New York: Springer.
Zhou, Yu, Liu Peng, and Cheng Zong. 2011. Approaches to improving corpus quality for statistical machine translation. *International Journal of Computer Processing of Languages* 23: 327–348.

Author Biographies

Miao-Hsia Chang (張妙霞) is a professor in the Department of English at National Taiwan Normal University. Her research interests include discourse analysis (and English language teaching), pragmatics (and English language teaching), grammaticalization, and corpus-based studies of spoken Taiwanese.

Jean Curran is a lecturer in the Department of English at National Taiwan Normal University. Her research interests include English as a lingua franca, pragmatics, and the teaching and testing of listening skills.

Yueh-Kuei Hsu (許月貴) is an associate professor in the Department of English at National Taiwan Normal University. Her research interests include language teacher development, young learner ELT, and teaching and researching autonomy.

Chih-Chun Hsu (徐芝君) is a post-doctoral researcher in the Center for Teaching and Learning Development at National Taiwan Normal University. Her current research focuses on cognitive psychology, educational psychology, and emotion.

Chapter 5
Politeness and Effectiveness of English Email Requests: Taiwanese Professors' Perspectives

Wan-jing Li and Yuan-shan Chen

Abstract This study investigated Taiwanese professors' perceptions of an email request to a faculty member. In this study, 13 Taiwanese professors at a university located in southern Taiwan who were proficient English speakers were asked to give their perceptions of the politeness and effectiveness of students' email writing. Content analysis was conducted to analyze these professors' perceptions in order to identify what they consider to be a polite and an effective email request to faculty. The findings showed that although Taiwanese professors have a high degree of tolerance toward nonstandard forms in email writing, they still believed that the formal, epistolary type of email writing to faculty is the best email style. In addition, most Taiwanese professors also tend to believe that when making a request to faculty, it would be better for students to give reasons first before they request, which indicated their support for modern standard Chinese information sequencing.

Keywords Politeness · Effectiveness · Email · Request

This study was adapted from the first author's unpublished master thesis, entitled "Politeness and Effectiveness of English Request Emails: Taiwanese Professors' Perspectives," National Chung Cheng University, 2013.

W. Li
Institute of Linguistics, National Chung Cheng University, Chiayi, Taiwan
e-mail: polestar0604@gmail.com

Y. Chen (✉)
Department of Applied English, National Chin-Yi University of Technology, Taichung, Taiwan
e-mail: yuanshan@ncut.edu.tw

Y. Chen et al. (eds.), *Email Discourse Among Chinese Using English as a Lingua Franca*, DOI 10.1007/978-981-287-888-5_5

5.1 Introduction

Computer-mediated communication (CMC) facilitates human communication. In CMC, email is most frequently compared to other means such as computer conferencing (Baron 1998). Nowadays, English has become a major medium of instruction in the English-as-a-lingua-franca context and email has become a common means of communication in academia (Baron 1998; Chang and Hsu 1998). Students frequently need to write emails to professors to request a deadline extension, a leave of absence, assistance with homework assignments, or opinions on course selection. There may be several reasons why students prefer writing emails to their professors. First, students can send messages to professors whenever they feel necessary without having to make an appointment in advance. Second, professors find emails to be "less intrusive" (Baron 1998, p. 159) because they can take time to consider and respond to students' requests whenever it is convenient for them. Finally, students prefer to write emails to their professors rather than talking to them face-to-face in order to minimize the face threat of a requesting behavior (Brown and Levinson 1987).

When writing email requests to faculty, students need to show politeness to acknowledge institutional hierarchy and minimize face threat (Biesenbach-Lucas 2007; Chen 2000). However, they should also pursue email effectiveness at the same time to increase the likelihood of the request being granted. Until now, a difference between a traditional letter and email is that the latter "is not yet governed by clear conventions and expectations" (Biesenbach-Lucas 2007, p. 61). Also, due to different cultural backgrounds, when students write English emails to professors, they may encounter some problems because of their limited English proficiency or unfamiliarity with the target culture norm (Chen 2006). For example, it has been found that nonnative speakers (NNS) of English tend to use "please" as a politeness marker when they write email requests (Biesenbach-Lucas 2004, 2007; Economidou-Kogetsidis 2011; Weasenforth and Biesenbach-Lucas 2001), but a request like, "Please answer me as soon as possible" may be considered inappropriate and impolite when addressed to a higher ranking person (Economidou-Kogetsidis 2011). Moreover, Sproull and Kiesler (1991) claimed that when people use the Internet as a communication tool, sending inappropriate emails would be one of the greatest dangers. This is because any misunderstandings created by emails usually have fewer opportunities to be clarified (Honeycutt 2001). In view of this, this study posed two research questions to be answered:

1. What constitutes a polite email? What expressions would be considered polite in an English email request by Taiwanese professors?
2. What constitutes an effective email? What expressions would be considered effective in an English email request by Taiwanese professors?

5.2 Theoretical Background

5.2.1 Email in Computer-Mediated Communication (CMC)

Computer-mediated communication (CMC) facilitates the frequency of cross-cultural communication. In CMC, email has the longest history and has been frequently used in business, academia, and everyday life (Baron 1998). One of the biggest characteristics differentiating email from traditional letters is the way of transmission. Taylor (2006) reported that email has the advantage of instant communication so that people can get email from others almost immediately after they send it. Thus, email is convenient not only because of the way of transmission but also its speed. The other characteristic which sets email apart from traditional letters is the style. Traditional letters usually adopt a formal style of writing. However, email has more flexibility, ranging from a very formal to a very informal, or even conversational style of writing (Baron 1998; Mackevic and Mamin 2010). The choice between formality and informality is usually dependent on the relationship between the email sender and recipient and the occasion under which the email is written and sent. These characteristics of email make it easier for global communication (Taylor 2009).

5.2.2 The Act of Requesting

Requesting behavior is one type of speech act, which serves as a pre-event, making "an attempt to cause an event or change one" (Blum-Kulka and Olshtain 1984, p. 206). Put simply, the function of a request is for the speaker to get the hearer to do what the speaker asks. When a speaker makes a request to a hearer, it is perceived as a face-threatening act (FTA). Brown and Levinson (1987) divided interlocutors' face wants into *positive face wants* and *negative face wants*. Positive face wants refer to the interlocutor's desires to be appreciated and approved of in order to increase their self-image. On the other hand, negative face wants refer to the interlocutor's desires to have "freedom of action and freedom from imposition" (p. 61). The act of requesting threatens the hearer's negative face wants because such an act violates his/her wants to be free from action and imposition. Therefore, in order to minimize the threat to the hearer's negative face while at the same time pursuing the speaker's communicative goal, it is important to make a request simultaneously polite and effective. A polite request can be achieved by minimizing the degree of face threat. One of the approaches is to adopt negative politeness strategies to convey the request in an indirect way. For example, the request forms "Can you…" or "May I…?" are considered as conventionally indirect request strategies which can diminish the illocutionary force of requesting and therefore help reduce the threat to the hearer's face to a minimum (Searle 1979). In addition to politeness, an effective request requires that the hearer recognize the speaker's intent and that the propositional content of the request be transparent to the hearer (Blum-Kulka et al. 1989).

5.2.3 Email Politeness

Watts (2003, p. 24) remarked: "Politeness has a 'chameleon-like nature.'" In order to be polite, people need to choose appropriate words and expressions to suit the needs of different cultures and languages. Just like a chameleon, people need to change themselves to adapt to a specific context. Problems may occur if people cannot change their language usage to fit the given context.

Previous investigations on email politeness have generally compared different politeness strategies employed by native (henceforth NS) and nonnative speakers (henceforth NNS) of English. For instance, Hartford and Bardovi-Harlig (1996) investigated the different ways of making requests between NS and NNS in email writings. They found that impoliteness may occur in NNS emails to faculty in terms of linguistic forms, downgraders, level of imposition, and content. Chang and Hsu (1998) studied the differences between American native speakers and Chinese learners of English in writing English email requests. They found that American native speakers structured their email request in a direct way (request + reason), but tended to use indirect linguistic forms to mitigate their requests. On the other hand, Chinese learners of English structured their email requests in an indirect way (reason + request), but tended to use direct linguistic forms to realize their requests. Therefore, some request samples written by the Chinese learners of English were judged as inappropriate or even impolite.

Chen (2001) examined the strategies used by American native speakers and Taiwanese learners of English and tried to explain the differences from cultural notions of politeness and the cultural identities each group would like to reflect in the emails. In another study, Chen (2006) investigated the emails written by a Taiwanese graduate student Ling to her professors during her stay in the United States. Ling indicated in the interviews that she thought it was polite to use formal discourse style and an inductive message structure containing many long, personal details before a request is issued. Chen's practice indicates transfer of indirectness in Chinese requesting (Zhang 1995) to email requests in English.

In addition to conducting text analysis and interviews to understand email writers' perceptions of politeness, some studies have investigated politeness from the perception of email recipients. For example, Hartford and Bardovi-Harlig (1996) categorized the students' emails into those which caused positive affect and those which caused negative affect on the part of the faculty recipient. Hendriks (2010) also did an experimental study on native speakers' perceptions in which they were asked to evaluate the degree of politeness of nonnative speakers' expressions in emails. Economidou-Kogetsidis (2011) similarly asked British native speakers to evaluate six email samples and to offer their perceptions of politeness and appropriateness of these emails.

However, none of above-mentioned studies investigated how Chinese faculty recipients evaluate students' English emails. Therefore, in the present study, we will explore how Chinese English speakers perceive email politeness from the perspective of faculty recipients.

5.2.4 *Email Effectiveness*

A good email request should be not only polite but also effective as well. An effective email is defined as one that leads to successful achievement of the email sender's goal. Previous studies have shown that email is an effective medium/tool (Chang and Hsu 1998; Liu 2008) and have examined the effectiveness of email. Turk and Kirkman (1989, p. 239) stated that a clear and useful letter should adopt "a direct and friendly tone, use simple, clear language, thoughtful tactics and a helpful layout." Moreover, Blumenthal (1985) stated that people should discuss only one point in a letter, or recipients would get confused because they do not know what to focus on. He also claimed that to write an effective request letter, people should make it as short as possible. Also, Tiffany and Carol (2005) claimed that every effective email should contain the following characteristics:

(1) The subject line of the email should capture the theme of the email.
(2) The content of the email should be concise.
(3) If there are questions in an email, they should be listed to elicit responses.
(4) An email should be no longer than one page.

Like Tiffany and Carol, Mitsuyo-Arimoto (2008) proposed similar tips for writing an effective email. First of all, an email should be concise and to the point because a long one is less likely to catch the recipient's attention. For instance, an email sender should not employ complex expressions if a word or sentence can be expressed in a simpler or more straightforward way. Therefore, it would be better to change a long sentence such as "It is with regret that this letter is written to inform you" to a shorter one such as: "We regret to inform you" (Mitsuyo-Arimoto 2008, p. 22). Second, if the sender has to discuss more than one thing within an email, he/she should list them out because it would be easier for the recipient to read and catch the main points. Taylor (2006, p. 48) also argued that an email sender cannot leave good impressions on the recipient unless he/she follows the "KISS (Keep It Short and Simple) principle." Moreover, she proposed an "ABC" principle (Taylor 2006, p. 52, 2009, p. 79), standing for "Accurate," "Brief," and "Clear," respectively. She claimed that this principle can: (1) save the recipient's time because he/she does not need to guess the purpose of the email; (2) avoid confusing the recipient; (3) create good impressions on the recipient; (4) enhance a good relationship with the recipient; and finally, (5) achieve the desired outcome.

To sum up, since email has become an important communication tool in academia, students need to know how to write an appropriate email request to faculty. Difficulties exist not only when students need to write emails to communicate with people in other countries. Even if the interlocutors are from the same L1 background, it is still important to avoid translating word for word from L1 to L2 without considering how L1 speakers would perceive the email written in L2. In view of this, the present study set out to explore how Taiwanese professors perceived politeness and effectiveness of email requests to faculty written by Taiwanese students.

5.3 The Study

5.3.1 Participants

In the present study, 13 Taiwanese professors were recruited to investigate how they perceived email politeness and effectiveness. Among them, six professors came from the Department of Foreign Languages and Literature (henceforth DFL) and seven professors from the Teacher Education Center (henceforth TEC) in a university in southern Taiwan.[1] Five were females and eight were males. These professors were selected because of the following conditions. First, all of them had previously studied in English-speaking countries like the United States or Britain for their doctoral degrees. Second, they had near-native English proficiency. DFL professors needed to use English to teach most of the time. TEC professors also needed to use English to write research papers and email for academic purposes.

5.3.2 Data Collection

The data was collected primarily through interviewing the 13 participants. They were given an English email request sample which a junior undergraduate student studying in a university of technology in central Taiwan wrote to the second author. This email was written under a special circumstance. At the beginning of the semester, this student, Emma,[2] chose an advanced listening course on the school internet but did not check to see if she was officially admitted to take that course. After the midterm exam, she got a notice from the Office of Student Affairs warning her that she had missed too many classes and would fail the course. She did not know the second author but tried to explain to her as follows:

---

[1]Pseudonyms are used for all the professors. The DFL professors were Derek, Meg, Belinda, Juliet, Jeanie, and Cherry. The TEC professors were Vic, Justin, Joe, Colin, Archie, Kevin, and Jennifer.

[2]A pseudonym.

Dear teacher:

I am Emma. I'm a junior student. I have a problem about attendances and scores in your Advanced Listening course. Because of my carelessness, I don't know I was officially admitted to take this course. Therefore, it caused I was always absent. Please teacher gives me a chance to make efforts on your course. Also, I am willing to do any assignments to complement the past achievements. Sincerely, hope teacher give me one chance again.

Thank you for your reading and hope you have a nice day.

Your student, Emma

Each participant met with and was interviewed individually by the first author. In the interview, the participant was asked first to read the sample email request. Then the first author conducted a semi-structured interview by asking both fixed questions and probes which naturally emerged as the interview went on.

The fixed questions consisted of 12 items, which can be divided into three types. First, items (1) to (7) were general questions for the participants to express freely their own opinions. Second, items (8) and (9) were specific questions about the use of address term 'Dear teacher' and 'teacher,' and about the importance of grammar, word choice and tone of voice in an email request to faculty. Finally, items (10) to (12) addressed the participants' personal experiences when receiving students' emails or when writing their own emails. Notice that item (3) was particularly related to politeness and items (2) and (7) were particularly related to effectiveness. The 12 questions[3] are listed below:

(1) What impressed you most when you read this sample email request for the first time?
(2) If you were the email recipient, would you grant her the request? Why would you give her the permission? Or why would not you give her the permission?
(3) Do you think this email sender is polite? Why or why not?
(4) What is (are) the strength(s) of this sample email request?
(5) What is (are) the weakness(es) of this sample email request?
(6) Do you think this sample email request is in general appropriate?
(7) What do you concern most when students write an email request to you?
(8) Do you think the address term 'Dear teacher' and 'teacher' used in this sample email request is appropriate? Why or why not?
(9) Which one do you think is the most important element for an English email? Grammar, word choice, or tone of voice?
(10) In your experience, what are the frequent problems of the English emails which your students sent you?

[3]The 12 questions were asked in English. However, the professors were free to respond in either English or Chinese.

(11) In your experience, have you ever replied to students' emails to tell him/her email etiquette due to the impoliteness?
(12) What problems did you encounter when you wrote English emails for the first time?

5.3.3 Data Analysis

The interviews were audio-taped and transcribed verbatim. Inductive content analysis was used to analyze the interview protocols. The first author categorized the perceptions to see if they would influence email politeness or email effectiveness. The second author helped check the coding. If there were any discrepancies, they discussed them to reconcile the differences and reach final consensus. Examples are listed as follows:

Perceptions coded as politeness
"The politeness is okay. But, the politeness of the email would be better if she provided sufficient reasons." (Vic)

Perceptions coded as effectiveness
"I wish the email content contained options for solutions. Otherwise, the teacher has to worry about it after getting her email." (Vic)

Under the politeness/effectiveness framework, the present study further categorized the perceptions into *content* and *form*, as proposed by Chen and Rau (2011). Content refers to *what to say*, while form refers to *how to say it*. When the professors' opinions were related to the elements which should be included in the email, they were categorized as "content." On the other hand, when the professors' opinions were related to the manner of writing the email, they were categorized as "form."

5.4 Results

5.4.1 Email Politeness

5.4.1.1 Email Politeness by Content

The professors regarded "content" as important to show politeness in an email request. Nine of the 13 professors (69 %) claimed that they would consider granting the request if the content of an email is appropriate. For instance, Juliet, a DFL professor, said,

> 我會根據內容回信。而不是因爲 language 影響 request 答應與否, 回信是爲了內容,而不是根據像文法、用字遣詞,語氣等…作回應。

> I would reply to emails according to their contents. Whether I grant requests or not is based on the content instead of language forms, such as grammar, word choice, or tone of voice.

From the interview protocols, we can also see that the appropriateness of content is usually judged by the request event and the student attitudes. In terms of request event, what seems to be of the greatest importance is that the request should be rational. Cherry, a DFL professor, remarked,

> 我通常都針對事情處理! 若不是自己該做的事情, 則學生怎麼 request 都沒用。
> I usually tackle the event itself. If it is not something that I should deal with, I would not grant her request no matter how hard the student requested.

Strikingly, 10 of the 13 professors (77 %) mentioned that in a high-imposition request, making an appointment with the professor is the first requirement for email politeness. Student senders should not expect to resolve a serious problem by email only.

In addition to being rational, 9 of the 13 professors (69 %) claimed that request events should be clear. Belinda, a DFL professor, said:

> Email 要有禮貌, 但是內容不能言不及意, 很空泛就不知道在說什麼。
> Emails should be polite but the contents cannot be vague or talk about nonsense.

Also, the occurrence of the reason/grounder for the request event is significant, too. Colin, a TEC professor, said,

> 這封信禮貌還不錯。因爲她的內容, 事件敘述的完整, 來龍去脈, 有提到原因。
>
> This sample email request is polite because the content of the request event is narrated completely with a beginning and a subsequent development. The reason was also mentioned.

Furthermore, Kevin, a TEC professor, said,

> 理由要充分。例如說:爲什麼自己一直都不知道。
> The reason should be sufficient. For instance, the student should explain why she did not know that she was not officially admitted to take the course?

Also noteworthy is the cultural differences in discourse pattern. Derek, a DFL professor, stated,

> 這封信是中式的禮貌。中式 discourse pattern, 先講原因…再 request, 這個學生是這種 indirect 的禮貌。
> (The sample email) uses Chinese politeness. It is the Chinese discourse pattern. At first, she told the reason, and then she requested. This is the kind of indirect politeness that the student expressed.

Derek further suggested that it would be better for students to be aware of the different expressions caused by cultural differences to avoid cross-cultural misunderstandings.

In addition to rationality and clarity of request events, showing a good attitude in an email request is important, too. Jennifer, a TEC professor, considered this sample email request to be polite because this student was willing to do any assignments to make up for the problem. She said:

這個學生態度佳，因爲主動處理這個問題，請教老師。有些學生甚至要老師去追學生。
The attitude of the student is good because she dealt with the problem actively. Some students would not take the initiative to ask their professor. Instead, the professor has to chase the student around.

Showing appreciation at the end of the email is also a way to indicate good attitudes. For example, Meg, a DFL professor, regarded this sample email request to be polite because it contained "Thank you for your reading." Meg commented:

這學生的表達寫法令人覺得真誠。
The expression of the student makes people feel she is sincere.

5.4.1.2 Email Politeness by Form

From the interview protocols, it is clear that the professors regarded formal address terms, self-identification, and appropriate tone of voice to be three important elements of email politeness by form.

In terms of the first important element, address terms, an email which does not address/greet professors in the beginning of the email is regarded as an impolite one and an email like this would offend professors. Belinda, a DFL professor, specifically pointed out the problem that some students write emails without address terms and that they start with the problem right at the beginning of the email. She said,

一開始沒有稱呼，一開始就直接寫問題,例如:「我忘了交作業」。一開始沒有稱呼和問候，太direct了。自己一看到 email，就覺得不太開心。
Some students do not have any greeting at all. They address their own problems at the very beginning such as 'I forgot to hand in the homework.' The email is too direct because there are neither terms of address nor greetings in the very beginning. Thus, I would feel a little unhappy if I see such an email.

With regard to expression, 12 of the 13 professors (92 %) responded that "Dear + title + last name" (e.g., "Dear Professor Lin") would be the most appropriate when writing email requests to faculty. However, one thing that should be noticed is that the use of "Dear teacher" was also considered as acceptable because the professors felt the use was (1) "better than no address term," (2) "a direct translation of Taiwanese culture," and (3) "showing politeness and respect." Belinda, a DFL professor, remarked,

Dear teacher 雖然像中文的寫法，但至少還有個開頭結尾。有些學生是沒有開頭結尾的。
Although the address term 'Dear teacher' is a Chinese expression, this email request contained at least the address term and the closing. Some students write emails without such elements.

Also, 11 of the 13 professors (85 %) said that "teacher" is a common address term in Taiwan. Finally, 7 of the 13 professors (54 %) pointed out that they could perceive the politeness conveyed by the student and feel whether they were respected by the student. Despite the fact that most professors acknowledged the use of "Dear Teacher," 2 of the 13 professors (15 %) considered using this address term was impolite because "teacher" did not have a definite and specific reference, so using "teacher" to address the recipient could not work in English.

The second element which influences email politeness is self-identification. Four of the 13 professors (31 %) mentioned that this sample email request seemed to be polite because it contained a self-identification. Juliet, a DFL professor, said,

> 要清楚自我介紹。不要當「藏鏡人」。
> Students should give self-identification clearly. Do not be a 'secret agent.'

Juliet emphasized that students should learn to take responsibility for their own words. Jeanie, a DFL professor, also mentioned,

> 如果寫出來的 email 卻沒有基本的 elements, 我就會很介意, 比如說有些學生連 Dear teacher、Professor Chen 之類的都刪掉,也不告訴我他是誰,就直接講 request, 那對這件事情,這封 email 反而成了阻礙這個 request 的很大的原因。
> I would mind very much if an email does not contain basic elements. For instance, some students would leave out address terms, such as *Dear Teacher* or *Dear Professor Chen*, and even do not tell me who he/she is but immediately make the request in the email. Such an email would actually become a big stumbling block for the request.

When asked what should be included in self-identification, Justin, a TEC professor, stated that the full name, or the student's ID number, should be essential information in an email request.

Finally, 11 of the 13 professors (85 %) also put emphasis on the tone of voice as one of the elements of email politeness. For instance, Belinda, a DFL professor, said,

> 我認爲語氣最重要,因爲有沒有禮貌是最重要的。
> I think tone of voice is the most important element of politeness in email writing.

Jennifer, a TEC professor, remarked,

> 語氣最重要,因爲英文不是母語,因此容易覺得不禮貌。
> Tone of voice is the most important because we are not native speakers of English. It is easy for us to let others feel our writing is impolite.

Vic, a TEC professor, also said,

> 語氣可以表達誠懇和禮貌度。
> Tone of voice can show our sincerity and politeness.

Concerning what exactly tone of voice is, Jeanie, a DFL professor, pointed out:

> 通常當信基本的 elements 都有, tone of voice 就不會太扯。
> Generally speaking, when an email contains the basic elements, the tone of voice won't be bad.

Tone of voice is also related to the degree of indirectness of request strategies. Archie, a TEC professor, and Meg, a DFL professor, suggested the use of *query preparatory* expressions (Blum-Kulka et al. 1989) such as "Would you please…" to reflect the appropriate tone of voice in email requests to faculty. Notwithstanding using *query preparatory* seemed to reflect politeness, it is also found that tone of voice is not fixed, but varies across cultures. For instance, when students use an imperative-like sentence, like "Please teacher gives me a chance to make efforts on your course," to make a request, the interviewees thought they could understand the politeness of this expression because it seemed to be a direct translation from Chinese to English. However, the same request may not be read the same way by English native speakers and may be perceived as impolite.

5.4.2 *Email Effectiveness*

5.4.2.1 Email Effectiveness by Content

The interview protocols showed that email effectiveness by content can be achieved by providing convincing and specific information and possible solutions. Derek, a DFL professor, mentioned the importance of providing convincing and specific information. He commented on this sample email request,

> 這封信雖然寫得算清楚,但不能確定是否事實真是如此,我要 confirm 之後,才會確定是否給機會。...若是要用這種理由說服,要有更具體的細節事實,給evidence。
> Although this email is clear, I cannot be sure if this is the fact. I will decide whether to give her a chance or not after I confirm the situation… If the student wanted to convince the professor by giving such a reason, she should provide more specific details and evidence.

Another way to increase email effectiveness is to provide possible solutions to the problem. Three of the 13 professors (23 %) stated that students should express clearly in the email the chances/opportunities they require. For instance, Joe, a TEC professor, pointed out the students should provide possible solutions to the problem for the professors to consider. However, he also said that if the professor cannot help her, the student should accept the fact.

> 我重視的是如何幫助他解決問題,所以學生應該自己提出一些可能的解決方案,若是學生問題真的無法解決,學生也應該接受不能解決的事實。
> What I pay attention to is how to help the student to solve the problem. So the student should propose some solutions him/herself. If the student's problem cannot be solved, he/she should also accept the fact that this problem cannot be solved.

5.4.2.2 Email Effectiveness by Form

Three of the 13 professors (23 %) stressed that subject lines influence email effectiveness. Meg, a DFL professor, indicated that the subject line of an email could catch her attention. She remarked,

> 學生寄來的 email 主旨會看一下,然後就會好奇,想點進去看。例如:「關於訪談」,就會想說是什麼。
> I would read the subject line of students' email, and then I would be curious about the email content. Thus, I will want to read it. For instance, when I saw the email subject line of "about interview," I would wonder what it might be about.

Jennifer, a TEC professor, also said,

> 可以研究主旨,因爲很多人都不知道怎麼寫。年輕人說話很簡短,一句就說完了。但是不寫主旨又會被忽略或是檔信,被放到垃圾信件匣。
> You can investigate the subject line because many people do not know how to write it. People in the younger generation say things briefly, so they may finish all of their words within one sentence. However, if they do not write a subject line, the email would be easily ignored by the email recipient or be blocked by the email system. Without subject lines, emails may even be put into the spam folder.

Kevin, a TEC professor, brought out the same issue. He commented,

> 可以討論"主旨",會決定要不要看或是看哪封。不然 email 這麼多,要在短時間內知道重點。
> A subject line makes me decide whether to read the emails or not and which one should be read. Otherwise, there are so many emails in my mailbox. I need to know the themes of the emails within a very short time.

The email title can make the email recipients decide to read the email immediately so that the email has the chance to be read and handled; and therefore, email effectiveness can be enhanced.

5.5 Discussion

The present study aims to investigate what constitutes email politeness and email effectiveness based on the interview results from 13 professors in the Department of Foreign Languages and Literature and Teacher Education Center at a university in southern Taiwan. The discussion will focus on essentials of writing a polite email and essentials of writing an effective email. Also pedagogical implications will be provided for teaching email pragmatics in a language classroom.

5.5.1 Essentials of Writing a Polite Email

In the present study, all the interviewees argued for the importance of setting the tone of voice before starting to write an email request to faculty. Taylor (2006, 2009) contends that it is difficult to use email to transmit our attitudes and emotions because it is a form of written communication. All we can control in email writing is the written words. There is no body language, eye contact, intonations, or gestures which could help us to understand the information of emails; thus, it is quite possible that if we use poor tone of voice, it would cause misunderstanding or offend the recipients. It is interesting that Taylor (2006, p. 53) suggested that people "never think you are talking to a computer" in email writing, and people always need to realize that there is a real person on the other side of the computer. A principle of expressing a good tone of voice is to be "empathetic." That is, email senders should respect the recipients and value the feelings of email recipients.

Tone of voice is subject to social hierarchy and social distance. Writing to a professor is different from writing to a peer. Writing to an unknown person is also different from writing to someone you know. Second, tone of voice is subject to degree of imposition. Writing a request event with high imposition (e.g., asking the professor to change semester scores) is different from writing a request event with low imposition (e.g., asking for an appointment to talk to the professor). Taylor (2009) specified three elements to be taken into consideration to set an appropriate tone of voice: (1) the relative social status of email sender and recipient, (2) the social distance between email sender and recipient, and (3) the content of the email message.

In addition to setting an appropriate tone of voice, following the expected email format is also important. The interview results in the present study showed that a complete format which includes subject, greeting, message, and closing is considered as the minimum requirement to ensure email politeness (cf. Chen 1987, 2001; Tiffany and Carol 2005; Wei 1995). The analysis also showed that the basic elements of an email request agreed upon by these professors include address terms, self-identification, request event and closing, each of which will be discussed in detail below.

In an email request to faculty, the occurrence of an address term is regarded as important. Taylor (2009) claimed that address terms serve two major functions. First, an address term can catch the recipient's attention. If an email recipient finds that the address term is different from his/her own name, he/she could check the reasons why he/she considers the email. Second, an address term indicates the perceived relationship between the sender and the recipient (Chen 2001), which is usually determined by closeness/distance between the sender and recipient, the frequency of communication between the sender and recipient, the number of recipients, and the status of the recipient (Taylor 2009). For example, "Dear Miss White" can be used in formal letters. On the other hand, "Dear Tiffany" or "Hi Jessica" can be used to address close friends (Tiffany and Carol 2005). In fact, an inappropriate address term could damage the relationship between the sender and the recipient. For example, if an email sender and an email recipient are close to each other, it would be impolite for the sender to address the email recipient in the most formal way because it seems that the email sender intends to maintain distance from the email recipient on purpose. When writing an email request to faculty, most professors in the present study recommended the use of 'Dear + academic title + last name,' a very formal address term. One thing worth mentioning is the use of 'Dear teacher' when writing an email request to faculty. In the present study, such an address term was considered to be polite by 11 of the 13 professors (85 %) being interviewed. Huang (2009) explained that using "teacher" to address professors is quite a common address term in the Taiwan society because to address a professor as "you" or "their given names" is considered as too direct or even rude.[4]

[4]Such a view may be specific in the Chinese-speaking context.

Self-identification is also necessary in an email request to faculty. The interview results showed that professors may consider the student sender to be irresponsible if he/she does not provide any information about him/herself. Their claims can be supported by Bou-Franch (2011), who indicated that self-identification is most likely to occur between people of unequal status. She also suggested that in addition to names, student senders should provide the courses in which they enrolled or student ID numbers.

Following address terms and self-identification is the request event. The biggest difference in writing between American and Chinese cultures is how information is sequenced. Chinese people tend to adopt a 'reason + request' sequence while Americans tend to adopt a 'request + reason' sequence (Zhang 1995). Such an indirect way of information sequencing in Chinese email performance may not be appreciated by Americans, as shown in Chang and Hsu (1998). However, in the present study, while only 3 of the 13 professors (23 %) mentioned that it would be better to structure an English email in a 'request + reason' sequence, 10 professors (77 %) expressed that email senders should provide clear reasons first, before the request, particularly in situations which are more complex or highly imposing.

What also relates to a request event is the choice of a request strategy. Chen (2006) stated that a *query preparatory*, such as "Can/Could/Would you…" which contains the question of asking ability, willingness, and possibility is generally considered more indirect and more polite than *want statements*, such as "I want/need/hope you…." According to Searle (1979), such conventionally indirect requests can decrease the illocutionary force of requesting and minimize the threat to the hearer's negative face wants (i.e., not wanting to be imposed). In an email request to faculty, the use of *query preparatory* allows the professor to be the final decision maker without feeling being imposed on by the student.

The last essential of a polite email is closing. The email closing also influences whether an email is considered polite or not. Email senders should show their appreciation to the email recipients because they request or impose on the recipients to do something for them. Thus, it is necessary for email senders to express appreciation to the recipients. Previous research has also indicated that showing appreciation to email recipients is crucial (Economidou-Kogetsidis 2011; Hartford and Bardovi-Harlig 1996). Waldvogel (2007) further observed that *Thanks* or *Thank you* may be developing into a ritualistic expression in closings.

5.5.2 *Essentials of Writing an Effective Email*

A clear subject line is the first essential to ensure email effectiveness. Adding a subject line of an email would increase the effectiveness of the email because it could catch the recipient's attention by showing the main purpose of the email. Lewis (2002) claimed that the email subject line is very important. He pointed out that when people write down the email recipient's name in the subject line, the response rate could increase. In the study of Bunz and Campbell (2004), in the part of the discussion on CMC influencing interpersonal communication, they mentioned that CMC may be more time consuming than face-to-face communication, especially, when there are a lot of SPAMs which email users need to delete while picking out useful ones at the same time. Therefore, writing a clear subject line would be the first step to make sure email recipients read and respond to the email more quickly.

The second essential for an effective email is to make sure the email sender's goal is attainable. The first consideration in this regard is to provide a feasible request. If a request is difficult to fulfill, it may be impossible for the recipient to grant the request no matter how hard the email sender tries. The second consideration is to provide convincing and specific reasons with strong evidence to support the request. Furthermore, the provision of evidence increases the credibility of the request. A request which has specific detailed information and persuasive argument would be more likely to convince the recipient to grant his/her request and therefore achieve the sender's goals.

The last consideration is to provide possible solutions for the recipient to choose from after stating the request. Blumenthal (1985) suggested that in effective letter writing, writers should mention actions that the sender plans to take or that he/she wants the recipient to take. He claimed that "If you want the recipient to take some action, say so, very clearly and specifically" (Blumenthal 1985, p. 41). Taylor (2006) suggested that good emails should be structured in the order of *introduction, details, response,* or *action*, and finally, *closing*. In the study, she pointed out that the *response or action* section should contain the specific actions which we hope the email recipient could carry out. This kind of information could increase the possibility that email recipients will do the action the sender asks. She further pointed out that the emails which are unclear about the actions the sender wants the recipient to take seldom achieve the sender's goals.

5.5.3 Pedagogical Implications

The analysis of the professors' perception of a sample email request leads us to the next question: What should language teachers do to improve L2 learners' politeness and effectiveness when writing email requests to faculty? Although Shang (2007) found that L2 learners' email exchanges on assigned readings would improve syntactic complexity and grammatical accuracy, it did not show how instruction should be implemented in a language classroom at a pragmatic level. Perhaps Chen (2014, 2015) can give us some insights into how explicit instruction in email pragmatics can be implemented in a language classroom and the extent to which L2 learners can make progress after the instruction. These two studies complement each other, with the former focusing on "quality of output" and the latter on "quality of life" (Allwright 2005, p. 353), thus providing a comprehensive picture of the implementation of email instruction in a language classroom in Taiwan. In these two studies, Y.-S. Chen worked with 28 intermediate-level Taiwanese students of English and employed a genre-based approach (Hyland 2007) to teach email pragmatics in an advanced writing course. The genre-based instruction lasted 6 h and was divided into four sessions, including *Setting the context*, *Modeling*, *Joint construction,* and *Independent construction*. Each session will be described in detail below.

In the first session, *Setting the context*, the goal was to explore students' current email competence. To achieve this goal, Y.-S. Chen used both direct and indirect approaches. In the direct approach, she designed four pre-instruction request situations in which the learners needed to write emails to their professors (e.g., Asking for a paper extension). In the indirect approach, she asked the learners to evaluate authentic emails in groups and then report their perceptions in class. Her assumption was that the learners "would judge the email messages against their developing L2 interlanguage system, thus, revealing their existing pragmatic competence" (Chen 2014, p. 4).

The second session was *Modeling*, in which the learners were instructed in email essentials in the order of *Subject, Greeting, Message,* and *Closing*. First, she analyzed the pragmatic features of each essential (Presentation), then she asked the learners to do a series of exercises to reinforce what they had learned (Practice), and finally she distributed a questionnaire to understand the learners' perceptions of this session (Reflection).

In the third session, *Joint Construction*, she asked the entire class to work collaboratively on an email prompt asking for a leave of absence. In the last session, *Independent Construction*, the learners were asked to respond to four post-instruction situations regarding email requests to faculty.

The quantitative analysis of the learners' pre- and post-instruction scores showed that they made significant progress after the instruction in their overall performances. However, qualitative analysis showed that they made greater improvements in terms of framing moves (*Subject, Greeting, and Closing*), but less progress in terms of content moves (*Request strategies* and *Request support*). Chen (2015) explained that this might be because framing moves are formulaic, and thus, more controllable and easier to acquire in a teaching context. However, content moves are idiosyncratic and may vary from context to context, making them more difficult to acquire.

Chen's studies have demonstrated that explicit instruction was effective in enhancing L2 learners' knowledge about email pragmatics. This success can be attributed to the scaffolded assistance provided to the learners at the beginning stage, and then gradually removed to allow learners to become independent email writers in the later stages. In this genre-based approach, however, such scaffolded assistance did not come from the teacher only, in the Modeling session, but also from the peers, in the joint construction session. This leads us to the importance of interaction in instructional pragmatics research.

Over the past two decades, research has examined the role of interaction in second language acquisition (Long 1983). From a sociocultural perspective, Vygotsky (1978) claimed that a person's cognitive development cannot be achieved alone and learning is basically a social enterprise. He proposed the notion of "zone of proximal development," which refers to "the distance between the actual developmental level as determined by independent problem solving and the level of potential development as determined through problem solving under adult guidance or in collaboration with more capable peers" (Vygotsky 1978, p. 86). Donato (1994) further extended Vygotsky's notion and argued that peers can also offer scaffolded assistance to each other during collaboration. Such "collective scaffolding" is analogous to "expert scaffolding."

Empirical studies have also demonstrated the effects of peer-peer collaboration in promoting second language acquisition. For example, Kim (2008) worked with 32 learners of Korean to examine if collaboration would affect their vocabulary acquisition. These learners were divided into two groups. Half of them worked individually, while the other half worked in pairs. All the learners completed a pretest, a dictogloss task, an immediate posttest and a delayed posttest. The think aloud protocols produced by individual learners and collaborative dialogues were transcribed verbatim. The results showed that those who worked in pairs outperformed those who worked individually, implying that collaboration did have a positive effect on L2 vocabulary acquisition.

The same can be applied to the acquisition of email pragmatics. Future classroom research may investigate the role of pair or group work in developing L2 learners' email pragmatic competence, to echo Donato's (1994, p. 39) argument: "The focus [in SLA] should be… on observing the construction of co-knowledge and how this co-construction process results in linguistic change among and within individuals during joint activity."

5.6 Conclusion

This study has provided a new way of investigating the issue of writing a polite and an effective email request by interviewing 13 professors directly. In addition, this study has also provided essentials for composing a polite and an effective email based on empirical findings.

One of the main limitations of the present study may be the small sample of interviewees. Since the interviewees came from either the English or education disciplines, the results should be interpreted with caution and may not be generalized to other disciplines. In future research, researchers could also interview professors who are in business management or international trade departments because they may also have opportunities to use English email for their work, and may have their own opinions about email politeness and effectiveness.

Acknowledgments The authors would like to express special thanks to Hsuan-Yu Tai (戴宣毓) for his kind assistance with the manuscript.

References

Allwright, Dick. 2005. Developing principles for practitioner research: The case of exploratory practice. *The Modern Language Journal* 89: 353–366.

Baron, Naomi. 1998. Letters by phone or speech by other means: The linguistics of email. *Language & Communication* 18: 133–170.

Biesenbach-Lucas, Sigrun. 2004. Speech acts in e-mail: A new look at pragmatic competence. Paper presented at the Annual Convention of the American Association of Applied Linguistics, Portland, OR.

Biesenbach-Lucas, Sigrun. 2007. Students writing emails to faculty: An examination of e-politeness among native and nonnative speakers of English. *Language Learning & Technology* 11(2): 59–81.

Blumenthal, Lassor, A. 1985. *The art of letter writing: The new guide to writing more effective letters for all occasions.* NY: Perigee Books.

Blum-Kulka, Shoshana, and Elite Olshtain. 1984. Requests and apologies: A cross-cultural study of speech act realisation patterns. *Applied Linguistics* 5: 196–213.

Blum-Kulka, Shoshana, Julian House, and Gabriele Kasper. 1989. *Cross-cultural pragmatics: Requests and apologies*. Norwood, NJ: Ablex.

Bou-Franch, Patricia. 2011. Openings and closings in Spanish email conversations. *Journal of Pragmatics* 43: 1772–1785.

Brown, Penelope, and Stephen C. Levinson. 1987. *Politeness: Some universals in language usage*. New York: Cambridge University Press.

Bunz, Ulla, and Campbell, Scott, W. 2004. Politeness accommodation in electronic mail. *Communication Research Reports* 21(1):11–25.

Chang, Yu-Ying, and Yi-Ping Hsu. 1998. Requests on e-mail: A cross-cultural comparison. *RELC Journal* 29(2): 121–151.

Chen, Chi-Fen. 2000. *Interlanguage requesting behavior in e-mail: A study of Taiwanese students' English written requests to U.S. professors.* Paper presented at the 7th International Pragmatics Conference, Budapest, Hungary.

Chen, Chi-Fen. 2001. *Making e-mail requests to professors: Taiwanese vs. American students.* Paper presented at the Annual Meeting of the American Association for Applied Linguistics in St. Louis.

Chen, Chi-Fen. 2006. The development of email literacy: From writing to peers to writing to authority figures. *Language Learning and Technology* 10(2): 35–55.

Chen, Guang-Lang. (陳光郎). 1987. <實用英文書信大全> [*Practical letter writing*]. Taipei: Yih Chyun Book Co., Ltd.

Chen, Yuan-Shan. 2014. Understanding the development of Chinese EFL learners' email literacy through Exploratory Practice. *Language Teaching Research*. doi:10.1177/1362168814562014.

Chen, Yuan-Shan. 2015. Developing Chinese EFL learners' email literacy through requests to faculty. *Journal of Pragmatics* 75: 131–149.

Chen, Yuan-Shan, and D.Victoria Rau. 2011. Investigating the complimenting behaviors of Chinese speakers of American English. *Language and Linguistics* 12(4): 917–950.

Chen, Zong-Yao. (陳宗堯). 2001. <外交暨一般英文書信> [*English letters for diplomacy*]. Taipei: Wu-Nan Book Inc.

Donato, Richard. 1994. Collective scaffolding in second language learning. In *Vygotskian approaches to second language research,* eds, James. P. Lantolf, and Gabriala Appel, 33–56. Norwood, New Jersey: Ablex.

Economidou-Kogetsidis, Maria. 2011. "Please answer me as soon as possible": Pragmatic failure in non-native speakers' e-mail requests to faculty. *Journal of Pragmatics* 43: 3193–3215.

Hartford, Beverly S. and Bardovi-Harlig, Kathleen. 1996. "At your earliest convenience:" A study of written student requests to faculty. In *Pragmatics and Language Learning*, ed. Lawrence. F. Bouton, 55–69, vol. 7. Urbana Champaign, IL: University of Illinois, Division of English as an International Language (DEIL).

Hendriks, Berna. 2010. An experimental study of native speaker perceptions of non-native request modification in e-mails in English. *Intercultural Pragmatics* 7(2): 221–255.

Honeycutt, Lee. 2001. Comparing email and synchronous conferencing in online peer response. *Written Communication* 18(1): 26–60.

Huang, Chao-Li. 2009. *Politeness in children's language use in EFL language classroom in Taiwan*. Unpublished MA thesis of the Department of English Language, Literature, and Linguistics, Providence University, Taichung, Taiwan.

Hyland, Ken. 2007. Genre pedagogy: Language, literacy and L2 writing instruction. *Journal of Second Language Writing* 16: 148–164.

Kim, Youjin. 2008. The contribution of collaborative and individual tasks to the acquisition of L2 vocabulary. *The Modern Language Journal* 92(i):114–130.

Lewis, Herschell, Gordon. 2002. *Effective e-mail marketing: The complete guide to creating successful campaigns.* New York: AMACON.

Liu, Yi. Chun. 2008. Email miscommunication between EFL and NES students in virtual communities: Interplay of asynchrony and asymmetry. In *Perspectives on college English: Transformation, reformation and innovation*, 77–96. The Second National Conference on College English: Foreign Language Center, National Chengchi University.

Long, Michael, H. 1983. Native speaker/non-native speaker conversation and the negotiation of comprehensible input. Applied Linguistics 4(2):126–141.

Mackevic, Vlad, and Mamin, Leonid. 2010. "Dear Mr. Smith" vs "Hi there": An investigation into the language of modern business emails. *Debut: the undergraduate journal of languages, linguistics and area studies* 1(2):68–77.

Mitsuyo-Arimoto. (有元美津世). 2008. <商務英文書信寫作> [*Effective business writing*]. Taipei: ALC Press Inc.

Searle, John. 1979. *Expression and meaning: Studies in the theory of speech acts.* Cambridge: Cambridge University Press.

Shang, Hui-Fang. 2007. An exploratory study of e-mail application on FL writing Performance. *Computer Assisted Language Learning* 20(1):79–96.

Sproull, Lee, and Kiesler, Sara. 1991. *Connections: New ways of working in the networked organization.* Cambridge, MA: MIT Press.

Taylor, Shirley. 2006. <英文商業書信&電子郵件寫作技巧與範例> [*Model business letters, e-mails & other business documents*] (劉秋枝、羅明珠, Trans.). Taipei: Pearson Education Taiwan Limited. (Original work published 2004).

Taylor, Shirley. 2009. *Email etiquette: A fresh look at dealing effectively with e-mail, developing great style, and writing clear, concise messages.* Singapore: Marshall Cavendish Business.

Tiffany and Carol 2005. <*Sweet Words*打動人心的英文書寫技巧> [*Sweet words-The writing skill of English letters to impress other people*]. Taipei: AiritiBooks Inc.

Turk, Christopher, and Kirkman, John. 1989. *Effective writing: Improving scientific, technical and business communication.* London: Taylor & Francis.

Vygotsky, Lev Semyonovich. 1978. *Mind in society: The development of higher psychological processes*. Cambridge, MA: Harvard University Press.

Waldvogel, Joan. 2007. Greetings and closings in workplace email. *Journal of Computer-Mediated Communication* 12: 456–477.

Watts, Richard, J. 2003. *Politeness.* Cambridge: Cambridge University Press.

Weasenforth, Donald, and Biesenbach-Lucas, Sigrun. 2001. Just a little bit longer: A contrastive pragmatic analysis of requests for late submission. Paper presented at the Annual Convention of the American Association of Applied Linguistics, St. Louis, MO.

Wei, Dong, Cheng. (魏東城). 1995. <如何寫好英文書信與卡片> [*How to write English letters and cards*]. Taipei: Commercial Press (HK) Cyberbooks Ltd.

Zhang, Yan, Yin. 1995. Indirectness in Chinese requesting. In *Pragmatics of Chinese as a native and target language*, ed. Gabriele Kasper, 69–118. Manoa, Hawaii: University of Hawaii Press.

Author Biographies

Wan-jing Li (李宛靜) graduated from the Institute of Linguistics, National Chung Cheng University in Taiwan. She is interested in sociolinguistics and teaching English as a foreign language. Her master's thesis is entitled *Politeness and Effectiveness of English Request Emails: Taiwanese Professors' Perspectives.*

Yuan-shan Chen (陳媛珊) has been involved in language teaching for many years. Her research interests primarily lie in the areas of interlanguage pragmatics and L2 writing research. She teaches as an associate professor at the Department of Applied English, National Chin-Yi University of Technology in Taiwan. Her recent publications include articles in *Journal of Pragmatics, Language Teaching Research, System,* and *Language and Linguistics*.

Part II
Emails from Students to the International Academic Community

Chapter 6
Emailing Requests to International Researchers: The Construction of Identity by Chinese EFL Graduate Students

Xinren Chen

Abstract While email communication has received a lot of scholastic attention and its relevance to second language acquisition has been explored to some extent, how Chinese EFL learners write emails for academic purposes remains unknown. Despite a sizable amount of literature on requesting as a speech act and on the acquisition of the speech act in L2, scant discussion has been directed to how email correspondents construct relational identity and individual identities as requesters and requestees. Thus, considering the varied findings concerning the (in) formality of email communication, it might be worthwhile to explore what level of formality characterizes request-making emails written by Chinese EFL graduate students. Also, it may prove beneficial to investigate how the students, in their email requests, construct their personal identity as student requesters and the identity of the international researchers as academic requestees, as well as their relational identity. A sample of 12 request-making emails written by 12 Chinese EFL graduate students to appointed hypothetical international researchers were collected as the data, together with the results of informal interviews with three students. Through qualitative analysis, the researcher found that (i) the students' emails were basically formal; (ii) the students constructed a deferent relational identity with the international researchers; and (iii) they identified themselves as reasonable requesters and their addressees as appropriate requestees. The learner writers' use of basically formal style might be explicable in terms of culturally biased identity awareness.

Keywords Email communication · Request · Style · Identity · Chinese student

X. Chen (✉)
Department of English, School of Foreign Studies, Nanjing University, Nanjing, China
e-mail: cxr3354182@163.com

Y. Chen et al. (eds.), *Email Discourse Among Chinese Using English as a Lingua Franca*, DOI 10.1007/978-981-287-888-5_6

6.1 Introduction

More than a decade ago, Chinese graduate students would write hard-copy formal letters to international researchers for a variety of purposes, e.g., making requests for a copy of their publication, applying for opportunities for further education, or seeking solutions to certain scientific problems. Using this method, it would take weeks or even months for the requests to reach the international researchers and for the requested information to reach the students. The emergence of email correspondence has, fortunately, made the requests and their fulfillment a much easier and faster process.

An ensuing question is what characterizes Chinese students' email writing style. While some studies (e.g., Baron 1998, 2001; Crystal 2001; see also Waldvogel 2001, p. 8) suggest that email communication in general tends to be informal and casual, others (e.g., Biesenbach-Lucas 2006, 2007; Bjorge 2007; Chen 2006) hold that the formality of email communication actually varies according to contextual factors, such as the relative status of the addressee and the relationship between the writer and the receiver. In view of this inconsistency of findings, it might be worthwhile to explore what level of formality characterizes request-making emails written by Chinese EFL graduate students. Besides, as the style of communication is an essential indicator of the bilateral relationship between the two sides in the communication, does it follow that Chinese students will construct a different identity than they did in the past in relation to the international researchers? Adopting Tracy's (2002) taxonomy of identity, the researcher looked into how they constructed their identity as student requesters and the identity of the international researchers as academic requestees, focusing as well on the type of relational identity explicitly or implicitly built, such as whether both sides were projected as equal or unequal and whether both sides were assumed to be close or distant.

A sample of 12 request-making emails written by 12 Chinese EFL graduate students to appointed hypothetical international researchers was collected as the data. Through qualitative analysis, the researcher sought to find out what level of formality was expressed in their emails (measured in terms of addressing terms, contractions, distribution of long/short sentences, elliptical sentences, etc.), what relational identity the students constructed with the international researchers, and how they identified themselves as requesters and addressees as requestees.

It is hoped that the study will shed light on how the advanced-level learners' use of proper genre might be explicable in terms of culturally biased identity awareness. Meanwhile, the study is expected to fill in a research gap in the literature, as little has been done to reveal the stylistic features of Chinese learners' email requests.

6.2 Research Background

Second language acquisition is not just about the accumulation of L2 linguistic knowledge, lexical, or grammatical, or the development of language skills such as speaking, listening, reading, or writing in L2. It is also about the learning of how to do things in L2 by recourse to linguistic knowledge or skills. As part of pragmatic competence (Bachman 1990; Chen 2009; Taguchi 2011), the ability to perform speech acts with appropriate L2 pragmalinguistic resources and in socio-pragmatically appropriate ways is one of the most important strands of competence for L2 learners to develop.

6.2.1 Chinese Learners' Performance of Requests

So far, much has been done in regard to how L2 learners perform speech acts, particularly how they differ from native speakers in the performance of the speech acts in question and what pragmatic failures they may commit. Among others, in the Chinese context, how learners issue requests in L2 has attracted a lot of attention. For example, Yang (2009) finds that high-level English learners use fewer direct request strategies and nonconventionalized indirect strategies than either native English speakers or native Chinese speakers, but employ more conventionalized indirect strategies; middle-level and low-level learners, however, use more direct strategies than either native English speakers or native Chinese speakers, but employ fewer conventionalized and nonconventionalized indirect strategies. Lin (2009) focuses more on the Chinese learners' use of pragmalinguistic forms in enacting requests and finds that they exhibit a sizable difference in this respect from the native speakers. She attributes this difference to the fact that the two languages vary greatly in the distribution of the pragmalinguistic forms for requesting although the strategies converge significantly.

While revealing, neither of the two studies gives adequate attention to the learners' use of address terms or vocatives prefacing requests. According to Lee-Wong (2000), the use of address terms is very central in Chinese culture, and any misuse may impress the interlocutors as impolite. Furthermore, inadequate attention has been paid to Chinese learners' performance of requests in written communication. Although Yang (2009) does incorporate the tasks of writing letters and leaving messages in her research design, her discussion focuses on natural spoken data only. It might be a serious oversight if we failed to look into how Chinese learners make requests in equally interactive written communication like letter or email writing. Indeed, Economidou-Kogetsidis (2010) has found, in her study of Greek English learners' email requests, that the learners often misuse address terms and overuse direct requests.

Another concern not covered in the existing studies is how Chinese learners as requesters in particular and all L2 learners in general identify themselves in their request discourse. So far, prominence has been given to either the requesting strategies in terms of directness or pragmalinguistic choices in terms of internal or external modification (e.g., in "Could you possibly give me your feedback no later than this Friday? It means a lot to me." the use of the modal verb "could" and that of the hedge "possibly" are instances of internal modification, whereas the use of the explanation "It means a lot to me" is an example of external modification), or both. Due consideration has also been given to factors that modulate the learners' performance of requests, such as relative social distance or power relations between the interlocutors, the rank of imposition incurred by the requests, and L2 proficiency. While these aspects and factors are important, attention must be paid to how Chinese L2 learners construct their identity in relation to their interlocutors in general and how they construct themselves as requesters and the interlocutors as requestees, in particular in online interaction. It is natural to presume that their ability to properly identify themselves and their interlocutors has a close bearing on the success of their requests (email requests in the present case).

6.2.2 Email Communication and Its Relevance to L2 Writing

Email, which was intended as a means of enabling researchers to share data, originated in the late sixties as an additional feature of APRANET, the first large-scale computer network. Once email was used to send electronic messages via the network, it developed rapidly and began to exert a huge impact on many aspects of our daily and workplace life. Some even say that "it is still irreplaceable in certain contexts such as the academic world (e.g., to contact researchers, exchange publications via attachments)" (see Zimmerman and Bar-llan 2009, cited in Yus 2011, p. 219).

While email is a relatively recent phenomenon and one form of a larger category of Internet discourse sometimes called computer-mediated discourse or more informally "netspeak" (Crystal 2001), it has surpassed many traditional means of communication as it enables the easy, reliable, rapid, and inexpensive transmission of information to large numbers of people at the same time, and offers access to people in a way that may be impossible in face-to-face communication (Waldvogel 2001, p. 9).

There are more fundamental and less visible effects of the use of email. In one study, Kiesler et al. (1987) find that the use of computer-mediated communication (CMC) changed group dynamics; specifically, members participated more equally and high status members did not dominate the interaction to the same extent as in face-to-face meetings. In this sense, email seems to have the potential to be a "democratizing medium" (Waldvogel 2001, p. 9). Although later research concerning gender issues and organizational politics lends more support to Mantovani's (1994) view that such a role depends on the social context in which email is used (Waldvogel 2001, p. 9), it remains true to some extent.

This might be accounted for by a commonly observed feature of email communication, i.e., its informality in terms of its linguistic style, indicating that people communicate with each other on a more equal footing. As Baron has argued, email is "an ideal tool for building and maintaining social relationships" (1998, p. 155) since "it has both the informality of speech and the ability to facilitate communication at any time or place" (Bloch 2002, p. 119). Although many studies (e.g., Baron 1998, 2001; Crystal 2001) claim that the language of email tends to be informal, as manifested by the use of first-name address form, greeting form "Hi" and complimentary closing form "Cheers" (Waldvogel 2007), some other studies (e.g., Biesenbach-Lucas 2006, 2007; Bjorge 2007; Chen 2006) suggest that the degree of formality of email communication varies according to contextual factors, such as the relative status of the addressee and the relationship between the writer and the receiver.

As a new way of communication and by far the most popular use for the Internet (Nie and Erbring 2000), email seems to be neither speech nor writing, or we can say it is both. True, it does provide a permanent record, but it is often perceived as being ephemeral and used instead of telephone or face-to-face conversation (Waldvogel 2001, p. 8). Thus, the language of email is unlike any other form of language, either written or oral. Baron (1998) describes the development of this language as a process of creolization, by which a new language is created from a mixture of established languages. Some other researchers compare email to spoken and written data bases (Collot and Belmore 1996; Yates 1996) and conclude it is like "a hybrid language that has arisen as an amalgam of components taken from other language varieties: postcardese, headlines and telegraphese" (Ferrara et al. 1991, p. 12). Interestingly, Moran and Hawisher (1998) compare email language to a newborn child who, although a unique individual, may resemble her or his parents or grandparents. Furthermore, many people view email as an informal means of communication in which mistakes do not matter (Waldvogel 2001, p. 8).

But such stylistic features of email as informality and casualness may have negative effects. As Mulholland (1999) has warned, these features could "damage interpersonal relations" (see Waldvogel 2001, p. 8) and "be very costly both in human and financial terms" (2001, p. 9). Negative outcomes such as depersonalization, impoliteness and "flaming" could be attributed to the technological nature of email, because the technology filters out certain personal, social, and behavioral cues used by people when they engage in face-to-face communication, e.g., voice and body language cues, to the extent that "clues to social status of participants are often missing, altering normal patterns of dominance" (Waldvogel 2001, p. 3).

As a popular means of communication, email has been used in L2 teaching as an extension of the writing course or part of a more general teaching program. Crystal (2001) mentions that email has already become an important component of language teaching to facilitate teacher/student interaction. It has been suggested that email can provide a variety of opportunities for interpersonal interactions that would otherwise be impossible inside the traditional L2 composition classroom (Bloch 2002). But other researchers see negative effects as well. For example, Baron (2001) worries that her students might be too informal and casual in their email messages, assuming that this informality is a result of the current "fashion" in composition that values meaning over form.

Thus, given a tension between the potential of email for undermining some social distinctions and for maintaining other social distinctions, using email as a form of communication necessitates a clear understanding of how language affects the relationship between the writer and the audience, of the differences between formal and informal writing, and of what is private and what is public (Bloch 2002, p. 120). Indeed, as Sproull and Kiesler (1991) argue, while flaming may arise from a specific goal of verbal attack, it may also stem from a miscalculation of the relationship between the writer and the reader of an email message.

The discussion above has implications for the present study. As more and more Chinese EFL learners write email to native speakers of English and even to the nonnative international community, it is worthwhile to observe how they do it, so as to provide feedback on classroom teaching. Specifically, we might take a look at how they make requests via email in the following areas: (1) the style of their emails; (2) the relationships they construct with their addressees; and (3) their self-identification and other identification, and reveal whatever problems they may have in these aspects.

6.3 Methodology

6.3.1 Research Questions

This study sought to investigate how advanced-level Chinese EFL learners phrase their requests via email, how the degree of formality used reflects the kind of identity relations they construct with their requestees and, in particular, how they identify themselves and their interlocutors. Thus, the research questions are as follows:

1. What level of formality characterizes the Chinese graduate students' request emails to international researchers? How is it pragmalinguistically manifested?
2. What relational identity does the level of formality used, along with other features, construct for the student requesters and the international researchers?
3. What personal identities do the students construct for themselves as requesters and for the international researchers as their requestees?

6.3.2 Participants

Considering the frequent demand among advanced-level Chinese EFL learners to write emails to the international community in today's China (for such purposes as making requests for a copy of their publication, applying for academic programs of further education, and seeking solutions to certain scientific problems), this study focuses its attention on Chinese postgraduate students. Although it might be more interesting to compare English majors and non-English majors at this level of education, I only selected participants from the former category due to ease of access. Thus, a total of 12 first-year graduate students majoring in English linguistics were recruited from the School of Foreign Studies, XX University (here and after, XX is used instead of the real name of the university for sake of anonymity), one of the top ten universities in China. It was assumed that these participants could represent advanced-level Chinese EFL learners who, nevertheless, had not been academically trained well enough to contact the international community in professionally mature ways.

Demographically, the 12 participants, 2 male, and 10 female, had studied English for an average of 10.5 years. Their specializations included second language acquisition, translation, cognitive linguistics, lexicography, and pragmatics. They had no work experience and no experience of a long stay (over 6 months) abroad. None had received systematic curricular training in academic writing. All had plenty of experience writing emails on a regular basis, including writing to their instructors as well as friends, yet they had never received any formal instruction on this genre of writing because it was not part of their curriculum.

6.3.3 Data Collection and Analysis

To collect the data, I assigned a writing task in an elective course, *Introduction to Pragmatics*, to the entire class in the early part of the semester. The students were required to write an email to a certain international researcher whose article had been published in a certain journal they had just found out about. They were asked to request that the researcher, whom they had never met before, give them access to the article in some way. For submission, all the students were asked to address their email to an email account I gave them. No directions were given regarding the format of the email (including terms of address, complimentary closing, and signature). After a couple of days, all the students finished writing their email and sent it to the designated account. Thus, a total of 12 emails, whose length ranged between 60 and 150 words, were gathered for analysis. In addition, three students were informally interviewed afterwards on specific points related to their writing.

To answer the research questions proposed above, I chose to use a more qualitative approach to analyze the emails, as the purpose of the study is to explore the various ways the students constructed their identities with the international researchers rather than to test a specific hypothesis. There were three steps in the process of analysis.

First, I addressed the issue of formality that the emails demonstrated. To do so, I discussed the emails in terms of the formality of diction, appearance of contractions, distribution of long/short sentences, use of elliptical sentences, etc., as these features are stylistically sensitive.

Second, I analyzed the relational identity as defined by Tracy (2002) that the students constructed with their international requestees in terms of familiarity or deference expressed in the emails. To do so, I depended on Brown and Levinson's face theory to explore whether, apart from the use of informal style, such features as familiar address terms, informal complimentary close, and informal signatures are present, or whether, apart from the use of formal style, such features as deferent addressing terms, formal complimentary close, and formal signatures were present. If the students inclined toward the former, it might be concluded that they tried to establish a familiar relational identity; if they tended toward the latter, it might be said that they favored a deferent relational identity.

Third, I extended the discussion of (relational) identity construction to the issue of (individual) self-identification and other identification; that is, I probed how the participants constructed themselves as student requesters and how they constructed their interlocutors as academic requestees. To do this, I checked specifically whether the students made clear the reason or purpose of their request and whether they showed they would be grateful to their requestees if their requests were to be granted; I also checked specifically whether the students stated that their addresses were the right people from whom they could ask a favor and whether they expressed the relevance, usefulness, or importance of the researchers' article to them. After all, these aspects under scrutiny might be considered habitual or conventional practices that we can expect from the identities of requesters and requestees, respectively. It has been shown that despite the increased amount of social interaction taking place via email, distinctions in social relations among the participants can have a profound effect on their email interaction (see Bloch 2002, p. 119). If this is true, then we could infer from the opposite direction that the students' way of interaction, specifically their self-identification as compared to their addressees, could reflect the type of relational identity they constructed as well as their individual identities.

6.4 Results and Discussion

This section consists of three parts, each addressing one research question raised in Sect. 3.

6.4.1 The Level of Formality Characteristic of the Students' Emails

On the whole, the emails written by the postgraduate students exhibited a high level of formality, as manifested below.

6.4.1.1 Use of Formal Diction

While the diction the students used in their emails was characterized by general-level formality, they occasionally used some formal words or expressions. For example,

(1) … the issues addressed in it are *of great interest* to me.
(2) What you *elaborate* in your thesis is quite useful for me.
(3) Recently, I have *been engaged in* writing my term paper and I have read with great interest the abstract of your article …

In (1), "of greatly interest" as a prepositional phrase is more formal than its adjectival counterpart "very interesting." The word "elaborate" in (2) is a term often found in academic writing, as is "been engaged in" in (3), for which an informal way of expression might be "been busy with."

6.4.1.2 Infrequent Use of Contractions

Contractions occasionally occurred in the collected data, as shown below:

(4) *I'm* writing to ask for your published article, *Euphemisms in African English.*
(5) *I've* read the abstract of your paper *Euphemisms in African English* recently.

However, contrary to expectations, the participants seemed to use relatively fewer contracted forms in their emails than assumed in the literature. Not every email involved the use of contractions. Moreover, where contraction was possible or acceptable, some students preferred complete forms, as exemplified below:

(6) If it is convenient for you, please send me your paper.
(7) It would help me a lot in my course paper which I am working on. However, it is hard for me to get access to the full version.

The two sentences might have been phrased as follows respectively:

(6') If *it's* convenient for you, please send me your paper.
(7') *It'd* help me a lot in my course paper which *I'm* working on. However, *it's* hard for me to get access to the full version.

Interestingly, a couple of participants were not consistent in the use or non-use of contractions. Look at the following longer example:

(8) ① *I'm* a postgraduate of School of Foreign Studies at Nanjing University, and I major in English Linguistics and literature. ② Recently, *I have* been engaged in writing my term paper and *I have* read with great interest the abstract of your article titled "Euphemism in African English" published in ***Linguistic Magazine. ③ *I am* greatly enlightened by the abstract of your article and I found it would help me finish my paper.

While the author of the email used contraction in Sentence ①, he did not do so in Sentences ② and ③. Instead, he opted for complete forms ("I have" and "I am").

Whether he consciously chose to be inconsistent or failed to be consistent, possibly as a result of carelessness or anxiety, remains unknown. Such variability also found expression in other aspects of the students' linguistic choices, as we shall demonstrate soon.

6.4.1.3 Rare Use of Elliptical Sentences

Another important indicator of linguistic formality that we observed from the participants' emails was the rare use of elliptical sentences. Two instances of apparent ellipsis are as follows:

(9) Looking forward to your reply!
(10) Thank you for your assistance!

However, we might as well dismiss the sentences as elliptical ones, for the reason that expressions like (9) are highly conventionalized as a token of wish while utterances like (10) are habitually used as a note of gratitude.

6.4.1.4 Extensive Use of Long and Complex Sentences

It was found that the students quite frequently chose to write long and sometimes complex sentences (nearly 70 % of the data). Consider, the following examples of long and complex sentences:

(11) I'm currently working on my course paper on euphemism, and find that your paper may prove to be one of the key references. However, I can't retrieve it in the electronic resources of our university despite painful searching, so that I can do nothing but turn to you for help.
(12) Lately I have been doing research paper about euphemisms, and the paper that you have written most recently *Euphemisms in African English* is really capturing my eye and sounds very related to my research, so I would love to read through it and hopefully get some inspiring ideas out of it.

In (11), the first sentence as a compound sentence comprises an object complement clause in the second clause; the second sentence, very long in itself, contains an adverbial clause of result and an implicit clause of concession. Example (12) is a compound sentence that contains three clauses, of which the second clause further comprises a relative clause and the third clause combines two subclauses.

What merits attention is that the way that most long sentences were formed was somewhat informal, as the students often employed the words "and," "so," or "but" in conjoining the clauses, rather than formal words like "however" in (10). This type of informality, however, might be attributed to a general dependence on these words among Chinese EFL learners to connect sentences. The problematic dependence might also be observed in their other types of writing including formal theses and dissertations.

To sum up, the discussion along the above lines all points to the conclusion that on the whole the Chinese advanced-level EFL learners acted formally in their email communication with the international researchers. This finding runs counter to some afore-mentioned researchers' observation that emails are usually informal (e.g., Baron 1998, 2001; Crystal 2001). It cannot be claimed, though, that the result conforms to the finding that the formality of email communication varies according to contextual factors (e.g., Biesenbach-Lucas 2006, 2007; Bjorge 2007; Chen 2006), as no emails to familiar people or peers as recipients were gathered for stylistic comparison. The uncovering of occasional use of informal language and inconsistent style in the data partially supports Bou-Franch's (2011) study that challenges the validity of claims that assume that language usage in emails is homogeneous due to its informality and its oral nature.

An ensuing question that we may ask is why the students write their emails in a formal way on the whole. To answer this question, we turn to the next subsection.

6.4.2 Relational Identity Constructed in Relation to the International Researchers

The writing task required the students to address their emails to a certain international researcher they had never met before. As communication between strangers tends to be formal, it was all too natural that the students chose a formal style of writing to address the international researchers who they did not know beforehand. However, I would argue that what more crucially determines their use of formality is the attempted deference rather than the perceived distance. In other words, the students' treatment of the international researchers as superior was even a more important factor underlying the overall formality of their emails.

Indeed, we could find evidence for this line of argument. Presumably, the students understood that their emails not only conveyed their requests, but also constructed certain identities for themselves, for the international researchers, and for both sides, which might affect the success of their requests. According to Bakhtin (1981), language is "not a neutral force but a means by which an individual constitutes himself or herself in a social context" (see Bloch 2002, p. 120). In regard to the identity relation between the two sides, the emails were used to construct a relational identity, which, according to Tracy (2002), refers to "the kind of relationship that a person enacts with a particular conversational partner in a specific situation" (2002, p. 19), such as whether both sides are projected as equal or unequal and whether both sides are assumed to be close or distant. Apart from the previous linguistic choices, some other features also indicated that the Chinese students constructed a deferent type of relational identity for themselves relative to their requestees.

One such usage was the terms of address. Almost all the participants used "Dear Professor XX" (where XX is either the last name or the first name plus the last name) to address their interlocutor, except that two of them used "Dear Prof. XX", which is a bit less formal as "Prof." is a contracted form. Both address terms were deferent in comparison with some alternatives like "Dear + first name" or "Dear + nickname". Actually, these alternatives were quite unlikely to be chosen, as the international researchers were assumed to be unfamiliar to the participants.

An interesting point that deserves special mention was the uniform use of "Professor" as part of the deferent address form. This was surprising, as there was no evidence available to the students that the international researchers were professors or associate professors. This suggested that the students held the international researchers in high esteem, while viewing themselves as learners. Underlying the students' attitude might be the influence of the Chinese culture: according to Gu (1990), both the self-denigration maxim and address maxim regulate Chinese people's verbal behavior; taken together, one needs to elevate others when addressing them. A follow-up interview as to why they used the address form contributed the following reports:

> 当然要称对方为教授啊,人家都在那么好的期刊上发表了文章,真了不起。我们作为研究生当然要向他们学习了。•在国际期刊上发文章太难了,中国很多老师都做不到的。
> Of course I need to call the requestee Professor. You know, she/he has published a paper in such a distinguished journal. It's a great achievement. We postgraduate students must learn from him or her. It's all too difficult to get one's paper published in international journals. Not many Chinese teachers can manage to do so.

> 估计能在这种高级别的期刊上发文章的人一般都是教授、副教授。再说了,即使对方不是教授或副教授,你称其为教授,对方也是乐于接受的。至少在中国,称呼对方高一些总不会错的。
> I reckon that those who can publish papers in such top journals must be full professors or associate professors. What is more, even if they are not, they like to hear you call them professors. At least in China, it is never wrong to address people with a higher title.

In the first excerpt, the student showed high respect for the international scholar, regarding his publication in a prestigious journal as a remarkable achievement. In the second excerpt, the student clearly mentioned that in China, it is a good policy to elevate others when addressing them. Thus, her choice of the address term was a culturally biased one.

Another deferent usage was the use of polite request formulae like the ones listed below:

(13) *I am wondering if* you *would be kind enough to* send me the full text of the article by email.
(14) So *I'm wondering*, could you please send me a copy?
(15) Therefore, I *would appreciate it very very much if* you can generously give me an access to this article and I believe it will be a great help to my paper.

"I am wondering if …" in (13), often used as a formulaic expression in performing requests, is a token of showing pessimism, a strategy of negative politeness according to Brown and Levinson (1987, p. 173), which offers deference to the addressee. Although it was a bit unusual to use the expression in the way as in (14), the same strategy was in operation. In (15), "would appreciate it very (very) much if …," also frequently found in requests, expressed the speaker's gratitude for the addressee's potential satisfaction of his or her request. The subjunctive mood as indicated by the modal word "would" also conveyed the notion of deference. Besides, only one in distant relation to the other would be so serious in voicing his or her gratitude for a favor of small or medium size like asking for an electronic copy of the other's published paper.

A further indicator of the deferent relational identity constructed by the students was that the majority of them employed deferential types of complimentary closings. Many used "Sincerely yours" or "Yours sincerely" (although a couple of them used incorrect capitalization as in "Sincerely Yours" and "Yours Sincerely"). Only one of the 12 students used "Yours," a much more familiar and informal option. For the latter, most of the students employed "Best regards," with only one student opting for an informal expression, "Good Day!" Thus, while cross-participant variability was observed in the data, the tendency was clearly towards the formal end. It is worthy of mention, though, that two students failed to use any complimentary closing. This might be due to the fact that they were not aware of the need rather than the consideration of being informal, as the rest of the emails were formal.

Finally, the signatures the students used also suggested deference. All except three signed their full Chinese name at the end of their email. Among the exceptions, two signed with their English name, whereas one did not sign at all. Compared with signature on a first-name basis, a full-name signature sounds more deferential.

To wind up this section, I found the students' performance of requests in their email provided evidence for Yus's argument that "…the style of e-mail and its (in) formality are influenced by a number of exogenous aspects such as the power relationship existing between the interlocutors" (2011, p. 237). Bou-Franch's finding that "email users in the corpus were especially careful in elaborating their comments in order to begin conversations, particularly when addressing users of higher institutional standing" (2011, p. 1779) leads to a conclusion similar to mine. Furthermore, a cultural note needs to be stressed. It is typical of Chinese culture that one keeps a distance from people one respects. As formality signals distance, the significant formality manifested in the students' emails conveys respect. The distant relational identity constructed by the Chinese students is essentially a deferent one in this case. As properly "positioning" oneself relative to the significant other is tremendously important in China, the students' discursive practice in large measure betrayed their cultural identity. Finally, the deference that the students showed in various ways to their requestees was a strategy of negative politeness, in Brown and Levinson's (1987, pp. 178–197) terms, which may be instrumental to the fulfillment of their requesting goal.

6.4.3 *Self-Identification as Student Requesters*

Next, let's move to the personal identities that the students constructed for themselves and the international researchers. According to Tracy (2002, personal quality refers to one's "personality, attitudes and character" (p. 18), which are "frequently contested" (p. 19) because "others do not automatically grant a person's claims to be honest, reasonable, thoughtful, and so on" (p. 19)

To make an appropriate request, one needs to identify oneself as a reasonable requester. One has to consider the following when issuing a request:

(1) What is the exact content of the request?
(2) Does one have a reason for making the request?

For email requests, one needs to consider further things like:

(3) Who am I?

From the data, I found that all the students clearly pointed out what paper they needed. Furthermore, almost all the students self-identified themselves as graduate students, as exemplified below:

(16) My name is M. S., and I am a graduate student of XX University in China.
(17) I am a year-one postgraduate major in English in XX University.
(18) I'm a graduate student from XX University, China. My major is English, and my research interest is in applied linguistics.

As the students were expected to direct their emails to international researchers, (16) was detailed enough to include such information as one's name, one's current status, affiliation (university), and nationality. While (17) included a further sort of information, i.e., one's major, it assumed the requestee's knowledge that XX University was in China. By comparison, (18) was the most informative.

What's more, most students also did well in grounding their requests, as shown below:

(19) Recently, I have been working on a course paper with the topic of euphemisms in different cultures and languages. I have read the abstract of your paper *Euphemisms in African English* and the issues addressed in it are of great interest to me. However, I tried my best but only got the access to the abstract rather than the full text.
(20) I'm currently working on my course paper on euphemism, and find that your paper may prove to be one of the key references. However, I can't retrieve it in the electronic resources of our university despite painful searching, so that I can do nothing but turn to you for help.

In (19), the author justified his request in three ways: first, he was working on a course paper, the topic of which was related to the requestee's paper being asked for; second, he was interested in the paper; third, he could only find the abstract of the paper but not the full text. These accounts could establish the author as a reasonable requester in normal cases. In (20), the author did similar things: asserting the requestee's paper was important to his writing at the moment; explaining that he had undergone painful searching elsewhere (in his own university).

While the majority of the students did a good job, there were problems in a couple of cases. One student failed to identify herself as a student requester, as illustrated in (21):

(21) I'm XXX from the English department of XX University, China. Recently, I've been working on a paper about the use of euphemism.

Clearly, the author could be misperceived to be a teacher from XX University.

In another case, a student neglected mentioning any reason for making her request, which would make the request sound non-justified and therefore impolite:

(22) I am a year-one postgraduate major in English in XX University. Days ago, I read a paper in which your thesis *Euphemisms in African English* has been cited. What you elaborate in your thesis is quite useful for me, but I cannot get it from the Internet. Therefore, I wonder whether you can kindly send me your thesis. I am looking forward to your reply.

In this mail, the author only vaguely said that the paper in question was "quite useful for me." There was no mention of the specific use to which the paper would be put. Considering the possibility that the paper might be misused, the international researcher might well ignore this request.

6.4.4 Other Identification as Academic Requestees

To succeed in making a request, in addition to the three questions discussed in the last section, one also has to consider the following:

(4) Is one making the request of the right person?

Specifically, in this "blind" request situation:Is one properly constructing the requestee as an academic person?

Over half of the students constructed their requestees as academic people. For instance,

(23) I'm currently working on my course paper on euphemism, and find that your paper may prove to be one of the key references.

(24) I found that many of the resources in this field refer to your paper *Euphemisms in African English* but I failed to find neither the downloadable version on the Internet nor the printed one in our library.

(25) I am always an admirer of your research talent and my research area also demands frequent reference to your research papers.

(26) I am greatly enlightened by the abstract of your article and I found it would help me finish my paper.

In (23), the author highlighted the requestee's importance or achievement by saying that his paper was "one of the key references", as being a key reference is presumably a mark of academic achievement. In (24), the author did a similar thing by mentioning the fact to the requestee that his paper was frequently cited, suggesting the success of his paper. In (25), the author followed a different path: she voiced her admiration for the requestee and stated her future dependence on his work. Clearly, this strategy might add to the positive face of the requestee as a researcher. Finally, in (26), the author highlighted the detail that she had been "enlightened" by the addressee's article and stated that she would benefit significantly from his or her paper. Again, such words would effectively elevate the requestee's positive face as an academic researcher. As an interviewee reported:

> 每个研究者都希望自己写的东西能引起别人的注意。如果知道自己的文章能被人引用、得到他人肯定就更开心了。所以,我在信中说得到对方文章的启发,应该会让他高兴的。也许他一高兴,就将文章发给我了。
> Every researcher hopes that their work can attract some attention. If they know their paper has been cited or well received by others, they feel even happier. So, I said in my mail that I had been enlightened by his paper. I guess this will please him. Perhaps he will feel glad and send me his paper.

While a couple of others pointed out the "usefulness" or "relevance" of the addressee's paper, two students made no explicit effort at constructing their addressees as academic researchers. Rather, they just expressed their need for the latter's papers for the reason that they could not find the full text. This absence of explicit construction of the addressees as researchers, parallel to the presence of identity construction of them as requestees, might not be very conducive to the success of the requests, as there was no compensation for the imposition caused to the international researchers. As is often the case, a request is not very likely to succeed when no facework is done, especially when the requester is not in a socially or emotionally favorable position (Chen 2013a).

Despite the problems I detected, I am still in a strong position to argue that the majority of the students did wonderful identity work in their emails most of the time. For one thing, they properly identified themselves as student requesters who were in need for help and who would be grateful if their needs were fulfilled. For another, though less successfully, they projected their addressees as excellent or even remarkable researchers. Clearly, what the students did in their emails was not just to objectively represent their own identity and that of their addressees. They also constructed shades or strands of identity, especially that of their addressees, that might not exist. In this sense, I would like to conclude that the students actually drew on identity representation and construction as enabling pragmatic resources (Chen 2004, 2013b) for getting their requests performed and met, as evidenced by the interviewees' report. Whether or to what extent they would succeed depended on, among other things, how successfully they could construct their own identity as student requesters and their addressees as academic requestees. The data suggested that while a few students might fail, the majority of them showed their pragmatic competence in properly "doing things with words".

6.5 Conclusion

Research on computer-mediated communication has undergone a recent shift from the linguistic approach, termed the "Internet Linguistics" approach, to one that emphasizes technological, social and contextual factors (Bou-Franch 2011). While previous studies on email communication have contributed to the understanding of the language of email, they have neglected the "the interplay of technological, social, and contextual factors in the shaping of computer-mediated language practices" (Androutsopoulos 2006, p. 421). As a result, more and more CMC researchers have begun to direct their attention towards such aspects as the building and maintaining of interpersonal relations in CMC communication (e.g., Bunz and Campbell 2002; Duthler 2006; Herring 1996). Yet what role language plays in this process fails to attract adequate attention. For this reason, the present paper has combined the two approaches by looking at the language of the emails first, and proceeding to analyze how the style of the email language used, together with other components of the emails, contributes to the construction of identities, relational and personal alike, in the context specified by the designated writing task. Such practice is more pragmatic by nature, as it embraces both the pragmalinguistic aspect and the sociopragmatic dimension of email communication.

I found that the language of the collected email data was basically formal, showing that the factor of identity relation between the two sides of the communication (students viz international researchers) may outweigh the role of the network medium, such that electronic communication is better viewed as socially situated discourse (Herring 2004, 2007). Quite importantly, the style of the email language used in the data was found to vary both interpersonally and intrapersonally. This finding lends partial support to what Crystal calls "the remarkable diversity and creativity" of Internet discourse (2001, p. 242), although this may result from the students' carelessness or anxiety. At least, the study shows that the "language of email" does not exist as a fixed set of linguistic features underlying all email communication.

In the study of how the students perform their request to international researchers, I found that they deliberately constructed a deferent relational identity, which is characteristic of the Chinese culture. Apart from the formal linguistic choices they used, they also selected some other strategies such as the use of elevating address forms and compliment giving, which is again characteristically Chinese. This is a definite indicator of the students' pragmatic competence in Chinese eyes, although not all of them seemed to be equally competent. It confirms the argument that to be successful email users we need more than just fluency; we also need to learn how to express ourselves by using a variety of language forms and rhetorical strategies and get to know when it is appropriate to use these different forms (Bloch 2002, pp. 131–132). Even in email communication, the use of language does not just reflect identities, but also constructs identities that might not exist. Thus, it is the 'people first, business second' email style (Bou-Franch 2011, p. 1783), rather than the 'business first, people second' email style (Waldvogel 2007, p. 17), that dominates, as evidenced by my data. What's more, the identities constructed by the students are meant to serve the purpose of getting their requests fulfilled.

It might be safer to be not as conclusive as I was above, as the size of the data set used in this study is rather small. More crucially, the highly formal style the participants demonstrated might be due to the task assigned to them, as requesting an article from an unfamiliar professor is not only an imposing act but also a difficult one. Furthermore, since the emails were addressed to "superior" interlocutors, they do not represent those written to familiar people, peers or an "inferior" audience. Thus, further effort is called for to address these situations. Nevertheless, the findings I have obtained have rich implications for the study of email communication and L2 writing practice.

References

Androutsopoulos, Jannis. 2006. Introduction: Sociolinguistics and computer-mediated communication. *Journal of Sociolinguistics* 10(4): 419–438.

Bachman, Lyle. 1990. *Fundamental considerations in language testing*. Oxford: Oxford University Press.

Bakhtin, Mikhail. 1981. *The dialogic imagination: Four essays by M.M. Bakhtin* (trans: Emerson, C. and Holquist, M.). Austin, TX: University of Texas Press.

Baron, Naomi. 1998. Letters by phone or speech by any other means: The linguistics of email. *Language & Communication* 18: 133–170.

Baron, Naomi. 2001. Put on a public face. *New York Times* (April 11).

Biesenbach-Lucas, Sigrun. 2006. Making request in email: Do cyber-consultations entail directness? Toward conventions in a new medium. In *Pragmatics and language learning*, eds. Bardovi-Harlig, Kathleen, et al. Honolulu, HI.: Second Language Teaching and Curriculum Center, University of Hawai'i.

Biesenbach-Lucas, Sigrun. 2007. Students writing emails to faculty: An examination of E-politeness. *Language Learning & Technology* 11(2): 59–81.

Bjorge, Anne. 2007. Power distance in English lingua franca email communication. *International Journal of Applied Linguistics* 17(1): 60–80.

Bloch, Joel. 2002. Student/teacher interaction via email: The social context of Internet discourse. *Journal of Second Language Writing* 11: 117–134.

Bou-Franch, Patricia. 2011. Openings and closings in Spanish email conversations. *Journal of Pragmatics* 43: 1772–1785.

Brown, Penelope, and Stepehen Levinson. 1987. *Politeness: Some universals in language usage*. Cambridge: Cambridge University Press.

Bunz, Ulla, and Scott Campbell. 2002. Accommodating politeness indicators in personal electronic mail messages. Paper presented at the association of internet researcher's 3rd annual conference, October 13–16, 2002, in Maastricht, The Netherlands. http://bunz.comm.fsu.edu/AoIR2002politeness.pdf.

Chen, Chi-fen. 2006. The development of e-mail literacy: From writing to peers to writing to authority figures. *Language Learning & Technology* 10(2): 35–55.

Chen, Xinren. 2004. On pragmatic balance. *Journal of Foreign Language Studies* 6: 42–47.

Chen, Xinren. 2009. *A new coursebook in pragmatics*. Beijing: Foreign Language Teaching and Research Press.

Chen, Xinren. 2013a. *Politeness theories and English learning*. Beijing: Foreign Language Teaching and Research Press.

Chen, Xinren. 2013b. *Identity and communication: The pragmatic perspective*. Beijing: Higher Education Press.

Collot, Milena, and Nancy Belmore. 1996. Electronic language: A new variety of English. In *Computer-mediated communication: Linguistic, social and cross-cultural perspectives*, ed. Susan Herring, 13–28. Amsterdam: John Banjamins.

Crystal, David. 2001. *Language and the internet*. Cambridge: Cambridge University Press.

Duthler, Kirk. 2006. The politeness of requests made via email and voicemail: Support for the hyperpersonal model. *Journal of Computer-mediated Communication* 11(2): 500–521.

Economidou-Kogetsidis, Maria. 2010. Cross-cultural and situational variation in requesting behavior: Perceptions of social situations and strategic usage of request patterns. *Journal of Pragmatics* 42: 2262–2281.

Ferrara, Kathleen, Hans Brunner, and Greg Whittemore. 1991. Interactive written discourse as an emergent register. *Written Communication* 8(1): 8–34.

Gu, Yueguo. 1990. Politeness phenomena in modern Chinese. *Journal of Pragmatics* 14: 237–257.

Herring, Susan. 1996. Two variants of an electronic message schema. In *Computer-mediated communication: Linguistic, social and cross-cultural perspectives*, ed. Susan Herring, 81–106. Amsterdam: John Benjamins.

Herring, Susan. 2004. Computer-mediated discourse analysis: An approach to researching online communities. In *Designing for virtual communities in the service of learning*, ed. Sasha Barab, Rob Kling, and James Gray, 338–376. Cambridge: Cambridge University Press.

Herring, Susan. 2007. A faceted classification scheme for computer-mediated discourse. Language@internet 4. http://www.languageatinternet.de/articles/2007/761/index_html/.

Kiesler, Sara, Jane Siegel, and Timothy W. McGuire. 1987. Social psychological aspects of computer-mediated communication. In *Information technology: Social issues. A reader*, eds. Ruth Finnegan, Graeme Salaman and Kenneth Thompson, 247–262. Seven Oaks: Hodder and Stoughton (in association with the Open University).

Lee-Wong, Song Mei. 2000. *Politeness and face in Chinese culture*. Bern: Peter Lang.

Lin, Yuh-Huey. 2009. Query preparatory modals: Cross-linguistic and cross-situational variations in request modification. *Journal of Pragmatics* 41: 1636–1656.

Mantovani, Giuseppe. 1994. Is computer-mediated communication intrinsically apt to enhance democracy in organizations? *Human Relations* 47(1): 45–59.

Moran, Charles, and Gaffe Hawisher. 1998. The rhetoric and languages of electronic mail. In *Page to screen: Taking literacy into the electronic age*, ed. Ilana Synder, 80–101. London: Routledge.

Mulholland, Joan. 1999. Email: Uses, issues and problems in an institutional setting. In *Writing business: Genres, media, and discourse*, ed. Francesca Bargiela-Chiappini, and Catherine Nickerson, 57–84. New York: Longman.

Nie, Norman, and Lutz Erbring. 2000. *Internet society*. Pala alto: Stanford institute for the quantitative study of society [Online]. http://www.standford.edu/group/siqss/Press_Release/Preliminary_Report-4-21.pdf. Accessed 30 July 2001.

Sproull, Lee, and Sara Kiesler. 1991. *Connections: New ways of working in networked organizations*. Cambridge: MIT Press.

Taguchi, Nako. 2011. Teaching pragmatics: Trends and issues. *Annual Review of Applied Linguistics* 31: 289–310.

Tracy, Karen. 2002. *Everyday talk: Building and reflecting identities*. London: The Guilford Press.

Waldvogel, Joan. 2001. Email and workplace communication: A literature review. *Language in the Workplace: Occasional Papers* 3: 1–12.

Waldvogel, Joan. 2007. Greetings and closings in workplace email. *Journal of Computer-Mediated Communication* 12(2): 456–477.

Yang, Xianjue. 2009. *Pragmatic development in a second language: A cross-sectional study on the acquisition of English requests by Chinese learners*. Beijing: National Defense Industry Press.

Yates, Simeon. 1996. Oral and written linguistic aspects of computer conferencing: A corpus based study. In *Computer-mediated communication: Linguistic, social and cross-cultural perspectives*, ed. Susan Herring, 29–46. Amsterdam: John Benjamins.

Yus, Francisco. 2011. *Cyberpragmatics: Internet-mediated communication in context*. Philadelphia: John Benjamins.

Zimmerman, Eric, and Judit Bar-Ilan. 2009. PIM @ academia: How e-mail is used by scholars. *Online Information Review* 33(1): 22–42.

Author Biography

Xinren Chen (陈新仁), professor of Linguistics at Nanjing University and co-editor of East Asian Pragmatics, specializes in pragmatics and SLA, and has (co-)authored 13 monographs and over 110 articles. He is currently executive vice-president of the China Pragmatics Association, and vice-president of China Association for Discourse Studies, and China English Language Education Association.

Chapter 7
Intercultural *Taoci* Email: New Wine in an Old Bottle

Lin Xiao and Yihong Gao

Abstract "*Taoci*" originally means building *guanxi* with targeted persons for practical goals, mainly through linguistic means. This word is rooted in Chinese culture, which highlights *guanxi* as a networking resource in social functioning. In the field of overseas education application in contemporary China, "*Taoci* email" has become a catch word referring specifically to applicants' personal email contacts with their targeted supervisors to increase their admission and scholarship opportunities. The present research examined what student applicants performed discursively in such *Taoci* email and the various types of strategies used. Further, the values underlying *Taoci* email were unpacked, as connecting to and departing from the original meaning of *Taoci*. Main data included 26 initial pieces and 11 packages of *Taoci* email written by 19 Chinese applicants to their potential supervisors in US universities; supplementary data included interviews with accessible applicants and meta-discourse about *Taoci* email writing from the Internet. Spencer-Oatey's rapport management model was adopted as the theoretical framework. Two major types of *Taoci* strategies were found: "*guanxi Taoci*" and "academic *Taoci*." While the former focused on interpersonal relations and was associated with *Taoci* in its original sense in Chinese culture, the latter focused on the individual's academic competence, and was associated with "quality face" which embedded Western values. Mixed use of strategies was not uncommon, but

According to *The New Testament* (Matthew), Jesus says, 'Neither do men put new wine into old bottles: else the bottles break, and the wine runneth out, and the bottles perish: but they put new wine into new bottles, and both are preserved.' This means new ideas do not fit into old forms; they should be expressed in new forms. After the 'May Fourth' (New Cultural Movement at the beginning of the twentieth century in China), a reversed meaning of the metaphor is developed, i.e., making use of existing forms to express new ideas. … (Xinhua Dictionary of Idioms 2013, p. 777).

L. Xiao · Y. Gao (✉)
Research Institute of Linguistics and Applied Linguistics,
Peking University, Beijing, China
e-mail: gaoyh@pku.edu.cn

L. Xiao
e-mail: lindaxiaopku@163.com

Y. Chen et al. (eds.), *Email Discourse Among Chinese Using English as a Lingua Franca*, DOI 10.1007/978-981-287-888-5_7

"academic *Taoci*" was clearly dominant in distribution. Such results create new meanings of *Taoci* in an (inter)cultural context. The phenomenon can be considered, based on a Chinese idiom contrary to the Biblical sense, "new wine in an old bottle."

Keywords *Taoci* · *Guanxi* · Rapport · Culture · Study-abroad application

7.1 Introduction

7.1.1 Taoci and Taoci Email

"*Taoci*" ("套磁" or "套瓷") was originally a colloquial term in Beijing dialect. According to dictionary explanations, *Taoci* means "trying to build up *guanxi* (relation, rapport), chum up with or cotton up to somebody, mainly through talking and chatting" (Gao and Fu 2001, p. 809).[1] Such rapport building has its targeted persons, and usually clear practical goals. The term *Taoci* has a derogatory connotation. In an earlier dictionary, it is even labeled as a "word used by hooligans in modern Chinese society" (Chen 1985, p. 268).[2] Conducted "mainly through talking and chatting" and therefore a speech act, *Taoci* is a form of general "*guanxi*" building ("*la guanxi,*" literally "pull *guanxi*") in Chinese culture. "Pulling-*guanxi*" is to place oneself into an effective interpersonal network in order to realize the intended goal (Wen 2012) through linguistic or nonlinguistic means.

Taoci as a concept in "modern Chinese society" (Chen 1985) is in fact situated in Chinese historical tradition where the hierarchical social structure and concentric relational circles of the family are central. As Confucius said, "There is government when the prince is the prince, and the minister is the minister; when the father is father, and the son is the son".[3] Each person possesses a proper position in the hierarchical network, which is a way to fulfill the principle of Chinese "*li*" (ritual, propriety) (Chen 2010; Yum 1988). Such social hierarchies are strengthened through linguistic practices such as the use of honorific address terms. *Taoci* as a form of "*la* (pull; pull close) *guanxi*" can be considered an approach to social networking complementary and alternative to the traditional maintenance of *li*. It creates opportunities to develop one's social resources outside (as well as inside)

[1] "套瓷" is also written in "套磁" in Chinese characters. It means pulling *guanxi* with other people. This word can be used as the following examples show: spend a long time doing *Taoci*, do *Taoci* with her. (Gao and Fu (eds.) 2001, p. 809).

[2] "套磁" (*Taoci*) means pulling guanxi with targeted persons for practical purposes. It is a catch word used by hooligans in modern Chinese society (Chen 1985, p. 268).

[3] This episode is from *Confucian Analects—Yanyuan*. It is Confucius's response to the duke Ching of Chi who asked about government. The English version is translated by Legge (2014, p. 122).

the legitimized hierarchical structure. Some unconventional methods may be used for network building with strangers. "*Guanxi*" means "relationship," but it is relationship employed as a useful social resource (Chang and Holt 1991). People in a *guanxi* network can manipulate *guanxi* to obtain practical benefits. In Bourdieu's (1986) term, *guanxi* is a "social capital," the aggregate of existing or potential resources deriving from membership. However, pulling *guanxi* will lead to the flow of social capital between different *guanxi* circles, and generate a rupture in the existing structured connection. Once the flow and rupture become more fixed in and digested by the new network, it will be inserted in the previous structure as expansion and enrichment. So in a paradoxical sense, *guanxi* building is both an alternative to and an expansion of the Confucian familism/clannism (家族主义), group formation based on patriarchal family networks. Through continued practice, the unconventional will turn into the conventional. *Taoci* as a form of *guanxi* building became a norm of communication, reified in dictionary entries (e.g., Gao and Fu 2001). It has become a "*habitus*" (Bourdieu 1986), or structuring structure for people's behavior in Chinese culture.

In the domain of cross-cultural communication, a number of value dimensions have been proposed for cultural classification. On a commonly adopted dichotomy/continuum of individualism–collectivism (e.g., Hofstede 1991; Gudykunst and Matsumoto 1996; Triandis 1990), Chinese culture on the whole is placed on the side of collectivism, in which "people stress fitting in with and belonging to the group, and they focus on a 'we' identity," whereas the United States is on the side of individualism, with "the emphasis on an individual's rights, such as individuality, independence, and freedom, … [while] family relations, loyalty, and harmony are perceived as less important" (Gao and Ting-Toomey 1998, p. 3). Such a cross-cultural contrast provides a reference point for the examination of intra-cultural *habitus* reproduction and transformation.

"*Taoci* email" is a contemporary genre of English writing for Chinese students applying for graduate programs abroad, referring to applicants' personal email contacts with their targeted supervisors so as to increase admission and scholarship opportunities (Baidu Baike).[4] With the increase of Chinese students going abroad, especially to English-speaking countries,[5] various Internet forums put up special columns to demonstrate and exchange ideas regarding how to write *Taoci* email as well as other application documents like personal statement and CV. Almost all overseas-program websites, such as New Oriental, Taoisha, Jituo, have a special space for *Taoci* email writing, where people can find *Taoci* tips, *Taoci* experience sharing, and *Taoci* FAQs. These put together constitute an online *Taoci*

---

[4]*Taoci* is a term which overseas education applicants are quite familiar with. It specifically refers to applicants' personal email contacts with their targeted supervisors so as to increase admission and scholarship opportunities. (from http://baike.baidu.com/view/1385927.html *Baidu Baike* is a Chinese online encyclopedia, also known as Baidu Wikipedia).

[5]America, Britain, Canada, and Australia are the favorite destinations for Chinese students to choose for study-abroad programs according to official statistics for the past 5 years. (from http://edu.sina.com.cn/a/2013-12-16/1446237588.shtml).

"meta-discourse," i.e., discourse about *Taoci* discourse, which informs applicants how to write *Taoci* email. *Taoci* meta-discourse also covers the communication between applicants and their peers, senior schoolmates, and (or) teachers about how to do *Taoci* with American professors. In an intercultural academic context of graduate program application, it is interesting to examine whether and in what ways the strategies in *Taoci* email have maintained the original meaning of *Taoci* in Chinese local culture, whether and in what ways new meanings have been adopted.

7.1.2 *Guanxi*

Jacob (1979) commented that under the Chinese culture context and perhaps cross-cultural context, *kuan-hsi* (*guanxi*) depended upon two or more persons having a commonality of shared attributes. The shared identification constitutes the most popular means to pull *guanxi* with familiars or the unfamiliar, like "locality (native place), kinship, coworker, classmate, sworn brotherhood, surname and teacher-student" listed by Ambrose (1991, p. 70). *Guanxi* can also be built through the exchange of gifts, favors, and banquets (Yang 1994), for example, Kipnis (1996) and Yan (1996) investigated the gift-giving practice to maintain *guanxi* in Chinese villages. Shenkar and Ronen (1987) summarized that keeping frequent contact, developing mutual understanding, giving gifts or favors, and establishing personal trust and mutual interest are examples of building a good relationship for Chinese people. Based on interview data, Chang and Holt (1991, p. 258) distinguished the following ways of Chinese *guanxi* building: by appealing to kinship relations and previous association, by going through one's ingroup members, by interacting with others, and by saying something good.

Farrer (2002) investigated the function of "idle talk" (written in Chinese as 闲话) among neighbors in a Shanghai residence community in delivering information, negotiating local moral standards and further shaping the network. Similar to gossip, small talk is also regarded as an important means to attend to relationship building and maintenance (Pavlidou 2007). Pavlidou suggested other means than phatic communion, such as redundancy, negative politeness, talking about the relationship itself and strategies of directness, which might affect the rapport.

7.1.3 Rapport Management

Spencer-Oatey (2002, 2007a, b) believed that the use of language is to promote, maintain, or threaten the harmonious social relations. She proposed the theory of "rapport management" in interpersonal relationship. Rapport refers to people's subjective perceptions of good and bad interpersonal relations. Based on her rapport-sensitive incident investigation (Spencer-Oatey 2002), she designed four interrelated components of rapport management: (1) "quality face," referring to the value people successfully claim for themselves in terms of personal qualities, skills, competence, appearance, etc.; (2) "identity face," which involves acknowledgment of social roles; (3) "equity rights," referring to the belief in freedom from imposition; and (4) "association rights," which is about entitlement to an association with others. The first two constitute "face management" to manage "the presentation of self" (Goffman 1959). The last two constitute "sociality rights management," which is concerned with personal and social expectancies, i.e., belief in the entitlement to social interaction, not being imposed and not being excluded. Peoples' psychological desire of face and rights can be found in textual lines, which is a pragmatic manifestation of the use of utterances.

Spencer-Oatey's rapport management model is similar to Brown and Levinson's (1987) politeness theory in which they both drew upon the concept of face from Goffman (1967) and stressed the importance of face concern. Spencer-Oatey's (2007c, p. 14) "equity rights" refers to the belief "that we are not unduly imposed upon, that we are not unfairly ordered about." With its focus on non-imposition, this definition is very similar to Brown and Levinson's (1987, p. 62) definition of "negative face": "the want of every 'competent adult member' that this action be unimpeded by others." Yet in Brown and Levinson (1987), face is pre-defined, static, and centered on the individual. Spencer-Oatey's model is more relation oriented, which compensates for Brown and Levinson's (1987) overemphasis on individual freedom/autonomy (e.g., Matsumoto 1988; Watts et al. 2005). Moreover, instead of "politeness" conventions, Spencer-Oatey's perspective focuses on "rights" to be obtained through interpersonal communication. The rapport management model is useful for the present study research as it addresses people's desire for face needs and rights entitlement from both personal and social dimensions, because Chinese applicants' *Taoci* email is aimed at a successful claim of face value as well as pulling close the relation with their potential supervisors.

The four components of rapport management can be embedded in both verbal and nonverbal communications. Spencer-Oatey (2007c) suggested five domains to inspect: (1) illocutionary domain, which concerns the illocutionary effect of a speech act; (2) discourse domain, which is about the discourse content and structure, such as topic choice and topic management; (3) participation domain, which concerns such procedures as turn-taking; (4) stylistic domain, which concerns choice of genre, choice of tone, address, etc.; and (5) nonverbal domain, which involves gestures, facial expressions, eye contact, etc. The five domains of strategy are affected by different types of rapport orientation: rapport enhancement, rapport maintenance, rapport neglect, and rapport challenge.

Regarding intercultural communication studies, Spencer-Oatey and Xing (2003) explored face issues in interactions between Chinese business people and a British company, validating both verbal and nonverbal factors important to explain sociality rights and face management. This study has demonstrated the significance of paying heed to face/rights expectations in different cultures. Gunthner (2007) inspected how topic, style, and conversational turn-taking could affect the social contact and rapport construction in German–Chinese students' conversation. In China, Ran (2012) used the rapport management framework to explain the conflicting discourse (rapport challenge orientation) in Chinese soap operas on TV. Liu (2011) employed the concepts of face management and sociality management in analyzing euphemisms of rapport building in a classic Chinese novel *A Dream of Red Mansions*. These two studies were the applications of the rapport management model to the Chinese context. However, the data used in the studies were from literary sources, hence, the validity problem of "real language use." Xiao (2014) applied the rapport management model to analyze the first Chinese email texts written by 34 Chinese Ph.D. applicants to a Chinese supervisor. It was found that the applicants resorted to both positive and negative quality face, and constructed multiple identity faces for themselves. But only positive quality face and identity face were ascribed to the supervisor. Speech acts like apologizing and thanking were used to soften the imposition to recover equity rights, and ingroup membership was claimed to seek equal association rights. Yet, the article barely touched the cultural connotation-laden aspects of Chinese *Taoci* email.

It appears that studies of *guanxi*-building conventions have identified major strategies of *guanxi* building in Chinese intra-group communication. Intercultural communication studies have demonstrated the special importance of *guanxi* in communication with Chinese people, while cross-cultural communication differences are identified between individualistic and collectivistic cultures. Nonetheless, language-specific *guanxi*-building details remain to be further explored. In addition, values and communication strategies not only differ across cultures, but also vary and change in a given culture. The traditional value attached to *guanxi* in China is possibly undergoing subtle transformations in the process of modernization, which goes hand in hand with English learning and the use of English as a lingua franca in the globalized academia (Jenkins 2014). Such possible transformations need to be closely examined. Spencer-Oatey's framework of rapport management (2002, 2007c) has been found to have explanatory power in empirical studies, paying more attention to interpersonal issues. It might be employed for the exploration of linguistic strategies for rapport building in specific domains of intercultural academic communication, and the underlying value traditions and transformations.

7.1.4 Research Questions

The present study investigated what student applicants performed discursively in their *Taoci* email. The research questions were as follows:

1. What did applicants do in *Taoci* email, in the rapport building with their targeted supervisors? What were the prominent discursive content and linguistic strategies?
2. In what ways, if any, did the "*Taoci*" in *Taoci* email converge to and diverge from *Taoci* in its traditional cultural sense as indicated in the dialect form?

7.2 Methods

Two types of *Taoci* data were collected. Main data consisted of 26 initial pieces and 11 packages of *Taoci* email written by 19 applicants; supplementary data consisted of 11 follow-up interviews with the applicants, and meta-discourses on *Taoci* email collected from the Internet.

All of the participants, except Jane Liu, who was a friend of one of the authors, were recruited through the Internet. Two rounds of data collection were carried out in Beijing.[6] The first round was conducted from April to May in 2013[7] and nine participants including Jane Liu were recruited. The second round was carried out in the same period during 2014, with ten participants enrolled. We contacted through email those who posted their application information on online bulletin boards of four universities and a public online forum, and asked whether they would be willing to provide their *Taoci* email and participate in follow-up interviews. In all, nineteen applicants were taken as participants; all were applicants for M.A. or Ph.D. programs in the USA. There were eight females and eleven males, all of whom had a relatively high level of English proficiency—their TOEFL scores were all over 90.[8] The *Taoci* texts collected also included those written to recipients other than their eventual supervisors. The dataset consisted of initial pieces of *Taoci* email (first contact email), full packages, i.e., all email contacts with their supervisors from the beginning to the admission notification, partial packages (several email exchanges with supervisors), and face-to-face or email interviews (Table 7.1). To protect participants' privacy, pseudonyms were used and sensitive personal information like university name was deleted or modified.

The interviews were conducted from April to July in 2013 and 2014, respectively, for the first and second round; some follow-up questions were asked through email after the applicants went abroad. Semi-structured face-to-face interviews were conducted individually, about *Taoci* experience, perceptions of, and reflections on *Taoci*. These interviews were carried out in campus cafeterias, each lasting about 30 minutes, recorded and transcribed afterward. For the applicants who were not then in Beijing, interviews were conducted through several rounds of email contact. Eight participants were inaccessible for interviews due to various reasons.

In data analysis, the 26 pieces of initial *Taoci* email were examined to figure out what kinds of strategies were employed. Then the full and partial *Taoci* packages were gone through to identify more possible strategy types. Interview excerpts were used to provide an emic perspective of the goals and *Taoci* strategies used in the email. Spencer-Oatey's (2002, 2007a, b, c) theory of rapport management was employed as the major analytical framework, but care was taken to attend to categories emerging from the data in a bottom-up manner.

---

[6]Beijing has the biggest number of successful applicants for overseas higher education programs. (from http://edu.sina.com.cn/a/2013-12-16/1446237588.shtml).

[7]Usually, by April 15, most US universities have released their final admissions. After that, good news about admission and scholarship are shared by applicants on the bulletin board.

[8]The full TOEFL (Test of English as a Foreign Language) score is 120.

Table 7.1 Data distribution

Participants (Pseudonyms)	Gender	English proficiency (TOEFL)	Initial *Taoci* email	*Taoci* package	Interview
201301 Jane Liu	F	>110	1 piece	/	/
201302 Master Miao	M	>90	1 piece	/	/
201303 Lily Si	F	>100	1 piece	/	/
201304 Francis Zhao	M	>100	2 pieces	One package	Face-to-face
201305 Shelly Chen	F	>95	3 pieces	/	Face-to-face
201306 Albert Yu	M	>90	1 piece	/	Face-to-face
201307 Brook Li	M	>95	1 piece	One package	Face-to-face
201308 Cindy He	F	>95	2 pieces	Two packages	Email
201309 Leo Gao	M	>95	2 pieces	Two partial packages	Email
201401 Grace Qi	F	>95	1 piece	/	/
201402 Tony Hu	M	>90	1 piece	/	/
201403 Aeron Xia	M	>90	1 piece	/	/
201404 Kate Zhou	F	>100	1 piece	One package	Face-to-face
201405 Smith Liu	M	>90	1 piece	/	/
201406 Richard Xu	M	>90	1 piece	/	Email
201407 Aubrey Fen	F	>100	2 pieces	One partial package	/
201408 Sam Wang	M	>95	2 pieces	One package	Face-to-face
201409 Jack Qu	M	>100	1 piece	One package	Face-to-face
201410 Julie Yi	F	>100	1 piece	One package	Face-to-face
Total	8F 11M	>90	26 pieces	8 (full) + 3 (partial)	11

The email content was examined at a clause-unit level to identify specific communication strategies. The coding was conducted independently by one of the researchers and her American friend, with an inter-coder reliability of 0.8. The remaining coding differences were all discussed until agreement was reached.

After the clause-level coding, rapport strategy types were coded according to their content. At first, open coding of each clause was adopted to generate relevant strategy types. Then two major axial themes (*guanxi Taoci* and academic *Taoci*) were developed to assemble the strategies found. In addition, strategies found other than clause-level (including participation structure, choice of tone, address terms) were added. For the statistics presented below, only the clause-unit coding of each participant's initial email was used in order to maintain consistency of the data. In the discussion of strategy types, qualitative data from interviews and online meta-discourse were used as supplementary evidence.

7.3 Findings

Two major types of *Taoci* strategies were found—*guanxi Taoci* and academic *Taoci*. *Guanxi Taoci* involves identifying and amplifying the actual or possible associations between the applicants and supervisors. It has two subcategories—power-oriented *Taoci* and solidarity-oriented *Taoci*; both involve the discourse domain, participation domain, and illocutionary domain. Academic *Taoci* highlights the individual applicant's educational and academic strengths, involving the stylistic domain, discourse domain, and illocutionary domain. *Guanxi Taoci* is oriented to Spencer-Oatey's association rights, but with some exceptions, while academic *Taoci* attends to applicants' needs for quality face.

7.3.1 Guanxi Taoci

7.3.1.1 Power-Oriented Strategies: Showing Respect

By showing respect to the supervisor or the targeted institution, the applicants placed the recipient in a superior position in a power relation. This might be realized in a number of ways.

Stating that Admission Would Be an Honor

(1) …, and wish to <u>have the honored opportunity</u> to work with you. (Jane Liu)
(2) <u>It would be an honor</u> if I had the chance to work with you. (Aubrey Fen)

Chinese teacher–student relationship is usually characterized as a hierarchical one under the influence of Confucianism, for example, "treat your teacher just as you treat your father[9]"; "He who teaches me for one day is my father for life[10]", with teacher amounting to the role of father, one of the Five Codes of Ethics (*Wulun* 五伦). Indeed, it was found that such a showing of respect was very common in Chinese applicants' *Taoci* email to Chinese supervisors written in Chinese (Xiao 2014). Comparatively, in our intercultural data in English, it was not common, appearing in only five email texts.

Using Formal Titles as Address Terms

Another way of showing respect was the use of formal address terms, such as academic titles. All of the initial *Taoci* email used respectful address terms like "Dear Professor ***," probably following a convention; most authors continued to use such address terms in following email contacts. In Brook Li's *Taoci* package, however, there was a shift in address term. The first email started with "Dear Prof. Kiong" (a Korean professor in America), but in the following contacts the author shifted to "Dear Kiong," "Hi Kiong," or even zero address term (with one exception in the thirteenth email) until email 19 where he began to reuse "Dear Professor". Brook reflected in his interview:

> (I worked part time in a western electronic company). All of my habits [of addressing others] are cultivated there. Whenever I write to Chinese or English speakers, I'm used to an equal relationship in addressing others. No matter he is my boss or big boss, we are equal, rather equal. So after chatting a little or four or five emails, I addressed them by their given names. But later, I felt that, Asian, or Korean, Chinese, or Japanese, or some Indians, probably do not like such kind of equality. They might expect you to respect your teacher much more. So suddenly one day, I felt that I should go back to use "Dear Professor" in the email. (Interview transcript 2013)

Making Compliments About the Supervisor's Work or Lab

Compliment is often resorted to lubricate the interpersonal relationship. It functions to boost positive face (Brown and Levinson 1987), to elevate others (Gu 1990, 1992), to maximize approbation for others (Leech 1983), and to maintain a harmonious relationship with other people (Chang and Holt 1991). Compliments were also frequently used in *Taoci* email, though sometimes implicitly.

(3) …, in which you gave a <u>thought-provoking</u> key-note speech. (Jane Liu)
(4) …, the former a <u>unique opportunity</u> on the recovery of deforestation, and the latter an <u>ambitious and grandiose prospect</u>. (Leo Gao)

---

[9]From "Encouraging Leaning" in Lü's *Commentaries of History*.

[10]Folk adage.

Jane Liu was complimenting the target supervisor's speech made at an academic conference. Leo Gao praised the professor's two current projects. The words underlined were laden with positive evaluative meanings, thus giving quality face to the supervisors. Compliments about the work done by the supervisor and his or her teams were viewed as more objective and therefore more appropriate than compliments on the supervisor directly. In contrast, one *Taoci* email complimenting the professor incurred much criticism and was considered "bizarre" on the Internet meta-discourse.[11]

> You are in my view one of the most knowledgeable and authoritative scholars in the area of self-assembling materials … Therefore I am eager to be your intern student and learn from you the most helpful research skills.

This *Taoci* email was written by a Chinese student applying for an intern position of an American university. The compliment "the most knowledgeable and authoritative scholars" was criticized in the meta-discourse as excessive flattery. In Chinese students' *Taoci* email to Chinese supervisors (Xiao 2014), compliments about the supervisors' character, morality, and reputation were pervasive, which nevertheless was absent in our English data.

Showing Magnetic Attraction of the Supervisor

The applicants stated that they were attracted by the supervisors' achievements or charisma ("ci" in *Taoci* means magnet[12]), and would therefore like to be recruited to their programs:

(5) I am fascinated to read your publications in this area, and wish to … (Jane Liu)
(6) Therefore I found your group at U University a dream place for me to start my graduate education and research. (Shelly Chen)

Jane Liu was attracted by the supervisor's publications. Shelly Chen felt attracted to the supervisor's research and regarded it as a dream place to realize her research ambition to "contribute to human welfare." Making the supervisor (or his/her lab) the magnetic center was a way of showing respect and appreciation, and amplifying the supervisor's quality face.

The ways of showing respect seemed to strengthen the quality face of the recipient while depreciating the sender, thus making the distance between them

---

[11]This *Taoci* email was posted on *Renren* (a Chinese equivalent of Facebook) and forwarded for many times. It was cited as a bad example of *Taoci* email writing with regards to its content, format, font, etc. (from http://page.renren.com/601573029/channel-noteshow-900408688?id=900408688&op=pre&curTime=1365667934000&pid=601573029&).

[12]*Taoci* is often written as "套磁" in the overseas application field, in which "磁" means magnetic force to draw the applicant and the targeted supervisor together. Another Chinese form, "套瓷," is also used, but not as popular as "套磁."

larger. However, it was aimed to "pull" the teacher–student relation closer through a paradoxical distancing.

7.3.1.2 Solidarity-Oriented Strategies

Taoci can also be exercised at the horizontal dimension to endear the two parties. This is related to Spencer-Oatey's association rights, the belief in the entitlement to an association with others that one feels appropriate or desirable.

Keeping Frequent Contact

By initiating or taking turns in the communication process, the applicants managed to keep contact with the supervisors. Turn-taking is one procedural aspect of participation domain in rapport building (Spencer-Oatey 2007c). In our analysis, a "turn" is defined as a battery of email contacts pivoting around a specific topic, which differs from the popular conception of "turn" in conversation analysis. Email turn-taking as such can be detected through a series of contacts. In Brook Li's package of 25 email texts, 15 were from Brook and 10 from the targeted supervisor Kiong. These were grouped into 9 turns, according to thematic relevance (Table 7.2).

Table 7.2 Turn sequencing in Brook's *Taoci* package

Turn	Range	Topical relevance	Who initiates?
Turn 1	Email 1–Email 4	Consulting about a possible Ph.D. position	Brook
Turn 2	Email 5–Email 7	Following up the application status (F1)	Brook
Turn 3	Email 8–Email 10	Updating resume	Brook
Turn 4	Email 11–Email 12	Giving a possible offer	Kiong
Turn 5	Email 13–Email 15	Following up the acceptance of the possible offer (F2)	Brook
Turn 6	Email 16–Email 18	Notifying the fellowship	Kiong
Turn 7	Email 19–Email 21	Following up the official offer (F3)	Brook
Turn 8	Email 22	Notifying the confirmation file	Brook
Turn 9	Email 23–Email 25	Seeking help about visa interview	Brook

Among the nine turns, seven were initiated by Brook and only two by the supervisor. There were three follow-ups by Brook about his application status, about accepting the possible offer, and about the official offer, when Brook had not heard from the supervisor immediately. The asymmetry of email number and turn-taking showed that Brook was a very proactive applicant, with an strong desire to be acknowledged for his personal quality of "taking initiative" by the supervisor, i.e., his quality face. Although the frequent initiation might inflict imposition on the hearer's freedom (equity rights), the action claims for association rights for further communication.

Resorting to Previous and Possible Association

a. To get acquainted with the unfamiliar person, the applicant might resort to previous roles connected with the targeted supervisor, for instance an encounter at an academic conference, a past contact through email, etc. For example, one applicant mentioned a previous association:

(7) … and I contacted with you last year. (Brook Li)

Brook Li had written an email to the targeted supervisor before. He tried to use this previous association as a resource for exploring overlapping zones between them. This might also be understood as a claim for association rights.

b. Claiming a similar cultural background was another way of claiming previous association. Among our data, only one applicant, Cindy, resorted to this strategy in both sets of her *Taoci* email because her targeted supervisors were Chinese working in America. For example:

(8) Happy Mid-Autumn Festival!:-) (Email 2 of Cindy Hu)

(9) Tonight is the Chinese new year' eve. I would like to take the chance to say happy spring festival and send you the best wishes. (Email 14 of Cindy Hu)

Cindy and Professor Huang sent each other wishes on two important Chinese traditional festivals—Middle Autumn Festival and Spring Festival. Cindy's move to share festival wishes symbolized a tie with the professor because of a shared cultural background. Their email contact covered the period from September 2012 to the first half of 2013. However, there was no exchange of Christmas wishes between them. The exclusive use of holiday greetings for traditional Chinese festivals in the discourse domain was meant to strengthen their cultural bonding.

c. Geographical closeness also shows intention to pull *guanxi.*

(10) I am attracted in your project in ** plain (** is my hometown). (Cindy Hu)

In this example, Cindy Hu's targeted supervisor had her research site in ** Plain, which was also Cindy's hometown. By disclosing this geographic coincidence, Cindy tried to claim an advantage over other applicants.

Creating Chances for Further Interaction

Chinese people attach much importance to the mutualness of interaction, *laiwang* (来往) i.e., to and fro, or reciprocation. A smart applicant would leave open the chance for further contact with the recipient through skillful wording. A question or a request, for example, would lead to a probable response.

(11) If you have available funds and consider me qualified, please let me know. (Lily Si)

(12) … and if you have any questions about me or my research, please let me know. (Julie Yi)

The two examples of request above were expected to bring about positive responses from the recipients. Request was one of the most frequent types of speech act in *Taoci* email, since applicants were petitioners for limited educational resources, and the counterparts were positioned as resource allocators.

Relating Oneself with Ingroup Members

Guanxi network is significant in which its expansion can create new relational ties. Therefore, outsiders might try to enter the network through ingroup members, for example, "I am your father's friend's best friend." This is what Chang and Holt (1991, p. 260) called "intermediaries," which are often employed in a more implicit way in the *Taoci* email. For example,

(13) During the last summer vacation, I was doing some work related to computational simulation under the guidance of Professor Jiang in *** Academy of Science. (Francis Zhao)

(14) Prof. Fanyang Sun is my current supervisor. (Sam Wang)

In Example (13), the named professor was a famous figure in the research field. This connection not only specified the applicants' academic background, but also brought the applicant closer to the potential supervisor. The intermediary model is like this: "The person I am acquainted with is a famous scholar in the professional field, whose reputation you must know very well. As you know him, and I also know him, you and I belong to the same respected professional group." Francis Zhao reflected in his interview, "In one letter, I mentioned Professor Jiang's name on purpose because he and the other supervisor had previous cooperation and met each other before".

By contrast, Example (14) demonstrates the ingroup membership in a more explicit way by articulating the intermediary's full name in the second paragraph of his email. Sam Wang mentioned in the interview that his supervisor in China knew the targeted supervisor well. Since he was Professor Sun's student, Sam was justifiably involved in a kind of *guanxi* networking.

The mentioning of Professor Jiang and Professor Sun brought the respective three parties into the same group so that the applicants' claim of association rights could be realized.

7.3.2 *Academic Taoci*

Academic *Taoci* refers to strategies of attracting the recipient's interest by resorting to academic aspects of the applicant. This can be carried out in two ways: (1) appealing to shared academic interest and reflecting association rights; and (2) resorting to personal strengths, corresponding to a claim of academic face needs.

7.3.2.1 Establishing Mutual Academic Interests

Mutual academic interests were verbalized so as to pull the two parties into the same community of practice. The shared interests were sometimes general but mostly specific so that the supervisor's academic community was squarely targeted. All of the 19 participants' email contained a reference to mutual interests in an academic topic or field as the following examples show:

(15) Seems my research interests really matches with your group research topics. (Kate Zhou)

(16) I am very excited to learn that you have done great research work in the areas I am passionate about. (Jack Qu)

The interviewees emphasized their perception that matched interest was a fundamental factor for admission and *Taoci* was employed to check whether the two parties fitted each other well. They also mentioned that the matched interest was the prerequisite for future cooperation. For example,

> Francis Zhou: … in *Taoci* email you need to make the professor know that your interests match… if it doesn't match, no matter how hard you try *Taoci*, it will not work. (Interview transcript 2013)
>
> Shelly Chen: Match with the lab covers various aspects, like your character, style, your gender … Certainly match is mainly about research interest. But if you don't contact the supervisor, you will definitely not know the "match" matter. (Interview transcript 2013)

7.3.2.2 Self-presentation

If mutual interest served as an introduction part of academic *Taoci*, self-presentation was the main stage to pose applicants' "front" (Goffman 1959, p.32). For postgraduate and Ph.D. programs, applicants' academic potential and competence were perhaps the most convincing factors for supervisors to take into account. To cater for this need, applicants tried hard to manifest their skills and competence. Their face need was to obtain positive evaluation of their academic abilities and potential from target supervisors. The following five aspects were generalized as the most frequent topics in terms of Spencer-Oatey's discourse domain, which would be further related to the style domain, a formal and serious wording as academic *Taoci*.

Academic Background

a. Education Names of universities to which the applicants belonged, associated with the ranking of universities in the nation's higher education system, were used as capital for applicants' self-presentation or self-promotion. To specify one's college educational background is to posit an aspect of learning ability.

(17) Before studying in XXX University, I received the degree of Bachelor of Science in XXX department of W University, China. (Master Miao)

(18) I did my M.Sc. in Artificial Intelligence at University of XXX and bachelor in Science and Technology of Intelligence at Beijing University of XXX. (Aeron Xia)

The universities mentioned in the above email texts were internationally well known as well as top-ranking in China. Student membership in such a university stood for excellence in academic competence, thus enhancing applicants' quality face as competent candidates.

b. Research or working experience Research and work experience constituted another aspect that applicants highlighted in their self-presentations to potential supervisors. In *Taoci* email, a review of past work was often used to claim this perceived advantage in admission.

(19) I spent the past year reading literature on phylogenetic niche conservatism and phylogenetic and/or functional structure of community … Currently I am working in Professor Liang's lab mainly on three projects: (1) performing further analysis on phylogenetic … digitizing data of woody plants distribution in China using *GIS*. (Shelly Chen)

(20) I have more than 3 years of experience in computational materials, both molecular dynamics simulations (with LAMMPS) and finite element analysis (with COMSOL Multiphysics). (Kate Zhou)

Past experience and current work were presented to indicate the applicant's research competence. The underlined technical terms also served to mark a professional identity in a highly specialized academic field.

Academic Achievement (Research Paper, Publications, Patent, Etc.)

Publication in journals, books and conferences, and patents could be the best ostensible proof of one's research ability, which was credited as their "hardware" or "hard stuff" mentioned by the participants in the interviews.

(21) At this stage, I have one first-authored international conference publication and several co-authored conference and journal publications. (Master Miao)

(22) And I have a paper for the field which was published in a workshop of Ubicomp 201*. (Smith Liu)

Although the two applicants used a representative speech act (Searle 1976) regarding publication, they were making a point to convince the recipients that they possessed the required academic skills and ability. This was another way to satisfy a positive quality face of the applicants.

Future Research Plan or Interest

In addition to claiming a mutual interest with the supervisor, the applicant also talked about their future research direction:

(23) I am going to start from the May Fourth Movement period and comb the development of feminism in Chinese literature and its historical influence. This will also be an important subject of my future graduate study. (Lily Si)

(24) …, and I really want to compare microsatellites abundance in the genome of clonal plants and non-clonal plants in the same genus … (Grace Qi)

The projects mentioned in Lily Si's and Grace Qi's email constituted part of their future research. They were mentioned in order to show that the applicants were (potential) researchers capable of independent thinking.

Discussing Academic Issues

In the view of the applicants, reading the targeted supervisor's publications and making relevant comments might leave a strong impression on the supervisor. Also, discussing specific academic issues such as a possible research direction would demonstrate independent thinking ability and research potentials. In the following examples, Francis Zhao was talking about his inspiration from reading the supervisor's paper, and Shelly Chen was consulting about a possible research direction with the counterpart.

(25) After reading the inspiring paper [the supervisor's paper] First principles study of the multiferroics $BiFeO_3$, Bi_2FeCrO_6, and $BiCrO_3$ published in 2005, I was amazed by the versatile properties of multiferroics. (Francis Zhao)

(26) now I am curious about the change of dominant community …, how they were altered …, what was the role of specific traits …, and what if we take herbivores and insects into consideration? (Shelly Chen)

But the strategy of discussing academic issues is not frequently used in the initial email, because usually applicants expressed their opinions and views about a specific academic issue in succeeding email exchanges after they received a positive response from the supervisors.

Possible Contribution

To make a convincing self-presentation, some applicants also claim their possible contribution to the field, to the supervisor's lab, or even to the human welfare.

(27) … and also contribute my knowledge and experience to your lab. (Shelly Chen)

(28) According to my understanding, if I had my Ph.D. study under your instruction, my previous research experience can benefit the research in your group. (Sam Wang)

Shelly Chen was explaining that her research background would be beneficial for the supervisor's lab, while Sam Wang articulated explicitly that his work would bring benefits to the supervisor's group. Sam Wang recalled the following:

> After I wrote [my Taoci email], I asked my supervisor Teacher Sun to have a look at it. He didn't make harsh comments on my writing but said that what I wrote wouldn't work… He said, "You should say what you will bring to the supervisor, what contribution you will make to his lab". So I followed his advice to rewrite my email. (Interview transcript 2014)

Teacher Sun's words indicated the stance of a supervisor as admission goal-keeper. To be a prospective candidate, the applicant should emphasize his or her possible contribution to the counterpart. This strategy also shows the quality face of a competitive applicant.

The strategies used in academic *Taoci* above were intended to promote the quality face of applicants, i.e., highlighting their academic preparation, competence, and potential. In doing academic *Taoci*, participants wove their claimed values into the textual lines in a more indirect way. Spencer-Oatey (2007a, p.651) cited Schwartz and Bardi's ten value constructs and relevant qualities under each construct to unpack the face-sensitive attributes for which people may be concerned about. Two constructs—achievement (e.g., success, competence, and ambition) and self-direction (e.g., independent thought, action choosing, creating, and exploring)—were particularly embraced by our participants. The data discussed above involved both of these aspects.

In the stylistic domain, academic *Taoci* was different from *guanxi Taoci* in which it featured technical terms, long sentences, formal wording, and very often an equal positioning with the counterpart. Such formal writing style itself might serve to demonstrate the applicants' competence in academic English, as one aspect of quality face.

7.3.3 Distribution of *Taoci* Strategies

Tables 7.3 and 7.4 present the distributions of *guanxi Taoci* and academic *Taoci*, respectively, focusing exclusively on the main body of the 26 initial email texts provided by the 19 participants. Packages were excluded from this section of the

Table 7.3 Distribution of *guanxi Taoci* strategies N (denominator) = 382

	Power-oriented			Solidarity-oriented		
Participants' email	Honor	Compliment	Magnetic attraction	Previous association	Further interaction	Ingroup member
Jane	1	1	1	/	4	/
Master	/	3	2	/	/	2
Lily	/	/	/	/	1	/
Francis 1	/	3	1	/	/	1
Francis 2	/	/	1	/	1	/
Shelly 1	/	/	1	/	1	/
Shelly 2	/	/	2	/	1	3
Shelly 3	/	/	1	/	2	1
Albert	/	/	/	/	1	/
Brook	/	/	2	1	/	/
Cindy 1	/	/	1	1	/	/
Cindy 2	/	/	/	/	/	1
Leo 1	/	/	1	/	2	3
Leo 2	/	/	1	/	2	/
Grace	/	1	1	/	1	2
Tony	1	/	/	/	3	1
Aeron	/	/	/	/	1	/
Kate	/	/	1	/	3	/
Smith	/	/	/	/	2	/
Richard	/	/	/	/	1	/
Aubrey 1	/	/	1	/	2	1
Aubrey 2	1	/	/	/	/	1
Sam 1	/	/	1	/	4	/
Sam 2	/	/	/	/	/	2
Jack	/	/	/	/	4	/
Julie	1	/	/	/	2	/
Total	4	8	18	3	38	18
Proportion (%)	1.1	2.1	4.7	0.8	9.9	4.7
Proportion (%)	7.9			15.4		
Proportion (%)	23.3					

Table 7.4 Distribution of academic *Taoci* strategies N (denominator) = 382

	Solidarity-oriented	Self-presentation				
Participants' email	Mutual academic interest	Academic background	Publication	Research plan	Possible contribution	Discuss academic issues
Jane	2	5	/	6	/	/
Master	2	10	3	/	/	/
Lily	/	10	/	7	/	1
Francis 1	/	9	/	1	/	4
Francis 2	/	2	/	/	/	/
Shelly 1	1	10	/	1	/	2
Shelly 2	1	11	/	1	1	/
Shelly 3	1	18	/	/	2	1
Albert	2	10	/	/	/	1
Brook	/	10	/	/	/	/
Cindy 1	1	3	/	/	/	/
Cindy 2	/	1	/	/	/	/
Leo 1	3	9	/	/	/	/
Leo 2	2	9	/	3	1	4
Grace	/	7	1	3	/	/
Tony	1	8	/	/	/	/
Aeron	/	9	/	1	/	/
Kate	3	5	2	/	/	/
Smith	2	4	2	1	1	/
Richard	1	8	/	/	/	/
Aubrey 1	/	4	/	/	/	/
Aubrey 2	1	3	/	/	/	/
Sam 1	2	6	3	/	1	/
Sam 2	/	14	/	/	6	/
Jack	2	7	/	/	1	/
Julie	1	11	/	1	/	/
Total	28	203	11	25	13	13
Proportion (%)	7.3	53.1	2.9	6.5	3.4	3.4
Proportion (%)	7.3	69.4				
Proportion (%)	76.7					

analysis since not every applicant provided a package. Frequencies of the strategies appearing in the main body of initial email texts were tabulated on a clause-unit base.

In the 26 email texts, 382 out of the total 525 clauses were identified as containing strategies. Therefore, sentences not falling into *Taoci* categories (such as "so

Fig. 7.1 General distribution of *Taoci* strategies

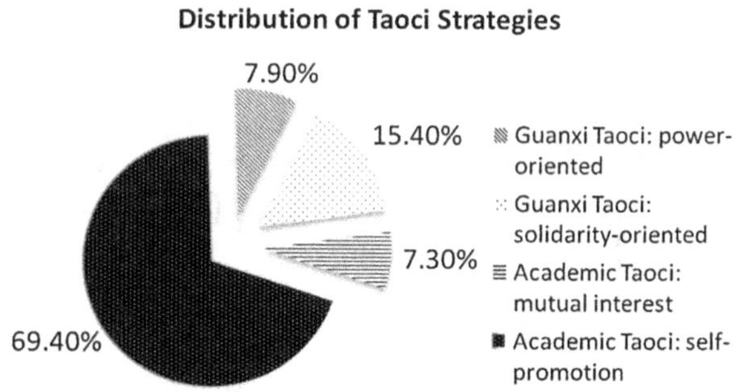

I would like to briefly introduce myself" and "My name is Lily") were excluded from our statistics in the above two tables, with 382 as the denominator for proportion. Among *guanxi Taoci* strategies (Table 7.3), "creating chances for further interaction" was the most prominent, accounting for 9.9 %, followed by "showing magnetic attraction of the supervisor" and "relating oneself with ingroup members" both with a percentage of 4.7 %. The percentage of solidarity-oriented strategies was almost double that of power-oriented ones. Among academic *Taoci* strategies (Table 7.4), revealing one's background was the most conspicuous, with a high percentage of 53.1 %, followed by mutual academic interest at 7.3 %. Probably because most participants were undergraduates and were just on the threshold of doing research, the use of academic achievement as an application strategy was rather infrequent, only 2.9 % of the total.

On the whole, academic *Taoci* was by far more prominent, amounting to 76.7 % of the total strategies used; *guanxi Taoci* comprised 23.3 % of the total. Among the four subcategories, self-presentation or promotion of quality face was the most frequently used, representing a giant share of 69.4 % (Fig. 7.1).

7.4 General Discussion

7.4.1 Modeling Taoci Relations as Embedded in the Strategies

In this section, we will try to model the applicant–supervisor relations into several *Taoci* types. Grounded in the above classification of strategies, the modeling attempts to provide a higher level of abstraction in response to Research Question 2 concerning in what ways *Taoci* email might converge to and diverge from Chinese cultural traditions.

As Figs. 7.2 and 6.3 show, there are altogether five *Taoci* types, which are grouped at a higher level into "*guanxi Taoci*" (Types a, b, and c in Fig. 7.2), and "academic *Taoci*" (Types d and e in Fig. 7.3). *Guanxi Taoci* resorts to either

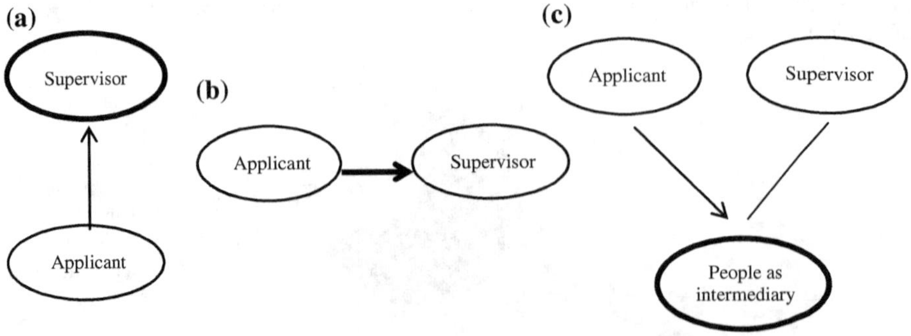

Fig. 7.2 *Guanxi Taoci* (*Arrows* represent directions of *guanxi* "pulling," and *bold lines* indicate prominence). **a**. Power-Oriented *Taoci*. **b**. Solidarity-Oriented *Taoci* (Focusing on form). **c**. Solidarity-Oriented *Taoci* (Focusing on content)

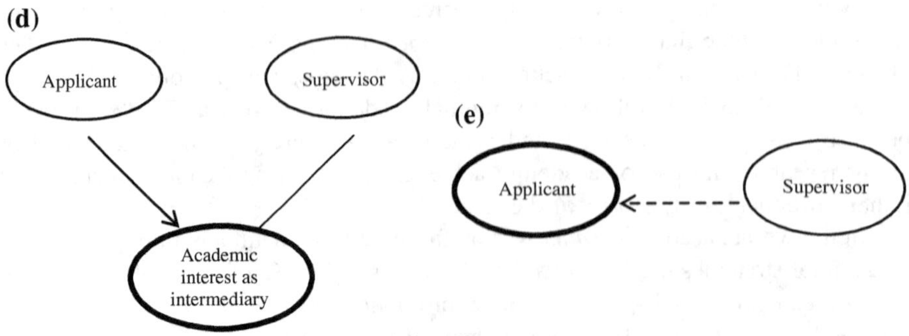

Fig. 7.3 Academic *Taoci* (*Arrows* represent directions of *guanxi* "pulling," *bold lines* indicate prominence, and *dashed lines* index indirect, expected relations). **d**. Interest *Taoci*. **e**. Self-presentation *Taoci*

existing hierarchical power or to a solidarity bond with the supervisor, whereas academic *Taoci* highlights the applicant's academic competence or interest.

In Type a (power-oriented *Taoci*), the applicant is related to the supervisor in a hierarchical relation, as represented by the "showing respect" strategy. The applicant looks up to the supervisor, whose competences and merits are highlighted.

In Type b (solidarity-oriented *Taoci*, focusing on form), forms of communication are highlighted. This corresponds to strategies of keeping frequent contact and creating opportunities for further interaction.

In Type c (solidarity-oriented *Taoci*, focusing on content), the applicant "pulls" him- or herself toward some interpersonal intermediaries associated with the supervisor. The intermediaries are general or personal rather than academic in nature; this can be cultural background, past experiences, personal interest, etc.

Type d (shared academic interest *Taoci*) is very similar to Type c regarding the use of intermediaries; however, the intermediaries are exclusively academic interests.

Type e (self-presentation *Taoci*) focuses on qualities of the applicant him- or herself. It is believed that when the self is presented as a competent candidate, attention and favorable consideration will be obtained from the supervisor. This type corresponds explicitly to quality face.

7.4.2 The Difference Between Taoci Email and Traditional Chinese Culture: Convergence and Divergence

As shown above, the pragmatic meanings of *Taoci* email are multiple, forming complex relations with traditional Chinese culture, convergence (in Types a, b, and c), as well as divergence (in Types d and e). First, the respect for hierarchical social status is maintained, as revealed in the power-oriented *guanxi Taoci* (Type a). Such respect for power is deeply rooted in the rituals or politeness (*li*) of Chinese cultural traditions. Second, much emphasis is put on attending to the other party in the relation or maintenance of interpersonal relations (Type b and Type c), which corresponds with the importance of *guanxi* in Chinese cultural traditions or collectivism in a broad sense. Third, the meaning of *Taoci* in Beijing dialect is preserved to some extent, i.e., trying to build up *guanxi* with someone for practical purposes, mainly through verbal means. However, the original derogative connotation in Beijing dialect is no longer present in the *Taoci* strategies in general. Moreover, the solidarity-oriented *guanxi Taoci* is related to association rights, which is not altogether "Chinese" in its traditional sense. Fourth, a brand new meaning is added, i.e., attracting the interest of others by focusing on a positive self-presentation of quality face. This is contrasted with traditional Chinese *li* in which the focus is no longer the *other* in the relation or the relational hierarchy itself, but *self*, the individual agent characterizing individualism in low-context culture (Hall 1976). This new meaning is particularly evident in the self-presentation of academic *Taoci* (Type d and Type e). The difference between Type d relation (academic interest *Taoci*) and Type c relation (solidarity-oriented *Taoci*, focusing on content) may appear trivial, as both types involve intermediaries. However, this difference is crucial, as there is a shift from the "we" identity in Type c, to the emerging "I" identity in Type d, a shift from collectivistic to individualistic orientation. Academic interest, while shared with the supervisor, nevertheless demonstrates individual characteristics.

The convergence and divergence discussed here might indicate an important change in the Chinese *habitus* of *Taoci* in the field of overseas higher education application, that is, from the dominance of respect for power hierarchy and *guanxi* construction, to more focus on self-presentation of individual strengths. The meaning of "*Taoci*" in *Taoci* email is no longer the same as in dictionaries of the Beijing dialect. Drawing on a Chinese idiom, we may say the individualism-based self-promotion is "new wine in an old bottle." On the whole, with little doubt, what the new signified bottle "*Taoci*" contains is a signified cocktail, i.e., mixture of old and new pragmatic strategies with respective cultural values, but the new is by far the larger proportion, and tastes much stronger. Sapir's metaphor of language as the instrument and thought as the product further captures this idea:

> The instrument makes possible the product, the product refines the instrument. The birth of a new concept is invariably overshadowed by a more or less trained or extended use of old linguistic material; … In most cases the new symbol is but a thing wrought from linguistic material already in existence in ways mapped out by crushingly despotic precedents. (Sapir 1921/2002, p. 14)

From a social constructivist perspective, the despotic "bottle" or "instrument" of language can be quietly transformed to accommodate new "wine" or "product" in subtle connection with the old.

Individual learning of *Taoci* strategies and the related changing of *Taoci* conventions are carried out through collective construction and consumption of discourse conventions in communities, especially with the help of information technology. Applicants' real-life *Taoci* experience was a result of interacting with the meta-discourse of *Taoci*. Interviews with the applicants indicated that all of them had a certain amount of knowledge about *Taoci*, from friends, classmates, teachers, website, or overseas education training organizations (e.g., New Oriental). For example,

> Brook Li: Certainly I have read other people's *Taoci* email. I googled some and also asked for an example version from my upper classmen. After I wrote it, I even asked my classmate and upper classman abroad to correct for me. Actually, the online resources are not very useful for me because it is too general. I think the opinion from my seniors and classmates are more focused and more advanced. (Follow-up email interview 2013)
> Cindy Hu: My best girl friend told me the success depends on both the hard staff (research competence, publications, GPA, etc.) and *Taoci* to let the supervisor know you very well. I kept that in my mind. (Email interview 2013)
> Shelly Chen: I didn't consult my teachers or classmates. But I have sought information on the Internet, for example I read an article on *Douban*[13] about how to write, what to write, what not to write. (Follow-up email interview 2013)
> Sam Wang: I didn't follow those *Taoci* models on the website. The training organization that I joined had given me some guidance. I just wrote it by myself and sent it to the professors… However this email (the second initial email he provided), I showed it to my supervisor here (in China). He said my writing wouldn't work… I followed his advice and modified. We discussed my writing for about four or five times through email. And this version you have is the final one sent to the (American) supervisor. (Interview transcript 2014)

Various types of meta-discourse influenced our informants' practice, by giving them guidance and providing writing tips. On the other hand, the continuous practice of making the new wine will further reinforce the transformation. Such practice, as the maintenance and transformation of cultural *habitus*, is perhaps a necessary characteristic of English as a Lingua Franca.

[13]Douban (豆瓣网) is a Chinese website mainly about film reviews and book reviews. It is also an important forum for people to communicate online. (http://www.douban.com/).

7.5 Conclusion

We have examined the specific *Taoci* strategies used by Chinese applicants in their *Taoci* email written to potential future supervisors, and classified them into two major types–*guanxi Taoci* and academic *Taoci*. While *guanxi Taoci* focuses on interpersonal relations and retains the dynamics of traditional cultural vestige, academic *Taoci* focused on the individual's academic competence, and was associated with "quality face" (Spencer-Oatey 2007a, b, c) which embeds Western values. Types of applicant–supervisor relations as embedded in these *Taoci* strategies were also generalized. In the collected data, mixed use of strategies was not uncommon, but "academic *Taoci*" was the most common. Such results indicate a prominent change in the speech act of "*Taoci*," creating new meanings in an (inter)cultural context. It can be considered, based on a Chinese secular idiom contrary to the Biblical sense, "new wine in an old bottle".[14]

However, our research is not impeccable. As we mentioned above, *Taoci* email is quite private and it is difficult for the researchers to have access to a larger scope of data. Furthermore, some participants provide more data and participated in our interviews while others did not, which resulted in no strict systematic correspondence between types of data collected. In addition, the present research did not have a reference group of similar email writing by students from other cultures. Future research might work on a wider scope of data, explore the historical dimension of discourse convention transformation, or make cross-cultural comparisons.

Acknowledgments We owe special gratitude to all research participants who provided email texts and (or) participated the interviews. We would also like to thank Dr. Yuanshan Chen and the reviewers for their valuable comments and suggestions for the revision of this paper.

References

Ambrose, Yeo-chi King. 1991. Kuan-hsi and network building: A sociological interpretation. *Daedalus* 120(2): 63–84.

Bourdieu, Pierre. 1986. The forms of capital. In *The handbook of theory and research for the sociology of education*, ed. John G. Richardson, 241–258. New York: Greenwood.

Brown, Penelope, and Stephen C. Levinson. 1987. *Politeness: Some universals in language usage*. Cambridge: Cambridge University Press.

[14]See Article note. The "May Fourth" (1919) signifies a New Cultural Movement or cultural and linguistic transition in China at the beginning of the twentieth century. During this period, many new ideas were imported from the West, and classical Chinese was replaced by modern Chinese. Nevertheless, during and after this transitional period, some old linguistic forms have been retained for creative formulation and expression of new ideas, thus constituting a positive tradition of "古为今用" (making the past serve the present). The positive (or neutral) meaning of "new wine in the old bottle" contrary to the Biblical sense was acquired during this period.

Chang, Hui-Ching, and G. Richard Holt. 1991. More than relationship: Chinese interaction and the principle of Guan-hsi. *Communication Quarterly* 39: 251–271.

Chen, Gang (ed.). 1985. *Beijing colloquial terms dictionary*. Beijing: The Commercial Press. (陈刚 (编) .1985.《北京方言词典》 北京:商务印书馆.).

Chen, Guo-Ming. 2010. Towards transcultural understanding: A harmony theory of Chinese communication. In *Study on Chinese communication behaviors*, ed. Guoming Cheng, 196–217. Hong Kong: China Review Academic Publishers.

Farrer, James. 2002. "Idle talk": Neighborhood gossip as a medium of social communication in reform era Shanghai. In *Social connections in China: Institutions, culture and the changing nature of guanxi*, ed. Thomas Gold, Doug Guthrie, and David L. Wank. Cambridge: Cambridge University Press.

Gao, Ge, and Stella Ting-Toomey. 1998. *Communicating effectively with the Chinese*. Thousand Oaks: SAGE Publication Inc.

Gao, Aijun and Ming Fu. (eds.) 2001. *Beijing dialect dictionary*. Beijing: Peking University Press. (高艾军、傅民(编). 2001.《北京话词典》北京:北京大学出版社).

Goffman, Erving. 1959. *The presentation of self in everyday life*. London: Penguin Group.

Goffman, Erving. 1967. *Interaction ritual: Essays in face-to-face behavior*. Chicago: Aldine Publishing Company.

Gu, Yue Guo. 1990. Politeness phenomena in modern Chinese. *Journal of Pragmatics* 14: 237–257.

Gu, Yue Guo. 1992. Politeness, pragmatics and culture. *Foreign Language Teaching and Research* 4:10–17. (顾曰国, 1992, 礼貌、语用与文化.《外语教学与研究》4: 10–17).

Gudykunst, William. B. and Matsumoto, Yuko. 1996. Cross-cultural variability of communication in personal relationships. In *Communication in personal relationships across cultures*, eds. William B. Gudykunst, Stella Ting-Toomey and Tsukasa Nishida, 19–56. Thousand Oaks: SAGE Publication, Inc.

Gunthner, Susanne. 2007. Argumentation and resulting problems in the negotiation of rapport in a German-Chinese conversation. In *Culturally speaking: Managing rapport through talk across cultures*, ed. Helen Spencer-Oatey, 217–239. Continuum: London. (republished by Shanghai Foreign Language Education Press).

Hall, Edward T. 1976. *Beyond culture*. Garden City, New York: Anchor.

Hofstede, Geert. 1991. *Cultures and organizations: Software of the mind*. London: McGraw-Hill.

Jacobs, J.Bruce. 1979. A preliminary model of particularistic ties in Chinese political alliance: Kang-ch'ing and Kuan-hsi in a rural Taiwanese township. *China Quarterly* 78: 237–273.

Jenkins, Jennifer. 2014. *English as a lingua franca in the international university*. New York: Routledge.

Kipnis, Andrew B. 1996. The language of gifts: Managing guanxi in north China village. *Modern China* 22(3): 285–314.

Leech, Geoffrey. N. 1983. *Principles of pragmatics*. New York: Longman.

Legge, James. (trans.). 2014. *The Chinese classics: Confucian analects, the great learning, the Doctrine of the mean*. Shanghai: Shanghai Sanlian Bookstore Press.

Liu, Xiao Ling. (2011). *Towards a pragmatic study of euphemisms in A Dream of Red Mansions: A rapport management approach* (unpublished PhD dissertation, Shanghai International Studies University.

Matsumoto, Yoshiko. 1988. Reexamination of the universality of face: Politeness phenomena in Japanese. *Journal of Pragmatics* 12: 403–426.

Pavlidou, Theodossia-Soula. 2007. Telephone conversations in Greek and German: Attending to the relationship aspect of communication. In *Culturally speaking: Managing rapport through talk across cultures*, ed. Helen Spencer-Oatey, 121–142. Continuum: London (republished by Shanghai Foreign Language Education Press).

Ran, Yong Ping. 2012. Rapport management in interpersonal communication and its violation (in Chinese). *Foreign Language Education* 33(4): 1–5. (冉永平, 2012, 人际交往中的和谐管理模式及其违反. 《外语教学》 33(4): 1–5.).

Sapir, Edward. 1921/2002. *Language: An introduction to the study of speech*. Beijing: Foreign Language Teaching and Research Press.

Searle, John R. 1976. A classification of illocutionary acts. *Language in Society* 5(1): 1–23.

Shenkar, Oded and Simcha Ronen. 1987. The cultural context of negotiations: The implications of Chinese interpersonal norms. *The Journal of Applied Behavioral Science* 23(2): 263–275.

Spencer-Oatey, Helen. 2002. Managing rapport in talk: Using rapport sensitive incidents to explore the motivational concerns underlying the management of relations. *Journal of Pragmatics* 34: 529–545.

Spencer-Oatey, Helen. 2007a. Theories of identity and the analysis of face. *Journal of Pragmatics* 39: 639–656.

Spencer-Oatey, Helen. 2007b. Introduction: Language, culture and rapport management. In *Culturally speaking: Managing rapport through talk across culture*s, ed. Helen Spencer-Oatey, 1–8. Continuum: London, (republished by Shanghai Foreign Language Education Press).

Spencer-Oatey, Helen. 2007c. Rapport management: A framework for analysis. In *Culturally speaking: Managing rapport through talk across culture*s, ed. Helen Spencer-Oatey, 11–46. Continuum: London, (republished by Shanghai Foreign Language Education Press 2007).

Spencer-Oatey, Helen, and Jianyu Xing. 2003. Managing rapport in intercultural business interactions: A comparison of two Chinese-British welcome meetings. *Journal of Intercultural Studies* 24(1): 33–46.

Triandis, Harry C. 1990. Cross-cultural studies of individualism-collectivism. In *Nebraska Symposium on Motivation*, ed. John J. Berman, Vol. 37, 41–133. Lincoln: University of Nebraska Press.

Watts, Richard J., Sachiko Ide and Konrad Ehlich (eds.). 2005. *Politeness in language: Studies in its history, theory, and practice* (2nd revised edition). Berlin and New York: Mouton de Gruyter.

Wen, Chong-yi. 2012. An investigation of Chinese national character: A value orientation perspective. In *Chinese characteristics* (3rd revised edition in simplified Chinese), eds. Yih-yuan Lee and Kuo-shu Yang, 40–71. Beijing: China Remin Univeristy Press. (李亦园、杨国枢(主编). 2012. 《中国人的性格》(第三版,简体中文版) 北京:中国人民大学出版社).

Xiao, Lin. 2014. Rapport management in Chinese "Taoci" email. *Linguistic Research* 15: 165–174. (肖琳,2014,中文 "套磁" 邮件中的人际关系管理.《语言学研究》 15: 165–174.

Xinhua dictionary of idioms. 2013. Beijing: The Commercial Press. (商务印书馆辞书研究中心(编). 2013. 《新华成语大辞典》. 北京:商务印书馆.).

Yan, Yun Xiang. 1996. The culture of guanxi a north China village. *The China Journal* 35: 1–25.

Yang, Mayfair Mei-hui. 1994. *Gifts, favors and banquets: The art of social relationships in China*. Ithaca: Cornell University Press.

Yum, June Ock. 1988. The impact of Confucianism on interpersonal relationships and communication patterns in East Asia. *Communication Monographs* 55: 374–388.

Author Biographies

Lin Xiao (肖琳) is a Ph.D. student in linguistics at the Research Institute of Linguistics and Applied Linguistics, School of Foreign Languages, Peking University in China. Her major academic interest is sociolinguistics and intercultural communication. Currently, she is working on Chinese study-abroad applicants' identity construction in intercultural email interaction.

Yihong Gao (高一虹) is Professor of Linguistics and Director of the Research Institute of Linguistics and Applied Linguistics, School of Foreign Languages, Peking University in China. Currently, she serves as vice president of China English Language Education Association. Her major research interest lies in the social psychology and socio-cultural contexts of English language learning and teaching.

Chapter 8
Strategies Used in Chinese University Students' ELF Emails to Remedy or Prevent Problems in Understanding

Wei Ren

Abstract Although there has been a steady growth of empirical studies investigating spoken English as a lingua franca (ELF) usage in institutional settings, less attention has been paid to written texts. Email communication, despite its popularity nowadays, has scarcely been examined. To extend the existing ELF research into email discourse, this study investigates Chinese university students' ELF emails in intercultural communication. The data were collected from 30 students in Mainland China, mainly consisting of inquiries about prospective programs, asking for help, financial disputes, and daily communication on campus. The paper analyzes and discusses the remedial and preemptive pragmatic strategies employed by the Chinese university students to remedy or prevent problems of understanding in their ELF emails. The results indicate that when the Chinese university students encountered misunderstanding in ELF emails, they employed metalinguistic comments to signal the problem. When they could not understand some utterances in the email they received, they tended to point them out straightforwardly using focused questions and metalinguistic comments. In addition, they often employed preemptive strategies such as 'building shared knowledge and common ground' and 'confirmation checks' to ensure the success of the ELF email communication.

Keywords English as a lingua franca (ELF) · Email communication · Remedial strategies · Preemptive strategies

8.1 Introduction

English as a Lingua Franca (henceforth, ELF) refers to the use of English as the communicative medium of choice in an interaction, which is not dominated by native speakers of English. Research on ELF started relatively recently. It was only

W. Ren (✉)
National Key Research Center for Linguistics and Applied Linguistics,
Guangdong University of Foreign Studies, Guangzhou, China
e-mail: renweixz@yahoo.com

Y. Chen et al. (eds.), *Email Discourse Among Chinese Using English as a Lingua Franca*, DOI 10.1007/978-981-287-888-5_8

discussed occasionally in the last century (e.g., Firth 1996; House 1999; Knapp 1987). A landmark of change was the publication of Jenkins' (2000) extensive study of ELF pronunciation. This book inspired more research into ELF, as witnessed by a dramatically increased interest in ELF since then, resulting in many monographs (e.g., Björkman 2013; Cogo and Dewey 2012; Jenkins 2007, 2014; Kirkpatrick 2010; Mauranen 2012; Seidlhofer 2011; Smit 2010), edited books (e.g., Archibald et al. 2011; Knapp and Meierkord 2002; Mauranen and Ranta 2009), and a large number of individual articles in journals and collected volumes. ELF has become a major focus of discussions and activities among both applied linguists and English language teaching professionals (Jenkins et al. 2011). The majority of the ELF research, however, has been devoted to spoken discourse in various settings, mainly academic and business settings (see Jenkins et al. 2011 for a state-of-the-art review of studies on ELF). Little attention has been paid to written discourse from an ELF perspective.

Even among the few available studies on written discourse in ELF research, the main focus is on the difficulty that ELF writers encounter in academic publishing (e.g., Flowerdew 2008; Ingvarsdóttir and Arnbjörnsdóttir 2013; Lillis and Curry 2010), aiming to call for more discussion on the appropriateness of adhering to English native speakers' standards (Flowerdew 2008; Ingvarsdóttir and Arnbjörnsdóttir 2013) or the necessity of applying findings of ELF research to writing pedagogy (Horner 2011). That is, research has to date barely investigated the characteristics of ELF written discourse. There is indeed an attitude that ELF is unhelpful and ELF users will be significantly disadvantaged when it comes to written language (Sowden 2012). Sowden, for example, argues that cultural sympathy and interpersonal skills are crucial for ELF speakers to communicate successfully. When writing is involved, however, in his words, "the need for clarity, and rhetorical coherence, in the absence of scope for interpersonal negotiation and with a potentially heterogeneous audience, forces both writer and reader to give greater weight to recognized rules of grammar and syntax" (Sowden 2012, p. 95). Until substantial empirical research carried out in real-life contexts becomes available, we will not be able to say with confidence what characteristics ELF written discourse possesses.

To shed light on this matter, it is necessary to examine in detail the nature of ELF written discourse in intercultural communication. This paper reports on the findings of an explorative study that was conducted to investigate Chinese university students' real-life ELF emails. The purpose of this study is to analyze the remedial and preemptive pragmatic strategies employed by Chinese university students in their ELF emails to solve and to avert problems of understanding to achieve communicative effectiveness. A remedial strategy refers to a pragmatic strategy occurring after the signals of trouble, whereas a preemptive strategy refers to a pragmatic strategy occurring without or before any signal of non- or misunderstanding has taken place.

The rest of the paper is structured as follows: first, I will discuss the working definition of ELF adopted in this study, followed by review of the literature on email discourse, ELF research on written language and on pragmatic strategies in oral communication. Definitions of understanding, non-understanding, and misunderstanding are also introduced, before I explain the methodology of this study. The findings are then presented, followed by discussion and conclusion.

8.2 Literature Review

8.2.1 Definition of ELF

As Jenkins (2014, p. 24) notes, defining ELF is "problematic and controversial." There is still disparity regarding the inclusion of native speakers of English (hereafter NESs) in ELF research. Some scholars (e.g., Firth 1996; House 1999, 2002; Meierkord 2002) do not include native speakers of English in their definition. For example, Firth (1996) describes ELF as follows (Firth does not use the exact term ELF): "*English is used as a 'lingua franca'* –a 'contact language' between persons who share neither a common native language nor a common (national) culture, and for whom English is the chosen *foreign* language of communication" (Firth 1996, p. 240, italics original). Likewise, House (1999) also excludes NESs in her early definition of ELF: "ELF interactions are defined as interactions between members of two or more different lingua cultures in English, for none of whom English is the mother tongue" (House 1999, p. 74).

By contrast, most ELF researchers do not exclude NESs from their definition of ELF (House 2014; Jenkins 2014; Mauranen 2012; Seidlhofer 2011; among others). Seidlhofer points out that ELF should be regarded as "*any use of English among speakers of different first languages for whom English is the communicative medium of choice, and often the only option*" (Seidlhofer 2011, p. 7; italics original). Native speakers of English are thus included in Seidlhofer's definition. Jenkins explicitly includes NESs in her definition. She refers to ELF as "the world's most extensive contemporary use of English, in essence, English when it is used as a contact language between people from different first languages (*including native English speakers*)" (Jenkins 2014, p. 2; italics added).

The present study focuses on pragmatic strategies employed in Chinese university students' email, rather than email discourses of both senders and recipients. An 'anonymous' medium such as the Internet raises problems for reliable information about participant's ethnicity, gender, age, social class, education level, etc. (Herring 2001, p. 621). There are many situations in which email senders are not certain whether their recipients are native speakers of English. In addition, as noted by Elder and Davies (2006), ELF may as well be understood as the use of English in an interaction where all the participants "share the same or (similar) first language" (Elder and Davies 2006, p. 282). Therefore, in the present study I shall include ELF emails sent by the Chinese university students regardless of whether they were addressed to native speakers of English or whether the receiver shares the same L1 (Chinese in this case).

8.2.2 Previous Research on Email Discourse

Email represents a popular means of electronic communication that is prevalent in university students' life today. Due to its virtual nature, it has been observed that email is a hybrid form of discourse which shares features with both spoken and written language (Crystal 2006, 2011; Herring 2001). Email discourse shares some of the attributes of face-to-face interaction such as an informal style (Félix-Brasdefer 2012). Nevertheless, Dürscheid and Frehner (2013) argue that email per se is 'text-based.' In emails, "there may be oral features, but these features are situated on the conceptual level and not on the medial one" (Dürscheid and Frehner 2013, p. 47).

Email is an asynchronous medium, which does not require that users be logged on at the same time in order to send and receive the message. With regard to its interactional structure, email discourse is characterized as 'disrupted turn adjacency' because "messages are posted in the order received by the system, without regard for what they are responding to, and lack of simultaneous *feedback* caused by reduced audiovisual cues" (Herring 2001, p. 618; italics original). In addition, email is a 'one-way' transmission (Herring 2001, p. 615): it is transmitted in its entirety as a single unit, which may convey what would have been communicated through multiple turns in face-to-face communication. The recipient does not know that an email is being addressed to him/her until it arrives. S/he therefore cannot provide simultaneous feedback to the email s/he receives. Furthermore, an email can also be edited or deleted without the knowledge of the intended recipient.

As email is becoming an accepted means of communication for both university students and their professors (and other faculty members), there have been many investigations into students' pragmatic competence in writing emails. Nevertheless, these studies primarily examine pragmatic performance of native and/or nonnative speakers of English and aim to identify similarities and differences between the two groups (e.g., Biesenbach-Lucas 2005, 2007; Chen 2006; Economidou-Kogetsidis 2011; Félix-Brasdefer 2012; just to name a few). To date little research has been carried out to investigate email discourse from an ELF perspective.

8.2.3 ELF Research on Written English

As stated above, the majority of ELF research to date has been devoted to spoken discourse, whereas less attention has been paid to written discourse. Among those few studies available, the primary concern is the difficulty of writing in English as an additional language for nonnative speakers of English (they do not necessarily use the term ELF). Flowerdew (2008), for example, highlights the disadvantages that writers of English as an additional language (EAL) experience in international publishing. It emphasizes that judgments regarding the acceptability and otherwise of EAL writers' English might better be accorded to intelligibility in individual disciplinary communities rather than conformity to 'standard English.'

Lillis and Curry (2010) report on the nature and politics of academic writing and publishing from the experiences and perceptions of academics who work in countries in the Expanding Circle (Kachru 1992). In these countries, English-medium publications are attributed higher status than publications in other languages. The authors explore the impact of the dominance of English on the writing, publishing, and achievements and ambitions of the multilingual scholars, for whom English is not the official or dominant language of communication. They not only face limited access to resources but also carry the additional burden of having to write at an appropriate level of English proficiency.

The extra burden of writing and publishing in English has also been observed in Ingvarsdóttir and Arnbjörnsdóttir's (2013) investigation into academic writing in Iceland. Ingvarsdóttir and Arnbjörnsdóttir describe the perceptions of Icelandic academics on using English in their scientific pursuits, based on a survey followed up by interviews. Even though the respondents claim that their general English is good, the majority confess to an added workload and needing assistance with their academic English. However, despite pressure from the university to increase international publication, no official writing support is offered. The paper calls for more discussion on the appropriateness of adhering to English native speakers standards by journals to which nonnative users of English contribute (Flowerdew 2008).

Unlike the above three studies focusing on academic publishing, Horner (2011) addresses the issue of ELF writing and writing pedagogy from the perspective of the field of U.S. composition studies. He argues the possibility of identifying how the attitude toward and strategies in ELF oral communication can be applied to writing instructions. Against the traditional transmission model of writing pedagogy "aiming to transmit a stabilized core of forms, practices and meanings" (Horner 2011, p. 301), the author calls for an ELF writing pedagogy that puts negotiation of meaning and an exploratory approach at the center of writing, "in which students have as much to contribute, and as much say, in determining acceptability" (Horner 2011, p. 307). However, Horner primarily takes as a focus the conceptual discussion of the possibility of an ELF writing pedagogy, rather than empirical investigation into the strategies employed in real ELF writings.

As the above review shows, available ELF studies on written language seem to investigate primarily either the attitudinal and/or pedagogical issues related to academic ELF writing and publishing, such as difficulties faced by academics from countries in the Expanding Circle in disseminating their research, or the possibilities and/or appropriateness of adopting strategies observed in ELF oral communication into ELF writing pedagogy. There is a need for more emphasis in empirical research on the nature of written ELF discourse (Ingvarsdóttir and Arnbjörnsdóttir 2013).

8.2.4 Pragmatics Strategies in Oral ELF Communication

This section reviews previous research exploring ELF speakers' pragmatic strategies in oral communication. Among the earliest pragmatic studies investigating ELF settings was Firth's work (Firth 1996), where Danish export managers and their foreign partners' business telephone conversations were examined through conversation analysis. A number of strategies have been identified in this ELF business situation. The first of these is termed the 'let-it-pass' strategy, where speakers let an unclear word or utterance pass. The second strategy is the 'make-it-normal' strategy, where the hearer treats the speaker's nonstandard usage as normal and produces reformulations of the other's opaque usage.

However, the 'let-it-pass' strategy has not been documented in Mauranen's (2006) study on ELF discourses in academic settings. Analyzing authentic academic ELF discussions, Mauranen observes that ELF speakers in her corpus do not let "vague or potentially incorrect understanding pass" (2006, p. 135). Instead, her participants cooperate toward achieving a sufficient basis in their mutual understanding to continue the discourse. Therefore, Mauranen argues that the 'let-it-pass' strategy may not be a feasible option in academic discussion. Although straightforward misunderstandings occur infrequently in Mauranen's corpus, when they occur, interlocutors employ various remedial strategies to solve the communication problem. For instance, the misunderstandings are signaled directly (by direct questions or repetition of the troublesome item) or indirectly (e.g., the minimal incomprehension signal 'hm?' or an unspecific question such as 'what?'). These remedial strategies indicate that ELF interlocutors exhibit a high degree of interactional and pragmatic competence to signal misunderstanding and/or non-understanding so as to solve the problem of understanding and ensure the effectiveness of communication (see Sect. 8.2.5 for distinction of non-understanding and misunderstanding). ELF speakers' employment of such remedial strategies have also been documented in Pitzl (2005), Watterson (2008), and Cogo and Dewey (2012).

In addition to the remedial strategies for non-understanding and/or misunderstanding, another focus of ELF pragmatics research has been on how ELF speakers employ proactive strategies to successfully preempt problems of understanding. For example, Mauranen (2006) notes that ELF speakers employ preemptive strategies such as clarification, self-repair, and repetition frequently to prevent misunderstandings and to ensure mutual intelligibility in academic ELF discussion. Likewise, Kaur (2009) highlights how her ELF students display a considerable amount of repetition and rephrasing as preemptive strategies to help avert problems of understanding in specific interactional contexts, such as after a prolonged silence, minimal response, or overlapping talk. Similar results have also been found by Cogo (2009, 2010), Kaur (2011b, 2012), and Cogo and Dewey (2012).

8.2.5 *Understanding, Non-understanding, and Misunderstanding*

When it comes to investigation into communicative problems, there has been a wide range of terminologies used in the literature to refer to various problems of communication. Adding to the complexity, there is lack of consistency in the use of these terms. Different researchers use different terms for the same phenomenon, whereas the same term may be used to refer to different phenomena (Gass and Varonis 1991; Tzanne 1999). Due to the limited space, this paper cannot review the vast array of terminology related to problems of understanding. Nevertheless, it is necessary to be explicit about how the terms 'understanding,' 'non-understanding,' and 'misunderstanding' are defined in the present paper.

Following a social perspective on understanding such as that of Roberts (1996), understanding in the present paper is referred to as an "interactive and jointly constructed" process (Roberts 1996, p. 17), which is dynamic and cooperative and which both sides of a conversation (or email exchange in the context of the present paper) actively engage in. Rather than placing all the responsibility for understanding on the listener/recipient, the speaker/sender is also responsible for both preempting anticipated problems of understanding and handling non- and/or misunderstandings when they arise.

Non-understanding occurs when the listener/recipient "realizes that s/he cannot make sense of (part of) an utterance," while misunderstanding refers to the situation where the listener/recipient "achieves an interpretation which makes sense to her or him—but it wasn't the one the speaker [sender] meant" (Bremer 1996, p. 40). The key to distinguish non-understanding from misunderstanding is the listener's or the recipient's awareness of the problem. This distinction between non- and misunderstanding is widely followed in ELF studies on problems of understanding (e.g., Cogo and Dewey 2012; Kaur 2011a; Pitzl 2005). However, it has to be reiterated that the distinction is neither absolute nor clear cut (Bremer 1996; Kaur 2011a). It is possible that the interlocutor misunderstands something uttered by the speaker but "neither of the speakers is aware or at least neither displays any awareness of it" (Cogo and Dewey 2012, p. 116). Furthermore, misunderstanding can result from partial or non-understanding of a prior utterance as well (Bremer 1996).

8.3 Methodology

8.3.1 *Research Questions*

The present study aims to contribute to the field of ELF research by investigating Chinese university students' real-life ELF emails. The purpose of the present study is to examine what pragmatic strategies Chinese university students employ to achieve understanding, negotiate non-understanding, and resolve misunderstanding in writing ELF emails in intercultural communication. To be specific, the study is designed to address the following three research questions:

1. When misunderstanding occurs in their ELF emails, what pragmatic strategies do Chinese university students employ to remedy the email communication?
2. When non-understanding occurs in their ELF emails, what pragmatic strategies do Chinese university students employ to remedy the email communication?
3. What pragmatic strategies do Chinese university students employ to preempt problems of understanding in their ELF emails?

8.3.2 Data and Participants

The data for the present study are a natural email corpus of 215 emails collected from 30 Chinese university students. The data collected in the present study consist entirely of authentic emails in the sense that none of them have been elicited for research purposes. The emails consist of inquires about prospective programs, financial disputes, appointment arrangements, asking for help, and daily communication. The participants were informed that it would be better to contribute both the emails they sent and the emails they responded to or received, in which the email exchanges would help understand the communication exchange. Nevertheless, regardless of whether emails from the other side were available, only the Chinese university students' emails were counted and analyzed. The participants contributed various numbers of emails, ranging from 1 to 34, with an average of 7.2.

The participants were recruited by employing "a friend of friend" technique (Milroy 1987). Fifteen of them were studying for their bachelor's degree, seven were studying for their master's degree, and eight were studying for their doctoral degree when they wrote the emails. Thirteen of them were receiving their education in an English-speaking country and the rest were studying in Mainland China. They all agreed to participate in the study by sharing email messages they sent for various purposes. They were informed that they were free to choose which emails they would like to share and they could delete whatever information they considered confidential.

Among the 215 emails collected, 88 (40.93 %) were sent to native speakers of English, 95 (44.19 %) were sent to speakers whose L1 was not English, and the other 32 (14.88 %) emails were sent to speakers whose L1 was hard to determine (the sender had no knowledge of the recipient's L1 background). As explained in Sect. 8.2.1, the present study focuses on pragmatic strategies in Chinese university students' email, rather than the email discourse of both senders and recipients. Therefore, all 215 emails were included in the present study.

Data presented in the present study will remain as they are in the original emails. That is, I did not correct any misspelling or change any linguistic features. To save space, I will use /…/ to indicate that irrelevant portions of messages are omitted, and *** to show that sensitive information (e.g., names) was deleted for confidentiality. In addition, italics are added for emphasis (refer to the Appendix for illustration of symbols used in the examples).

8.3.3 Data Analysis

This study focuses on the remedial and preemptive pragmatic strategies Chinese university students employ in their ELF emails to avert problems of understanding and to resolve non- and misunderstanding when they occur. I first carefully read all the email interactions collected. Then I identified the instances indicating problems of understanding in the emails, including signaling non-understanding and/or misunderstanding, and the resolution of those problems. In addition, I also looked for pragmatic strategies working toward understanding by preempting anticipated problems of understanding.

As observed in previous studies (e.g., Mauranen 2006), straightforward misunderstandings occur infrequently in ELF communication. ELF speakers often employ various proactive strategies to prevent problems of understanding. Analysis only focusing on remedial pragmatic strategies employed in instance of non-understanding or misunderstanding may overlook instances in which ELF users employ preemptive strategies to prevent problems of understanding, thus cannot reveal the whole picture of the ELF users' pragmatic competence. Therefore, the present study analyzed both remedial strategies engaged in by the author to signal or solve a prior non- or misunderstanding, as well as preemptive strategies employed to avert potential understanding problems.

8.4 Findings

This section presents findings of the pragmatic strategies employed in the Chinese university students' ELF email data by concentrating first on remedial strategies, then moving on to preemptive strategies. All names of the participants used in the examples are pseudonyms.

8.4.1 Remedial Strategies Signaling Misunderstanding

As discussed in Sect. 8.2.5, following Bremer (1996, p. 40), misunderstanding in the present study refers to the situation where the recipient achieves an interpretation of part of an email discourse which makes sense to him or her—but it was not the one the sender meant. The present study investigated the Chinese university students' ELF email discourse, thus this section only analyzes situations where the

Chinese university students noticed a problem in their recipient's interpretation of their previous emails, to explore what pragmatic strategies they employed to signal the misunderstanding, and to remedy the email communication.

Only two instances of straightforward misunderstanding (out of 215 emails) were observed in the present study, both sent by the same student. In the first example, the student Hao had emailed an administrative staff member at a university he applied to, inquiring about how to pay his application fee, as shown in (1):

(1) Hao: /…/ I write to inquire about how to send the application fee.
Now I am preparing the application to ***. Since I don't have an international credit card yet, I have to make a draft through the bank. So I wonder who shall I send it to. /…/

However, Hao received a reply from the admission office simply telling him how to apply to the university. Therefore, in another email, Hao pointed out the misunderstanding, as follows:

(2) Hao: /…/ Thanks for your reply.
However, *I think you might misunderstand me*. I have chosen the program and contacted the supervisor. Now I want to send my application fee through draft. So I want to know who shall I send this draft to. /…/

In this situation, Hao's first email was intended to inquire to whom he should send his application fee. The reply he received, however, did not contain the information he needed. The administrative person (given that the university was in an English-speaking country, it is likely that the administrator would be a native speaker of English) only replied to Hao concerning how to apply to the university generally, which did not help answer Hao's specific question at all. The reason the administrative officer missed Hao's question is unknown and beyond our discussion in this paper. In the student's second email, the misunderstanding was pointed out straightforwardly by the explicit metalinguistic comment, '*I think you might misunderstand me.*' Hao then explained his problem by telling his recipient which stage of application he was at and what kind of help he was seeking. As Vasseur et al. (1996) argue, metalinguistic queries and comments are the most explicit, direct, and specific means to signal the understanding problem. This example thus indicated, when misunderstanding occurred in the Chinese student's email exchange and had been recognized, the student was capable of taking action to remedy the problem, in the above example by the most explicit means—'metalinguistic comments,' plus elaboration of the situation.

As one reviewer pointed out, alternatively, the student could have put the blame on himself by saying "I probably did not make myself clear in my previous email." There was, however, no such 'blame of the speaker him/herself' observed in the present study. In the other case of signaling misunderstanding, the Chinese student Hao did blame himself by writing "Sorry for the misunderstanding I had" when he replied to his tutor concerning the length of a proposal he was expected to submit.

However, it was different from "blame of the speaker him/herself" pointed out by the reviewer. In the latter case, Hao was the interpreter for the assignment requirement. Although he took responsibility for the misunderstanding, he was the recipient rather than the sender of the misunderstood requirement. Since the present study was an explorative study with a small dataset (only two instances of signaling misunderstanding were observed in the present study), we cannot draw any conclusion regarding whether this kind of 'blame of the speaker him/herself' occurs in ELF email communication. Future studies including a large number of ELF emails would be needed to explore whether ELF users distinguish 'blame of the recipient' (e.g., 'you might misunderstand me') from 'blame of the sender him/herself' (e.g., 'I did not make myself clear').

8.4.2 Remedial Strategies Signaling Non-understanding

In this section, I will present the Chinese students' pragmatic strategies for negotiating non-understandings in their ELF emails to remedy their email communication. To recapitulate, non-understandings refer to situations when the recipient realizes that s/he cannot make sense of (part of) an utterance. In the present study, non-understandings were signaled by two strategies: focused questions and metalinguistic comments.

8.4.2.1 Focused Questions

As Mauranen (2006, p. 132) observes, "direct, focused questions on an expression or its meaning are perhaps the easiest to detect and also the most unequivocal signs of lack of understanding." In the next example, the student Jia received an email which stated that she had overdue invoices on her account. She had made all her payments thus she did not understand what the invoices were for. Therefore, she pointed out the problem explicitly in her reply, as in (3):

(3) Jia: /…/ *What is this overdue about? if is about the tuition, i have payed the tatal tuition fee 2 months age. i do not think i have ant overdue.* thank /…/

As displayed in example (3), Jia explicated the problem of understanding by a specific and direct question about the overdue payment, and then made clear that she had paid her tuition fee two months before. Afterward, Jia received another email from her university, telling her that the email had been sent to her in error and restating that her tuition fees had been paid in full. Thus a mutual understanding was successfully negotiated.

Focused questions do not necessarily take the form of special questions. As shown in example (4) below, the student Tao also successfully negotiated a situation of non-understanding, although he did not use a *wh*-question.

(4) Tao: /…/ I consulted the school website and found the deadline for *** is June 1 while in your last email you wrote 13 May. *I wonder is there any mistake?* /…/

As stated in Tao's email above, the student was preparing his application for a scholarship. The school website said that the deadline was June 1, whereas his tutor (NNES, L1: Dutch) told him the deadline was May 13. Tao thus emailed his tutor regarding the contradictory date. His request, although taking the form of a conditional clause (Blum-Kulka et al. 1989), '*I wonder is there any mistake,*' served as a focused question about the application due date in this context.

8.4.2.2 Metalinguistic Comment

Another strategy signaling non-understanding observed in this study is metalinguistic comment. In example (5), Yue's pen pal (NNES, L1: Arabic) emailed her in Arabic which she could not understand. So she emailed back and explained the problem:

(5) Yue: hello! sorry, *i don't understand the language.* but i am happy to receive your email. /…/

This example indicated that the Chinese student Yue was quite specific in the trouble source of the non-understanding: 'the language' in (5). The metalinguistic comments, with specification of the source of non-understanding, explicitly directing the recipient's attention to the problem, served as the most explicit, direct, and specific means to signal the understanding problem (Vasseur et al. 1996) (see Sect. 8.4.1 for metalinguistic comments employed to signal misunderstanding).

8.4.3 Preemptive Strategies to Avert Problems of Understanding

The above two sections analyzed remedial pragmatic strategies the Chinese students employed to solve problems of understanding when they occurred. This section deals with the ways in which the Chinese university students employed preemptive pragmatic strategies to guard against non- or misunderstanding.

8.4.3.1 Building Shared Knowledge and Common Ground

The first type of preemptive pragmatic strategies observed in the data to avoid problems of understanding is to build shared knowledge and common ground with the recipient. The Chinese students anticipated that some topics containing their local cultures might cause problems to the recipient's understanding. Thus, they elaborated the cultural issues to fill the gap in the knowledge of their recipient so as to build shared knowledge and common ground between their recipient and themselves. The next extract illustrates one such example:

(6) Yue: /…/ it [the number 8] lies in its pronunciation in chinese "ba", and it sounds like "fa" which means a big fortune will come. so almost everybody in China like the number 8. /…/

In example (6), the student Yue was explaining to her Arabic friend why Chinese people were so fond of the number 8. The reason that the pronunciation of the number 8 was similar with the Chinese word "fa" (big fortune as Yue explained), was well known by Chinese people but might be unknown to a person who was not familiar with Chinese culture. Yue anticipated that her friend, being Arabic, might not have the related knowledge of Chinese culture and language. She therefore introduced the knowledge necessary to her friend before moving to her conclusion that "almost everybody in China like the number 8."

Not taking the recipient's knowledge for granted is further exemplified in the next extract:

(7) Hao: /…/ As for my name, *** is my family name while *** is the given name. Chinese say their family names first, opposite to Western culture. I guess you will know much more about China and Chinese when I get there. Haha (Chinese word means laughing, I don't whether English is the same one?) /…/

In this example, the student Hao first explained his family name and given name, and the Chinese traditional way to present names. In the end, because email lacked nonverbal expression such as facial expression, he would like to use an onomatopoeia word "haha" to indicate the informal atmosphere. Despite the simplicity of the word "haha," Hao did not presume the universality of understanding toward the word as indicating laughing. He thus decided to explicate the meaning of the word, to guarantee his recipient could understand the word so as to ensure the smooth communication of the email exchange.

8.4.3.2 Confirmation Checks

Confirmation checks are a well-documented strategy in ELF oral communication (Mauranen 2006; Watterson 2008). It has been observed that in ELF speech, confirmation checks can take the form of a minimal check (e.g., 'yeah?') or a more explicit one (e.g., 'did I understand right?') (Mauranen 2006). In addition, Watterson (2008) documents that at times the listener may reformulate what s/he guesses the speaker has said and utter his/her guess as a comprehension check. The strategy of confirmation checks also occurred in the present study, as exemplified in the following:

(8) Wei: /…/ As I read in your last email, I might apply for the grant via email. *Am I right?* /…/

This example illustrated how the Chinese student negotiated meanings and prevented misunderstandings and breakdowns in communication. Using the confirmation checks, the sender ensured the recipient followed the point and gave the recipient an opportunity to clarify the issue. If the assumption were correct, the email communication would be successful. Otherwise, if the assumption was incorrect, the recipient could detect the misunderstanding right away and fix the problem accordingly.

8.5 Discussion

The present study investigated remedial and preemptive pragmatic strategies employed by Chinese university students to achieve understanding, negotiate non-understanding, and resolve misunderstanding in writing emails in ELF communication. Only a few instances of problems of understanding (misunderstanding and non-understanding) were observed in the present study. When the Chinese university students encountered problems of understanding in their ELF communication, they did not let the problems pass (cf., Firth 1996), mirroring the findings in previous studies on oral communication in academic settings (e.g., Cogo and Dewey 2012; Kaur 2009, 2011b, 2012; Mauranen 2006).

In the present study, when the Chinese students encountered misunderstanding in their ELF email, they tended to point them out explicitly using specific metalinguistic comments. However, it must be acknowledged that given the low frequency of misunderstanding observed in the present study, the analyses and interpretations should be treated with caution and can only be considered tentative. It does not mean that in ELF email communication, misunderstandings are only signaled by metalinguistic comments. The result that only metalinguistic comments are observed may result from the low frequency of misunderstandings found in the present study, which is a small-scale explorative investigation only consisting of 215 emails. In addition, some of the emails are very short, for example, emails for daily greetings. Future studies involving more data are encouraged to examine whether other remedial pragmatic strategies would be employed to signal misunderstandings in ELF email communication.

The Chinese students also employed metalinguistic comments in their ELF emails when non-understanding occurred, in addition to questions focused on the part that caused non-understanding. Likewise, as discussed in the last paragraph, given the low frequency of non-understanding and the small scale of the present study, the findings should be treated with caution and should not be generalized to all Chinese students' emails in ELF communication.

The low occurrence of understanding problems resonates with previous findings of oral communication in ELF research, in which few misunderstandings and/or non-understandings are found (e.g., Firth 1996, 2009; Mauranen 2006). It appears that ELF users are aware of the lean nature of text-based email discourse (Dürscheid and Frehner 2013). Therefore, they tend to employ the two most direct remedial strategies to signal problems of understanding (Vasseur et al. 1996) in their ELF emails: metalinguistic comments and specific questions, rather than other strategies observed in oral ELF communication (see Cogo and Dewey 2012; Mauranen 2006 for pragmatic strategies in oral ELF discourse). In addition to the two remedial pragmatic strategies to signal problems of understanding, the students often added elaborated comments to explain the situation. This may result from their awareness of the 'one-way' transmission in email that precludes simultaneous feedback from the recipient (Herring 2001). The Chinese students therefore chose to write all relevant information in one email to enhance communication efficiency, which might be more appropriate in multi-turns in oral communication.

The present study also investigated preemptive pragmatic strategies employed by the Chinese university students to avert problems of understanding in their ELF email. The results indicated that the Chinese students, in ELF communication, did not take their recipient's knowledge for granted, reflecting the findings in oral ELF communication (Cogo and Dewey 2012; Mauranen 2006). The Chinese university students were aware that there might be gaps in their knowledge of some topics and the knowledge of their email recipients. Therefore, they often elaborated the cultural issues related to the incoming topics, to fill in the gaps and to build shared knowledge and common ground. In addition, they employed confirmation checks in their email to prevent potential misunderstandings and breakdowns in communication, to direct their recipient's attention, to provide the recipient an opportunity to clarify, and to guarantee communication success. As noted by Cogo and Dewey (2012, p. 128), these preemptive strategies may be used not only to prevent breakdowns in communication but also as general strategies to facilitate understanding and ensure communicative effectiveness.

As reviewed before (see the Introduction section), there is doubt in the literature concerning whether ELF is helpful and whether ELF users will be disadvantaged when written language is concerned (e.g., Sowden 2012). The findings of the present study have partially answered such questions. As shown in the present study, even without interpersonal negotiation and with a potentially heterogeneous audience, ELF users are still capable of manipulating their linguistic repertories to employ appropriate pragmatic strategies in their ELF email communication. They are not disadvantaged in email communication. More substantial empirical research is needed before we can say with confidence what the nature of ELF email discourse is. Before that, nevertheless, researchers should not assume that ELF is unhelpful, as discussed in the Introduction section (e.g., Sowden 2012), and should not assume that ELF users are disadvantaged in either email or written communication. More importantly, ELF users' pragmatic competence should not be evaluated against the 'native speaker norm.' As the present study has revealed, ELF email communication has its own characteristics and few understanding problems occur in ELF email communication.

However, the present study only analyzed the Chinese university students' email from the analyst's perspective. To date, although introspective research methods such as retrospective verbal reports (Cohen 2012; Gass and Mackey 2000; Jourdenais 2001) are widely used in language-learning research (see Gass and Mackey 2000 for a summary), they are rarely employed in ELF pragmatics research (but see Cogo 2012; Watterson 2008 for examples of using retrospective interviews in ELF research). It would benefit ELF research if retrospective verbal reports were included to triangulate findings based on analysis of discourses collected in ELF communication, and to shed light on the reasons why certain strategies are employed.

8.6 Conclusion

This study adds to the existing ELF literature on pragmatic strategies in email communication by examining a corpus of real-life emails written by Chinese university students. The study investigated both remedial pragmatic strategies to signal problems of understanding, i.e., misunderstanding and non-understanding, and preemptive pragmatic strategies to prevent problems of understanding. Findings include that when the Chinese university students encountered misunderstanding in their ELF communication, they employed metalinguistic comments to signal the problem. When they could not understand some utterances in the email they received, they tended to point them out straightforwardly by focused questions and metalinguistic comments. In addition, they did not assume homogeneity in writing emails in ELF communication. They often employed preemptive pragmatic strategies such as 'building shared knowledge and common ground' and 'confirmation checks' to ensure the success of the email communication.

As previously stated, little research has been conducted to examine ELF users' email discourse, and more generally, their written discourse. Findings from the present study have demonstrated the unique characteristics of ELF email communication. Investigating ELF users' authentic emails can provide insights into the nature of ELF email discourse and ELF users' pragmatic competence in intercultural communication.

For future research, it is recommended that more data are to be collected and analyzed from a wider range of ELF users (academics, business professionals, etc.). In addition, future research may also investigate emails from both sides (the sender and the recipient). If possible, retrospective verbal reports can be included to triangulate findings based on the email, and to uncover the reasons why certain strategies are employed.

Acknowledgments This work is supported in part by the National Social Science Fund of China (13CYY030) and the Special Financial Grant from China Postdoctoral Science Foundation (2014T70797).

Appendix: Symbols in the Examples

/.../	speech not included in the example
***	sensitive information (e.g., names) are deleted for confidentiality
Italics	used here to highlight parts of the email discussed in the text

References

Archibald, Alasdair, Alessia Cogo, and Jennifer Jenkins. 2011. *Latest trends in ELF research*. Newcastle upon Tyne: Cambridge Scholars Publishing.

Biesenbach-Lucas, Sigrun. 2005. Communication topics and strategies in e-mail consultation: Comparison between American and international university students. *Language Learning and Technology* 9(2): 24–46.

Biesenbach-Lucas, Sigrun. 2007. Student writing emails to faculty: An examination of e-politeness among native and non-native speakers of English. *Language Learning and Technology* 11(2): 59–81.

Björkman, Beyza. 2013. *English as an academic lingua franca: An investigation of form and communicative effectiveness*. Berlin: Mouton de Gruyter.

Blum-Kulka, Shoshana, Juliane House, and Gabriele Kasper. 1989. *Cross-cultural pragmatics: Requests and apologies*. New Jersey: Ablex Norwood.

Bremer, Katharina. 1996. Causes of understanding problems. In *Achieving understanding: Discourse in intercultural encounters*, ed. Katharina Bremer, Celia Roberts, Marie-Thérèse Vasseur, Margaret Simonot, and Peter Broeder, 37–64. London: Longman.

Chen, Chi-Fen E. 2006. The development of email literacy: From writing to peers to writing to authority figures. *Language learning & Technology* 10(2): 35–55.

Cogo, Alessia. 2009. Accommodating difference in ELF conversations: A study of pragmatic strategies. In *English as a lingua franca: Studies and findings*, ed. Anna Mauranen, and Elina Ranta, 245–273. Newcastle upon Tyne: Cambridge Scholars Publishing.

Cogo, Alessia. 2010. Strategic use and perceptions of English as a lingua franca. *Poznań Studies in Contemporary Linguistics* 46(3): 295–312.

Cogo, Alessia. 2012. ELF and super-diversity: A case study of ELF multilingual practices from a business context. *Journal of English as a Lingua Franca* 1(2): 287–313.

Cogo, Alessia, and Martin Dewey. 2012. *Analysing English as a lingua franca: A corpus-driven investigation*. London: Continuum.

Cohen, Andrew. D. 2012. Comprehensible pragmatics: Where input and output come together. In *New perspectives on individual differences in language learning and teaching*, ed. Miroslaw Pawlak, 249–261. Berlin: Springer.

Crystal, David. 2006. *Language and the Internet*. Cambridge: Cambridge University Press.

Crystal, David. 2011. *Internet Linguistics: A Student Guide*. London: Routledge.

Dürscheid, Christa, and Carmen Frehner. 2013. Email Communication. In *Pragmatics of computer-mediated communication*, ed. Susan C. Herring, Dieter Stein, and Virtanen Tuija, 35–54. Berlin: Mouton de Gruyter.

Economidou-Kogetsidis, Maria. 2011. "Please answer me as soon as possible": Pragmatic failure in non-native speakers' e-mail request to faculty. *Journal of Pragmatics* 43: 3193–3215.

Elder, Catherine, and Alan Davies. 2006. Assessing English as a lingua franca. *Annual Review of Applied Linguistics* 26: 282–301.

Félix-Brasdefer, J.César. 2012. E-mail requess to faculty: E-politeness and internal modification. In *Interlanguage request modification*, ed. Maria Economidou-Kogetsidis, and Helen Woodfield, 87–118. Amsterdam: John Benjamins.
Firth, Alan. 1996. The discursive accomplishment of normality: On "lingua franca" English and conversation analysis. *Journal of Pragmatics* 26: 237–259.
Firth, Alan. 2009. The lingua franca factor. *Intercultural Pragmatics* 6(2): 147–170.
Flowerdew, John. 2008. Scholarly writers who use English as an additional language: What can Goffmann's 'stigma' tell us? *Journal of English for Academic Purposes* 7: 77–86.
Gass, Susan, and Alison Mackey. 2000. *Stimulated recall methodology in second language research*. Mahwah, NJ: Lawrence Erlbaum.
Gass, Susan, and Evangeline Varonis. 1991. Miscommunication in nonnative speaker discourse. In *Miscommunication and Problematic Talk*, ed. Nikolas Coupland, Howard Giles, and John M. Wiemann, 121–145. London: Sage.
Herring, Susan C. 2001. Computer-mediated discourse. In *The Handbook of Discourse Analysis*, ed. Deborah Schiffrin, Deborah Tannen, and Heidi E. Hamilton, 612–634. Oxford: Balckwell.
Horner, Bruce. 2011. Writing English as a Lingua Franca. In *Latest trends in ELF Research*, ed. Alasdair Archibald, Alessia Cogo, and Jennifer Jenkins, 299–311. Newcastle upon Tyne: Cambridge Scholars Publishing.
House, Julian. 1999. Misunderstanding in intercultural communication: Interactions in English as *lingua franca* and the myth of mutual intelligibility. In *Teaching and learning English as a global language*, ed. Claus Gnutzmann, 73–89. Tubingen: Stauffenburg.
House, Julian. 2002. Developing pragmatic competence in lingua franca English. In *Lingua franca communication*, ed. Karlfried Knapp, and Christiane Meierkord, 217–244. Frankfurt: Peter Lang.
House, Juliane. 2014. English as a global lingua franca: A threat to multilingual communication and translation? *Language Teaching* 47(3): 363–376.
Ingvarsdóttir, Hafdís, and Birna Arnbjörnsdóttir. 2013. ELF and academic writing: A perspective from the expanding circle. *Journal of English as a Lingua Franca* 2(1): 123–145.
Jenkins, Jennifer. 2000. *The phonology of English as an international language*. Oxford: Oxford University Press.
Jenkins, Jennifer. 2007. *English as a lingua franca: Attitude and identity*. Oxford: Oxford University Press.
Jenkins, Jennifer. 2014. *English as a lingua franca in the international university: The politics of academic English language policy*. London: Routledge.
Jenkins, Jennifer, Alessia Cogo, and Martin Dewey. 2011. Review of developments in research into English as a lingua franca. *Language Teaching* 44(3): 281–315.
Jourdenais, Renee. 2001. Cognition, instruction and protocol analysis. In *Cognition and second language instruction*, ed. Peter Robinson, 354–375. Cambridge: Cambridge University Press.
Kachru, Braj B. 1992. *The other tongue: English across cultures*. Baltimore: University of Illinois Press.
Kaur, Jagdish. 2009. Pre-empting problems of understanding in English as a lingua franca. In *English as a lingua franca: Studies and findings*, ed. Anna Mauranen, and Elina Ranta, 107–123. Newcastle upon Tyne: Cambridge Scholars Publishing.
Kaur, Jagdish. 2011a. Intercultural communication in English as a lingua franca: Some sources of misunderstanding. *Intercultural Pragmatics* 8(1): 93–116.
Kaur, Jagdish. 2011b. Raising explicitness through self-repair in English as a lingua franca. *Journal of Pragmatics* 43: 2704–2715.
Kaur, Jagdish. 2012. Saying it again: Enhancing clarity in English as a lingua franca (ELF) talk through self-repetition. *Text & Talk* 32(5): 593–613.
Kirkpatrick, Andy. 2010. *English as a lingua franca in ASEAN: A multilingual model*. Hong Kong: Hong Kong University Press.
Knapp, Karlfried. 1987. English as an international lingua franca and the teaching of intercultural communication. In *Perspectives on language in performance*, ed. Wolfgang Lörsche, and Rainer Schulze, 1022–1039. Tübingen: Narr.

Knapp, Karlfried, and Christiane Meierkord. 2002. *Lingua franca communication*. Frankfurt: Peter Lang.

Lillis, Theresa, and Mary Jane Curry. 2010. *Academic writing in a global context: The politics and practices of publishing in English*. London: Routledge.

Mauranen, Anna. 2006. Signaling and preventing misunderstanding in English as a lingua franca communication. *International Journal of the Sociology of Language* 177: 123–150.

Mauranen, Anna. 2012. *Exploring ELF: Academic English shaped by non-native speakers*. Cambridge: Cambridge University Press.

Mauranen, Anna, and Elina Ranta. 2009. *English as a lingua franca: Studies and findings*. Newcastle upton Tyne: Cambridge Scholars Publishing.

Meierkord, Christiane. 2002. 'Language stripped bare' or 'linguistic masala'? Culture in lingua franca conversation. In *Lingua franca communication*, ed. Karlfried Knapp, and Christiane Meierkord, 109–133. Frankfurt: Peter Lang.

Milroy, Lesley. 1987. *Language and Social Networks*. Oxford: Blackwell.

Pitzl, Marie-Luise. 2005. Non-understanding in English as a lingua franca: Examples from a business context. *Vienna English Working Papers* 14(2): 50–71.

Roberts, Celia 1996. A social perspective on understanding: Some issues of theory and method. In *Achieving understanding: Discourse in intercultural encounters*, eds., Katharina Bremer, Celia Roberts, Marie-Thérèse vasseur, Margaret Simonot, and Peter Broeder, 9–36. London: Longman.

Seidlhofer, Barbara. 2011. *Understanding English as a lingua franca*. Oxford: Oxford University Press.

Smit, Ute. 2010. *English as a lingua franca in higher education: A longitudinal study of classroom discourse*. Berlin: Mouton de Gruyter.

Sowden, Colin. 2012. ELF on a mushroom: The overnight growth in English as a Lingua Franca. *ELT Journal* 66(1): 89–96.

Tzanne, Angeliki. 1999. *Talking at Cross-Purposes: The dynamics of miscommunication*. Amsterdam: John Benjamins.

Vasseur, Marie-Thérèse, Broeder, Peter, and Roberts, Celia. 1996. Managing understanding from a minority perspective. In *Achieving understanding: Discourse in intercultural encounters*, eds. Katharina Bremer, Celia Roberts, Marie-Thérèse vasseur, Margaret Simonot, and Peter Broeder, 65–108. London: Longman.

Watterson, Matthew. 2008. Repair of non-understanding in English in international communication. *World Englishes* 3(4): 378–406.

Author Biography

Wei Ren (任伟) is Professor of Applied Linguistics at the National Key Research Center for Linguistics & Applied Linguistics, Guangdong University of Foreign Studies, China. His recent publications include articles in *Applied Linguistics*, *Journal of Pragmatics*, *Pragmatics*, and a monograph *L2 Pragmatic Development in Study Abroad Contexts*.

Part III
Emails from Peer to Peer

Chapter 9
Openings and Closings in Intercultural Email Communication: A Case Study of Taiwanese, Japanese, and Italian Students

Hsin-chou Huang

Abstract This study investigates the distinct features of email openings and closings that emerge when EFL students interact with their global peers in cross-cultural exchanges. The data are drawn from two email exchange projects—one between Taiwanese and Italian students and the other between Taiwanese and Japanese students—which took place over the course of 2 years. Using conversational analysis and discourse analysis, this study analyzed a corpus of 768 emails and revealed interaction patterns in openings and closings among the different ethnic groups. Results showed that the most frequently used opening strategies were *salutation + name*, followed by *greeting*, *question*, *no opening*, and *gratitude*. Closing strategies included *signature*, *farewell/ending salutation*, *expectation*, *no closing*, and *gratitude*. Ethnic differences in the use of opening and closing strategies were also identified. By highlighting the variability of email communications, this paper can provide a preliminary understanding of electronic discourse in pragmatic terms.

Keywords Computer-mediated communication · Email · Pragmatics · Openings · Closings · EFL

9.1 Introduction

Recent decades have shown growing interest in computer-mediated communication (CMC). Among the many kinds of CMC, the most popular application for language teaching has been email because (1) it provides easy access to global peers without the need for special equipment, (2) it is able to quickly transcend time and space barriers, and (3) it delivers a platform for authentic language and direct interaction

H. Huang (✉)
Institute of Applied English, National Taiwan Ocean University, Keelung, Taiwan
e-mail: joehuang@ntou.edu.tw; jo65huang@gmail.com

Y. Chen et al. (eds.), *Email Discourse Among Chinese Using English as a Lingua Franca*, DOI 10.1007/978-981-287-888-5_9

with the target culture (Levy and Stockwell 2006). Language teachers have adopted a wide variety of email tasks with fruitful outcomes in language development and increased cross-cultural understanding (Appel and Gilabert 2002). Relatively, few studies have reported on the new stylistic and linguistic conventions of email discourse (Waldvogel 2007), so it is necessary to investigate the empirical validity of such language uses. The analysis of the language of CMC interactions in previous studies has mostly centered on the variation of email discourse in response to power relationships in the workplace (Waldvogel 2007) and in academic settings (Bou-Franch 2011). The writers of the emails have been mostly homogeneous ethnic groups, such as Spanish lecturers writing to their colleagues or their graduate students (Bou-Franch 2011) or English speakers writing to a Public Library about user inquiries and responses (Park et al. 2010). Relatively, a few studies have examined email discourse among different ethnic groups in intercultural communication. Because greetings and closings in email play an important social role in easing the strain of interacting online in a foreign language with someone from another culture (Eckert and McConnell-Ginet 2003, p. 105), research in this field has become urgent. As defined by Waldvogel (2007), greetings are how the writer constructs his social identity and relationship with the addressee. A closing can consolidate the relationship and build a basis for encounters in the future. Studies on email greetings and closings can shed light on how learners interact with their global peers in intercultural, computer-mediated settings. The patterns of language usage of different ethnic groups can provide learners with knowledge about how to best interact with exchange partners, better communicate with them, and understand the way they convey their messages.

This study aims to identify the patterns of interactions in openings and closings in email communication and examine whether there are ethnic differences in language use. This study asks the following research questions:

1. What are the opening and closing formulae of Taiwanese, Japanese, and Italian students in email discourse?
2. Do Taiwanese students use different opening and closing routines from their Japanese and Italian counterparts?

9.2 Background of the Study

9.2.1 *Email: Asynchronous Computer-Mediated Communication*

Computer-mediated communication (CMC) can be defined as "communication that takes place between human beings via the instrumentality of computers" (Herring 1996, p. 1). With the booming of the Internet, using computers as a medium to communicate either contributes to communicating immediately (synchronous

CMC) or at a delayed point (asynchronous CMC) (Levy and Stockwell 2006). Synchronous CMC allows active exchange of information in real time such as chat, online conferencing, and MOOs. Asynchronous CMC gives more time for participants to reflect on their partners' utterance, to plan, and produce their own response, and includes email, discussion boards, and mailing lists (Kitade 2008). Among all CMC forms of interaction, emails have been used most widely in language teaching, mainly because email exchanges require simple technology, provide relatively easy access to global peers, and do not necessitate matching participants' class times (Levy and Stockwell 2006). As for CMC's linguistic features, due to its informality, openings and closings are not pervasive (Herring 1996).

Collaborative, intercultural email exchanges are the computer-based activities used most widely by ESL teachers to increase student language proficiency (Greenfield 2003). Hertel (2003) suggested that an email exchange is a student-centered activity because students can play an active rather than a passive role in the learning process. During the exchange process, students need to initiate and discuss topics that are of their own interest. Within such a highly individualized interaction, students are then motivated to learn about the target cultures and the target language. Liaw (1998) investigated the effectiveness of integrating email writing into two Taiwanese EFL classrooms. The students from the two advanced English classes were randomly paired up to be email partners and each class contained 26 students. Data were collected from questionnaires, face-to-face group interviews, and the correspondence between students. The findings showed that due to the short duration of the project, email writing did not seem to have a great effect on improving reading skills. However, the students perceived improvements in their writing skills. Students also regarded advancing computer skills and cultivating potential friendships with mysterious partners as a valuable experience. Overall, students showed positive responses toward their experiences of email exchanges and believed that if they kept on writing email messages to their peers, their English proficiency would make progress.

O'Dowd (2003) reported on a year-long email exchange between five pairs of Spanish and English second-year university students. The ultimate goal of this research was to investigate how email exchanges influenced students' attitudes toward the target and home cultures. The results revealed that students valued the opportunity to express their feelings and views about their own culture to their intercultural partners. Students were encouraged to reflect critically on their own culture through questions asked by their partners, and to engage in dialogic interaction about both the home and target cultures. This led to a growing awareness of differing viewpoints on the two cultures' practices. Students who successfully developed their intercultural communicative competence had better chances to express their cultural identity to their receptive audience.

Successful intercultural exchanges require careful task design. Task preparations ensure successful communication between two groups of students if the topics assigned for communication are relevant for their lives. For example, Appel and Gilabert (2002) investigated the motivational effects of task planning on Irish and

Spanish learners. Results showed that when tasks were more closely connected to students' experiences, students were more motivated and the length of email messages was longer. Friermuth and Huang (2012) investigated the task attractiveness for Japanese and Taiwanese English learners in online chatroom communication. Results showed that having specific tasks in mind motivated learners to complete the interaction.

9.2.2 English as a Lingua Franca

Research into English as a lingua franca (ELF) is a relatively new activity. However, English has been used as a lingua franca in parts of Asia (e.g., Singapore) and Africa (e.g., Nigeria) since they were colonized by the British (Jenkins et al. 2011). According to Jenkins (2006), ELF is part of the Global Englishes paradigm, that is, most speakers of English are nonnative speakers and all English varieties are evaluated in their own right, not against the native speakers' benchmark. From this perspective, nonnative speakers are no longer learners of English; they are not failed native speakers. In other words, they are different rather than deficient. They are highly skillful communicators who can make good use of multilingual resources that native speakers may not have.

Sifakis (2006) views the terms English as an international language (EIL) and English as an intercultural language (EIcL) as being either N-bound (i.e., norm-bound) or C-bound (i.e., communication, comprehensibility, and culture based). Norm-bound interactions view native speakers as the owners of the target language, with nonnative speakers merely learners, whose L1 hinders communication. Norm-bound approaches provide rule-based accounts of languages based on lexical, synthetic, morphological, phonological, and socio-cultural analysis of the language use of native speakers. In contrast, a C-bound approach dictates communication as interactions between speakers and owners of the target language; the influence of nonnative speakers' L1 is inescapable and an important feature of their cultural identity. Language communication in an N-bound approach requires the message produced to be communicated. This characterizes EIL communication, in which syntactic, semantic, and phonological knowledge of the language needs to be addressed. This is more in-class communication. Real-life NNS–NNS and NNS–NS communication has always been C-bound. Communication depends on parameters such as speakers' individual language skills, attitudes toward language, and their attitudes toward interlocutors' cultural backgrounds (Byram 1997). This characterizes ElcL, which is situation specific. ESOL practitioners are familiar with N-bound classes that concentrate on the teaching of English as a second or foreign language. To teach in an N-bound way means to involve students in suitable communicative activities to produce and understand written and spoken discourse along the fluency and accuracy continuum (Sifakis 2006). To teach in a C-bound way means to expose students to authentic NNS ways of communicating. In this respect, technology is useful to link students to a wider community since teachers can encourage learners to seek communication with their global peers via email or teleconferencing (Warschauer and Healy 1998). This study thus utilizes a C-bound approach using emails to encourage users of English as an international language to communicate in the language. In particular, this study seeks to examine the interactional patterns of openings and closings in email exchanges.

9.2.3 Linguistic Politeness and Greetings and Closings in Asynchronous CMC

Brown and Levinson's (1987) politeness theory proposed the following strategies for performing face-threatening acts (FTAs): (1) do the act on record (i.e., direct speech act), (2) positive politeness to show solidarity, (3) negative politeness to show deference, and (4) do the act off record (i.e., indirect speech act). The choice of the strategy used is based on the speaker's assessment of the total weightiness of the FTA, that is, the parameters of the relative power of the speaker over the hearer, the social distance between the speaker and the hearer, and the degree to which such an act is rated an imposition in a given culture. Brown and Levinson (1987) came up with the formula, "*Social Distance + Power Differential + Degree of Imposition = degree of face threat to be compensated by appropriate linguistic strategy.*" Brown and Levinson's (1987) five strategies ranked from the most impolite, *do the act on record* without any linguistic compensation, through an escalating politeness, with *positive* and *negative politeness*, toward *don't do the act at all.* A speaker will choose strategies according to the power and distance relationship between hearers and the degree of imposition.

Openings and closings can be used for linguistic politeness in personal communication. In opening discourse, address forms and greetings are the most common linguistic features. Address forms contain first names (John, Mary), kinship names (brother, daddy), job titles (doctor, professor), or combination of title and name (Dr. Chang) (Park et al. 2010). The use of address forms varies from formality to informality. For example, in formal situations, a combination of title and last name is used to show deference. In informal situations, people may address each other using first names (Mary) or endearment terms (honey) to show solidarity. In addition, greetings and closings fulfill an important social role (Waldvogel 2007). In CMC, interlocutors employ a wide variety of nonverbal cues to show interpersonal solidarity (Park 2007). These strategies include emoticons, capitalization of letters, and contractions. Emoticons signal acknowledgement, display of happiness, and gratitude, which can support interpersonal relationship in an online community.

Several empirical studies have examined patterns of openings and closings in email-based online library interactions (Park et al. 2010), in asynchronous discussion boards (Abrams 2008), email communication (Bou-Franch 2011), workplace emails (Waldvogel 2007), and academic settings (Margaret and Levy 2006). Park et al. (2010) suggest that openings and closings can be used strategically to show linguistic politeness and interpersonal communication. They summarized widely used linguistic elements for openings and closings as follows: verbal politeness markers (e.g., acknowledgement, *thank you*), structural politeness markers such as greeting words (*hi, hello*), addressing by name, and leave-taking conventions (*take care, sincerely*, and *regards*). For opening discourse, address forms and greeting expressions represent the most frequent language use. Address forms, which often occur at the beginning of the sentence, include personal names, kinship terms, or job titles. These forms serve as interpersonal affective stances to show intimacy, formality, or informality. In formal situations, address forms come with the title, whereas in informal contexts address forms often begin with the person's first name or terms of endearment such as *dear* or *sweetie*.

Abrams (2008) examined opening and closing sequences of CMC among 78 undergraduate first-year learners of German at an American public university. Students logged into Blackboard, a course management system, to interact with peers and the teachers about the topics covered in course textbook. Analyses of the asynchronous sessions showed that opening sequences were similar, with a greeting followed by a request for information. The question and answer pairing reflected students' communicative needs to complete the assigned activities. Students' language use was modeled on the textbooks' face-to-face conversation samples but in a less formal way. Closing sequences were more elaborate and often asked the instructor for permission to leave. This study also showed that students can be asked to examine the transcript of their interaction and identify the opening and leave-taking sequences to learn more about register variation.

Bou-Franch (2011) investigated the stylistic language choice of openings and closings in a corpus of 240 Spanish email communications in academic settings. This study looked into how the power relationships shaped email discourse. Results showed that the opening sequences included greeting, self-identification, and personal comment. The closing sequence included gratitude, leave-taking, and signature. Contrary to previous studies on the absence of openings and closings in electronic communication due to the informal nature of the medium, this study found a high percentage of openings (over 85 %) and closings (97 %) in the email correspondence. As for density of opening and closing sequences, closings showed greater density than openings. This study found that closings sent to equals were the most compact because users tended to be more direct when writing to non-dominant equals. Closings sent to people with higher positions were the least dense because less powerful email users tended to be verbose when writing to more powerful addresses.

Waldvogel (2007) examined greetings and closings of 515 emails written in an educational organization and a manufacturing factory in New Zealand. The results showed that greetings and openings were more widely used in workplaces than in educational organizations. As for types of greetings, in educational organizations, 59 % did not have any greetings, and 21 % started with the person's name, followed by "*greeting word + first name.*" In a manufacturing plant, only 17 % did not have greetings at all, and 53 % used "*greetings + first name.*" As for closings, over one-third (34 %) of emails in the educational organization did not have any closing.

The most prevalent closing (38 %) used the writer's name. In the manufacturing plant, on the other hand, only a small percentage (10 %) had no closing and the majority corpus (46 %) used a "*farewell formula + name,*" followed by "*thanks + name*" (27 %). This study suggested that the more frequent use of openings and greetings in the workplace signals that the workplace culture presents a friendly working environment where greetings and openings show comradeship and open relationships.

Margaret and Levy (2006) investigated politeness strategies in email communication among 122 general and academic staff in an Australian metropolitan university and 16 Korean academics at seven universities in Korea. Participants needed to respond to an Intercultural Email Questionnaire to comment on their perceptions of politeness when they email people overseas they do not know. Results showed that Korean participants showed more concern about the use of correct titles than Australians. The full address form, such as *Dear Professor*, is much more important for Koreans than for Australians.

In summary, the use of openings and closings reflects linguistic politeness in email communication and it can be culture specific. This study then seeks to investigate such differences across cultures.

9.3 Methodology

The email discourse was gathered from two intercultural projects between Taiwanese students and Italian and Japanese counterparts. These two projects aimed to enable EFL learners in Taiwan to use English as a communication tool to learn more about the culture of their global peers.

9.3.1 The Email Corpus

The first project was between 11 Taiwanese college freshman speakers of English and 13 third-year senior high school Italian speakers of English (see Table 9.1). Both groups of students were low-intermediate EFL learners with at least 6 years of English learning experiences. Data were collected during a semester-long Freshman English course. The researcher as the instructor cooperated with the Italian partner teacher through international email classroom connections (IECC). Both teachers worked on collaborative syllabi to have students write to communicate on topics such as introducing food of their own culture, holiday traditions, and their school life. Students were paired up to write to their keypals at least biweekly and sent copies of their emails to their instructors. The first Taiwanese–Italian project analyzed a total of 151 email messages, of which 65 were written by the Taiwanese students and 86 were written by the Italian students.

Table 9.1 Profile of the two intercultural exchange projects

	Number of students	Number of emails	Number of openings	Number of closings
Project (I)				
Taiwanese	11	65	47	48
Italian	13	86	83	81
Subtotal	24	151	130	129
Project (II)				
Taiwanese	29	341	235	257
Japanese	26	276	187	217
Subtotal	55	617	422	474
Total	79	768	552	603

As with the first Taiwanese–Italian intercultural email project, the second email exchange took place between 29 Taiwanese college freshmen and 26 Japanese counterparts. All of the participants were low intermediate-level college EFL students with limited experience with email exchanges. This cross-cultural email project also involved students writing to communicate on topics such as food culture, festivals, and their school life. The second project yielded a total of 617 email messages, of which 341 were written by the Taiwanese students, whereas 276 were written by the Japanese participants.

In summary, the corpus of email message analyzed in this study included a total of 768 emails written by 79 students across two projects, which produced a total of 552 openings and 603 closings. The profile of these two exchange projects is shown in Table 9.1.

9.3.2 Data Collection and Analysis Procedures

A corpus of 768 email messages was the source for analysis, among which 151 messages were from the Taiwanese–Italian keypal project and 617 emails were from the Taiwanese–Japanese project. The coding procedure was based on conversation analysis (Schegloff and Sacks 1973) and discourse analysis (Sinclair and Coulthard 1975) in which both the sequences and the moves were the units of analysis. The coding scheme was adapted from Park et al.'s (2010) and Bou-Franch's (2011) studies. In their schemes, the opening taxonomy included *no opening, greeting expressions, acknowledgement, address forms/naming*, and *self-introduction*. The closing categories were *no closing, acknowledgement, thanking, farewell/ending solutions, signature using the sender's name*, and *follow-up*. Email transcripts were analyzed at a sentence level, which is regarded as the smallest linguistic unit to assign categories. Two raters who were pursuing their master degrees in TESOL and working as research assistants on the project coded the email messages. Prior to the coding, they attended training sessions with the researcher to ensure their familiarity with the coding process. During the actual coding, they read through the email messages, identified the openings and closings of each message, and assigned categories. After coding, they examined the results and, if differences arose, went back to the original data, discussed these differences, and finally reached consensus. The inter-rater reliability reached 0.86, which is considered reasonable reliability for research purposes (Muijs 2004, p. 73). These categories were not finite and additional categories were added based on the actual email exchange data.

The first round of coding yielded categories, such as *address form + name, greetings, questions, no opening, gratitude, self-identification, apology,* and *personal feelings*. The closing categories were *signature, farewell/ending salutation, expectation, no closing, gratitude, request,* and *question*. As suggested by Bou-Franch (2011), to have a more focused analysis on the most representative patterns of interaction, the researcher decided to analyze only the moves that occurred in at least 50 % of the datasets. Based on this criterion, the raters went through the categories again and selected the categories that were common in both projects and occurred in at least of 50 % of the total emails in their respective datasets. The second round of coding then yielded five categories: *opening, including address form + name, greeting, question, no opening,* and *gratitude*. The category items, descriptions, and examples are shown in Table 9.2. These five categories made up 56.70 % (N = 313) of the total dataset (N = 552). As for closings, the five refined categories were *signature, farewell/ending salutation, expectation, no closing,* and *gratitude*. The category items, descriptions, and examples are shown in Table 9.3. This refined set of data made up of 71.64 % (N = 432) of the original 603 closings.

Table 9.2 Coding categories and examples for openings

Category	Description	Text
1. Salutation + name	Greeting salutation followed by the name of the email recipient	Hi Giulia Dear Fabry  Hello Carol!!!
2. Greeting	Greeting salutation	Hello!/Hi!
3. Question	Asking questions of the email recipient	Did you receive the e-birthday card? How often do you have a family meal?
4. No opening	Not using any of the greetings or other sentences to engage in conversation before mentioning the major content in an email message	None
5. Gratitude	Showing gratitude for the recipient's message	Thanks for your blessing. Thank you for your e-mail!!

Table 9.3 Coding categories and examples for closings

Category	Description	Text
1. Signature	Showing the sender's name	Penny  Chiara and Giulia
2. Farewell/ending salutation	Expressing farewell to end the email	ok....see u !! Ciao! Cheers,
3. Expectation	A follow-up confirmation to show further interest in future communication	I hope we'll become good friend, too. We hope to hear from you soon
4. No closing	Not using any of the closings or other sentences to end the conversation	None
5. Gratitude	Showing thankfulness for the recipient's email	Many thanks!!!!! Thank you

9.4 Results and Discussion

9.4.1 *Openings*

A total of 313 openings were included in the corpus for analysis. Among the five categories of openings, the category of "*salutation + name*" was the most frequently used formula, covering almost half of the opening usage (47.28 %) (see Table 9.4). Students mostly started the email correspondence with a salutation and the recipient's name, such as "*Dear Fabry*" as a formal way to open the dialog. The second highest category was "*greeting*"—students used greeting salutations only to show their friendliness in the opening (22.04 %). The use of "*hello*" or "*hi*" was seen as an in-group identity marker and used as a positive politeness strategy to show the sender's interest toward the recipient and to narrow the distance between them (Park et al. 2010). The third highest category was "*question*" (11.82 %). Participants also asked questions to show their interest in their recipient's life (i.e., *How often did you cook for yourself*?) or to check if their partners had received the previous mail (i.e., *Did you receive the birthday card I sent you*?). The "no opening" routine only occurred in a small number of email exchanges (9.58 %).

Table 9.4 Frequency and percentages of opening categories

Category	F	%
Salutation + name	148	47.28
Greeting	69	22.04
Question	37	11.82
No opening	30	9.58
Gratitude	29	9.27
Total	313	100

The last formula was "*showing gratitude for what the recipient had done*" (9.27 %), which only occurred in less than 10 % of the exchanges.

Unlike many CMC studies which have found that openings and closings are absent due to the informal nature of online communication (Herring 1996), this study showed the pervasive use of openings and closings in intercultural email interactions. There was an overwhelming higher percentage (90.42 %) of openings than no openings (9.58 %). Recent studies have also shown a tendency for high-frequency usage of opening strategies. For example, Bou-Franch (2011) found a high percentage of openings (85 %) and closings (97 %). Park et al. (2010) also demonstrated 100 % use of openings in user replies in virtual public library email correspondence. The above findings are consistent with the findings of this intercultural exchange, which showed a high percentage of over 90 % for both openings and closings. It could be interpreted that both Bou-Franch's (2011) and this present study were conducted within academic institutions—the former between university lecturers and between undergraduate students and their lecturers and the latter between college/high school students from different parts of the world. Likewise, just as librarians in the context of a virtual public library in Park et al.'s (2007) study wanted to show their friendliness to user inquiries via greetings, intercultural speakers in this study also seemed to want to display their comradeship via a variety of opening strategies. However, more research needs to be completed in different institutional settings to confirm this observation (Bou-Franch 2011).

As for the types of linguistic tactics used in opening an email, this study showed a high percentage of "*address form + name*" and "*greeting*," which made up almost 70 % of the opening rituals. As Park et al. (2010) suggested, the use of *Hello* can be interpreted as an in-group marker and a combination of address form and addressee's first name can strengthen the warm welcoming atmosphere. The intercultural writers in this study wanted to convey their interest in knowing more about their partners and thus showed their politeness using the more emphatic "*address form + name*" more frequently than the "*greeting*." In written discourse such as emailing when facial expressions and verbal cues are absent, it is not surprising to find that students in this study frequently employ "*address form + name*" to show their politeness. In addition, the use of the "*question*" strategy supports Abram's (2008) finding that greetings were mostly followed by requests for information.

With regard to cultural differences, Table 9.5 shows the distribution of the five opening strategies among the three student groups: Taiwanese, Italian, and Japanese. The strategies in the Taiwanese group were calculated by adding up the strategies used by Taiwanese students in the two projects. Chi-square tests of homogeneity showed that students across cultures used different proportions of opening strategies in email messages (χ^2 = 34.62, df = 8, p = 0.000). When further post-hoc analyses were performed, it was found that such differences were due to the use of two strategies: "*address form + name*" and "*greeting*." Italian students used the strategy of "*address form + name*" less frequently than either the Taiwanese or Japanese students (Taiwanese: 54.50 %, z = 1.3; Italian: 23.60 %,

$z = -2.6$[1]; Japanese: 49.00 %, $z = 0.3$). The expected proportion for the "*address forms + names*" strategy was 47.3 %. With regard to the strategy of "*greetings*," Italian students used this comparatively more frequently than the Taiwanese and Japanese students (Taiwanese: 16.70 %, $z = -1.4$; Italian: 49.10 %, $z = 4.3$[2]; Japanese: 15.70 %, $z = -1.4$). The expected proportion for the "*greeting*" strategy was 22.0 %.

The email corpus in this study reveals interesting ethnic differences in opening strategies. The Italian students used comparatively more "*greeting*" and fewer "*address form + name*" strategies than the Taiwanese and Japanese students. "*Greetings*" only are regarded as a more casual and informal way to open the discourse to show informality and solidarity (Waldvogel 2007). The opening strategy of "*salutation + name*" was regarded as a more formal marker to show deference. This study showed that the Italian students showed more use of the informal marker, "*greeting*," than the Taiwanese and Japanese students. The Italian students also used the formal marker of "*salutation + name*" less frequently than the Taiwanese and Japanese students. This interesting phenomenon showed distinctive features of the Italian students' use of less formal opening strategies to display solidarity. Such ethnic differences were also found in Margaret and Levy's (2006) study, in which Australians used less formal titles to address their email correspondents than Koreans did. This finding might give intercultural partners a clue that people from different cultures may have different expectations about how they are to be addressed and greeted. In this study, the use of more informal opening strategies characterizes Italian students' choice to express solidarity. When engaging in communication with Italian speakers, intercultural partners might need to be aware of such a unique feature of Italian stylistic choice of opening strategies and not regard the use of "informal" opening markers as too loose. However, as this study involved only a small sample of Italian speakers, more research needs to be completed and to include larger samples to examine if such differences are valid.

[1]When results of a Chi-square test show significant differences, researchers may use a residual analysis to determine which particular cell(s) cause(s) the deviation. The standardized residuals are regarded as approximately forming a normal distribution, which has a mean of 0 and a standard deviation of 1. This allows researchers to compare individual standardized residuals with a cut-off line of +/−1.65 for the standardized normal distribution. Therefore, if the standardized residuals are greater than 1.65 or smaller than −1.65, researchers can then determine this cell would be regarded as significantly larger or smaller. In this case, the standardized residual for the cell of Italian students' use of the strategy of "address form + name" was smaller than −1.65 ($z = -2.6$). This means that compared to the Taiwanese and Japanese students, Italian students used significantly fewer strategies of "address form + name".

[2]The standardized residual for the cell of Italian students' use of the strategy of "greetings" was greater than 1.65 ($z = 4.3$). This means that compared to the Taiwanese and Japanese students, Italian students used more strategies of "greeting," and this difference was significant.

Table 9.5 Openings among different ethnic groups

Category		Ethnic groups			Total
		Taiwanese	Italian	Japanese	
Address form + name	Count	85	13	50	148
	Expected frequency	73.8	26.0	48.2	148.0
	Percentage	54.5	23.6	49.0	47.3
	Standardized residual	1.3	−2.6[a]	0.3	
Greeting	Count	26	27	16	69
	Expected frequency	34.4	12.1	22.5	69.0
	Percentage	16.7	49.1	15.7	22.0
	Standardized residual	−1.4	4.3[b]	−1.4	
Question	Count	15	8	14	37
	Expected frequency	18.4	6.5	12.1	37.0
	Percentage	9.6	14.5	13.7	11.8
	Standardized residual	−0.8	0.6	0.6	
No opening	Count	17	2	11	30
	Expected frequency	15.0	5.3	9.8	30.0
	Percentage	10.9	3.6	10.8	9.6
	Standardized residual	0.5	−1.4	0.4	
Gratitude	Count	13	5	11	29
	Expected frequency	14.5	5.1	9.5	29.0
	Percentage	8.3	9.1	10.8	9.3
	Standardized residual	−0.4	0.0	0.5	
Total	Count	156	55	102	313
	Expected frequency	156.0	55.0	102.0	313.0
	Percentage	100.0	100.0	100.0	100.0

[a]The proportion is significantly smaller than the other two groups
[b]The proportion is significantly larger than the other two groups

9.4.2 Closings

Among a corpus of 432 closing strategies, the use of "*signature*" (i.e., the name of the email writer) dominated, comprising almost half of the closing usage (44.68 %) (see Table 9.6). The next most frequently used closing strategy was "*farewell/ending salutation*," which occupied over a quarter of the closings (26.85 %). Writers said good-bye to their global peers using words such as *See you*, *Cheers*, or *Regards*. The next most popular category of closings was "*expectation*," which made up 12.27 % of the used strategies. Writers expressed their wish to continue friendship or their hope to receive a response by using phrases such as *Hope to hear from you soon* and *hope to become your friends* (12.27 %). Finally, no closing only occurred in 9.22 % of the exchanges and expressing "gratitude" (i.e., *Thank you!*) was the least used strategy (6.48 %).

Table 9.6 Frequency and percentages of closing categories

Category	N	F
Signature	193	44.68
Farewell/ending salutation	116	26.85
Expectation	53	12.27
No closing	42	9.22
Gratitude	28	6.48
Total	432	100

Similar to the overwhelming percentage of openings (over 90 %), closings were also present in over 90 % of the emails in this study. In other words, closings (90.78 %) also significantly outnumbered no closings (9.22 %). This finding is consistent with Bou-Franch's (2011) research on email conversations in an educational context among university lecturers and students in Spain, in which closings had a high percentage of 97 %. The ubiquitous usage of closings in this study also corroborates Waldvogel's (2007) finding of closings appearing in 90 % of the emails analyzed. Similar tendencies are shown in Park et al.'s (2010) Internet public library study where closings occurred in 95 % of the interactions. The frequent use of closings, like openings, shows that intercultural speakers in this study have used linguistic tokens such as closing formulas to show their intention to create friendly interactions in email communication.

Patterns of closing strategies share similarities and differences with previous studies on email discourse. With regard to the most frequently used strategy, this study's findings on the dominant use of "*signature*" are consistent with previous studies on email discourse in academic settings (Bou-Franch 2011; Gains 1999) in which signature was likewise the most widely used strategy. Leave-taking expressions such as *Good-bye* and *Regards* were also used frequently in this study to end a message. Bou-Franch's (2011) also found that leave-taking was used in 75 % of the email correspondence analyzed. The use of expectation strategy in this study was also found in Park et al.'s (2007) study where follow-up invitations showed the writer's wish to continue the interaction with his/her interlocutor.

With regards to differences, in our corpus, "*gratitude*" was the least frequently used strategy, less than 10 %. This finding is inconsistent with Waldvogel's (2007) email discourse collected from a manufacturing plant, where gratitude was a popular strategy consisting of 29 % of the entire closing strategies. It also sharply contrasts with Park et al.'s (2010) finding that thanking and acknowledgment are frequently used (95 %). This may be because Waldvogel's (2007) corpus was written either between administrators and employees or between colleagues, where social status was clearly defined even in email communication. The use of the gratitude strategy in closings shows deference and respect; therefore; it is not surprising to find gratitude strategies widely used in workplaces. Likewise, in Park et al.'s (2010) study, the heavy use of gratitude shows the librarian's intention to give an impression of approachability. The corpus in this study, however, was collected in academic settings and writers were all students on an equal basis. These student writers probably did not perceive their social status as being different and so did not frequently use politeness markers such as gratitude strategies to end a message. This might explain why "gratitude" was the least used strategy in this study.

As for cultural differences in the use of closing strategies, the chi-square test of homogeneity showed students across cultures used different strategies in closing email messages (χ^2 = 19.90, df = 8, p = 0.011) (see Table 9.7). When further post-hoc analyses were performed, it was found that such differences were due to the use of two strategies: "*farewell/ending salutation*" and "*no closing*." In terms of the strategy of "*farewell/ending salutation*," the Taiwanese students used this strategy less frequently than the Italian and Japanese students (Taiwanese: 20.1 %, z = −1.9[3]; Italian: 37.5 %, z = 1.4; Japanese: 32.7 %, z = 1.5). The expected proportion of "*farewell/ending salutation*" strategy was 26.9 %. With regard to the strategy of "*no closings*," it was found that the Taiwanese students used the "*no closing*" strategy comparatively more frequently than their Italian and Japanese counterparts, while the Japanese students used the "*no closing*" strategy comparatively less frequently (Taiwanese: 14.2 %, z = 2.1[4]; Italian: 6.3 %, z = −0.8; Japanese: 4.8 %, z = −2.0[5]). The expected proportion of "*no closing*" strategy was 9.7 %. In other words, when writing emails, "*no closings*" were mostly used by the Taiwanese, followed by the Italian and then by the Japanese. The Japanese employed closing strategies most frequently. Here are three email correspondences written by Taiwanese students to show how Taiwanese students ended emails without closing. To preserve authenticity, the following messages were not edited. The first sample shows that this student simply introduced herself without addressing her keypal or closing the email. The second sample shows that this student just let her counterpart know about her typical breakfast without closing the email. The third sample shows that this student seems to talk to himself without any closing.

"I am pepper by English name, because my Chinese name is sound piper nigram.

I am eighteen years old. We have lived in Taipei for eighteen years. It is my favorite city.There are four members in my family. My father is a painter, he is the breadwinner of my family. My mother is a good cook. Therefore we love to dine at home. I have an elder sister. There are only one year between my sister. My sister

---

[3]The standardized residual for the cell of Taiwanese students' use of the strategy of "farewell/ending salutations" was smaller than −1.65 (z = −1.9). This means that compared to the Japanese and Italian students, Taiwanese students used significantly fewer strategies of "farewell/ending salutation".

[4]The standardized residual for the cell of Taiwanese students' use of the strategy of "no closings" was larger than 1.65 (z = 2.1). This means that compared to the Japanese and Italian students, Taiwanese students used significantly more strategies of "no closing".

[5]The standardized residual for the cell of Japanese students' use of the strategy of "no closing" was smaller than -1.65 (z = −2.0). This means that compared to the Taiwanese and Italian students, Japanese students used significantly fewer strategies of "no closings".

Table 9.7 Closings among different ethnic groups

Category		Ethnic groups			TOTAL
		Taiwanese	Italian	Japanese	
Signature	Count	98	20	75	193
	Expected frequency	97.8	21.4	73.7	193.0
	Percentage	44.7	41.7	45.5	44.7
	Standardized residual	0.0	−0.3	0.1	
Farewell/ending salutation	Count	44	18	54	116
	Expected frequency	58.8	12.9	44.3	116.0
	Percentage	20.1	37.5	32.7	26.9
	Standardized residual	−1.9[a]	1.4	1.5	
Expectation	Count	28	6	19	53
	Expected frequency	26.9	5.9	20.2	53.0
	Percentage	12.8	12.5	11.5	12.3
	Standardized residual	0.2	0.0	−0.3	
No closing	Count	31	3	8	42
	Expected frequency	21.3	4.7	16.0	42.0
	Percentage	14.2	6.3	4.8	9.7
	Standardized residual	2.1[b]	−0.8	−2.0[a]	
Gratitude	Count	18	1	9	28
	Expected frequency	14.2	3.1	10.7	28.0
	Percentage	8.2	2.1	5.5	6.5
	Standardized residual	1.0	−1.2	−0.5	
Total	Count	219	48	165	432
	Expected frequency	219.0	48.0	165.0	432.0
	Percentage	100.0	100.0	100.0	100.0

[a]The proportion is significantly smaller than the other two groups
[b]The proportion is significantly larger than the other two groups

and I get along very well. She loves to go to KTV.I have got a part-time job in SUSHI BAR. I like this working environment very much, but this job makes me tired. I have decided to resign.I am fond of watching cartoons,I enjoyed detective fiction best(Holmes). I am very fond of playing PC games,such as Final Fantasy, Tomb…… I like horror films and comedies best. I go to the movie this summer vacation,for example JORASSIC PARK3 and TOMB. JORASSIC PARK is my favorite movie. Those in saurs and like meal one. I like 3D movies and 3Dgames.

I am interested in computer,because it cam make dreams come true." (Student #3)

"Hi:dear
How are you?
Thanks for your recipe.
In Taiwan, we usually eat "Taiwan's bread with egg" in the morning!
I usually drink "milk" and eat "Taiwan's bread with egg" (Student #11)
"Hi ~ ~ ~ ^^"

sorry ~ ~
three weeks not yet reply to you
Because....my computer get a computer virus ~>" < ~ everything wasn,t doing....
to follow a midterm examination
so, i was preparing for every subject in a curriculum
up to now, it was almost unacquainted with every subject.
it must be to suffer from one's own actions....
but....luckily,the midterm examination finally passed^^"
To feel happy y^^y
ah...." (Student #28)

Closings are comparatively more difficult than openings (Zhang 2013). Bardovi-Harlig et al. (1991) also indicated that knowing how to close a conversation in one's L1 does not necessarily lead to knowing how to do it successfully in the L2 because closings are culturally specific. In this study, Taiwanese students showed comparatively fewer closing strategies than the other ethnic groups. This might be interpreted as being in line with Bardovi-Harlig et al.'s (1991) finding that the act of transforming L1 closing strategies to the L2 posed considerable challenges. The Taiwanese students know the ending formula in Mandarin but fail to apply that knowledge when they use English to communicate. Another explanation might be that the Taiwanese students might put more emphasis on sending the messages without thinking of how to end the conversations wisely with more politeness markers. Unlike the Taiwanese students' underuse of closing strategies, the Japanese students used the most closing strategies of the three groups. This may be because the Japanese students are influenced by their native language, which makes elaborate use of closings. As more of the emphatic politeness strategies are already deeply rooted in their language, it seems natural for them to end the conversation with more of the politeness devices. Such cultural differences in applying linguistic formulas to end a conversation deserve more large-scale research to support the findings.

In addition to the overall underuse of opening strategies, the Taiwanese students also used fewer farewell/ending salutations. These farewell markers, such as *regards*, *best wishes*, and *sincerely*, are regarded as politeness signals to end a conversation. It seems that more instruction on ending a message politely will be necessary to ensure the flow of conversation.

In summary, the ethnic differences in opening strategies were reflected in the Italian students' more frequent usage of "*greetings*" and less frequent usage of "*address form + name*" than the Taiwanese and Japanese students. Differences in closing strategies were evident in the Taiwanese students' use of fewer closing strategies than the Italian and Japanese students, particularly with regard to the use of "*farewell/ending salutations*." Such differences among these three ethnic groups may draw the attention of intercultural speakers to the stylistic choice of language use in email discourse. Italian students employed more informal opening strategies to consolidate friendship; Taiwanese students used the least number of closing strategies and Japanese used the most closing strategies. A large-scale research to collect cross-cultural exchange data is needed to examine whether such patterns of variations persist.

9.5 Conclusion

The two intercultural exchange projects in this study took a C-bound approach to language use, in which language communication between nonnative speakers is valued (Sifakis 2006), and demonstrated the value of promoting authentic language use through real interactions with intercultural speakers as suggested in previous intercultural studies (Greenfield 2003; Liaw 1998; O'Dowd 2003). Through carefully designed tasks (Appel and Gilabert 2002; Friermuth and Huang 2012), students are more willing to communicate. In particular, this study explored the opening and closing rituals among three ethnic groups in email communication. The findings showed that politeness markers such as openings and closings are widely employed by English as a lingua franca speaker among Taiwanese, Italian, and Japanese students. The pervasive use of opening and closing strategies also demonstrates that these intercultural speakers seek to build up a friendly atmosphere in interacting with their partners and wish to maintain a good relationship. These politeness tactics in opening and ending an email message, whether informal or formal, are all tools to encode social relationship and solidarity. In future email interactions, teachers might explicitly teach students how to use these markers wisely to make their communication go smoothly and have their meaning conveyed.

This study also identified ethnic differences in the use of opening and closing strategies. However, due to its exploratory nature, this study has the following limitations. First, based on a corpus of 768 email correspondences, this study has shown some patterns of opening and closing strategies among Taiwanese, Italian, and Japanese students. The small size of the corpus limits the universal applicability of this study's findings to a wider context. Future studies might include more samples of email communication to investigate linguistic variability across cultures. Second, because this study aimed to explore the possible overall patterns of openings and closings among three ethnic groups, it did not differentiate the emails into initial or non-initial positions. Previous research has shown polarized findings —one, for example, showed no differences in greeting rituals regardless of whether the emails were initial interactions or in response to earlier emails (Waldvogel 2007) and another showed obvious differences (Bou-Franch 2006). Future studies may need to re-examine the data to determine whether patterns of openings and closings vary according to the email position within an exchange. Third, this study did not look into gender differences in openings and closings. As gender differences may be a factor in opening and closing strategies, future studies can look into whether there are any differences between males' and females' choices when opening or closing an email message. It is hoped that these study's preliminary findings will shed light on how intercultural speakers employ linguistic politeness strategies to open and close email interactions. Pedagogical implications from this study's findings will encourage teachers to raise EFL speakers' awareness of cultural differences in opening and closing rituals and thus help to develop effective communication strategies in email discourse.

Acknowledgments This study was supported by the Ministry of Science and Technology, Taiwan, ROC, Project No. MOST 103-2628-H-019-001.

References

Abrams, Zsuzsanna I. 2008. Sociopragmatic features of learner-to-learner computer-mediated communication. *CALICO Journal* 26: 1–27.

Appel, Christane, and Roger Gilabert. 2002. Motivation and task performance in a task-based and web-based tadem project. *ReCALL* 14: 16–31.

Bardovi-Harling, Kathleen, Beverly A.S. Hartford, Rebecca Mahan-Taylor, Mary J. Morgan, and Dudley W. Reynolds. 1991. Developing pragmatic awareness: Closing the conversation. *ELT Journal* 45: 4–15.

Bou-Franch, Patricia. 2006. Solidarity and deference in Spanish computer-mediated communication: A discourse-pragmatic analysis of students' emails to lecturers. In *Ways into discourse*, ed. Patricia Bou-Franch, 61–79. Comares: Granada.

Bou-Franch, Patricia. 2011. Openings and closings in Spanish email conversations. *Journal of Pragmatics* 43: 1772–1785.

Brown, Penelope, and Stephen. C. Levinson. 1987. *Politeness: Some universals in language usage*. Cambridge: Cambridge University Press.

Byram, Michael. 1997. *Teaching and assessing intercultural communicative competence.* Clevedon: Multilingual Matters.

Eckert, Penelope, and Sally McConnell-Ginet. 2003. *Language and gender.* Cambridge: Cambridge University Press.

Freiermuth, Mark. R., and Hsin-chou Huang. 2012. Bringing Japan and Taiwan closer electronically: A look at an intercultural online synchronic chat task and its effect on motivation. *Language Teaching Research* 16: 61–88.

Gains, Jonathan. 1999. Electronic mail—a new style of communication or just a new medium?: An investigation into the text features of e-mail. *English for Specific Purposes* 18(1): 81–101.

Greenfield, Roseanne. 2003. Collaborative e-mail exchange for teaching secondary ESL: A case study in Hong Kong. *Language Learning & Technology* 7: 46–70.

Herring, Susan C. 1996. Two variants of an electronic message schema. In *Computer-mediated communication: Linguistic, social and cross-cultural perspectives*, ed. Susan C. Herring, 81–106. Amsterdam: John Benjamins.

Hertel, Tammy. 2003. Using an e-mail exchange to promote cultural learning. *Foreign Language Annals* 36: 386–396.

Jenkins, Jennifer. 2006. Points of view and blind spots: EFL and SLA. *International Journal of Applied Linguistics* 162: 137–162.

Jenkins, Jennifer, Alessia Cogo, and Martin Dewey. 2011. Review of developments in research into English as a lingua franca. *Language Teaching* 44: 281–315.

Kitade, Keiko. 2008. The role of offline metalanguage talk in asynchronous computer-mediated communication. *Language Learning & Technology* 12: 64–84.

Levy, Michael, and Glenn Stockwell. 2006. Computer-mediated communication. In *CALL dimensions: Options and issues in Computer-assisted language learning*, ed. Michael Levy, and Glenn Stockwell, 84–109. Mahwah, NJ: Lawrence Erlbaum.

Liaw, Meei-Ling. 1998. Using electronic mail for English as a foreign language instruction. *System* 26: 335–351.

Muijs, Daniel. 2004. *Doing quantitative research in education with SPSS*. London: Sage Publications.

O'Dowd, Robert. 2003. Understanding the "other side": Intercultural learning in a Spanish-English e-mail exchange. *Language Learning & Technology* 7: 118–144.

Park, Jung-ran. 2007. Interpersonal and affective communication in synchronous online discourse. *Library Quarterly* 77: 133–55.

Park, Jung-ran, Guisu Li, and Amy Burger. 2010. Opening and closing rituals of the virtual reference service of the internet public library. *Journal of Documentation* 66: 807–823.

Schegloff, Emanuel A., and Harvey Sacks. 1973. Opening up closings. *Semiotica* 8: 289–327.

Sifakis, Nicos. 2006. Teaching EIL—Teaching international or intercultural English? What teachers should know. In *English in the world: Global rules, global roles*, eds. Rani Rubdy and Mario Saraceni, 151–168. New York: Continuum.

Sinclair, John M., and Richard M. Coulthard. 1975. *Towards an analysis of discourse*. Oxford: Oxford University Press.

Waldvogel, Joan. 2007. Greetings and closings in workplace email. *Journal of Computer-Mediated Communication* 12: 456–477.

Warschauer, Mark, and Deborah Healey. 1998. Computers and language learning: An overview. *Language Teaching* 31: 57–71.

Zhang, De. 2013. More than "hello" and "bye-bye": Opening and closing the online chats in mandarin Chinese. *Computer Assisted Language Learning*. doi:10.1080/09588221.2013.776966.

Author Biography

Hsin-chou Huang (黃馨週) is Professor of English as a Foreign Language at the Institute of Applied English at National Taiwan Ocean University. Her research focuses on using computer technology for language teaching and learning, second language reading and writing, and teacher education.

Chapter 10
Apologies in Emails: Interactions Between Chinese EFL Learners and Their Foreign Peers

Jianda Liu and Wei Ren

Abstract This paper examines and compares apologies in emails between two groups of Chinese university students, namely first-year non-English major university students and third-year English major university students, to see if there are any patterns in the development of pragmatic competence in terms of apologies. Comparisons between the two groups are made for the perception of sociopragmatic variables as well. Data for this study were obtained from two scenarios eliciting apologies to an equal status. The participants were asked to write emails to their foreign peers to make apologies according to the scenario. A metapragmatic questionnaire was also constructed to examine the participants' perception of the contextual constraints. The results showed that the Chinese learners of different proficiency levels perceived the sociopragmatic variables similarly in the situation of offense. Their preference of general apology strategies over situation-specific strategies also showed similar patterns. By contrast, the low group learners employed significantly more strategies of IFID (Illocutionary force indicating device) and taking responsibility but significantly fewer upgraders than did their high group counterparts. Consequently, the low group's emails were significantly longer than those of the high group.

Keywords Apology · Email · Strategy · Perception · Sociopragmatic variable

---

J. Liu (✉)
National Key Research Center for Linguistics and Applied Linguistics, Guangdong University of Foreign Studies, Guangzhou, China
e-mail: ahda_liu@aliyun.com

W. Ren
National Key Research Center for Linguistics and Applied Linguistics, Guangdong University of Foreign Studies, Guangzhou, China
e-mail: renweixz@yahoo.com

Y. Chen et al. (eds.), *Email Discourse Among Chinese Using English as a Lingua Franca*, DOI 10.1007/978-981-287-888-5_10

10.1 Introduction

The speech act of apology is of critical importance for successful social interaction and relational management. It "is perhaps the example *par excellence* of politeness at work" (Grainger and Harris 2007, p. 1) and has been widely investigated in pragmatics research for many years (e.g., Bergman and Kasper 1993; Blum-Kulka et al. 1989; Chang 2010; Fraser 1981; García 1989; Holmes 1990; Warga and Schölmberger 2007; just to name a few). However, few studies have been carried out to explore how Chinese perform apologies, either in their first language (L1) Chinese or second language (L2), excluding Kádár's (2007) investigation into apologies in historical Chinese. Pan and Kádár (2011, p. 101) argue that little work on apologies in Chinese is a reflection of the so-called "no-apologizing culture" developed in Mainland China, where apologies are more often achieved "by means other than linguistic expression, such as taking redressive action or doing something for the person offended to mend the relationship" (Pan and Kádár 2011, p. 101). However, given the large number of Chinese learners of English and the increasing importance of China in intercultural communication, it is necessary to investigate how Chinese speakers express their apologies in English.

On the other hand, the majority of pragmatics research on apology takes spoken discourse as its focus, either based on naturalistic data (e.g., Aijmer 1996; Holmes 1990; Márquez Reiter 2008; Robinson 2004) or elicited data (e.g., Bergman and Kasper 1993; Chang 2010; Flores Salgado 2011; Márquez Reiter 2000; Ogiermann 2009; Rose 2000). Although email represents a popular means of electronic communication prevalent in university students' lives (or people's lives in general) today, L2 pragmatics research on speech acts produced through emails mainly examines the speech act of request (e.g., Chen 2006; Economidou-Kogetsidis 2011; Félix-Brasdefer 2012; Pan 2012), with other speech acts less investigated. Little attention to date has been paid to apologies in emails. The limited number of studies on L2 learners' performance on apologies in emails reveals an important research area yet to be explored.

The present study aimed to contribute to the existing L2 pragmatics literature by investigating the apology performed in emails by Chinese English learners sent to their foreign peers. L2 pragmatics research has dealt with two main areas. Pragmalinguistic studies address the relationship between linguistic forms and their functions, whereas sociopragmatic studies investigate the relationship between linguistic actions and perception of variables in the social context. This paper examines and compares apology strategies in emails between two groups of Chinese university students, namely first-year non-English major students and third-year English major students in university, to investigate if there are any patterns in variation of pragmatic competence in terms of apologizing in emails. In addition, their perception of sociopragmatic variables, such as power, social distance, and the imposition of speech acts (Brown and Levinson 1987), is examined as well.

The rest of the paper is organized as follows. Section 10.2 defines the speech act of apology, and reviews recent studies on email apologies, on L2 learners' pragmatic development in apologies, and on the perception of sociopragmatic variables. Section 10.3 introduces the methodology of this study. The results and discussion are presented in Sects. 10.4 and 10.5, respectively, followed by the conclusion in Sect. 10.6.

10.2 Literature Review

10.2.1 The Speech Act of Apology

The apology can be defined as a compensatory action or remedial work for an offense committed by Speaker/Writer who has affected Hearer/Recipient. By apologizing, the Speaker/Writer wishes to transform "what could be seen as offensive into what can be seen as acceptable" (Goffman 1971, p. 139) in order to reestablish social harmony. This conceptualization is supported by Leech (1983), for whom the speech act of apology is a convivial speech act whose goal coincides with the social goal of maintaining harmony between Speaker and Hearer by providing some benefit for the Hearer and some cost to the Speaker. Similarly, under the framework of Brown and Levinson (1987), apologies are considered to be 'face-saving' for Hearer/Recipient and 'face-threatening' for Speaker/Writer (Fraser 1981; Olshtain 1989) because through apologies the Speaker/Writer acknowledges and expresses regret for a fault or offense to the Hearer/Recipient (Coulmas 1981). Apologies are thus generally perceived as 'negative politeness' in that they "express respect rather than friendliness" (Márquez Reiter 2000, p. 45).

Apologies fall into the group of expressives defined by Searle (1979, p. 15) as speech acts which express "the psychological state specified in the sincerity condition about a state of affairs specified in the propositional content." It is often assumed that the offense must occur prior to the apology. Nevertheless, some research shows that apology can also be anticipatory and disarming in orientation (Aijmer 1996; Davies et al. 2007). Olshtain and Cohen (1983) define a 'speech act set' for apology. They note that an illocutionary force indicating device (IFID), that is, the formulaic form containing "the explicit, performative verbs which express an apology" (Olshtain 1989, p. 157), is an indicator of an apology but is not essential. For example, an IFID "I apologize" can be considered as an apology. An expression of speaker's responsibility (e.g., "My fault.") can realize an apology in any situation as well. Olshtain (1989) lists a set of strategies, any of which can be used on their own or in combination to produce an apology. The strategies are divided into two general strategies which can be used in all contexts, and three situation-specific strategies which are context bound, as displayed below (adapted from Olshtain 1989, p. 157):

Two General Strategies

1. IFID or formulaic apology forms
2. Expression of Speaker's responsibility

Three Situation-Specific Strategies

1. An explanation
2. An offer of repair
3. A promise of forbearance

These strategies are further divided into substrategies which are listed in Blum-Kulka et al. (1989, pp. 290–294) with examples and definitions. The IFID can be intensified internally by various means, for example, intensifying adverbials, emotional expressions, please, etc.

The taxonomy of apology in Blum-Kulka et al. (1989) forms the foundation of coding apologies in the literature and has been adopted in various studies (e.g., Bergman and Kasper 1993; Chang 2010; Flores Salgado 2011; Márquez Reiter 2000; Rose 2000; Warga and Schölmberger 2007). The existence of a well thought out, well-defined classification system for a speech act, enables researchers to produce comparable analyses and results that are expressed in terms of the same categories (Ren 2012). Therefore, the data collected in the present study were coded according to the cross-cultural speech act research project (CCSARP) (Blum-Kulka et al. 1989) wherever possible. If any data could not be included in the taxonomy scheme, grounded theory was used to code the data (see Sect. 10.3.3 for detail of coding apologies).

10.2.2 Recent Research on Email Apologies

As previously stated, pragmatics research on speech acts has mainly focused on oral discourse, although the data may be collected through written discourse completion tasks (DCT). Email discourse has received comparatively less attention. Among the studies on speech acts performed through emails, the majority have examined the speech acts of requests (e.g., Chen 2006; Economidou-Kogetsidis 2011; Félix-Brasdefer 2012; Pan 2012), whereas fewer studies have investigated apologies in emails.

Hatipoğlu (2004) was one of the earliest studies to explore and compare the characteristics of apologies used in emails with those in spoken and written language, based on a corpus of 126 emails collected from British English speakers. It was found that in one-to-one emails the strategy 'expression of regret' formed the majority of the corpus (85.7 %), parallel to one most commonly observed in spoken communication (Aijmer 1996; Owen 1983). By contrast, in professional emails, where the writers were apologizing either as required by their post or as a spokesperson on behalf of the offender, 96.9 % of the corpus were realized by the strategy 'offer of apology.' In the emails sent to many recipients while the sender was apologizing for his/her own mistake, the writers tended to use the two strategies with a similar frequency (52.2 % for 'offer of apology' and 45.6 % for 'expressions of regret'). Unlike apologies in spoken or written language, some unique qualities in email apologies were documented in this study. For example, apologies were found to be used for duplicate messages or for irrelevant messages sent to the recipients. In addition, examination of content of the strategy 'offer of apology' revealed that the noun form was preferred over the verb form and bare forms were used more frequently than the modified forms (e.g., 'my apologies'). The author argued that the popularity of noun form and particularly bare form was due to the syntactic constraints of English. With the nominal form, the inclusion of personal or possessive pronouns was not a must. The apologizer therefore was allowed to remain unidentified, while s/he was still able to fulfill the goal to offer an apology and to remedy the situation (Hatipoğlu 2004, p. 26).

Davies et al. (2007) focused on students' email apologies to academic staff based on 100 naturally occurring emails by British undergraduate speakers of English. This study found that email apologies could refer to not only a past event but also a present or future event (Aijmer 1996). In addition, apologies might refer to an event either internal or external to the email message. Much of the data in this study consisted of apologies occurring alongside other speech acts (particularly requests), with only 26 % of the emails as apology only. Employing the concepts of equity and equilibrium (Clark 1996; Holmes 1990), the authors explicated that the students could write apologies to "pay debts and gain credit" within the student–lecture relationship. Furthermore, a previous undescribed apology strategy, 'But-Justification,' was analyzed and discussed, which focused on improving the writer's standing as a good student. The authors argued that the nature of the medium (email in this case) might increase its utility for students' identity work.

In a more recent study, Harrison and Allton (2013) explored apologies in email discussions with academic or professional themes. The study included apology emails to individual, and to the whole group or a subgroup (Hatipoğlu 2004). In this study, the word 'apologies' was the most frequently used form (42.1 %) and 'sorry' was the second most frequently used form (33.1 %). The authors proposed two possible explanations for the prevalence of 'apologies' in the email discussion data. One possibility was that the data were written rather than spoken (cf. Aijmer 1996). Another possibility was that the use of the noun from enabled the writer to avoid the personal pronoun thus creating a distance between the writer and the possibility for the offense (Hatipoğlu 2004). Almost all the apologies in the study related to the content or language of email discussions, or to the technology that supported email discussions. Moreover, apologies in the email discussions explicitly referred to the offense. According to the authors, this was necessary because (a) the communication took place asynchronously and (b) the communication was in writing.

As the above three studies indicate, apologies in emails have displayed unique characteristics. It is necessary that more empirical studies be implemented to explore the pragmatic strategies employed in apology emails. In addition, coincidentally the three studies on email apologies have all focused on British English speakers. Very little is known about apology use in emails by speakers from other cultures. The present study aimed to contribute to the existing literature by exploring the apology emails written to their foreign peers by Chinese English learners of two different proficiency levels, and then comparing and contrasting the apologies performed by the two groups.

10.2.3 Recent Research on Pragmatic Development in L2 Learners' Apologies

Because the present study compared email apologies written by Chinese learners of English at two different proficiency levels, in this section we review empirical studies investigating learners' pragmatic development in their L2 English apologies, focusing on cross-sectional and longitudinal studies only.

One of the earliest studies on learners' apology was Trosborg's (1987) investigation into apologies made by Danish English speakers of three proficiency levels (intermediate, lower advanced and higher advanced) and two groups of native speakers (English and Danish) using role plays. Regarding the frequency of apology strategies, the results showed that the learners differed significantly from the English native speakers in a number of strategies, whereas no statistically significant differences were found between the two groups of native speakers, implying that L1 inference was not the most likely cause of deviations in the choice of strategy between the learners and the English native speakers. Trosborg's (1987) learners employed direct apologies more frequently than the English native speakers. However, the differences between the learners and the English native speakers reached statistical significance only for the higher-advanced learners. With regard to internal lexical modifications, the English native speakers employed more internal modifiers than the learners, and the difference was significant when compared to the intermediate learners. When the three groups of learners were compared, there was an increase in the employment of internal lexical modifiers relative to increasing L2 proficiency.

Later Trosborg (1995) conducted a larger cross-sectional investigation into three speech acts (requests, complaints, and apologies). With regard to apology strategies, nonlinear development was observed. The intermediate and the higher-advanced groups employed more direct apologies than the native speakers, with the higher-advanced group using highest number. Distinct from her earlier findings (Trosborg 1987), the differences were not significant in this study. Concerning the use of internal modification, some improvement was observed relative to increasing proficiency, despite the significant failure in learners to employ internal modifiers in all three communicative acts.

Using DCTs, Sabaté i Dalmau and Curell i Gotor (2007) compared apologies by Catalan learners of English at three proficiency levels (intermediate, advanced, and proficient) and by Catalan native speakers and English native speakers. The effect of proficiency was found in the repertoire of apology expressions, with higher proficiency learners attempting a greater variety of apology strategies and decreasing in non-L2-like apology expressions, although the correlation was not linear (Trosborg 1987, 1995). With regard to internal modifiers, the acquisition of apology intensification happened very gradually and at a very late stage. Even the proficient group did not employ all the intensifiers available in English. Instead, they relied heavily on a few lexical forms to mark pragmatic intent unambiguously, indicating that the learners' pragmalinguistic competence was not sufficient.

Using a modified version of the cartoon oral production task developed by Rose (2000), Flores Salgado (2011) investigated apologies in Mexican Spanish learners of English across three levels of proficiency: basic, intermediate, and advanced (requests were also examined in this study, but the review here focuses on apologies only). Basic learners were found to employ the fewest strategies per apology, while intermediate learners used fewer strategies than advanced learners and native speakers of American English, both of whom used the most apology strategies per apology. The most commonly used strategy for the three groups of language learners was the IFID. Advanced learners employed more IFIDs than their intermediate counterparts, and the basic group less than intermediate group. From the three substrategies of IFID, the most common expression employed by the three groups of learners was the strategy 'expression of regret.' The author argued that the simplicity and explicitness of 'expression of regret' contributed to the common use of this strategy (Flores Salgado 2011, p. 193). The second most common expression used by the three groups was 'request for forgiveness,' and they employed the strategy more frequently with the increase of their English proficiency. However, this strategy was the least preferred by American speakers. For the substrategies under 'Taking responsibility,' the three groups of learners and the native English speakers most frequently selected 'admission of facts.' Concerning the length of apologies, the results showed a developmental process. A positive correlation was observed between the length of the learners' responses and the increase of their English proficiency.

Unlike the above-mentioned studies investigating learners of English, Warga and Schölmberger (2007) examined longitudinally the development of apologies of seven Austrian learners of French during a 10-month stay in Montreal. DCTs were employed six times for the learners at 2-month intervals (the last time after their return to Austria) and once for the two native speaker groups: native speakers of Quebecois French and native speakers of Austrian German. Residence in the L2 community was demonstrated to trigger important developments in the learners' L2 pragmatic competence. While some of these developments led to an increasingly L2-like pragmatic competence, not all changes over the year abroad necessarily represent developments toward the L2 norm. In addition, learners' acquisition of pragmalinguistic forms remained largely unchanged.

To date only two studies have explored Chinese learners' pragmatic development of apologies in English (cf. Liu 2007) for assessing Chinese English learners' pragmatic knowledge in relation to apologies. Rather than investigating adult learners, Rose (2000) examined Chinese young learners of English in Hong Kong with respect to speech acts of requests, apologies, and compliment responses (only findings of apologies are reviewed here), using a cartoon oral production task. Three groups of primary school students, P2, P4, and P6 (approximately 7, 9, and 11 years old) took part in this study. Rose coded the first strategy in each utterance 'main strategy' and any subsequent strategies 'adjuncts.' No differences among the three groups were found for main apology strategies. By contrast, distribution of apology adjuncts across groups offered some evidence of developmental trends, with a tendency for both a higher frequency and wider range of apology adjuncts in P6 group. There was, however, little evidence of situation variation for any of the three speech acts.

Also using DCTs, Chang (2010) investigated Chinese English learners' L2 apology across four proficiency levels: low beginners (3rd graders, 9 years old), high beginners (6th graders, 12 years old), low intermediate (10th graders, 16 years old), and high intermediate (college freshmen, 19 years old). With regard to apology strategies, the results showed a significant difference across groups only for three scenarios (the total number was eight), whereas with regard to apology adjuncts, the effect of proficiency was significant for all scenarios. The range of the apology strategies utilized by the learners widened with the increasing proficiency, while the employment of adjuncts was related to both proficiency and context.

It is interesting that those studies on learners with L1 Danish (Trosborg 1987, 1995), L1 Catalan (Sabaté i Dalmau and Curell i Gotor 2007), and L1 Mexican Spanish (Flores Salgado 2011) investigated adults learners, whereas studies on learners with L1 Chinese (Chang 2010; Rose 2000) focused more on younger learners. The present study thus attempted to add to the body of L2 learners' pragmatics research on apologies by investigating Chinese university students.

10.2.4 Research on the Perception of Sociopragmatic Factors

Pragmatic research on speech acts to date has primarily investigated learners' production data. Only a few studies have examined the perception of sociopragmatic factors, often as a part of study investigating learners' production data. Olshtain (1989), for example, analyzed the realization patterns of apologies among Hebrew, Australian English, Canadian French, and German across seven apology situations using DCTs. Each situation varied according to the sociopragmatic factors of power, social distance, and the severity of the violation. The situations were presented to native speakers who evaluated each of the sociopragmatic factors on a scale (see Olshtain 1989 for detail). As Olshtain (1989) noted, such an assessment was important because the independent variables embedded in the situations were expected to have an important effect on choices of realization patterns of apologies. However, Olshtain (1989) only presented the evaluation of sociopragmatic factors by Hebrew speakers. Thus a cross-cultural comparison of evaluation of sociopragmatic factors was not possible.

Blum-Kulka and House (1989) also assessed the perception of the social parameters for the request situations in their study. They compared three languages (Hebrew, German, and Argentinean Spanish) and included six social dimensions (social dominance and distance, rights and obligations, degree of difficulty, and likelihood of compliance) in five requesting situations. The results indicated that there were cross-cultural differences in the way different groups rated the social dimensions in specific request situations. A correlation was found between how the participants rated the situations and the level of directness displayed in the requests offered in the DCT. Specific cultural correlations were observed as well.

Bergman and Kasper (1993) investigated the perception of apologies and performance of apologies of Thai graduate students and native speakers of American English. Thirty American native speakers and thirty Thai graduate students were asked to rate a five-point rating scale for four context-internal factors (severity of offense, offender's obligation to apologize, likelihood for the apology to be accepted, offender's face loss) and two context-external actors (social distance and dominance). Context-external factors refer to variables that can be incorporated into the description of the situation, whereas context-internal variables refer to the features specific to the speech act elicited (Blum-Kulka et al. 1989). The results revealed that Thai and American raters perceived context-external and context-internal factors as unrelated but context-internal factors in offense contexts as highly related. Different ratings of severity of offense were observed in various specific situations between the two groups. Although both groups assessed the relationships between student and professor as medium Distance, for the Thais, student–professor tended more toward the low end of the medium Distance category, whereas for the Americans, it approximated closer to the high end of medium Distance.

Cultural differences in perception of the student–professor relationship were also observed in Spencer-Oatey's (1993) exploration of British and Chinese participants. Her focus was on the role relationship of tutor-postgraduate student and people's prototypical conceptions of the relationship, which was subdivided into three aspects: superordination/equality, distance/closeness, and rights and obligations. Participants were asked to provide likelihood ratings on a seven-point Likert scale for the items probing tutor superordination and social distance/closeness and to provide closeness ratings for the social distance/closeness items. Results demonstrated cross-cultural differences in the perception of the social factors involved. Only nationality and role had a statistically significant effect on the ratings, with, for example, teacher's ratings indicating a greater power differential than those of students, and Chinese participants' ratings revealing a perception of less distance than those of British participants.

In a more recent study, Maeshiba and colleagues (Maeshiba et al. 1996) examined whether pragmatic transfer in apologies was constrained by contextual factors or affected by learners' proficiency levels. A total of 120 participants (30 intermediate Japanese EFL learners, 30 advanced Japanese EFL learners, 30 English native speakers, and 30 Japanese native speakers) were asked first to answer a 20-item dialog construction questionnaire followed by an assessment questionnaire with the same offense contexts. Each context was rated on a five-point scale for five context-internal factors (severity of offense, offender's obligation to apologize, likelihood of the apology being accepted, offender's face loss, offended party's face loss) and two context-external factors (social distance and dominance). Comparison of the contextual assessments provided by the English native speakers and Japanese native speakers showed that there was strong agreement in the two groups' perception of status, obligation to apologize, and likelihood of apology acceptance.

10.2.5 Issues About Native Speaker Norm

As indicated in the review (Sect. 10.2.3), the majority of studies on learners' apologies compare learners' responses with those of native speakers, which are considered to be the baseline. This 'native norm model' in L2 pragmatics has been criticized by many scholars (e.g., Dewaele 2007; Mori 2009; Yates 2010) and challenged by empirical findings (e.g., Barron 2003; Xu 2009). In addition, the world's most extensive contemporary use of English is as a lingua franca (ELF) (Jenkins 2014; Seidlhofer 2001), defined as English "used as a contact language between people from different first languages (including native English speakers)" (Jenkins 2014, p. 2). The English users' discourse in lingua franca communication should be regarded as existing in its own, not with reference to any English native norm (refer to Jenkins et al. 2011 for a state-of-the-art review of ELF research).

The present study adopted the perspective of ELF (Cogo and Dewey 2012; Jenkins 2007, 2014; Mauranen 2012; Seidlhofer 2011), considering L2 English as different rather than deficient, and treats the Chinese learners of English as multi-competent L2 users (Cook 1992, 2002). In intercultural communication, the participants should be treated on an equal footing rather than native speaker norms being prioritized as a yardstick for evaluating L2 users' behavior (Chang and Haugh 2011). The study thus aimed to depict how apologies are produced in Chinese university students' emails sent to their foreign peers rather than comparing their usage with that of a group of native speakers.

To be specific, the purpose of the present study is to address the following research questions:

1. To what extent does the perception of sociopragmatic factors differ across Chinese learners of English with different proficiency levels?
2. To what extent does the length of apology emails produced by Chinese learners of English with different proficiency levels differ?
3. When Chinese learners apologize in emails, what apology strategies do they prefer? Are there any differences in the use of strategies across Chinese learners of English with different proficiency levels?

10.3 Methodology

10.3.1 Participants

The participants included two groups of university students: 40 Chinese first-year students and 40 Chinese third-year students, recruited at a university in south China. The age range of the former group was from 18 to 20, with an average of 19.65, and that of the latter group was from 20 to 23, with an average of 21.55. The first-year students were from various majors but not English related (Law, Finance, Accounting, and Auditing), whereas the third-year students were all English majors (English Language and Literature or English Education). Although no standardized tests were employed in the present study, the third-year English major students were generally more proficient in English than the first-year non-English major students. Thus, in the present study, the first-year university students were considered as intermediate learners (low group), whereas the third-year university students were considered as low-advanced learners (high group).

10.3.2 Instrument

The research instrument in the present study comprised two discourse production tasks validated by Liu (2006), eliciting students' ability to produce apologies in emails. Participants were given only one of the two tasks and were asked to write emails to their foreign peers to make apologies according to scenarios. The following exemplifies one of the situations.

Scenario 1.

Write a hypothetical email message to one of your classmates. His name is Mike Richter. He is from the United States.

Here's the situation:

- Mike came to China to learn Chinese. He loves Chinese songs very much.
- You promised Mike to teach him a Chinese pop song on Thursday afternoon. But you forgot.
- Today is Saturday. Your classmate Zhang Jie told you that Mike had waited for you in the classroom for 1 h on Thursday afternoon.
- Mike has left for another city.

Write your email message to Mike expressing your apology. When finished writing it, send it directly to Mike by email <***@hotmail.com>.

We were aware that discourse production tasks might not produce data that were used in actual email interaction (Félix-Brasdefer 2012), particularly that the elicitation tasks did not address the notion of consequentiality (Bardovi-Harlig and Hartford 2005). However, as noted by Grainger and Harris (2007, p. 3): "unlike requests and certain other common speech acts, they [apologies] are difficult to come across (and record) in naturally-occurring language." Since the present study aimed to examine email apologies of Chinese English learners across two different proficiency levels, it would be more difficult to collect enough naturally occurring apologies in emails from comparable situations (Ogiermann 2009). It was therefore necessary to apply elicitation tasks.

In addition to the production task, a metapragmatic questionnaire was also constructed to examine the participants' awareness of the sociopragmatic constraints (Brown and Levinson 1987). For each scenario, the participants were asked to rate the severity of the situation and their familiarity with the offended on a 5-point rating scale and to choose the social status between the recipient and themselves from a 3-choice multiple choice.

10.3.3 Data Analysis

As stated in the previous section, data for the present study mainly included two parts: the production of email response and the perception of three sociopragmatic variables (power, social distance, and the imposition of speech acts). Analysis of the perception data was straightforward as the answers were objective ratings or choices. With regard to the production data, the emails were analyzed using Grounded Theory (Glaser and Strauss 1967; Strauss and Corbin 1998) to explore the pragmatic features, with considerations of the CCSARP coding scheme (Blum-Kulka et al. 1989) wherever possible. The coding procedures were as follows.

The emails obtained were first coded into 'opening,' 'main texts,' and 'closing' (Gains 1999). Open coding (Strauss and Corbin 1998) was then conducted for the main texts. Memos were kept for some codes to keep the researchers' thoughts on a specific code in the open coding stages. After coding and recoding all the data, we obtained 25 coding categories. We then grouped the strategies with similar functions into a main category, based on review of research on coding apologies (Bergman and Kasper 1993; Blum-Kulka et al. 1989; Olshtain and Cohen 1983). The final coding scheme is illustrated as follows:

1. Illocutionary force indicating device (IFID)
   - 1.1 Expression of regret
   - 1.2 Offer of apology
   - 1.3 Request for forgiveness
2. Taking on responsibility
   - 2.1 Explicit self-blame
   - 2.2 Lack of intent
   - 2.3 Expression of embarrassment
   - 2.4 Admission of fact but not of responsibility
   - 2.5 Acknowledgement

3. Explanation
4. Offer of repair
5. Promise of forbearance
6. Showing concern for the offended
7. Efforts to appease
8. Downgraders: cajoler, appealer, alerter
9. Intensifiers: adverb, structure, please
10. State hearer facts
11. Phatic expressions
12. Ask for response
13. Opening
14. Closing

As the present study aimed to explore Chinese university students' apologies in email, the analysis therefore focused on apology strategies and modifications (i.e., strategies 1–9 listed above). In addition, the length of the participant's email was also calculated (number of words) and examined.

Each of the participant's responses was coded into one of the categories, and frequencies of responses within each main category were then obtained for each group. Regarding inferential statistics, the Kolmogorov–Smirnov test (the K–S test) and Levene's test were first computed to analyze the normality of the data and homogeneity of variance, respectively, two significant assumptions of a parametric test. The results showed that the assumption of the normality of the data was not met. Therefore, a nonparametric test, a Mann–Whitney U-test, was employed in order to yield appropriate test results. With regard to categorical data, the Chi-square test was used. The probability value was set at $p < 0.05$.

10.4 Results

10.4.1 Perception of Sociopragmatic Variables

This section presents results concerning the learners' perception of the three sociopragmatic variables, starting with the context-internal factor 'severity of offence' followed by the two context-external factor 'power' and 'social distance.'

Table 10.1 displays ratings of severity of offense by the two groups of participants. On average the two groups rated the offense of the situation similarly (3.58 for the low group and 3.85 for the high group). In the high group, 62.5 % of the participants (25 out of 40) rated the offense above 3 (40 % rated 4 and 22.5 %

Table 10.1 Rating of severity of offense across the low and high groups

Group	No. of students	Min	Max	Mean	SD
Low	40	1	5	3.58	0.781
High	40	3	5	3.85	0.770

Table 10.2 Rating of social distance across the low and high groups

Group	No. of students	Min	Max	Mean	SD
Low	40	2	5	3.25	0.809
High	40	2	5	3.23	0.768

rated 5), indicating that the majority of the high group considered the offense rather severe. Similarly, among the low group participants, 23 (57.5 %) rated the offense above 3 (50 % rated 4 and 7.5 % rated 5). None of the high group participants rated the offense lower than 3, whereas two participants in the low group rated the offense lower than 3. Mann–Whitney U-test showed that there was no significant difference between the two groups concerning their rating of severity of offense.

Although the two scenarios were designed to elicit apologies in emails among Chinese English learners toward their foreign peers (i.e., equal status), the learners' choices of their social status with their foreign peers revealed interesting results. The majority of the participants considered were in the same social status as their foreign peers (62.5 and 67.5 % for the low and the high group, respectively). Thirteen participants in each group (32.5 %) considered that they were in a lower ranking than their foreign peers. In the low group, two participants (5 %) considered themselves in a higher-ranking status. Chi-square test showed that there was no statistical difference between the two groups in terms of choice of power.

Table 10.2 presents the two groups' rating of the social distance between their foreign peers and themselves.

As shown in Table 10.2, both groups of participants rated their relation with the foreign peers as neutral (m = 3.25 for the low group and m = 3.23 for the high group). Three participants (7.5 %) in the low group considered their foreign peers as very intimate (rating the relationship 5) while only 1 (2.5 %) in the high group rated it 5. Mann–Whitney U-test showed that there was no significant difference between the two groups concerning their rating of social distance.

10.4.2 Apology Emails

This section analyzes the learners' email responses. The length of the participants' email responses is first examined, followed by analyses of apology strategies.

10.4.2.1 Length of Emails

Table 10.3 summarizes the descriptive statistics of length of the emails collected across the two groups of participants.

According to Table 10.3, on average the low group's email was approximately 113 words (m = 112.45), whereas the high group's email contained approximately 71 words (m = 70.98). The result indicated that the low group wrote longer emails

Table 10.3 Length of email apologies across the low and high groups

Group	No. of students	Min	Max	Mean	SD
Low	40	55	211	112.45	39.965
High	40	26	123	70.98	27.122

to apologize to their foreign peers than did the high group, and the difference reached a significant level ($U = 307$, $Z = -4.75$, $p < 0.0001$). This finding contradicts Flores Salgado (2011), in which the length of English apologies among the Mexican Spanish learners showed a positive relation with the increase of learners' L2 proficiency. We will discuss this in detail in Sect. 10.5.

10.4.2.2 Apology Strategies in Emails

The two groups' employments of apology strategies and modifications are displayed in Table 10.4. As shown in the table, both the low group and the high group participants employed significantly more general apology strategies than situation-specific apology strategies (205 vs. 67, chi-square = 70.02, $p < 0.001$ for the low group and 156 vs. 52, chi-square = 52, $p < 0.001$ for the high group). Chi-square test showed that there was no significant difference between the two groups with regard to the proportion of general strategies against situation-specific strategies employed in the two groups' email apologies.

In terms of frequency of overall apology strategies and modifications, the low group employed many more strategies than did the high group (324 vs. 279), but

Table 10.4 Overall distributions of apology strategies among low group and high group apologies

Strategy	Low		High	
	Frequency	Percentage	Frequency	Percentage
General strategies	205	63.27	156	55.91
IFID	119	36.73	93	33.33
Taking responsibility	86	26.54	63	22.58
Situation-specific strategies	67	20.68	52	18.64
Explanation	11	3.40	11	3.94
Offer of repair	36	11.11	30	10.75
Promise of forbearance	8	2.47	1	0.36
Showing concern for the offended	8	2.47	5	1.79
Efforts to appease	4	1.23	5	1.79
Subtotal	272	83.95	208	74.55
Upgrader	45	13.89	63	22.58
Downgrader	7	2.16	8	2.87
Total	324	100	279	100

the difference did not reach a significant level. In terms of individual strategies (strategies less than 5 % are not examined by inferential statistics), significant differences were observed between the two groups in the frequency of 'IFID' (119 vs. 93 for the low and high groups, respectively, $U = 563$, $Z = -2.39$, $p < 0.05$), the frequency of 'Taking responsibility' (86 vs. 63 for the low and high groups, respectively, $U = 573$, $Z = -2.30$, $p < 0.05$), and the frequency of upgraders (45 for the low group and 63 for the high group, $U = 1038$, $Z = 2.441$, $p < 0.05$). That is, the low group employed the strategy 'IFID' and the strategy 'Taking responsibility' (the two general apology strategies) in their emails significantly more frequently than did the high group. By contrast, the high group learners employed significantly more upgraders to intensify their apologies than did their low group counterparts. Considering that upgraders were used to intensify the force of IFID internally, the results indicated that the high group employed upgraders much more frequently than the low group to intensify the force of the strategy IFID in their email apologies. The increase in employment of apology upgraders with increasing L2 proficiency supports the findings of previous studies in the literature (Sabaté i Dalmau and Curell i Gotor 2007; Trosborg 1987, 1995).

The pragmatic development was also evidenced in the employment of the substrategies under 'Taking responsibility.' Table 10.5 displays the frequency of use of the five subcategories under the strategy 'Taking responsibility' across the two groups of learners.

As shown in Table 10.5, the two groups showed different preferences in the employment of various individual substrategies under the strategy 'taking responsibility.' For the low group, 'explicit self-blame' and 'admission of facts but not of responsibility' were employed in relatively high proportions in their apology emails (30.23 and 46.67 %, respectively). 'Lack of intent' and 'expression of embarrassment' were used moderately (10.47 and 9.30 %, respectively), whereas 'acknowledgement' was used less frequently (2.33 %). By contrast, the high group showed a strong preference in employing 'admission of facts but not responsibility' (74.60 %) over the other four substrategies. Chi-square test showed that the two groups were significantly different in terms of distribution of substrategies in 'taking responsibility' (chi-square = 17.00, $p < 0.002$). The strong preference of the

Table 10.5 Frequency and percentage of each subcategory in 'Taking responsibility' of the low group and the high group

Taking responsibility	Low		High	
	Frequency	Percentage	Frequency	Percentage
Explicit self-blame	26	30.23	7	11.11
Lack of intent	9	10.47	6	9.52
Expression of embarrassment	8	9.30	0	0.00
Admission of facts but not of responsibility	41	47.67	47	74.60
Acknowledgement	2	2.33	3	4.76
Total	86	100	63	100

substrategy 'admission of facts but not of responsibility' reflected that when the Chinese students employed the strategy 'taking responsibility,' the high group preferred using the substrategy 'admissions of facts but not of responsibility,' indicating that they tended to distance themselves from the offense and simultaneously perform their intention to maintain interpersonal harmony with the recipient.

10.5 Summary and Discussion

The present study was designed to investigate the speech act of apology performed in emails by Chinese English learners across two different proficiency levels. In addition, their perception of sociopragmatic variables was also analyzed.

The first research question examined the Chinese learners' perception of the three sociopragmatic factors (i.e., severity of offense, power, and social distance) in the two scenarios. With respect to severity of offense, both groups of learners considered the offense rather severe (3.58 for the low group and 3.85 for the high group). None of the high group participants rated the offense lower than 3, and only two in the low group rated the offense lower than 3. In terms of power, the majority of the two groups considered that they were in an equal status with their foreign peers (62.5 % and 67.5 % for the low and the high group, respectively). It is, however, interesting that 32.5 % of the participants in each group ranked their foreign peers as a higher status position. Concerning social distance, both groups rated their relation with the foreign peers as neutral ($m = 3.25$ and $m = 3.23$ for the low and the high groups, respectively), with few of them (3 in the low group and 1 in the high group) rating their foreign peers as very familiar. No significant difference was found between the two groups concerning their ratings of the three sociopragmatic variables.

The results revealed that the Chinese learners of the two proficiency levels perceived similarly the sociopragmatic factors (severity of offense, power, and social distance) in the two scenarios examined in the present study. This indicates that L2 English proficiency levels did not influence the Chinese learners' perception of sociopragmatic variables in the situation of offense. It is intriguing that although the scenarios described the foreign peers as classmate/friend, approximately one-third of the learners in both groups considered their foreign peers in a higher status position. Future research is encouraged to explore why Chinese learners perceived their foreign classmate/friend unequally in terms of social status. In the two scenarios, the foreign peers are described as native speakers from the United Kingdom or the United States. It is possible that their native English ability would put them in a higher status position in interaction with nonnative speakers of English in intercultural communication, particularly in contexts such as Chinese universities, where Chinese learners are required to learn English as a compulsory course. Furthermore, few of the Chinese learners in either group considered their foreign peer as very familiar. In Chinese universities, foreign students normally live separately from local Chinese students. In most cases, they do not have classes together with local Chinese students either. Therefore, it is not surprising that few participants in the present study rated the foreign peer as very familiar. Although the hypothetical situation may make it hard for the participants to imagine their relationship with their peer, in future studies we will include introspective instruments (Ericsson and Simon 1993) such as think-aloud (Bowles 2010; Gass and Mackey 2000) or retrospective verbal reports (Cohen 2012; Cohen and Olshtain 1993; Woodfield 2010) to incorporate the learners' emic views to shed light on reasons why they perceive the sociopragmatic variables in a certain way.

The second research question examined the length of apology emails produced by the two groups of Chinese learners. The results showed that on average the low group's apology email was significantly longer than that of the high group ($m = 112.45$ and $m = 70.98$ for the two groups, respectively, $U = 307$, $Z = -4.75$, $p < 0.0001$). This finding contradicts Flores Salgado's (2011) results in her investigation into apologies made by Mexican Spanish learners of English across three proficiency levels. In Flores Salgado (2011), a positive correlation was observed between the length of the learners' responses and the increase of their English proficiency, echoing the investigation of learners' request in Blum-Kulka and Olshtain (1986). That is, advanced Mexican Spanish learners produced longest apologies, whereas basic learners' apologies were shortest. The discrepancy between Flores Salgado (2011) and the present study may result from the different data collection methods. In the former study, the Mexican learners' apologies were collected through a modified version of the cartoon oral production task developed by Rose (2000). It is likely that the oral production task was more cognitively stressful to the L2 learners (Chang 2010; Kasper and Rose 2002), particularly to those with limited L2 proficiency. Therefore, the length of a learner's apology depends on the grammatical competence that they possess (Flores Salgado 2011). By contrast, the present study examined Chinese learners' apologies in emails. The asynchronous characteristic of email allowed the Chinese learners sufficient time to mediate and to compose. The discrepancy thus further supports previous findings that apologies in email discourse may display different features from those in spoken or written language (Davies et al. 2007; Harrison and Allton 2013; Hatipoğlu 2004).

There are two possible explanations why the low group's apology emails were significantly longer than those of the high group in the present study. One plausible explanation is that the low group participants lacked sufficient pragmatic competence to express themselves clearly. They may feel 'insecure' when performing their apologies in email so that they would like to write as much as possible (Edmondson and House 1991), worrying that they had not apologized enough. By contrast, the high group learners had higher pragmatic competence to express their apologies more clearly (for example, through upgraders), thus resulting in a shorter email. Another explanation is that the low group was more influenced by their L1 Chinese culture than their high group counterparts. That is, the low group showed more 'negative transfer' (Kasper 1992) in their English apology emails. As Chang and Haugh (2011) argue, for Chinese, repetition of the apology is a means to show '*chengyi*' (sincerity) of an apology to indicate the offender's sincerity (Gu 1990). This argument is supported by Zhu et al.'s comment on Chinese culture: "the initiator of an action, be it a gift offer, *apology*, or expression of gratitude, repeats the action several times to show what s/he intends to do is genuine" (Zhu et al. 2000, p. 99, emphasis added). The repetition of apologies unsurprisingly resulted in longer emails. As in the present study, more apology strategies indeed were observed in the low group's emails, for which we now turn to the third research question.

The last research question explored the strategies in Chinese learners' apology emails. Both the low group and the high group learners employed significantly more general apology strategies than situation-specific apology strategies. Overall, the low group employed many more strategies than did the high group. To be specific, the low group employed significantly more 'IFID' and 'Taking responsibility' than did the high group in their emails. By contrast, the high group employed significantly more upgraders to intensify their apologies than did their low group, indicating a pragmatic development reported in previous studies (Sabaté i Dalmau and Curell i Gotor 2007; Trosborg 1987, 1995). Because the speech act of apology is conventional and routinized (Aijmer 1996), L1 speakers often employ upgraders as a useful way to sound more sincerely in their apologies (Bergman and Kasper 1993). The result in the present study thus indicates that the high group was more capable of manipulating their linguistic competence to produce more appropriate intensified apologies than their low group counterparts. More employment of upgraders but less apology strategies may also explain why the high group' emails are shorter than those of the low group discussed above.

It must be remembered that even the low group learners are first-year university students at an intermediate level of English proficiency. Low frequency of upgraders in their apology emails revealed that internal modifiers of speech acts may be challenging to L2 learners' pragmatics acquisition. This echoes previous findings in L2 pragmatics on various speech acts that internal modifiers are acquired slowly and at a very late stage, e.g., requests (Bella 2012; Göy et al. 2012; Schauer 2009; Woodfield 2012), apologies (Sabaté i Dalmau and Curell i Gotor 2007), and refusals (Ren 2013). The difficulty of acquisition of internal modifiers in apologies thus highlights the need for pedagogical intervention in support of learners' pragmatic competence on these aspects.

10.6 Conclusion

The present study has investigated Chinese learners' apologies in email across different English proficiency levels. The results showed that L2 proficiency did not influence the Chinese learners' perception of sociopragmatic variables in the situation of offense. L2 proficiency did not influence the participants' preference of general apology strategies over situation-specific strategies in their apology email either. By contrast, L2 proficiency had an impact on the frequency of the two general apology strategies (IFID and Taking responsibility) and upgraders employed in the Chinese learners' apology emails. The low group learners employed significantly more strategies of IFID and Taking responsibility but significantly fewer upgraders than did their high group counterparts. The high group learners' ability to write more intensified apologies in a shorter email indicates pragmatic development in these aspects at least. However, the low group learners' difficulty to acquire internal modifiers highlights the necessity of pragmatics instruction.

As little research has explored L2 learners' apologies in emails and few studies (Chang 2010; Rose 2000) have investigated Chinese learners' pragmatic development in the speech act of apology, analyzing how learners perform various speech acts in emails would benefit the pragmatics literature. The present study has contributed to the existing literature by exploring Chinese English learners' perception and production of apologies in emails sent to their foreign peers, particularly in relation to pragmatics research in computer-mediated communication (Herring 2013). Nevertheless, the present study elicited data based on hypothetical situations. Thus the conclusions need to be treated with caution. In addition, the study only employed a production task and a metapragmatic assessment. Future research is needed to include introspective methods to shed light on reasons influencing learners' perception and responses.

References

Aijmer, Karin. 1996. *Conversational routines in English: Convention and creativy*. London: Longman.

Bardovi-Harlig, Kathleen, and Beverly Hartford. 2005. Institutional discourse and interlanguage pragmatics research. In *Interlanguage pragmatics: exploring institutional talk*, ed. Kathleen Bardovi-Harlig, and Beverly Hartford, 7–36. Mahwah, NJ: Lawrence Erlbaum.

Barron, Anne. 2003. *Acquisition in interlanguage pragmatics: Learning how to do things with words in a study abroad context*. Amsterdam: John Benjamins.

Bella, Spyridoula. 2012. Pragmatic development in a foreign language: A study of Greek FL requests. *Journal of Pragmatics* 44: 1917–1947.

Bergman, Marc L., and Gabriele Kasper. 1993. Perception and performance in native and nonnative apology. In *Interlanguage pragmatics*, ed. Gabriele Kasper, and Shoshana Blum-Kulka, 82–107. New York: Oxford University Press.

Blum-Kulka, Shoshana, and Julian House. 1989. Cross-cultural and situational variation in requesting behavior. In *Cross-cultural pragmatics: requests and apologies*, ed. Shoshana Blum-Kulka, Julian House, and Gabriele Kasper, 123–154. Norwood, New Jersey: Ablex.

Blum-Kulka, Shoshana, Julian House, and Gabriele Kasper (eds.). 1989. *Cross-cultural pragmatics: Requests and apologies*. Norwood, New Jersey: Ablex.

Blum-Kulka, Shoshana, and Elite Olshtain. 1986. Too many words: Length of utterance and pragmatic failure. *Studies in Second Language Acquisition* 8: 47–61.

Bowles, Melissa. 2010. *The think-aloud controversy in second language research*. New York/London: Routledge.

Brown, Penelope, and Stephen C. Levinson. 1987. *Politeness: Some universals in language usage*. Cambridge: Cambridge University Press.

Chang, Wei-lin Melody, and Michael Haugh. 2011. Evaluations of im/politeness of an intercultural apology. *Intercultural Pragmatics* 8(3): 411–442.

Chang, Yuh-Fang. 2010. 'I no say you say is boring': The development of pragmatic competence in L2 apology. *Language Sciences* 32: 408–424.

Chen, Chi-Fen E. 2006. The development of email literacy: From writing to peers to writing to authority figures. *Language learning & Technology* 10(2): 35–55.

Clark, Herbert H. 1996. *Using language.* Cambridge: Cambridge University Press.

Cogo, Alessia, and Martin Dewey. 2012. *Analysing English as a lingua franca: A corpus-driven investigation.* London: Continuum.

Cohen, Andrew D. 2012. Research methods for describing variation in intercultural pragmatics for cultures in contact and conflict. In *Pragmatic variation in first and second language contexts: Methodological issues,* eds. J. César. Félix-Brasdefer and Dale April Koike, 271–294. Amsterdam: John Benjamins.

Cohen, Andrew D., and Elite Olshtain. 1993. The production of speech acts by EFL learners. *TESOL Quarterly* 27: 33–56.

Cook, Vivian. 1992. Evidence for multicompetence. *Language Learning* 42(4): 557–591.

Cook, Vivian. 2002. Backgroud to the L2 user. In *Portraits of the L2 user*, ed.Vivian. Cook, 1–28. Clevedon: Multilingual matters.

Coulmas, Florian. 1981. "Poison to your soul": Thanks and apologies contrastively viewed. In *Conversational Routine: Explorations in standardized communication situations and prepatterned speech*, ed. Florian Coulmas, 69–91. The Hague: Mouton.

Davies, Bethan L., Andrew John Merrison, and Angela Goddard. 2007. Institutional apologies in UK higher education: Getting back into the black before going into red. *Journal of Politeness Research* 3: 39–63.

Dewaele, Jean-Marc. 2007. Context and L2 Users' Pragmatic Development. In *Language learning and teaching as social interaction*, ed. Hua Zhu, Paul Seedhouse, Wei Li, and Vivian Cook, 162–183. Basingstoke: Palgrave Macmillan.

Economidou-Kogetsidis, Maria. 2011. "Please answer me as soon as possible": Pragmatic failure in non-native speakers' e-mail request to faculty. *Journal of Pragmatics* 43: 3193–3215.

Edmondson, Willis, and Julian House. 1991. Do learners talk too much? The waffle phenomenon in interlanguage pragmatics. In *Foreign/Second Language Pedagogy Research: a Commemorative volume for Claus Faerch*, ed. Robert Philipson, Eric Kellerman, Larry Selinker, Michael Sharwood-Smith, and Merrill Swain, 273–287. Clevedon: Multilingual Matters.

Ericsson, Anders, and Herbert Simon. 1993. *Protocol analysis: Verbal reports as data.* Cambridge, MA: MIT Press.

Félix-Brasdefer, J.César. 2012. E-mail requess to faculty: E-politeness and internal modification. In *Interlanguage request modification*, ed. Maria Economidou-Kogetsidis, and Helen Woodfield, 87–118. Amsterdam: John Benjamins.

Flores Salgado, Elizabeth. 2011. *The pragmatics of requests and apologies: Developmental patterns of Mexican students.* Amsterdam: John Benjamins.

Fraser, Bruce. 1981. On apologizing. In *Conversational Routine: Explorations in standardized communication situations and prepatterned speech*, ed. Florian Coulmas, 259–271. The Hague: Mouton.

Gains, Jonathan. 1999. Electronic mail –A new style of communication or just a new medium?: An investigation into the text features of E-mail. *English for Specific Purposes* 18(1): 81–101.

García, Carmen. 1989. Apologizing in English: Politeness strategies used by native and non-native speakers. *Multilingua* 8(1): 3–20.

Gass, Susan, and Alison Mackey. 2000. *Stimulated recall methodology in second language research.* Mahwah, NJ: Lawrence Erlbaum.

Glaser, Barney, and Anselm Strauss. 1967. *The discovery of grounded theory: Strategies for qualitative research.* Chicago: Aldine.

Goffman, Erving. 1971. *Relations in public.* New York: Basic Books.

Göy, Elif, Deniz Zeyrek, and Bahar Otcu. 2012. Developmental patterns in internal modification of requests: A quantitative study on Turkish learners of English. In *Interlanguage request modification*, ed. Maria Economidou-Kogetsidis, and Helen Woodfield, 51–86. Amsterdam: John Benjamins.

Grainger, Karen, and Sandra Harris. 2007. Apologies: Introduction. *Journal of Politeness Research* 3: 1–9.

Gu, Yueguo. 1990. Politeness phenomena in modern Chinese. *Journal of Pragmatics* 14: 237–257.

Harrison, Sandra, and Diane Allton. 2013. Apologies in email discussions. In *Pragmatics of computer-mediated communication*, ed. Susan C. Herring, Dieter Stein, and Tuija Virtanen, 315–338. Berlin: Mouton de Gruyter.

Hatipoğlu, Çiler. 2004. Do apologies in emails follow spoken and written norms?: Some examples from British English. *Studies about Languages* 5: 21–29.

Herring, Susan C. 2013. *Pragmatics of computer-mediated communication*. Berlin: Mouton de Gruyter.

Holmes, Janet. 1990. Apologies in New Zealand English. *Language in Society* 19(2): 155–199.

Jenkins, Jennifer. 2007. *English as a lingua franca: Attitude and identity*. Oxford: Oxford University Press.

Jenkins, Jennifer. 2014. *English as a lingua franca in the international university: The politics of academic English language policy*. London/New York: Routledge.

Jenkins, Jennifer, Alessia Cogo, and Martin Dewey. 2011. Review of developments in research into English as a lingua franca. *Language Teaching* 44(3): 281–315.

Kádár, Dániel Z. 2007. On historical Chinese apology and its strategic application. *Journal of Politeness Research* 3: 125–150.

Kasper, Gabriele. 1992. Pragmatic transfer. *Second Language Research* 8: 203–231.

Kasper, Gabriele, and Kenneth R. Rose. 2002. *Pragmatic development in a second language*. Oxford: Blackwell.

Leech, Geoffrey. 1983. *Principles of pragmatics*. London: Longman.

Liu, Jianda. 2006. *Measuring interlanguage pragmatic knowledge of EFL learners*. Frankfurt am Main: Peter Lang.

Liu, Jianda. 2007. Developing a pragmatics test for Chinese EFL learners. *Language Testing* 24 (3): 391–415.

Maeshiba, Naoko, Naoko Yoshinaga, Gabriele Kasper, and Steve Ross. 1996. Transfer and proficiency in interlanguage apologizing. In *Speech acts across cultures*, ed. Susan Gass, and Joyce Neu, 155–187. Berlin: Mouton de Gruyter.

Márquez Reiter, Rosina. 2000. *Linguistic politeness in Britain and Uruguay: A contrastive study of requests and apologies*. Amsterdam: John Benjamins.

Márquez Reiter, Rosina. 2008. Intra-cultural variation: Explanations in service calls to two Montevidean service providers. *Journal of Politeness Research* 4: 1–30.

Mauranen, Anna. 2012. *Exploring ELF: Academic English shaped by non-native speakers*. Cambridge: Cambridge University Press.

Mori, Junko. 2009. Commentary: The social turn in second language acquisition and Japanese pragmatics research: Reflection on ideologies, methodologies and instructional implications. In *Pragmatic comptence*, ed. Naoko Taguchi, 335–358. Berlin: Mouton de Gruyter.

Ogiermann, Eva. 2009. *On apologising in negative and positive politeness cultures*. Amsterdam: John Benjamins.

Olshtain, Elite. 1989. Apologies across languages. In *Cross-cultural pragmatics: Requests and apologies*, ed. Shoshana Blum-Kulka, Julian House, and Gabriele Kasper, 155–173. Norwood, New Jersey: Ablex.

Olshtain, Elite, and Andrew D. Cohen. 1983. Apology: A speech act set. In *Sociolinguistics and language acquisition*, ed. Nessa Wolfson, and Elliot Judd, 18–35. Rowley, M.A.: Newbury House.

Owen, Marion. 1983. *Apologies and remedia exchanges: A study of language use in social interaction*. Berlin/New York: Mouton de Gruyter.

Pan, Ping Cathy. 2012. Interlanguage requests in institutional e-mail discourse. In *Interlanguage request modification*, eds. Maria. Economidou-Kogetsidis and Helen Woodfield, 119–161. Amsterdam: John Benjamins.

Pan, Yuling, and Dániel Z Kádár. 2011. *Politeness in historical and contemporary Chinese*. London: Continuum.

Ren, Wei. 2012. Pragmatic development in Chinese speakers' L2 English refusals. In *EUROSLA Yearbook (vol. 12)*, eds. Leah Roberts, Christina Lindqvist, Camilla Bardel and Niklas Abrahamsson, 63–87. Amsterdam: John Benjamins.

Ren, Wei. 2013. The effect of study abroad on the pragmatic development of the internal modification of refusals. *Pragmatics* 23(4): 715–741.

Robinson, Jeffrey D. 2004. The sequential organization of "explicit" apologies in naturally occurring English. *Research on language and social Interaction* 37(3): 291–330.

Rose, Kenneth R. 2000. An exploratory cross-sectional study of interlanguage pragmatic development. *Studies in Second Language Acquisition* 22: 27–67.

Sabaté i Dalmau, Maria, and Hortènsia Curell i Gotor. 2007. From "Sorry very much" to "I'm ever so sorry": Acquisitional patterns in L2 apologies by Catalan learners of English. *Intercultural Pragmatics* 4(2): 287–315.

Schauer, Gila. A. 2009. *Interlanguage pragmatic development: The study abroad context*. London: Continuum.

Searle, John R. 1979. *Expression and meaning: Studies in the theory of speech acts*. Cambridge: Cambridge University Press.

Seidlhofer, Barbara. 2001. Closing a conceptual gap: The case for a description of English as a lingua franca. *International Journal of Applied Linguistics* 11(2): 133–158.

Seidlhofer, Barbara. 2011. *Understanding English as a lingua franca*. Oxford: Oxford University Press.

Spencer-Oatey, Helen. 1993. Conceptions of social relations and pragmatics research. *Journal of Pragmatics* 20: 27–47.

Strauss, Aaselm, and Juliet Corbin. 1998. *Basics of qualitative research: Grounded theory procedures and techniques*, 2nd ed. Newbury Park: SAGE.

Trosborg, Anna. 1987. Apology strategies in native/non-natives. *Journal of Pragmatics* 11: 147–167.

Trosborg, Anna. 1995. *Interlanguage pragmatics: Requests, complaints, apologies*. Berlin: Mouton de Gruyter.

Warga, Muriel, and Ursula Schölmberger. 2007. The acquisition of French apologetic behavior in a study abroad context. *Intercultural Pragmatics* 4(2): 221–251.

Woodfield, Helen. 2010. What lies beneath? Verbal report in interlanguage requests in English. *Multilingua* 29: 1–27.

Woodfield, Helen. 2012. "I think maybe I want to lend the notes from you": Development of request modification in graduate learners. In *Interlanguage request modification*, ed. Maria Economidou-Kogetsidis, and Helen Woodfield, 9–49. Amsterdam: John Benjamins.

Xu, Wei. 2009. *Gaining pragmatic competence in English as a second and a foreign language: The effects of the learning environment and overall L2 proficiency*. (unpublished Ph.D. Dissertation), University of Nevada, Reno.

Yates, Lynda. 2010. Pragmatic challenges for second language learners. In *Pragmatics across languages and cultures*, ed. Anna Trosborg, 287–308. Berlin: Mouton de Gruyter.

Zhu, Hua, Wei Li, and Yuan Qian. 2000. The sequential organisation of gift offering and acceptance in Chinese. *Journal of Pragmatics* 32: 81–103.

Author Biographies

Jianda Liu (刘建达) is a professor and dean of the National Key Research Center for Linguistics and Applied Linguistics, Guangdong University of Foreign Studies, China. He is currently the vice president of Guangdong University of Foreign Studies and vice dean of the National Educational Examinations Authority. He has worked in designing, developing, and validating language tests in China. His research interests include language testing, pragmatics, and second language acquisition. He has published many papers in different academic journals. His recent book entitled *Measuring Interlanguage Pragmatic Knowledge of EFL Learners* was published by Peter Lang.

Wei Ren (任伟) is Professor of Applied Linguistics at the National Key Research Center for Linguistics and Applied Linguistics, Guangdong University of Foreign Studies, China. His recent publications include articles in *Applied Linguistics*, *Journal of Pragmatics*, *Pragmatics*, and a monograph *L2 Pragmatic Development in Study Abroad Contexts*.

Part IV
Emails in the Workplace

Chapter 11
Status-Congruence in Request E-Mail Discourse of Professional Secretaries in a University of Taiwan

Pi-Hsia Lü

Abstract This study investigated the status-congruence of request e-mails composed by professional secretaries serving in a private university departmental office in Taiwan. It first explored the degree of directness and internal and external modification used in their discourse, and then examined the politeness standards of 'cultural insiders.' The results showed that senior professionals tended to use more direct strategies and more internal and external modification devices, while a novice professional used more conventionally indirect strategies and fewer modifiers. The difference in choice of request strategies revealed that senior professionals take for granted the right to make requests for information or action on behalf of the administrative body, thus giving faculty the impression of having no choice in matters. Relative to the interactional function of request e-mails, conventionally indirect expressions which showed regard for them as persons were favored by the faculty. The study also made evident the novice professional's lack of assurance in her identity as a practicing professional in the asymmetrical academic context.

Keywords E-mail communication · Requests · Interlanguage pragmatics · Status-congruence

11.1 Introduction

Electronic mail has become a powerful tool for written communication in academic settings, functioning as a primary medium of intercommunication. Bicultural academic workplaces, in particular, require professionals to use English e-mails in their work environment. This paper investigates how professionals, i.e., secretaries, in a private university departmental office in Taiwan made requests to their faculty in

P.-H. Lü (✉)
Department of English Language, Literature and Linguistics, Providence University, Taichung, Taiwan
e-mail: bhlu@pu.edu.tw

Y. Chen et al. (eds.), *Email Discourse Among Chinese Using English as a Lingua Franca*, DOI 10.1007/978-981-287-888-5_11

e-mail communication. In general, people in secretarial positions function as "servers" for the department communication, both relaying messages and controlling and filtering messages, just like a nerve center or a computer mainframe. They act like mediators between the school administration and teachers and between the school administration and students (Lü 2012). On the one hand, secretaries respond to academic-related requests from teachers. On the other hand, due to their job responsibility, they frequently need to make requests of teachers to ask them either to provide information that the school needs or to perform a particular task.

Given the asymmetrical relation between faculty and secretaries in the work context, making requests of faculty is not only a highly imposing act for secretaries, but also involves a complex psychological struggle. This linguistic behavior poses difficulties for the professionals, who are stuck in the middle, trying to fulfill school administrative requirements by writing to addressees who may not want to comply with the request.

The present research investigates differences between professionals and foreign faculty in their use of request strategies. Further exploration of novice versus senior professionals reveals additional distinctions. In addition to the linguistic features shown in request e-mail discourse, a close look at representative e-mail messages reveals the professionals' pragmalinguistic competence on the one hand, and their eagerness to show politeness to authority figures based on sociopragmatic knowledge on the other hand.[1]

Based on the view that any single setting can provide a rich background for investigation (Bardovi-Harlig and Hartford 2005), the exploration of professionals' request e-mail discourse in a particular working environment can shed light not only on interlanguage pragmatics research, but also on the understanding of insiders' 'emic' viewpoints, providing far-reaching revelation to outsiders. By investigating institutional discourse, the researcher can observe novice participants as they become experts and observe how institutional talk and institutional rules are taught and learned (Scollon and Scollon 1995). The findings of this study will help language learners cope with the features of language and develop the competency needed to function in a workplace (Basturkmen 2006).

This study attempts to address the following research questions:

1. How does a novice secretary differ from senior secretaries in using request strategies?
2. How do faculty perceive the request e-mail discourse sent by secretaries and what is deemed as an appropriate request e-mail in the academic context?

[1]The term "pragmalinguistics" refers to the linguistic resources needed by a speaker to express illocutions. The resources include lexical, syntactic, and prosodic means of softening or strengthening the force of an utterance and means of expressing it formally and informally. The term "sociopragmatics" refers to the speaker's ability to use and interpret speech acts appropriately according to social norms. Thus, knowing how linguistically to form a polite request is pragmalinguistics, whereas knowing what, when and from whom it is polite to request is sociopragmatics (Leech 1983).

11.2 Rationale

E-mail has become an effective and popular means of written communication, providing professionals with a convenient way to obtain feedback, clarification, and information. Such professionals are often faced with uncertainties regarding style and politeness strategies in e-mail interaction (Crystal 2001; Barron 2002, 2003; Biesenbach-Lucas 2006) especially in hierarchical relationships where the power asymmetry needs to be maintained.

The request act in written business communication means "a legitimate attempt by the writer to get the reader to perform an action required by the business circumstances through evoking the reader's need for compliance on the grounds of corporate and personal motivators such as necessity, duty and goodwill" (Bargiela-Chiappini et al. 1996, p. 640). Writing e-mails to authority figures requires high pragmatic competence and awareness of politeness conventions and e-mail etiquette (Biesenbach-Lucas 2007), and people usually need to spend more time planning and composing status-unequal e-mails in which various face-threatening acts are usually involved (Chen 2006). Therefore, drafting an appropriate and language-congruent e-mail to an authority figure often involves a lot of guesswork and can be an even greater challenge for nonnative speakers who often lack "the sophisticated pragmatic competence in the L2 and critical language awareness of how discourse shapes and is shaped by power relations, identity, and ideologies established in the target culture" (Chen 2006, p. 36).

In this institutionally unequal relationship, faculty members have "power of control" (Brown and Levinson 1987) over secretaries. By virtue of the institutionalized role, professionals are expected to use status-congruent language that properly acknowledges their own lower institutional status and the professor's higher institutional status (Hartford and Bardovi-Harlig 1996; Biesenbach-Lucas 2007). More specifically, status-congruent requests in academic settings are usually characterized by higher formality, avoidance of imperative requests, a fairly high level of mitigation and acknowledgment of the imposition involved (Economidou-Kogetsidis 2011).

Professionals need to be able to judge the relationship they have with the faculty and assess correctly the degree of imposition of their e-mail requests, taking into account the rights and obligations of the parties involved. They need to be able to express their e-mail requests both to avoid putting at risk their own positive face (their desire to have their public self-image appreciated, understood, liked, approved of and ratified), and their professor's negative face (the faculty's desire to be free from imposition and distraction, to have their territory respected and their freedom of action unimpeded) (Brown and Levinson 1987). The actions requested fall within the work responsibilities of the addresser and the collaboration of the addressee (Vine 2009). It is a goal-oriented activity to get someone to do something, or to get something out of someone. The language used in conveying the (potentially) face-threatening act of a request reflects the addresser's perception of his/her own status and that of the addressee (Bargiela-Chiappini and Harris 1996, p. 637). As requests are typically situated in ongoing contexts of social relations and of activity, their form and interpretation are dependent on both.

Interlanguage research has shown that confusion or problems can occur in L2 communication, including e-mail communication, due to nonnative speakers' limited linguistic ability and unfamiliarity with the norms and values of the target culture. In Chen's (2006) longitudinal case study, a Taiwanese graduate student's e-mail practice in English was examined during her studies at a US university for two and a half years. The study reveals the complexity of an L2 learner's evolving e-mail practice and struggle for appropriateness in her e-mail communication with professors. Lee (2004) studied the request e-mail discourse constructed by Chinese learners of English and focused on the use of request strategies and potential grounders. The findings showed that the learners mainly used direct requests when communicating with their teachers, applying linguistic politeness devices that conform to the traditional teacher-student hierarchical relationship in Chinese culture. Requestive hints, consisting of a potential grounder before a request, ranked second. It appears that the learners tended to give facts or reasons before making requests.

Pragmatic research has so far centered on the investigation of speakers' strategies, namely the performance of interlocutors' speech acts, and on speakers' strategy choice and linguistic forms used to convey illocutionary meaning and politeness (Economidou-Kogetsidis 2011). As requests are "inherently imposing" (Blum-Kulka et al. 1989), they call for considerable face work. Blum-Kulka et al. (1989) in their Cross-Cultural Speech Act Realization Project (CCSARP) compare the use of request strategies by native speakers of different languages and find that while individuals of some cultures tended to make requests using conventionally indirect strategies like 'preparatory' and 'suggestory formula,' those of some other cultures preferred more direct ones such as 'mood derivable' and 'want statement' (Blum-Kulka et al. 1989, p. 125).

Economidou-Kogetsidis (2011) examined e-mail requests sent by Greek Cypriot university students (learners of English) to faculty at a major English-medium university in Cyprus over a period of several semesters. The study examined forms of address (salutations), the degree of directness employed, and the degree and type of supportive moves and lexical/phrasal modifiers used by students in order to soften or aggravate their e-requests. Findings showed that the NNS students' e-mails are characterized by significant directness, an absence of lexical/phrasal downgraders, an omission of greetings and closings and inappropriate or unacceptable forms of address. The study argued that such e-mails can be perceived as impolite and discourteous and therefore capable of causing pragmatic failure[2]

[2]Jenny Thomas defines pragmatic failure as "[…] the inability to understand what is meant by what is said" (1983, p. 93). Two types of failure are normally distinguished according to Leech's (1983) differentiation between pragmalinguistic and sociopragmatic aspects of language usage: *pragmalinguistic failure* and *sociopragmatic failure*. Instances of the former type arise when

(Thomas 1983). This is primarily due to the fact that they appear to give the faculty no choice in complying with the request and fail to acknowledge the imposition involved.

In most interlanguage and cross-cultural studies on requests, data have been collected primarily through the employment of either a discourse completion test (DCT) (Takahashi 1992; Le Pair 1996; Economidou-Kogetsidis 2009) or oral role plays (Hassall 2001; Felix-Brasdefer 2007). However, few studies on request e-mails have focused on the examination of authentic e-mail messages or on the exploration of authentic speech act performance (Biesenbach-Lucas 2007, p. 62), and due to ethical and privacy concerns, only a few messages sent to the researchers themselves have been included in such studies (e.g., Bloch 2002; Economidou-Kogetsidis 2011; Hartford and Bardovi-Harlig 1996; Lee 2004; Li et al. 2011; Warschauer 1999; Danet 2001; Biesenbach-Lucas 2006).

So far, most research investigating request e-mails has focused on the student-professor relationship (Bloch 2002; Biesenbach-Lucas 2006; Chen 2006; Glater 2006; Hartford and Bardovi-Harlig 1996; Hendriks 2010; Li et al. 2011; Economidou-Kogetsidis 2011). Few studies have collected authentic speech act data in workplaces, especially requesting behavior (Ho 2009, 2010; Kong 2006). Kong (2006) examined the making of requests through e-mail. He looked particularly at the use of accounts in the request e-mails exchanged among the employees of a corporation and found that employees in different capacities accompanied their requests with accounts that were either pre-posed (inductive rhetorical approach) or post-posed (deductive rhetorical approach) to different extents.

Ho (2009) investigated the generic structure and discourse strategies employed by the leaders of a multicultural group of educators in making downward requests through internal e-mails. Later, Ho (2010) discussed the construction of personal identities through the request e-mail discourse by a group of professional English language teachers at a public education institution in Hong Kong. It was found that the teachers constructed for themselves the identity of a responsible, hardworking member, as well as a member with authority and power.

The present study aims to examine the English request e-mail discourse performed by secretaries to professors (local Chinese and foreign speakers) in academic contexts and to investigate those linguistic features that might render their e-mails status-incongruent. The study additionally investigates the perceptions of faculty and secretaries about secretaries' request e-mails in the same work setting. The aim of the perception questionnaire is to understand the politeness embedded in request e-mail discourse and the appropriateness of language use as perceived by

(Footnote 2 continued)

non-native speakers or L2 learners inadequately transfer linguistic strategies from their L1 to the L2. It may also arise when non-natives do not identify or express meaning correctly or use wrong suprasegmental/prosodic features (Thomas 1983; Tran 2006). Sociopragmatic failure, on the contrary, originates when non-native speakers unknowingly abide by their L1 rules of speaking and their communicative behavior is therefore influenced by their sociocultural competence in the L1 (Padilla Cruz 2013, pp. 26–27).

the community members. The data further disclose the emic knowledge of the 'cultural insiders,' i.e., the members of the culture under investigation (Eelen 2001, p. 77).

11.3 Methodology

11.3.1 E-Mail Data and Participants

This is a case study of e-mail communication taking place in a bicultural academic context. When the study was carried out, the faculty comprised six foreign teachers and 21 local Chinese teachers. Secretaries as professionals in the academic context dealt quite often with academic-related requests, such as requests for information about courses or faculty research, and requests for actions like updating publication lists or posting course syllabi on the web.

The e-mail data were collected when three secretaries, Alice, Helen and May,[3] all Chinese, served in the department office. Alice and Helen had worked in the department office for more than 10 years while May, a novice secretary, had just begun working in the office. In this intercultural office, where English and Chinese are used interchangeably, in addition to face-to-face exchanges with foreign teachers, secretaries need to deal with e-mail communication every day. As English is a lingua franca in the setting, even some local Chinese teachers commonly used English to communicate with secretaries by e-mail. Hence, there was a very high chance that secretaries would use English as the medium of e-mail communication. To understand the request e-mail discourse used by the members of the target academic context, i.e., faculty and secretaries, authentic e-mail data were collected spanning a period of 6 months.[4] Both the secretaries and faculty involved in the study gave written consent to allow the researcher to use the e-mail data for analysis and promises were given that no personal information would be disclosed. E-mail messages that contained sensitive or confidential information were excluded from the study.

The e-mail data consisted of 240 English e-mail messages that the three secretaries sent to faculty members, with 80 messages collected from each secretary. Eighty e-mail messages that foreign faculty sent to secretaries were collected to compare the request strategies and politeness realization between secretaries and foreign faculty. A contrastive study would allow for more definitive claims concerning the interlanguage-specific features embedded in novice and senior

[3]For ethical reasons (Punch 1994; Stake 1994), pseudonyms are used for the participants.

[4]The researcher was a secretary in the department office when the study was carried out. To avoid skewing the results, the researcher's own e-mail data were excluded from the study.

secretaries' e-mails. All the e-mails were "self-contained" requests and were not part of longer exchanges (Economidou-Kogetsidis 2011).

11.3.2 E-Mail Analysis Procedures

As the years of service for the senior secretaries, Alice and Helen, and the novice secretary, May, were saliently different; the senders of collected request e-mails were categorized based on three groups: senior data collected from Alice and Helen, novice data from May, and foreign data from foreign faculty.

The request e-mails were then analyzed and coded with regard to the degree of directness (direct requests, conventionally indirect requests, or hints), internal modification (lexical/phrasal downgraders and upgraders), and external modification (mitigating supportive moves and aggravating moves added to the head act). Following the coding scheme for degree of directness contrived by Economidou-Kogetsidis (2011), the researcher investigated the request strategies used by the participants (see Appendices 1 and 2). Requests for action and requests for information were analyzed separately. Both e-mail requests for action and request for information for each group were analyzed along the main directness levels of (a) most direct strategies, (b) conventionally indirect strategies, and (c) nonconventionally indirect strategies (e.g., hints). The data classification scheme for internal and external modifications adopted in the study was also based on Economidou-Kogetsidis (2011) (Appendices 3 and 4 for internal modification and Appendices 5 and 6 for external modification). The use of address forms in e-mails is not discussed in this study.

11.3.3 Perception Questionnaire and Participants

The participants in the perception questionnaire were five foreign teachers (3 female, 2 male), five local Chinese teachers (3 female, 2 male) and the three secretaries. The age of foreign teachers ranged from 40 to 60 s, the age for Chinese teachers from 40 to 55 s, and the age for secretaries from 30 to 40 s. The questionnaire was administered to the participants in person or by e-mail. They were asked to offer their perceptions of the politeness and/or appropriateness of the eight e-mail messages which appear in Appendix 7. The eight e-mail messages[5] were authentic e-mails selected from the e-mail corpus of the present study, written by the secretaries. Each secretary was asked to select two to three messages which she perceived were polite and appropriate from the corpus mentioned in 3.1. The

[5]In the questionnaire, the e-mails written by the novice secretary were placed first, followed by those from senior secretaries.

secretaries were then interviewed about their experience of making requests in the academic context. In addition, they were asked to evaluate the eight e-mail messages on a 5-point Likert scale in terms of the dimension of politeness (i.e., 1 = not at all, 5 = very much), and they were then asked to qualitatively explain their choice for ranking the e-mail by making reference to specific linguistic features from the messages.

Foreign teachers and local Chinese teachers were instructed to imagine that they received the eight e-mails from one of the secretaries. They were asked first to evaluate each message based on the above-mentioned scale and dimension, and they were then asked to qualitatively make explanations for their choice. Statistical Package for Social Sciences (SPSS) was used for statistical testing of the results of evaluation. Aside from descriptive statistics, one-way ANOVA was also employed. Further clarification and elaboration followed in order to understand the politeness realization and appropriateness of request strategy use in the academia.

11.4 Results

The results showed that the novice secretary and senior secretaries used different request strategies in terms of degree of directness, internal modification, and external modification. Regarding the perception questionnaire, there were no significant differences found among the three groups (secretaries, Chinese faculty, and foreign faculty) toward the perception of the eight e-mail messages. A close look at the e-mails and retrospective interviews revealed the emic knowledge of appropriate request e-mails in the academic setting.

11.4.1 Degree of Directness

Analysis of e-mail requests for information (Tables 11.1, 11.2 and 11.3) and requests for action (Tables 11.4, 11.5 and 11.6) are presented below. In the corpus, it was found that requests made by the secretaries for action outnumbered requests for information.

11.4.1.1 Request for Information

In making requests for information, the three groups used different request strategies, as indicated below.

As shown in Table 11.1. For the most part, the senior secretaries, Alice and Helen, used a direct strategy (74 %), more specifically, "please" plus imperative (mood derivable: 52 %), as in example (1) below.

Table 11.1 Degree of requestive directness: request for information from senior data (N: 88)

Most direct	Mood derivable	46/88 (52 %)	Total: 65/88 (74 %)
	Direct question	12/88 (14 %)	
	Need statement	4/88 (5 %)	
	Performative	3/88 (3 %)	
Conventionally indirect	Query preparatory (ability, willingness, permission)	22/88 (25 %)	Total: 22/88 (25 %)

Table 11.2 Degree of requestive directness: request for information from novice data (N: 40)

Most direct	Direct question	12/40 (30 %)	Total: 12/40 (30 %)
Conventionally indirect	Query preparatory (ability, willingness, permission)	23/40 (58 %)	Total: 23/40 (58 %)
Hints	Mild hints	6/40 (15 %)	Total: 6/40 (15 %)

Table 11.3 Degree of requestive directness: request for information from foreign data (N: 35)

Most direct	Direct question	18/35 (51 %)	Total: 25/35 (71 %)
	Elliptical	2/35 (6 %)	
	Mood derivable	5/35 (14 %)	
Conventionally indirect	Query preparatory (ability, willingness, permission)	10/35 (29 %)	Total: 10/35 (29 %)

Table 11.4 Degree of requestive directness: request for action from senior data (N: 127)

Most direct	Imperative/Mood derivable	70/127 (55 %)	Total: 94/127 (74 %)
	Need statements	10/127 (8 %)	
	Reminder request	6/127 (5 %)	
	Performatives	4/127 (3 %)	
	Want statements	4/127 (3 %)	
Conventionally indirect	Query preparatory (ability, willingness, permission)	30/127 (24 %)	Total: 30/127 (24 %)
Hints	Mild hints	3/127 (2 %)	Total: 3/127 (2 %)

Table 11.5 Degree of requestive directness: request for action from novice data (N: 59)

Most direct	Imperative/mood derivable	5/59 (8 %)	Total: 9/59 (15 %)
	Need statements	4/59 (7 %)	
Conventionally indirect	Query preparatory (ability, willingness, permission)	34/59 (58 %)	Total: 34/59 (58 %)
Hints	Mild hints	16/59 (27 %)	Total: 16/59 (27 %)

Table 11.6 Degree of requestive directness: request for action from foreign data (N: 56)

Conventionally indirect	Query preparatory (ability, willingness, permission)	35/56 (63 %)	Total: 35/56 (63 %)
Most direct	Imperative/mood derivable	12/56 (21 %)	Total: 14/56 (25 %)
	Need statements	2/56 (4 %)	
Hints	Mild hints	7/56 (12 %)	Total: 7/56 (12 %)

(1)
Subject: Proposal for offering a new course
Dear Prof. H,
We are going to have the meeting for curriculum on March 22. If you would like to offer a new course, *please let me know before March 15.* You will need to send your proposal to me soon.
[FN]

The conventionally indirect strategy inquiring about the recipient's ability, willingness, or permission, ranked second in frequency. The e-mail below is a typical example.

(2)
Subject: Your computer problems
Dear Prof. A,
About the computer problems you mentioned yesterday, I have contacted Mr. Wu of the Computer Center. *Could you please* let me know when you are around so the computer person can go check for you?
With best regards,
[FN]

The e-mail data collected from May, a novice secretary, began when she first started to work in the department office. The data were collected over 6 months, and therefore show how a newcomer tried to acculturate to this new environment. As shown in Table 11.2, for the most part, she used a conventionally indirect way (query preparatory: 58 %). The strategy of using direct questions for information ranked second. The two most frequently used strategies are illustrated below.

(3)
Subject: The oral exam on November 15th
Dear Prof. B,
We are going to have an entrance exam for MA program on November 15th.
We need to invite three committee members for each program including Literature, Linguistics, and Education.
Would you please be one of the committee members for the oral exam, please?
Sincerely
[FN]

(4)
Subject: The speech contest on November 12
Dear Prof. C,
When will you come to the office, room 213?
[FN] needs to give your paper about the speech contest on November 12.
By the way, I need your ARC and copy one for the payment.
Thanks
[FN]

As indicated in Table 11.3, for the most part, foreign teachers used a direct strategy (71 %), and more specifically, direct questions for information (51 %), as shown in Table 11.3. The conventionally indirect strategy of inquiring about the recipient's ability, willingness, or permission ranked second (29 %). The two most frequently used strategies are shown below.

(5)
Subject: slides
Dear [FN],
I would like to use slides for the graduate class this afternoon. *Is there a beamer in that room?* (And, if so, do just I need to save the slides on a disk?)
Best,
[professor's name]

(6)
Subject: course numbers
Dear [FN],
Could you give me my four course numbers for Fall 2013, so I can check the enrollment? I do not know where to find the numbers. Thanks. I'll appreciate it.
With best regards,
[professor's name]

11.4.1.2 Request for Action

When making requests for faculty to do something, both senior secretaries and the novice secretary used more divergent strategies than when making requests for information.

As indicated in Table 11.4, for the most part, senior secretaries used a direct strategy when requesting action (74 %), and more specifically, "please" plus an imperative (imperative/mood derivable: 55 %). The indirect strategy of inquiring about the recipients' ability, willingness and permission was the second most common (24 %). Typical examples of the two most frequently employed strategies are indicated below.

(7)
Subject: Please check your proposal
Dear Prof. D,
Attached is your proposal, which will be discussed in the department curriculum committee this Thursday noon. *Please check it carefully*. If you find any mistakes, *please let me know by 17:00 tomorrow (October 23).* Thank you very much for your cooperation.
Best regards,
[FN]

(8)
Subject: Receipt of your visa application
Dear Prof. C,
I am wondering if you have made an application for your visa application. For your information, we will have a short break from July 15–19, and the Office of Budget and Finance requires the receipt of the application by July 21. *Would you please send it to me as soon as possible*? Thanks a lot. Have a nice vacation!
Best regards,
[FN]

As indicated in Table 11.5 from novice data, most frequently, the indirect strategy of inquiring about the recipients' ability, willingness, or permission was used (58 %), with mild hints ranked second (27 %). Typical examples of the two most frequently used strategies are indicated below.

(9)
Subject: Announcement for the composition contest
Dear Faculty,
Forwarded is the composition contest from Cave Bookstore. We need to encourage students to participate in the contest. *Would you please help us promote the information in [your] composition class?* Thanks for your help.
Best regards,
[FN]

(10)
Subject: The evaluation of written references
Dear Prof. E,
Thanks for your help of admission via recommendation.
[FN] will give you the written references as soon as possible.
The deadline for the evaluation will be on November 23.
Sincerely,
[FN]

As indicated in Table 11.6, for the most part, foreign teachers used a conventionally indirect strategy of inquiring about the recipient's ability, willingness, or permission (Query preparatory: 63 %). The strategy of "please" plus imperative was the second most common method (imperative/mood derivable: 21 %). Examples of the two most frequently used strategies are shown below.

(11)
Subject: syllabi
Dear [FN].
Could you help me again putting the syllabi on the web for this semester? (or at least remind me how to do it myself?) Attached are the syllabi for graduate courses.
Thanks!
Best regards,
[professor's name]

(12)
Subject: Need assistance
Dear [FN],
Would you please put the document that you want to give me in an envelope and have a work student slip it under my office #105 door in the research building? Also, *please check with [another secretary's FN] to see if your office or the Personnel Office already has a copy of my ARC.*
Thanks,
[professor's name]

11.4.2 Internal Modification

Internal modifiers are "elements within the request utterance proper (linked to the head act), the presence of which is not essential for the utterance to be potentially understood as a request." (Blum-Kulka 1989, p. 60). They may act either as downgraders to soften the request or as upgraders to intensify the coerciveness of a request. The use of lexical/phrasal downgraders and upgraders is indicated in the following subsections.

Table 11.7 Internal modification: lexical/phrasal downgraders from senior data

Marker "please"	129/215(60 %)
Subjectivizers	19/215 (9 %)
Consultative devices	17/215 (8 %)
Downtoners	9/215 (4 %)

Table 11.8 Internal modification: lexical/phrasal downgraders from novice data

Marker "please"	54/99 (55 %)

Table 11.9 Internal modification: lexical/phrasal downgraders from foreign data

Marker "please"	36/90 (40 %)
Consultative device	15/90 (17 %)
Downtoners	6/90 (7 %)
Subjectivizers	5/90 (6 %)

11.4.2.1 Internal Modification: Lexical/Phrasal Downgraders

The employment of downgraders by the three groups is explicitly shown in the following three tables.

Senior secretaries used the lexical or phrasal devices downgraders, such as the marker "please," subjectivizers, consultative devices, and downtoners, as shown in Table 11.7. In making requests for using imperative/mood derivables, "please" was always attached to show the sender's politeness while requesting that the recipient comply. Therefore, "please" could be found in, "*Please* sign your name at the bottom of the first page…" and, "Could you *please* look at your schedule to check if December 3 is available for you to…?" Subjectivizers were the second most common downgrader, found in the messages such as, "*I wonder* if I could get your revised one [translation] on Wednesday morning…" and, "*I am afraid* that I need to double check with the travel agent." Consultative devices such as "do you think," "may I know," "I could," and "would you like" were employed in messages such as, "*Do you think* we need to prepare a microphone since the Chair needs to host the meeting during the lunch time?", "*May I know* when you need the copies?", "I am wondering if *I could* get your revised one [translation] on Wednesday morning…" and, "*Would you like* to reschedule an appointment for the afternoon on the same day?" The downtoner "may" was used in the message such as, "You *may* check your e-portfolio to find the information you need."

As opposed to the senior secretaries, who used a variety of lexical/phrasal downgraders when making requests, May, a novice secretary, only used the marker "please" in most cases of the conventionally indirect strategy, as shown in Table 11.8. Examples include, "Would you *please* be one of our three judges for the [English] speech contest on December 10 and 26?" and, "Would you *please* fill in the attached form for me?"

Foreign faculty employed the same lexical/phrasal downgraders as senior secretaries, but there was a difference in frequency. The downgraders used by foreign faculty included the marker "please," consultative devices, downtoners, and subjectivizers, as shown in Table 11.9. The marker "please" was found in messages such as, "*Please* let me know where the contest will be held and how many students are involved" and, "Would you *please* put the document that you want to give me in an envelope and have a work student slip it under my office #105 door in the research building?" Consultative devices such as "would you mind," "could you" and "do you think" were found in the messages such as, "*Would you mind* to[6] send this to the copy staff? It is a final exam for A class and there are 30 students in the class.," "*Could you* have someone check and see if my name is on one of the lists up there and what room I have to go to?" and, "*Do you think* we will be able to get these signed by the department chair?" Downtoners like "may," and "any chance" could be found in, "You *may* check with the computer person if he is available tomorrow afternoon" and, "*Any chance* someone around the campus might be able to assist?" In addition, subjectivizers like "I wonder" and "I am afraid" were used in messages such as, "*I wonder* if you could delete that description and use mine for this semester only." and, "*I am afraid* we need to update the departmental website."

11.4.2.2 Internal Modification: Upgraders-Intensifiers

An internal upgrader device is used to intensify the coerciveness of a request. Senior secretaries only used the time intensifier (21 %). Devices such as "soon," "as soon as possible," "today," "tomorrow," or specific dates were found in messages like, "Please send me the confirmation of your travel information by *March 31*," "Please let me know your opinion on this *as soon as possible*," and, "If you have any questions, please let me know *soon*." No upgraders were found in the data collected from the novice secretary or foreign faculty.

11.4.3 External Modification

External modification appears in the form of supportive or aggravating moves occurring either before or after the head act. It might therefore serve to either soften or emphasize the force of the whole request (Economidou-Kogetsidis 2011, p. 3199). The use of modification is indicated in the following subsections.

[6]It was an authentic message found in the foreign data, but it seems wrong from super-standard English grammar.

Table 11.10 External modification: supportive moves from senior data

Greeting/opening	6/160 (4 %)
Grounders (reasons, explanation)	124/160 (78 %)
Disarmer	5/160 (3 %)
Getting a precommitment	3/160 (2 %)
Apology	4/160 (3 %)
Pre-closing/thanks	128/160 (80 %)
E-mail closing	151/160 (94 %)

Table 11.11 External modification: supportive moves from novice data

Grounders (reasons, explanation)	44/80 (55 %)
Getting a precommitment	1/80 (1 %)
Pre-closing/thanks	43/80 (54 %)
E-mail closing	59/80 (74 %)

Table 11.12 External modification: supportive moves from foreign data

Greeting/opening	4/80 (5 %)
Grounders (reasons, explanation)	25/80 (31 %)
Disarmer	2/80 (3 %)
Getting a precommitment	4/80 (5 %)
Pre-closing/thanks	36/80 (45 %)
E-mail closing	71/80 (89 %)

11.4.3.1 External Modification: Supportive Moves

The use of the supportive moves by the three groups is indicated in Tables 11.10, 11.11 and 11.12. From the results, some important findings could be gleaned as stated below.

(1) Senior secretaries and foreign teachers sometimes opened the e-mail with a greeting (e.g., "Good morning!" or "I hope this letter/note finds you well"). This move could not be found in the data collected from the novice secretary.
(2) Grounders (reasons, explanation) and pre-closing/thanks were highly used by all three groups. Comparing the two moves used by the three groups, it was found that senior secretaries have a higher occurrence (grounders: 78 %, pre-closing/thanks: 80 %), and foreign teachers have a lower occurrence (grounders: 31 %, pre-closing/thanks: 45 %) Examples of grounders and pre-closing/thanks can be found in examples (1)–(10) and (1), (4), (6)–(9), (11), (12), respectively.
(3) The majority of senior secretaries' and the novice secretary's e-mails used an e-mail closing (e.g., Best, Best regards), which is an important component in email messages. The percentages for the two groups were 94 and 74 %, respectively.

Table 11.13 External modification: aggravating moves from senior data

Emphasis on urgency	4/160 (3 %)

(4) Disarmers and apology were found only in senior data (e.g., disarmer: "I hope you can understand." apology: "I am sorry to ask you to read the translation.")

11.4.3.2 External Modification: Aggravating Moves

Aggravating moves were found only in a few e-mails by senior secretaries, to characterize how urgent the assigned task was, as shown in Table 11.13. The emphasis on urgency could be found in messages such as, "I need to send the materials to the Curriculum Division in 5 days."

11.4.4 Results of Perception Questionnaire

Based on the eight selected e-mails written by secretaries, the perceptions of secretaries, Chinese faculty and foreign faculty on a 5-point Likert scale in terms of the dimension of politeness (1 = not at all, 5 = very much) were examined by SPSS. One-way ANOVA analyses yielded no significant effects for the three groups (secretaries, Chinese faculty, and foreign faculty) (Email 1: $F(2, 10) = 0.962$, $p > 0.05$; Email 2: $F(2, 10) = 0.436$, $p > 0.05$; Email 3: $F(2, 10) = 0.275$, $p > 0.05$; Email 4: $F(2, 10) = 0.769$, $p > 0.05$; Email 5: $F(2, 10) = 0.604$, $p > 0.05$; Email 6: $F(2, 10) = 0.162$, $p > 0.05$; Email 7: $F(2, 10) = 0.769$, $p > 0.05$; Email 8: $F(2, 10) = 1.031$, $p > 0.05$). The means and standard deviations for the perceptions of the eight e-mail messages were shown in Table 11.14.

Table 11.14 Perception of the politeness of emails by different groups

Email number	Secretaries	Chinese faculty	Foreign faculty
1	3.00 (0.00)	2.80 (0.84)	2.40 (0.55)
2	4.67 (0.58)	4.60 (0.55)	4.00 (1.73)
3	4.00 (1.00)	3.80 (0.84)	3.40 (1.52)
4	4.00 (1.00)	3.40 (0.89)	3.20 (0.84)
5	3.67 (0.58)	3.20 (0.84)	3.60 (0.55)
6	3.67 (0.58)	3.40 (0.55)	3.40 (0.89)
7	5.00 (0.00)	4.20 (1.30)	4.00 (1.22)
8	3.67 (0.58)	3.60 (0.55)	3.00 (1.00)

11.5 Discussion

The present study serves as a preliminary investigation aiming to explore how novice and expert professionals use requests in the academic setting and what is deemed to be appropriate language use in e-mail communication. The collected data were all naturally occurring e-mail messages from which participant interaction could be gleaned. E-mails sent by secretaries tended to be bland and impersonal since the topics covered were usually related to academic-related matters, closely associated with the secretaries' responsibilities. It seemed that the request e-mail discourse is institutionally sanctioned, although it is still face threatening (Brown and Levinson 1987) since the intention of the letters is to get the addressee to do what is requested.

One salient finding was that, in the asymmetrical communication, senior secretaries failed to follow the principles of deference politeness or 'negative politeness' (Brown and Levinson 1987) held in Western society, which include acknowledgement of imposition, sufficient mitigation and a preference for conventional indirectness (Economidou-Kogetsidis 2011). Instead, direct strategies, such as using imperatives preceded by "please," direct question, need statement, and performative, were frequently employed in both requests for information and action, which is in line with the findings of Biesenbach-Lucas (2002, 2004) and Chen (2006), both of whom point out their NNSs (non-native speakers of English) tended to employ direct strategies. Among the strategies, "please + imperative" was heavily used. The high density of direct strategies seemed to express pragmatic infelicities since they did not give the faculty any choice but to comply with the request. In addition, the marker "please" alone does not serve as a strong enough mitigator to soften the force of the imperative (Hartford and Bardovi-Harlig 1996). Using imperatives preceded by "please" did not address the imposition involved. The interview data showed that senior secretaries, as part of their job responsibility, subconsciously imposed the pressure that they received from a higher authority on the faculty, interpreting the requesting behavior as their own right and the faculty member's obligation, as has been found in other NNS (nonnative speakers of English) research on faculty-student relations (Chen 2006; Economidou-Kogetsidis 2011). This could also explain the co-occurrences of internal time intensifier and external aggravating moves, with their emphasis on urgency, which were used by the senior secretaries. The seniority of the secretaries might grant them more status in issuing direct requests as they are seasoned "care-takers" of the department. The high percentage of the occurrence of "please + imperative" might result from L1 transfer (Chen 2006), i.e., *qing* "please" is the initial word used when making requests in Chinese.

Conversely, May, a novice secretary, surprisingly realized the force of imposition incurred by employing direct strategies, and thus refrained from using them in request e-mail discourse. Acculturation to the new environment made her pay special attention to the directness and politeness embedded in the requesting behavior at the institution. While interacting with faculty, she, as a newcomer, was particularly aware of the asymmetrical relation between faculty and secretaries. May, reflecting on her experience in e-mail communication with faculty in the retrospective interview, expressed that, "*I dare not ask teachers to do anything. If needed, I will do it indirectly. So I inquire about their willingness and even seek their permission for complying with the requested tasks. Sometimes I will use a notification replacing a request in the e-mails.*" Thus, when making requests both for information and for action, mild hints were found in her request e-mail data instead of need or want statements, as when she said, "This is the reminder that the oral exam will be held on November 22 (Saturday). *That will start from 9:00 am in SP 411 and each student has about ten minutes for the oral.*" "Thanks for your help of admission via recommendation. [FN] will give you the written references as soon as possible. By the way, *the deadline for the evaluation will be on November 23.*" (example (10)). In a couple of e-mails, the subject appearing in the e-mails tended to be flexible as she sometimes interchanged between "I" and her first name in the discourse, as shown in "When will you come to the department office? *[FN]* needs to give your paper about the speech contest on October 10. By the way, *I* need your ARC and copy one for the payment." The uncertainty in the subject represented her lack of assurance in her identity as a secretary. In addition, the first name in the discourse seemed to function as a solidarity marker, attempting to shorten her relations with the faculty.

Need and want statements, both direct strategies, seemed to convey a help-needed tone, implying that the speaker's intention was to get attention, seeking help from people in a higher position (Chen 2006; Biesenbach-Lucas and Weasenforth 2000; Chang and Hsu 1998; Hartford and Bardovi-Harlig 1996), and a coercive tone, failing to show status-appropriate politeness in asymmetrical communication (Chen 2006). In previous research (Chen 2006; Biesenbach-Lucas and Weasenforth 2000; Chang and Hsu 1998; Hartford and Bardovi-Harlig 1996), both need and want statements were subsumed under the category of want statements. In workplaces, written business communication is a goal-oriented activity; the writer aims to get people with inherent status to do something, or to get something out of someone (Bargiela-Chiappini et al. 1996). The use of the two devices could present the sender's claim or opinions. Need statements were only used by senior secretaries in messages, such as, "*I need to know the information as soon as possible*" in making requests for information, and need and want statements were used in requesting for action, such as, "*I would like to seek your assistance in submitting the following documents by this Friday so ...*" To show the degree of politeness of a request, 'metaphorical space,' or the distance between the speaker and the listener (Haverkate 1992), was found in request e-mail discourse in the use of an impersonal pronoun or the indexical *we* as in, "Thank you for your quick reply. On the letter you need the stamp and the authorized signature from the Bureau of Consular Affairs in Taipei. Can *we* put the stamp and the authorized signature from the English Department who is in charge of the conference?" (request for information). Need statements and want statements were also found in May's request emails. She only used need statements in requesting action, such as "*I need a photocopy of your*

ARC for the payment." She also made use of 'metaphorical space' by using "*We* need to invite three committee members for each program…" (example (3)).

For professionals working in the academic institution, using unmitigated need and want statements denoted granted right behind the linguistic devices: as one of the senior secretaries said, "*We need to deal with many tasks at the same time and every task is expected to be completed before a certain date. Every day we need to meet different deadlines set by different administration offices.*" Using this direct, speaker-oriented request strategy could seem improper, given the status of the professionals in this asymmetrical communication, for they did not observe the principles of deference politeness (or "negative politeness," Brown and Levinson 1987) prevalent in Western societies; however, from a Chinese cultural perspective, although making requests to higher-ups with need and want statements is direct, it does not necessarily indicate impoliteness as the level of indirectness and politeness is associated with the type of and the number of supportive moves employed before the request act (Zhang 1995). In this study, even though senior secretaries used need and want statements in their request e-mail discourse, a variety of supportive moves were employed in the discourse.

The result showed that the novice professional secretary has less knowledge of how to use mitigating devices to redress the force of the request. Internal modifiers served as downgraders to soften the request or as upgraders to intensify the coerciveness of a request. May, a novice secretary, only used the marker "please"; however, Alice and Helen, senior secretaries, used a variety of lexical/phrasal downgraders, such as the marker "please," subjectivizers, consultative devices, and downtoners. The time intensifier was only used by senior secretaries. In addition, senior secretaries used more external supportive or aggravating moves before or after the head act to soften or emphasize the force of the whole request than the novice secretary. Although senior secretaries used more direct strategies to make requests, they knew how to make use of internal and external modifiers to mitigate the threatening force of the requesting behavior. The acquisition of modifiers in the workplace appears to be essential for professionals, especially newcomers to the environment, in smoothing interaction with faculty.

Grounders, an external supportive move, were heavily used by the secretaries. To seek faculty's compliance with the request act, secretaries tended to use more reasons or explanations before making requests for the sake of indirectness. According to the interview data, the novice secretary, May, noted that she dare not make requests without providing sufficient background information or explanation first. Senior secretaries also expressed that they needed to let teachers understand why they requested information or actions from them. The inductive approach made their request sound more indirect and polite (Chen 2006), as in example (1)–(3) and (7)–(9). Conversely, foreign faculty tended to use the deductive approach to structure their e-mail messages; that is, making requests followed by reasons and elaborations, as in example (6) and (11).

Regarding the perception questionnaire conducted to understand the politeness embedded in request e-mail discourse and the appropriateness of language use as perceived by 'cultural insiders,' although there were no significant differences found among the three groups toward the perceptions of the eight e-mail messages, a close examination of the messages and retrospective interview reveals the emic views on the status-congruence of request e-mails.

E-mails 2 and 7 were scored above 4.0 by secretaries and 4.0 by foreign teachers as these two e-mails sounded either overly solicitous or overpolite, which indicated power dynamics; namely, it was too obvious that the sender sought something from the recipient. In Chinese culture, "extreme politeness" is also part of face saving in that being rude would cause the addressee to feel disrespected (Samovar et al. 2007). In E-mail 2, the novice secretary used the conventionally indirect strategy, writing "Would you please…?" "do me a favor" (though it was overelaborate), "may," "Please … thanks a lot." In E-mail 7, the senior secretary initiated the e-mail with a direct question, followed by making apologies twice for asking the faculty to help proofread translation during her leisure time. More linguistic devices were used by the senior secretary such as "I am wondering if" and "I am afraid …" As a foreign teacher noted, "The sender is almost self-debasing in being so apologetic in the message." E-mail 1 was scored the lowest since it sounded like an order to the faculty even though the novice secretary treated it as a notification. One foreign teacher said that it seemed that she needed to get permission to come to the departmental office. "Please …" and "Please thank you" appearing in E-mail 3 sounded strange to the faculty. Most of the Chinese faculty did not notice its ungrammaticality, but felt it was polite. Foreign faculty, on the other hand, felt it overly solicitous. One foreign teacher noticed the usage and then said, "'please'… 'Please thank you' [sic!] Not grammatically perfect, but obviously trying to be polite." *Please* in Chinese can be interpreted as *baituo* 'request someone to do something' in this case although it is a linguistic error. In terms of the requesting behavior in academia, the novice secretary has the need to make requests as the behavior is purposeful and the faculty has the obligation to comply with the request act. On the other hand, she sensed the power relationships between faculty and secretaries. The attempt to show sociopragmatic competence in the expressions of the request act in the asymmetrical context was evident. The politeness conventions needed in the work context were carefully followed by the novice professional.

L1 transfer was found in a couple of expressions, such as "Please attend the meeting on time," in E-mail 4, "I am sorry that I have to occupy your leisure time again," in E-mail 7, and "Would you please come to the office and do me a favor?" in E-mail 2, in which the request was not a favor to the sender at all. According to the foreign faculty, the first expression seemed unnecessary in the context, or could be revised as "The meeting will begin promptly at (time). Thank you for your consideration." And the second expression could be revised as "I know you are busy. But when you have a chance, could you please send the information to me?"

Conventionally indirect expressions, i.e., "Would you (please) tell me … ?" were favored by Chinese and foreign faculty, as they think that it is more polite to make requests using them. The data collected from academia showed that senior professionals often used more direct strategies such as "please + imperative" followed by a time intensifier, which sounded abrupt to the faculty and might cause pragmatic infelicities. Some participants mentioned in the retrospective interview that this strategy did not sound impolite to them since they just interpreted it as information about a deadline. Nevertheless, they suggested indirect expressions be used for making requests. Three foreign teachers expressed their views on use of "please + imperative" followed by time intensifiers by secretaries.

> These do not sound impolite if they are preceded by the word "please." Or are phrased like this: "The department would like your response as soon as possible." By using the non-personal word "department" and the conditional expression "would like", the writer softens the command phrase, "as soon as possible" or "by May 25." It gives it a softer sound and so sounds more polite. (female foreign teacher)
>
> The direct expression sounds like a demand. Actually some indirect expressions can be used, such as "Would you please…? Could you please…? It would be nice if you could…, It would be better if you could…, I would appreciate it if you could…, It is important for you to do …." The suggested ways of expressions are more polite, but from my observation, most of the secretaries neglect them. It is a problem of culture. (female foreign teacher)
>
> It depends on the situation. If there is enough time for me to do whatever they want, then it is polite to me. For using *as soon as possible* by secretaries, it seems that they have been managing their own time well, so the last minute they are working on something is making me feel rushed. (female foreign teacher)

The use of "please + imperative" followed by time intensifiers seemed to be ambiguous in the academic contexts. On the one hand, secretaries acted on behalf of the administrative body to make requests of faculty and her emails tended to be impersonal and direct. The insiders perceived that the ideational function of the request emails composed by secretaries outweighs the interactional function on the one hand, and on the other hand, they also treated secretaries as persons hoping that more polite, indirect expressions were used to present status-congruent language and avoid risking their own negative face (Brown and Levinson 1987).

To be polite is always "to act appropriately" (Eelen 2001, p. 128). The collected data showed that informal expressions such as "thanks" or "thanks a lot" were found in a large number of request e-mail discourse. One foreign teacher suggested that no matter how well secretaries know the people in the workplace, it is suggested to always use a more formal approach in a business communique. However, most teachers expressed different viewpoints. It seems that familiarity overrides formality in this working setting.

> The formality of language used in e-mails depends on who is writing to whom and the nature of the e-mail. But generally speaking, for any e-mails that I involve with and that I write to secretaries or secretaries write to me, "thanks" is often used. I think it's friendly and polite. (female foreign teacher)
>
> It depends on how often you see the persons and how close you are to them. Since we meet secretaries every day, the informal "thanks" used in e-mails by secretaries sound comfortable. For those I don't have too much contact with, I will use "thank you. (female foreign teacher)
>
> We are so familiar with each other since we meet almost every day. I think "thanks" is fine to me in e-mail exchanges. (Chinese male teacher)

11.6 Conclusion

This study has investigated the status congruence of request e-mails composed by professionals serving in a private university departmental office in Taiwan. It examined their degree of directness and use of internal and external modification. Politeness considerations held by 'cultural insiders' were then explored. Many of the secretaries' request e-mails address institutional topics that fall within their duties. It is often the case that requests upwards require more mitigation and less directness. Therefore, e-mail messages addressed upwards are expected to be characterized by greater formality, less directness and a greater degree of external and/or internal mitigation (Holmes and Stubbe 2003). The results showed that senior professionals tended to use more direct strategies and more internal and external modification devices, while the novice professional used more conventionally indirect strategies and less modifiers. The selection of request strategies seems to represent senior professionals' granted right to request information or action from the faculty without giving them choices. They serve as mediators helping the administrative body make requests of faculty. The ideational and interactional functions of request emails composed by them appear to make the e-mails more ambiguous. Given the fact that they use more direct request strategies, conventionally indirect expressions were actually favored by the faculty. It also manifests the novice professional's naïveté, as she was in the process of acculturating to the institutional culture.

Written business communication is viewed as a complex goal-oriented activity which is context-dependent. To act politely means to adopt an acceptable behavior in a given cultural context within the constraints of socially defined norms (Bargiela-Chiappini and Harris 1996). Politeness conventions practiced in different cultural work settings may vary. So far there are few established conventions for linguistic behavior in e-mail communication (Biesenbach-Lucas 2006). Hence, academic syllabi related to e-mail writing devised especially for professionals in academia are badly needed.

The present study reveals the significance of using authentic written requests collected at work. In addition, the retrospective interviews with the cultural insiders shed some light on the socially sanctioned norm of appropriate request e-mail discourse. For professionals, knowing how to make requests politely and appropriately under the asymmetrical relations is essential in boosting effective communication. For future study, it would be intriguing to find out how the addressee, i.e., faculty, responds to the request e-mails and the degree of compliance from the faculty based on the relations. In addition, it would also be worth observing how department chairs make requests of faculty to avoid risking their own positive face and faculty's negative face.

Appendix 1: Degree of Directness—Coding Categories for E-Requests for Information

Directness level	Request strategies	Examples
Most direct	Direct questions	Did you get my project?
	Elliptical	Any news?
	Mood derivable	Please let me know if you have to withdraw me from class
	Performatives	I would like to ask if…
	Want statements	I would like to know what your policy is on…
	Need statements	I will need to know…
Conventionally indirect	Query preparatory (ability, willingness, permission)	Could you tell me…
Hints	Strong hints/mild hints	I tried very hard to find your office but could nots find it

Appendix 2: Degree of Directness—Coding Categories for E-Requests for Action

Directness level	Request strategies	Examples
Most direct	Imperative/mood derivable	Please note what changes should be made
	Elliptical requests	Any comments?
	Performatives	I have to ask for an extension for a week
	Want statements	I would like your suggestion
		I want to have an extension
	Need statements	I will need a little more time
	Expectation statements	I hope you'll give me the weekend to finish my assignment
		I look forward to hearing from you
	Reminder requests	I would like to remind you of my reference letter
	Pre-decided statements	I will hand my assignment in tomorrow
Conventionally indirect	Query preparatory (ability, willingness, permission)	Can/could…/Would you mind…
		I would appreciate it if…
Hints	Strong hints/mild hints	Attached is a draft of my work
		I have some trouble understanding the essay question

Appendix 3: Internal Modification: The Classification Scheme—Lexical/Phrasal Downgraders

Name	Explanation	Devices
Marker 'please'	"An optional element added to a request to bid for cooperative behavior" (Blum-Kulka et al. 1989, p. 283)	'Please'
Consultative devices	"expressions by means of which the speaker seeks to involve the hearer directly bidding for cooperation" (Blum-Kulka et al. 1989, p. 283)	'Would you mind', 'do you think', 'would it be all right if', 'is it/would it be possible', 'do you think I could…', 'is it all right?'
Downtoners	"modifiers which are used by a speaker in order to modulate the impact his or her request is likely to have on the hearer" (Blum-Kulka et al. 1989, p. 284)	'Possibly', 'perhaps', 'just', 'rather', 'maybe', 'by any chance', 'at all'
Understaters/hedges	"adverbial modifiers by means of which the speaker underrepresents the state of affairs denoted in the proposition" (Blum-Kulka et al. 1989, p. 283)	'A bit', 'a little', 'sort of', 'a kind of'
Subjectivizers	"elements in which the speaker explicitly expresses his or her subjective opinion vis-à-vis the state of affairs referred to in the proposition, thus lowering the assertive force of the request" (Blum-Kulka et al. 1989, p. 284)	'I'm afraid', 'I wonder', 'I think/suppose'
Cajolers	"conventionalized, addressee-oriented modifiers whose function is to make things clearer for the addressee and invite him/her to metaphorically participate in the speech act" (Sifianou 1992, p. 180)	'You know', 'You see…'
Appealers	Addressee-oriented elements occurring in a syntactically final position. They may signal turn-availability and "are used by the speaker whenever he or she wishes to appeal to his or her hearer's benevolent understanding" (Blum-Kulka et al. 1989, p. 285)	'Clean the table dear, *will you?* ……*ok/right?*'

Appendix 4: Internal Modification: The Classification Scheme—Upgraders-Intensifiers

Name	Explanation	Examples
Intensifier	"Adverbial moodier that stresses specific elements of the request" (Schauer 2009, p. 91)	I *truly/really* need this extension
		I had *such* a high fever
Time intensifier	"Employed to emphasize the temporal aspect of the speaker's request" (Schauer 2009, p. 91)	As soon as possible
		Urgent
		Right now
Overstater	"Exaggerated utterances that form part of the request and are employed by the speaker to communicate their need of the request being met" (Schauer 2009, p. 91)	I'm in *desperate* need of material for my essay

Appendix 5: External Modification: The Classification Scheme—Supportive Moves

Name	Explanation	Examples
Greeting/opening	The writer opens the e-mail with a greeting	'Hi/Hello/Good morning'
		'How are you?'
Self introduction	The writer introduces himself/herself	'I'm Alan from your literature class'
Grounder	A clause which can either precede or follow a request and allows the speaker to give reasons, explanations, or justifications for his or her request	'I would like an assignment extension *because I could not deal the typing time*'
Disarmer	A phrase with which "the speaker tries to remove any potential objections the hearer might raise upon being confronted with the request" (Blum-Kulka et al. 1989, p. 287)	'*I know that this assignment is important but could you…?*'
		'*I hope you understand my situation…*'
Preparator	The speaker prepares the hearer for the ensuing request	'I really need a favor…'
Getting a precommitment	The speaker checks on a potential refusal before performing the request by trying to get the hearer to commit	'Could you do me a favor?'
Promise	The speaker makes a promise to be fulfilled upon completion of the requested act	'Could you give me an extension? *I promise I'll have it ready by tomorrow*'

(continued)

(continued)

Name	Explanation	Examples
Imposition minimizer	"The speaker tries to reduce the imposition placed on the hearer by his request" (Blum-Kulka et al. 1989, p. 288)	'I would like to ask for an extension. *Just for a few days*'
Apology	The speaker apologizes for posing the request and/or for the imposition incurred	'*I'm very sorry* but I need an extension on this project'
Orientation move	Opening discourse moves which serve an orientation function but do not necessarily mitigate or aggravate the request in any way	'It's about our midterm exam'
		'I have a question about the essay…'
Complement/sweetener	"Employed to flatter the interlocutor and to put them into a positive mood" (Schauer 2009, p. 92)	'Your opinion counts', 'I hope you feel better'
Pre-closing/thanks		'Thanks for your time', 'I look forward to hearing from you'
E-mail closing		Best, Sincerely

Appendix 6: External Modification: The Classification Scheme—Aggravating Moves

Name	Examples
Complaint/criticism	'I sent you an e-mail 3 days ago and never replied'
Emphasis on urgency/positive outcome	'I need to have the reference letter in 3 days'
	'I will expect your positive reply'

Appendix 7 Perception survey
(E-mail 1)
Subject: The midterm papers
Dear Prof. A,
You can come to the office, room 111, and get the midterm papers.
Best regards,
[FN]

(E-mail 2)
Subject: the new computer
Dear Prof. B,
Would you please come to the office and do me a favor? You may need to sign one document about the new computer. The content will explain the details about the ownership.

Please…thanks a lot
Best regards,
[FN]

(E-mail 3)
Subject: The new computer
Dear Prof. C,

Here comes the new computer. The vender would like to make an appointment with you. Please we need to make sure when you will in the office. They also would like to make sure whether the computer needs to be hung on the wall?

Please thank you.
Sincerely,
[FN]

(E-mail 4)
Subject: Meeting notice for the dept. curriculum committee
Dear Faculty,

The department curriculum committee will be scheduled for next Monday, December 24, 12:10, in Room 215, Good Will Hall. Please attend the meeting on time.

Best regards,
[FN]

(E-mail 5)
Subject: Your personal portfolio
Dear Prof. D,

Please check your personal portfolio, as shown in the attachment. If you find anything wrong, please let me know by next Monday. Thanks.

Best,
[FN]

(E-mail 6)
Subject: Meeting
Dear Prof. E,

Forwarded is the message from the Center for Teaching Development. You are invited to attend an advisory committee on teaching evaluation scheduled for Monday, October 21, 12:10, in Room 223, Good Will Hall. Please reply to the Center the kind of food you need, regular food or vegetarian food, by September 26. Thanks.

Best regards,
[FN]

(E-mail 7)
Subject: Proofread translation
Dear Prof. F,

Have you received the letter I sent last Friday? I am sorry that I have to occupy your leisure time again!

The meeting is on Thursday noon, and I am wondering if I could get your revised translation on Wednesday morning. In doing so, I could send it to Helen before the meeting. I am so sorry that I write this letter to rush you because I will have Wednesday afternoon off and I am afraid that my absence will cause trouble to the meeting.

Thank you so much!

[FN]

(E-mail 8)

Subject: your suggestion

Dear Prof. G,

I try to double check the percentage of each course we discussed at the last meeting and I found there is a course without any changes. Could you please tell me your suggestion on this course?

[The form indicating the percentage of each course is attached.]

Thanks a lot!

[FN]

References

Bardovi-Harlig, Kathleen H., and Beverly S. Hartford (eds.). 2005. *Interlanguage pragmatics: Exploring institutional talk*. Mahwah, NJ: Lawrence Erlbaum.

Bargiela-Chiappini, Francesca, and Sandra J. Harris. 1996. Requests and status in business correspondence. *Journal of Pragmatics* 28(5): 635–662.

Barron, Naomi. 2002. Who sets e-mail style? Prescriptivism, coping strategies, and democratizing communication access. *The Information Society* 18: 403–413.

Barron, Naomi. 2003. Why e-mail looks like speech: Proofreading pedagogy and public face. In *New media language*, ed. Jean Atchison, and Diana M. Lewis, 85–94. New York: Routledge.

Basturkmen, Helen. 2006. *Ideas and options in English for specific purposes*. Mahwah, NJ: Lawrence Erlbaum.

Biesenbach-Lucas, Sigrun, and Donald Weasenforth. 2000. Please help me: L1/L2 variations in solicitations in electronic conferences. Paper presented at the 20th Annual Second Language Research Forum (SLRF), Madison, WI.

Biesenbach-Lucas, Sigrun. 2002. How's tomorrow? Pragmatic features of student requests for appointments. Paper presented at the Annual Convention of the American Association of Applied Linguistics (AAAL), Salt Lake City, UT.

Biesenbach-Lucas, Sigrun. 2004. Speech acts in e-mail: A new look at pragmatic competence. Paper presented at the Annual Convention of the American Association of Applied Linguistics, Portland, OR.

Biesenbach-Lucas, Sigrun. 2006. Making requests in e-mail: Do cyber-consultations entail directness? Toward conventions in a new medium. In *Pragmatics and language learning,* eds. Kathleen Bardovi-Harlig, César Felix Brasdefer and Alwiya S. Omar, 81–107. Vol. 11. [National Foreign Language Resource Center] Honolulu: University of Hawaii Press.

Biesenbach-Lucas, Sigrun. 2007. Students writing e-mails to faculty: An examination of e-politeness among native and non-native speakers of English. *Language Learning and Technology* 11(2): 59–81.

Bloch, Joel. 2002. Student/teacher interaction via e-mail: The social context of Internet discourse. *Journal of Second Language Writing* 11(2): 117–134.

Blum-Kulka, Shoshana. 1989. Playing it safe: The role of conventionality in indirectness. In *Cross-cultural pragmatics: Requests and apologies*, ed. Shoshana Blum-Kulka, Juliane House, and Gabriele Kasper, 37–70. New York: Ablex.

Blum-Kulka, Shoshana, Juliane House, and Gabriele Kasper (eds.). 1989. *Cross-cultural pragmatics: Requests and apologies*. Norword, NJ: Ablex.

Brown, Penelope, and Stephen L. Levinson. 1987. *Politeness: Some universals in language usage*. Cambridge: Cambridge University Press.

Chang, Yu-Ying, and Yi-Ping Hsu. 1998. Requests on e-mail: A cross-cultural comparison. *RELC Journal* 29: 121–151.

Chen, Chi-Fen Emily. 2006. The development of e-mail literacy: from writing to peers to writing to authority figures. *Language Learning and Technology* 10(2): 35–55.

Crystal, David. 2001. *Language and the internet*. Cambridge: Cambridge University Press.

Danet, Brenda. 2001. *Cyberpl@y: Communication online*. Oxford: Oxford University Press.

Economidou-Kogetsidis, Maria. 2009. Interlanguage request modification: The use of lexical/phrasal downgraders and mitigating supportive moves. *Multilingua* 28(1): 79–112.

Economidou-Kogetsidis, Maria. 2011. Please answer me as soon as possible: Pragmatic failure in non-native speaker's e-mail requests to faculty. *Journal of Pragmatics* 43: 3193–3215.

Eelen, Gino. 2001. *A critique of politeness theories*. Manchester: St. Jerome.

Felix-Brasdefer, César. 2007. Pragmatic development in the Spanish as a FL classroom. *Intercultural Pragmatics* 4(2): 253–286.

Glater, Jonathan D. 2006. To: Professor @University.edu subject: why it's all about me. The New York Times. http://www.nytimes.com/2006/02/21/education/21professors.html. Accessed 22 July 2010.

Hartford, Beverly S., and Kathleen Bardovi-Harlig. 1996. At your earliest convenience: A study of written student requests to faculty. In *Pragmatics and language learning*, ed. L. Bouton, 55–69, Vol. 7. Urbana-Campaign: Division of English as an International Language, University of Illinois.

Hassall, Tim. 2001. Modifying requests in a second language. *International Review of Applied Linguistics (IRAL)* 39: 259–283.

Haverkate, Henk. 1992. Deictic categories as mitigating devices. *Pragmatics* 2(4): 505–522.

Hendriks, Berna. 2010. An experimental study of native speaker perceptions of non-native request modification in e-mails in English. *Intercultural Pragmatics* 7(2): 221–255.

Ho, Victor. 2009. The generic structure and discourse strategies employed in downward request e-mails. *The Linguistics Journal* 4(1): 46–66.

Ho, Victor. 2010. Constructing identities in the workplace through request e-mail discourse-how does one benefit from it? *GEMA OnlineTM Journal of Language Studies* 10(2): 3–18.

Holmes, Janet, and Maria Stubbe. 2003. *Power and politeness in the workplace: A sociolinguistic analysis of talk at work*. London: Longman.

Kong, Kenneth. 2006. Accounts as a politeness strategy in the internal directive documents of a business firm in Hong Kong. *Journal of Asian Pacific Communication* 16(1): 77–101.

Le Pair, Rob. 1996. Spanish requests strategies: A cross-cultural analysis from an intercultural perspective. *Language Sciences* 18(3–4): 651–670.

Lee, Cynthia. 2004. Written requests in emails sent by adult Chinese learners of English. *Language, Culture and Curriculum* 17(1): 58–72.

Leech, Geoffrey. 1983. *Principles of pragmatics*. London: Longman.

Li, Wan-Jing Grace, Yuan-shan Chen, and D. Victoria Rau. 2011. What constitutes an appropriate email request? In *Multimedia-based multicultural instruction and research: Innovative 21st-century approaches via literature and language*, ed. Ying-Hsiung Chou, 69–83. Taipei: Crane.

Lü, Pi-Hsia. 2012. A nexus analysis approach toward Taiwanese secretaries' ESP needs and communicative strategies. Unpublished doctoral dissertation, National Kaohsiung Normal University.

Padilla Cruz, Manuel. 2013. Understanding and overcoming pragmatic failure in intercultural communication: From focus on speakers to focus on hearers. *IRAL* 51: 23–54.

Punch, Maurice. 1994. Politics and ethics in qualitative research. In *Handbook of Qualitative Research*, ed. Norman K. Denzin, and Yvonna S. Lincoln, 83–97. Thousand Oaks, CA: Sage.

Samovar, Larry A., Richard E. Porter, and Edwin R. McDaniel. 2007. *Communication between Cultures*, 6th ed. Belmont, CA: Thomson-Wadsworth.

Schauer, Gila. 2009. *Interlanguage pragmatic development: The study abroad context*. London: Continuum.

Scollon, Ron, and Suzanne W. Scollon. 1995. *Intercultural communication: A discourse approach*. Oxford: Blackwell.

Sifianou, Maria. 1992. *Politeness phenomena in England and Greece: A cross-cultural perspective*. Oxford: Clarendon Press.

Stake, Robert E. 1994. Case studies. In *Handbook of Qualitative Research*, ed. Norman K. Denzin, and Yvonna S. Lincoln, 236–247. Thousand Oaks, CA: Sage.

Takahashi, Satomi. 1992. Transferability of indirect request strategies. *University of Hawaii Working Papers in ESL* 11(1): 69–124.

Thomas, Jenny. 1983. Cross-cultural pragmatic failure. *Applied Linguistics* 4(2): 91–112.

Tran, Giao Q. 2006. *The nature and conditions of pragmatic and discourse transfer investigated through naturalized role-play*. Muenchen: Lincom.

Vine, Bernadette. 2009. Directives at work: Exploring the contextual complexity of workplace directives. *Journal of Pragmatics* 41: 1395–1405.

Warschauer, Mark. 1999. *Electronic literacy: Language, culture, and power in online education*. NJ: Lawrence Erlbaum Associates.

Zhang, Yanyin. 1995. Indirectness in Chinese requesting. In *Pragmatics of Chinese as naïve and target language*, ed. Gabriele Kasper, 69–118. Honolulu: Second Language Teaching & Curriculum Center, University of Hawaii at Manoa.

Author Biography

Pi-Hsia Lü (呂碧霞) is Adjunct Assistant Professor of English at Providence University, Taiwan. Her main interests include English for Specific Purposes (ESP), interlanguage pragmatics, sociolinguistics, and discourse analysis.

Chapter 12
A Study on Symbolic Competence and Face in ELF Email Communication

Hsuan-Yu Tai

Abstract Unlike much of the previous research on email, which has examined how students wrote emails to make requests of faculty, this study investigated how an editor demonstrated her symbolic competence and negotiated face with contributors through email communication in a context where English was used as a lingua franca. The major data were collected from the editor's email during the 2-year editorial process. An interview was also conducted to elicit her understanding of her relationship with the contributors, changes of relationship, and particular events during the editorial process. The data were analyzed based on symbolic competence and face constituting theory. The findings revealed that, in terms of symbolic competence, the editor showed subjectivity by positioning herself in different roles, historicity by referring to her past experience, performativity to create a reality, and reframing by reestablishing the situation. In terms of face, the findings showed that face was not only realized as co-constituted interactional processes but also realized as individual wants.

Keywords Symbolic competence · Face · Editorial process · English as a lingua franca · Email

12.1 Introduction

English is undoubtedly the most widely used language in the world at present. Communication in English is not restricted to native speakers (NSs) or communication between native and nonnative speakers (NNSs). Fairly frequently English is used among (NNSs) who may or may not share a first language. In other words, English now has become a lingua franca in various settings. In recently years, there has been a growing body of research on English as a lingua franca (ELF), including

H.-Y. Tai (✉)
Institute of Linguistics, National Chung Cheng University, Minxiong, Taiwan
e-mail: tsuyoshi730411@hotmail.com

Y. Chen et al. (eds.), *Email Discourse Among Chinese Using English as a Lingua Franca*, DOI 10.1007/978-981-287-888-5_12

studies in lexicogrammar (Cogo and Dewey 2006; Bjorkman 2008; Breiteneder 2009; Meierkord 2004; Ranta 2006), pragmatics (Cogo and Dewey 2006; Firth 1996), phonology (Jenkins 2000), lexical and organizational features (Kao and Wang 2014) and word class variation (Osimk-Teasdale 2014) in spoken English. However, English nowadays is not only used for speaking. According to Crystal (2003), there is extensive use through the Internet, such as email and academic publication.

Using English is recognized as a significant outlet for publishing research articles among scholars and it has become an interesting terrain to investigate. Relevant studies have examined perceptions of using English for publication (Braine 2005; Flowerdew 1999), case studies of the process of socializing into the discourse community of publication (Cheung 2010; Li 2007a; Flowerdew 2000), or editorial services (Li 2007b). These research studies have implications for English for specific purposes (ESP) and English for academic purposes (EAP) to teach graduate students how to successfully publish research papers. While there have been many studies on contributors' perspectives, very little attention has been given to the process of editorial review (Feak 2009; Godsden 1995, 2001, 2003; Swales 1996) in which referees' comments and authors' responses were analyzed. Even within the few studies on editorial processes, none has dealt with email communication. Therefore, there is a need to investigate how ELF users construct their emails in the process of academic publication.

Email has received some attention from second language acquisition scholars. Not surprisingly, their research is mostly targeted to how native and nonnative students address emails to faculty, because writing emails to professors or supervisors to request permission for late submission or to get feedback on assignments are fairly common in the educational setting (Hartford and Bardovi-Harlig 1996; Biesenbach-Lucas 2007; Biesenbach-Lucas and Weasenforth 2002). Nevertheless, emails are not only used between students and professors in academic settings, they also serve as a way to communicate among scholars. Also, as English has become a lingua franca in today's world, there is a need to shift the focus from a language learning perspective to how the language is used in real contexts such as academic publication. In addition, when communicating through emails, some less studied but crucial aspects, such as symbolic competence (Kramsch and Whiteside 2008) and face (Arundale 1999, 2010), ought to be taken into consideration as well, in that senders and receivers constantly need to negotiate a task, an event, or opinions meticulously without offending each other.

Accordingly, this study focused on how an editor used English to communicate with contributors in the process of editing a book. By investigating this under-researched territory, one could learn how symbolic competence and facework are important in academic email discourse to get one's work accepted for publication.

12.2 Literature Review

12.2.1 *English as a Lingua Franca*

English as a Lingua Franca can be defined as "any use of English among speakers of different first languages for whom English is the communicative medium of choice, and often the only option" (Seidlhofer 2011, p. 7). In other words, in ELF contexts, either NSs or NNSs may be included as participants in the communication. Furthermore, ELF is not only restricted to interlocutors from different language background, it also encompasses "the use of English in an interaction where all the participants are NNSs and all share the same (or similar) first language" (Elder and Davies 2006, p. 282).

In ELF literature, much research to date has been dedicated to spoken discourse (Bjorkman 2008, 2014; Breiteneder 2009; Cogo and Dewey 2006; Firth 1996; Kao and Wang 2014; Meierkord 2004; Osimk-Teasdale 2014; Ranta 2006; Walkinshaw and Kirkpatrick 2014). Research on ELF written discourse is relatively scarce. Among the few studies on ELF written discourse, scholars have mainly been concerned about the attitude of using English for publication in an expanding circle (Ingvarsdóttir and Arnbjörnsdóttir 2013), disadvantages and implications of using English as an additional language for international publication (Flowerdew 2008) as well as attitudes toward the legitimacy and identity of using ELF and pedagogical responses (Erling and Bartlett 2006). However, little is known as to how communication is maintained in ELF written discourse. Consequently, the current study attempts to investigate how ELF communication is maintained through email interactions.

12.2.2 *Research on Email*

The past two decades have seen an increasing body of research on emails. A small number of studies were carried out in business settings among staff, attempting to discover how various social factors, such as power, social status, and gender affected the formulation of emails (Callahan 2011; Murphy and Levy 2006; Waldvogel 2007). There are also many second language acquisition scholars who have conducted research on email interactions between students and professor (Hartford and Bardovi-Harlig 1996; Biesenbach-Lucas 2007; Biesenbach-Lucas and Weasenforth 2002; Bou-Franch 2011; Economidou-Kogetsidis 2011; Hallajian and David 2014). Specifically, researchers have taken a contrastive perspective in looking at how NNSs of English differed in email formulation when they wrote to faculty. As such, those studies purported to provide pedagogical implications for teaching ESP. An earlier study by Hartford and Bardovi-Harlig (1996) compared 34 NSs of English students and 65 NNSs of English students who wrote emails to their faculty. The results showed that NNS students seemed to be more influenced by a high degree of imposition. They also used fewer downgraders and referred to "my time," which had a negative affect.

Biesenbach-Lucas and Weasenforth (2002) explored how NSs and NNSs of English demonstrated their negotiation through writing emails to an American professor. The findings showed that NSs used more contexts for proposal and justification, made clearer requests, provided alternative suggestions, and initiated actions as well as producing more and longer clauses. Furthermore, the findings showed that NSs' proposals contained the use of hedging, e.g., perhaps, modals, and alternative options, while NNSs' proposals did not contain alternative options and mostly the clauses were short. As for the requests, NSs used lexical items that were related to response such as suggestions while NNSs seemed to portray themselves as helpless by using "help" frequently.

Biesenbach-Lucas (2007) investigated request strategies, politeness features, and preferred linguistic realization between NSs and NNSs who formulated emails to their faculty ranging from high to low imposition situations. The findings revealed that NSs and NNSs showed similar pattern of request strategies and lexical modifiers in response to different impositional situations. However, NSs and NNSs differed in certain aspects such as the use of politeness features, preferred linguistic realization, the use of impersonal form, constructions and so on.

Economidou-Kogetsidis (2011) explored pragmatic failure in email requests written by NNSs of English to faculty at a university in Greece. The results demonstrated that NNSs employed a large amount of direct requests and the typical sentence structures were direct questions, imperatives/mood derivable, and want statements. The results also showed that there was a lack of downgraders and that "please" served as a frequent marker, which might cause pragmatic failure. In terms of moves, greeting/opening, and closing were less used in the NNS emails. As for forms of address, the majority of emails lacked an address form or contained incorrect academic title + last name, which contradicted Hallajian and David's (2014) study in which Iranian students' email requests were considered formal.

In addition to researchers who are interested in interlanguge pragmatics or cross cultural difference in emails, Bou-Franch (2011) looked at opening and closing sequences of Spanish emails and their relationship with social (power relationship) and interactional (position of an email in a conversation) factors between university lecturers and their colleagues and undergraduates. The results showed that the position of an email could affect the occurrence of openings, the density of openings and closings and the use of self-identification. For instance, openings decreased considerably when email position was non-initial. Also, although power relationship seemed not to affect the occurrence of openings and closings, it affected the density of openings and closings, the use of self-identification, and the use of thanking moves.

Notwithstanding that it appears email research is well established, there are still some aspects that can be taken into consideration. First, as Crystal (2003) stated, English is a language that is used by more NNSs than NSs, although the definition of NSs simply based on early child exposure is problematic (Davies 2004). A new attitude and perspective is to see NNSs as legitimate native English users (Seidlhofer

2001). Therefore, previous research on interlangauge pragmatics in email, though still valuable for language teaching, does not take into consideration how ELF users formulate their emails. Second, the majority of the research has paid a great deal of attention to looking at "requests." Nonetheless, other aspects such as how senders negotiate with receivers and how face is shown in email communication deserve attention as well. Hence, given the aforementioned research gaps, this study is set in a context in which English is used as a lingua franca between a book editor and contributors, focusing on how the editor demonstrated her symbolic competence (Kramsch and Whiteside 2008), and how face was negotiated in emails.

12.2.3 Symbolic Competence

According to Kramsch and Whiteside (2008, p. 664), symbolic competence means "to display a particularly acute ability to play with various linguistic code and with the various spatial and temporal resonances of these codes." It is also the ability "to shape the very context in which the language is learned and used." Therefore, when analyzing symbolic competence in discourses, researchers can look at four aspects, i.e., subjectivity, historicity, performativity, and reframing. Subjectivity refers to how speakers use language to position themselves. Also, when producing language, language users not only demonstrate what they intend to say, but also reveal their cultural memories and histories, that is, how they construct their historicities through language with others. In addition, using certain discourses not only shows how language users perform their roles or meaning, it can also create realities or results in what they express and hence affect performativity. Finally, symbolic competence refers to the ability to change contexts such as changing a face-threatening context into a context in which language users regain their power in the communication. Such ability is called reframing.

One significance of adopting symbolic competence in the present study is that in the situation where English is used as a lingua franca, the notion of a single norm of culture or ways of communication is questionable. Symbolic competence in intercultural communication then goes beyond understanding others in their cultures or sharing common goals or interests but "presupposes a lack of understanding due to divergent subjectivities and historicities" (Kramsch 2011, p. 356). Consequently, everyone is seen as a unique individual in communication, possessing his/her subjective experience and stories with which he/she performs his/her roles by creating discourses that brings about realities and/or frames or reframes events.

12.2.4 Face as Relational and Interactional

Like face-to-face communication, email communication also requires a sender/receiver to be aware of the face of the other. Brown and Levinson (1987) claimed that face was a reflection of the pre-existing social and cultural practices and face was a basic want that everyone desires. However, Arundale (2006) criticized Brown and Levinson's point of view as being restricted to a monadic individual and merely placing focus on a single isolated utterance when doing analyses. Hence, he proposed Face Constituting Theory (Arundale 1999), which regarded face as a co-constituting model and as interactional and relational.

In his theory, Arundale (2010) mentioned three types of face interpreting. The first is *projected/interpreted face*, which means the provisional interpreting of a recipient's interpretation when a speaker designs and produces his first utterance. This provisional interpreting will be later confirmed when the recipient provides his utterances. The second is called *evolving face interpreting*, which is the interpreting of the relationship of the connectedness and separateness that identify the relationship from the prior discourse to the current moment. The third is *contextual face interpreting*, which is defined as "one's expectation for the interpreting of connectedness with and separateness from the other person that applied in the current context" (Arundale 2010, p. 2092). This is important because it may involve current evolving face as well as different expectations with others or societies. One can sense that the three interpretings are related to past (evolving face), present (contextual face), and future (projected/interpreted face). The three evaluations of face interpreting are of significance in interpreting face as threatening, in stasis, or supportive.

When evaluating face as in stasis, supportive or threatening, speakers, and recipients need to compare the situated shift and the proffered shift. Situated shift refers to the difference in connectedness and separateness between one's contextual face and evolving face interpreting at the current moment in conversation. Proffered shift means the differences in connectedness and separateness between one's projected face and evolving face at the current moment. When a situated and a proffered shift do not involve convergence or divergence, the projected/interpreted face is interpreted as *in stasis*. When a situated shift involved convergence or differentiation, and a proffered face involves the same, the projected/interpreted face is interpreted as *supportive*. Once there is an inequality between the proffered shift and the situated shift in terms of divergence or convergence, the projected/interpreted face might be *threatening*.

Adopting Arundale's theory, researchers then can interpret face, facework, and politeness in the context where what precedes and follows an utterance or discourse is relevant and crucial. Also, this allows researchers to shift from interpreting an utterance or sentence as culturally derived and inherently face-threatening to seeing that face is the evaluation of a participant in the moment. As a result, face is emergent from the on-going discourses and it is conceptualized in terms of the relationship that is co-constituted between persons rather than by independent individuals. More specifically, face is seen in a dialectic yin/yang way because the interpreting of face is realized through each other in a non-resolute process. Each utterance can define or be defined by other utterances. Furthermore, because of the dialectic yin/yang nature, face involves an interdependent relationship of connectedness and separateness between two or more persons where the relationship is inseparable from and always reflexively linked with each other.

12.2.5 Research Questions

Based on the previous literature, two research questions are presented as follows.

1. How do international English users demonstrate symbolic competence in their negotiation of revision?
2. How does the editor care for face in the discourse between her and the contributors?

12.3 Methods

12.3.1 Participants

In line with ethical protocols and so as not to disclose their identities, pseudonyms are used for all participants in this study. The primary participant is one of the editors of a book, Prof. Chen Mei Hua. In the process of editing a book, she needed to regularly contact different scholars from China, Taiwan, and America, most of whom she had not met before. Although there were many contributors, in this study, I primarily focused on the interactions between Prof. Chen and two contributors, Kevin and Prof. Wang, because, as the data in the following sections show, there was much symbolic competence and facework needed in these interactions, which served as good examples for analysis. Furthermore, the researcher also obtained permission from Kevin and Prof. Wang to use their emails and they were informed that their identities would not be disclosed.

12.3.2 Data Collection

There are two types of sources of data. One is email and the other is an interview with the editor. The email data are mostly gathered from the email exchanges between Prof. Chen and the contributors. Some emails are interactions between her and other scholars who participated in the reviewing processes. The total number of emails received by and sent from Prof. Chen is 960. However, because the current study is interested in how the editor used ELF to communicate with contributors I only analyzed emails that were written by Prof. Chen and by Kevin. Hence, the number of the emails counted as data is 574. The emails are all in English. The book editing process commenced in January, 2013 and I obtained Prof. Chen's permission to access to her email account in July, 2014. The period of email data collection is from January, 2013 to November, 2014.

Regarding the interview data, I arranged an interview with Prof. Chen through Skype on October 21, 2014. By this time, most of the contributors had submitted their papers for external review. The whole process was audio-recorded and the length of the interview was 26 min, 48 s. There were five questions (see Appendix), covering the process of writing emails to different receivers during the editing process, her relationship with the contributors and the influence of her teaching and research background in writing emails.

12.3.3 Data Analysis

Email data were first sorted according to different contributors and different periods of time to facilitate a more in-depth investigation. In addition, in order to investigate how the editor demonstrated her symbolic competence and facework with different contributors, I first read and observed every email carefully, and produced summaries of each event and my observations (Duff 2008). After that, I identified a few critical events. In terms of symbolic competence, I referred to the ecologically oriented analysis suggested by Kramsch (2008) and Kramsch and Whiteside (2008) that treats both self and other as pluralistic, meaning as emergentism expressed by multiple timescales, and patterns of activities are fractal (Larsen-Freeman 1997). Later, I included every email in each critical event to construct comprehensive contexts and investigate the editor's subjectivity, historicity, performativity, and how she framed/reframed the contexts. With regard to facework, I adopted Arundale's (2006, 2010) framework and thus email interactions are seen as conversation. Hence, emails are not analyzed in an isolated manner, but what precedes and follows should also be included as a whole in a single event. For example, in analysis of an event such as negotiating an extension of submission, a contributor would initiate a request, followed by the editor's suggestion of deadline and final consensus. Therefore, there may be two or more emails in a single event.

For the analysis of the interview data, I first listened to the audio-file and identified general themes and transcribed them. Subsequently, I provided interpretations that correspond to the transcriptions. The transcriptions covered issues that related to symbolic competence and face, including the editor's experiences of interacting with the contributors, her relationship with them, concerns when writing emails, and any changes that she noticed during the process in terms of writing emails or relationships. Finally, I examined what terms or themes in the interview were associated with my observation from the email interactions for triangulation.

12.4 Results

In this section, I will present two cases that demonstrate how the editor used symbolic competence and facework to negotiate with the contributors. The first case involves interactions between Prof. Chen and Kevin. The second case is an email sent to Prof. Wang.

12.4.1 How Do International English Users Demonstrate Symbolic Competence in Their Negotiation of Revision?

The first case presented here was a tug of war between Professor Chen and one of the initial potential contributors, Kevin. Kevin initially joined the submission process in 2013 but withdrew from this process for personal reasons. However, in May, 2014, Professor Chen emailed him and asked about whether he would still like to contribute his paper. After receiving this invitation, Kevin was interested in contributing a paper again. After finishing his paper in July, it was sent for internal review. In this internal review process, the other editor was concerned about the quality of his paper and suggested that a serious reorganization of his results and discussion sections were needed. Hence, Professor Chen emailed him to request a revision.

A problem arose at this time, as Kevin seemed not to understand some comments he received and was not certain about the reviewing process and hence, he queried what he should do. To deal with this problem, Professor Chen then emailed him a fairly long email, as shown in Email (1).

Email (1): Responding to Kevin's problems, 15/07/2014

> Dear Kevin:
> If you do not understand the comments, you may tell me which one and I'll try to explain more clearly to you.
> This volume operates on a two-tier review system. First, the chapters will be reviewed by the editors, and then we will send your paper to two external reviewers to ensure the quality of the book.
> We have discussed your paper. The main areas which you need to revise are the way you presented the statistical findings. They are more like something in a mathematics paper, but in applied linguistics or SLA research, we do not write that way. Second, we hope that you can provide more discussion about your statistical results. The results are interesting, but we would like to hear how you explain the results and what insights they can give us, and so forth. The best value of a research paper lies not only in the findings, but also in how a researcher interprets them, how they relate to previous research, how they differ from previous research, or what insights you obtain from doing this research.

> I hope all this can help. If you have any further questions, please do not hesitate to contact me. I'm not sure if this is the first paper you submit to a book or journal, but all of us experienced researchers have gone through similar review process when we want to publish a paper. So please do not be discouraged when you see so many comments. We're willing to help you in any way possible.
> Thank you for your patience.
> Meihua

In this email, at first Professor Chen took an editor's role in explaining the reviewing process. Nonetheless, in the second paragraph she changed this discourse into a professor-student consultation by using "in applied linguistics or SLA research, we do not write that way" as well as discussing how to write a research paper by saying, "The best value of a research paper lies not only in the findings, but also in how a researcher interprets them, how they relate to previous research, how they differ from previous research, or what insights you obtain from doing this research." The reason why she wrote this professor-student like suggestion was because she realized that Kevin was a PhD candidate at that moment and probably needed more guidance in how to write a research paper.

Finally, in closing this email, Prof. Chen then switched her discourse to consolation by referring to her own and other scholars' experience of becoming an experienced researcher who often needed to go through tedious and arduous processes. By saying this, she accepted Kevin as a legitimate researcher in academia rather than an outsider. In the end, she ended this email by saying "So please do not be discouraged when you see so many comments. We are willing to help you in any way possible." This final supportive ending is a stark contrast from the beginning of the email in which she positioned herself as an editor as well as an applied linguistics professor. Instead, the ending is more like a friend's talk.

Upon receiving this email, Kevin replied on the same day, as shown in Email (2). However, he appears to have misinterpreted Prof. Chen's intentions.

Email (2): Kevin's reply

> Hi MeiHua,
> Do you mind if I ask you where you are? It would be helpful to meet. I am flexible with time and distance.
> To be honest, I am a teacher, not a researcher or publisher, per se, and this is the first time I have ever attempted to do this!

Recall that Prof. Chen mentioned the process that "experienced researchers" all have. The purpose of saying that was to make Kevin feel better. However, he interpreted it in a different way, claiming that "he is a teacher, not a researcher or publisher." Here, it appears that Kevin would like to create a separate relationship with Prof. Chen because he did not want to be associated with the research community or felt he was not yet in that role.

After his reply, Kevin thought he needed some extra assistance so he and Prof. Chen arranged a time to discuss his problems in person. Before the day of their personal talk, he proposed an alternative suggestion to Prof. Chen. He asked if she would like to be his co-author because he had difficult time revising his paper. In response to this request, Prof. Chen emailed him back, as shown in Email (3).

Email (3): Reply to Kevin's co-author proposal

> I have an idea. Since your paper is part of your dissertation, i'm wondering if I can see your dissertation so I may have a clue of what you can do to extract something from your dissertation. Your literature is fine, but we both think that your results and discussion should be strengthened.
> Meihua

Notice that in this email there is no address term, which might suggest that the relationship between them is not as distant as it used to be. She did not turn down his request directly but rather provided an alternative solution to his problem.

Later, Kevin revealed that he in fact had not finished his dissertation and felt overwhelmed by the publication process. After reconsidering, he decided he should put his dissertation as the top priority and decided to withdraw from contribution completely.

In these events, it is evident that both of them demonstrated their symbolic competence. In the email shown in Email (1), Prof. Chen actually showed her subjectivity (Kramsch and Whiteside 2008) by positioning herself in different roles, e.g., editor, researcher, and teacher. Also, historicity was also revealed when she referred to the topic of "experienced researchers," the discourse clearly showed her memory of being a researcher along the way to the current moment. In the following Email (2), Kevin showed his subjectivity as well by positioning himself as merely a teacher, refusing to be categorized as a researcher. Through the use of "researcher," Kevin actually reframed the whole event and performed an alternative reality and balanced the symbolic power between him and Prof. Chen. In Email (3), in response to Kevin's co-author proposal, Prof. Chen also reframed the event into a professor-student context where she probably could provide some assistance during the time of consultation and hence the use of "I have an idea," "I'm wondering if I can…" is not only a suggestion or a request. In addition, notice that the modal verbs she used in the sentence "I'm wondering if I can see your dissertation so I may have a clue of what you can do to extract something from your dissertation" are *can* and *may* instead of *could* and *might*. This also indicates that she created realis for the future because she knew what she would do and that she would have the ability to do it (Scollon 2008). Taken together, Email (3) shows performativity and reframing because she reestablished the relationship and created a different reality.

12.4.2 How Does the Editor Care for Face in the Discourse Between Her and Contributors?

In this section, I will focus on two cases. The first case is the interactions between Kevin and Prof. Chen, which I have shown above. The second case is an email sent to Prof. Wang. First, I will refer to Kevin's case. Email (1) and (2) reveal how much facework Prof. Chen did. If we adopt Brown and Levinson's (1987) account, then the sentence "all of us experienced researchers have gone through similar review process when we want to publish a paper" is considered as positive face because Prof. Chen used an inclusive "us" in the publication activity. However, according to Arundale (2006, 2010), face interpreting is a jointly co-constituted interactional and relational process and thus preceding and following discourses should be taken into account. By doing so, we can see that in Email (1), the interpreting of the face was still provisional because Kevin had not provided his reply. After Prof. Chen received Kevin's reply, her interpretation of face became operative and would subsequently need to be modified. Moreover, if we look at Email (2) in association with Email (1), while the situation at the moment involved convergence, Kevin's response showed divergence and thus Prof. Chen's sentence was seen as threatening. As a result, the interpreting of face emerged at that moment. The sentence then should be seen as separation face as Kevin attempts to show divergence and differentiation.

Another interesting case is shown in Email (4), in which Prof. Chen asked a contributor, Prof. Wang, to revise his paper. The reason why this critical incident is selected is because prior to sending this email, Prof. Chen first asked the other editor to see if this email was appropriate or not, suggesting that a high degree of facework was required. Moreover, she mentioned in the interview that she deliberately formulated this email in order not to be face-threatening.

The connection between Prof. Chen and Prof. Wang was different from the others in that it was Prof. Wang who sent an email showing his interest in contributing a book chapter. He introduced himself as a friend of one of the contributors. As an editor, Prof. Chen welcomed his submission. However, toward the deadline for submission, he needed an extension because he admitted that he was occupied with his teaching and meetings. Finally, after submitting his first draft, the editors decided that he needed to revise it considerably because there were serious adjustments that needed to be made both in terms of content and language. In fact, she emailed the other editor about the difficulty in understanding his paper. She wrote, "I spent hours yesterday reading Wang's paper again."

Email (4): Asking Prof. Wang to revise his work, 16/07/2014

> Dear Dr. Wang:
> Thank you for submitting your paper to our book. To ensure the best quality, we decided to operate on a two-tier review system, which means that the editors will review each paper first before it goes to external review.
> Your paper discusses email data used for research, which is valuable because unlike DCTs or role plays, email has been under-represented in ILP research. However, it seems to us that your paper can be roughly divided into two separate ones: one seems to be an opinion essay using secondary research data and lots of literature to support your view; and the other seems to be an experiment in which you collected data directly from your own students. Either way is fine and fits the scope of the book, but we are afraid that putting them together may distract our readers. Therefore, we would like to recommend that you make a choice between these two types. If you prefer the first type, you may argue why email is useful and valid data for L2 pragmatists by giving strong theoretical and empirical support. What is more, relate it to Chinese native speakers of English since this is the scope

of our book. If you prefer the second type, then please follow the format of a regular experimental study, starting with introduction, literature, method, results, discussion and conclusion.
Attached please find (1) editors' comments on your paper, (2) a response sheet, and (3) an authors' guide for your reference. We would appreciate it very much if you could do the following before submitting your second draft for anonymous external review:

1. Please use the response sheet to react to the editors' comments.
2. Please prepare a new word file with the revised version of your paper. Highlight all the changes you made in BLUE. Make the format consistent with that specified in the authors' guide.
3. Please submit your revised version no later than 8/5.

Thank you very much for your time and consideration.
Happy Summer Vacation!
Meihua

In the attempt to ask him to make major changes, Prof. Chen wrote an email to him, as shown in Email (4). In this email, in order to take care of his face, Prof. Chen started off by addressing the contributor as "Dear Dr. Wang" and summarizing two main foci in his research and said "Either way is fine and fits the scope of the book" to recognize that the directions were acceptable. This serves the function of paving the path for the later recommendation. However, interpreting the two recommendations, one can see that the major problems of his paper include lack of focus, lack of arguments, lack of theoretical and empirical evidence, lack of relation with the scope of this book, and not conforming to the style of research writing. These recommendations could be quite face-threatening for a professor, but Prof. Chen strategically used the subjunctive "if," the modal "may," the lexical modifier "please" and receiver's perspective "you" to show her politeness.

Interview Excerpt (1): Prof. Chen's reflection on the email to Prof. Wang[1]

Prof. Chen: Sometimes I would need to think about it. That is. For example, the email I wrote to Prof. Wang. The comments (I wrote). Because his writing was a little odd..and…I did not intend to reject his submission or something like that. But, I just wanted to ask him to revise. But, I was afraid….because we are all scholars and professors, I couldn't put it like….you know. You just need politeness. Politeness is very important. I think it's politeness. Politeness was a very big concern in writing the email. So like Prof. Wang.. you…I wrote a very long email to him, right? I thought about how to write that email. It took him longer time to write it.
Researcher: Do you mean the content?
Prof. Chen: Because you, you just need to be courteous and polite. And you can't be too… anyway you need to be circumlocutory! Right, be circumlocutory. And then…don't be too…that. Can't put it like…you are criticizing the person or something like that. Even if he/she did not do very well, it can't be too face threatening. So sometimes I would use some strategies.

[1]The interview was conducted in Chinese. All the excerpts were translated into English.

In the interview extract shown in Interview Excerpt (1), she mentioned how she really thought about this email. Evidently, she kept repeating the importance of politeness and how she thought about the relationship between her and Prof. Wang so that she needed to tactfully use some strategies to make her request. Therefore, her self-report confirmed the observations on the linguistic features for face and politeness in her email.

After receiving this email, Prof. Wang said he would revise and resubmit his work as soon as possible, but he did not do so and presumably withdrew from submission because Prof. Chen had no contact with him since then. Back to the issue of how face was interpreted and presented in this email, there appear to be two different aspects of how face is shown according to the email and the interview data. First, based on Arundale (2010), it is found that in the evaluation of Prof. Chen's projected/interpreted face, she thought of her email as not threatening as she meticulously designed this email by using subjunctive mood and modal, which are considered strategies to show politeness (Brown and Levinson 1987), by using lexical modifier "please," a common feature to show mitigation in requests, though not considered effective in all studies (Biesenbach-Lucas 2007; Economidou-Kogetsidis 2011; Hartford and Bardovi-Harlig 1996), and by using hearer's perspective.

Interview Excerpt (2): Prof. Chen's interaction with the contributors

> So at first when I emailed them, I used a more formal style. And I think I should be formal as an editor. But, after that, we had frequent communication. After we had frequent communication…I would feel…eh…he/she…was a little… I don't know if you ever noticed the change of addressing terms. Right. For example, I initially used Dr., Dear Dr. or something for some people. But after a while I felt they were not…some people were not as formal. Then, I thought I could…hm…establish a relationship. So, later sometimes I used first name. Also, I didn't use sincerely for the closing part. Probably I would just use Best or Regards.

Moreover, when Prof. Chen chose to address the potential contributor as "Dear Dr. Wang," it showed her evolving face, that she interpreted this relationship as separateness at that point in terms of distance. This interpretation of their relationship is further supported in Excerpt (2) as Prof. Chen mentioned that she changed her terms of address as time progressed because she felt they she established a relationship with some contributors; however, this change was not found in the interaction with Prof. Wang. Therefore, it is reasonable to assume that their relationship was considered as separate from the beginning to that moment. In addition, the term of address also shows her contextual face, in that she positioned herself as an editor in this email so she needed to keep some distance from the contributor.

Finally, interpretations to whether this email is threatening, in stasis, or supportive appear to be not absolute. One could interpret the email for revision as threatening based on the consequence because he disappeared without further reply. Alternatively, he might have decided that he did not have sufficient time for extensive revision requested, which would have no relation to whether the email was face-threatening or not. If the former interpretation is adopted, it could be interpreted that the situated shift involved mild divergence but the proffered shift involved too much separation, presumably because of the suggestions, and hence, Prof. Wang interpreted his projected/interpreted face as threatening to their relationship. This interpretation is in stark contrast to Prof. Chen's projected/interpreted face.

Albeit from the analyses of the email, one could interpret face as emergent according to Arundale's (2010) theory, a noteworthy and intriguing fact was that in Excerpt (1), Prof. Chen explicitly stated that she thought that politeness was crucial when she constructed this email and she did not want it to be face-threatening. This was reminiscent of Brown and Levinson's (1987) politeness theory in which face was considered as a want. In other words, every member knows what other members desire. Therefore, it appears to be fair to state that it may be too biased to claim that face is only exclusively achieved through co-constituted interactions because to some degree, face is something that people want inherently.

In summary, the findings of the present study revealed that face and its meaning were emergent and face was conjoint co-constituting and interactional achievement. By examining the preceding and ensuing discourse, one can determine face as threatening, in stasis or supportive. Furthermore, the findings also suggest that Brown and Levison's (1987) theory has a place as well in that Prof. Chen clearly mentioned that she did not intend to offend the contributors, which reflects that face cannot merely be understood through interactions, but could exist as a basic want. Moreover, email communication is subject to how senders and receiver interpret the relationship, which could change and develop over time.

12.5 Discussion

This study focused on several critical events in academic publication in ELF email interactions. Specifically, I focused on how the editor negotiated with the contributors as they revised and resubmitted their papers. In examining these critical events, the findings showed that there were metaphoric tussles between the two parties in which the editor and the contributors employed symbolic competence and facework to tactfully negotiate and reach the goal. What is interesting from the findings is that both parties are recognized as different individual as each possesses their own subjectivity and historicity. In an ELF context like this, this demonstrates that each individual has different understandings of the world. Hence, similar to ELF spoken discourse (Bjørge 2012), not only consensus, but also conflicts can be discovered in ELF written discourse. Also, the inconsistency that resulted from the different concepts held by Prof. Chen and Kevin in effect echoes the fact that in intercultural communication, it is the lack of common subjectivity and historicity that symbolic competence is all about (Kramsch 2011). Notwithstanding that diversity of subjectivity and historicity of participants in communication is not uncommon, the differences might be even more huge in ELF communication in that the interlocutors are usually not from the same country or speech community and do not share the same cultural norms. Thus, taking one's subjectivity and historicity into account in ELF communication can shed more light on realizing how meaning is negotiated and understood.

Recognizing the importance of one's subjectivity and historicity will further lead us to understand that these two elements are not merely unitary. One can see that besides the editor's role, Prof. Chen also assumed multiple identities such as a professor or a researcher. This echoes Larsen-Freeman's (1997) statement that everyone's identity is pluralistic. Furthermore, by adopting ecologically oriented analysis, one can see that identity is not discourse external (Uryu et al. 2014), it is rather a relational and interactional phenomenon and it is emergent through interactions (Kramsch and Steffensen 2008). Hence, how Prof. Chen positioned herself was associated with how Kevin responded to her. Also, these identities not only refer to the present, but also to different timescales, showing that our discourses are recursive (Kramsch 2008).

In addition, by looking at symbolic competence in the ELF email data, one can also realize how both parties showed their performativity and context reframing. In other words, language here serves as a medium of making meaning and constructing knowledge and experiences (Swain 2006). Revealing that he was only a teacher and rejecting the title of a researcher, Kevin's statement did not merely say what the statement intends to say, it also symbolized himself as who he was as well as how he thought about the roles of himself and a researcher. More importantly, the refusal and unwillingness in his email then demonstrated performativity and created a power to reframe the contexts.

Given that language is used as a medium to show performativity and reframing, what accompanies is the issue of facework. In light of the results of the study, face is interactional, relational and non-summative on the one hand, but it can also be attributed to individual and social expectations on the other. In the negotiation between Prof. Chen and Kevin, one can see that face cannot be interpreted only by means of one email from one party nor can we understand face as predetermined by a certain norm. The fact is that the norm of appropriate politeness in ELF contexts is rather suspended (Walkinshaw and Kirkpatrick 2014) and co-constructed (Seidlhofer 2011). Hence, Arundale's (2006, 2010) theory did make a contribution in understanding face in ELF written discourse.

However, Prof. Wang's example appears to be more controversial if we attempt to provide an account in terms of Arundale's proposal. One could contend that the email sent to Prof. Wang was face-threatening because he withdrew from this process. In this regard, face could be interpreted as relational and interactional if we adopt a broader concept of interaction (Spencer-Oatey 2007). Alternatively, one could argue that his withdrawal was because he did not have time for the extensive revision required. Therefore, it is irrelevant to face-threatening. Moreover, from Prof. Chen's interview, she clearly stated that she understood she needed to be polite. That is, she did care about Prof. Wang's face because he was a professor and there were things that would be regarded as face threatening when requesting a professor to considerably revise his paper. In other words, there would be "a sense of what is normal" that is recognized by members of society (Leech 2014, p. 5). Therefore, it would be too biased to claim that face is only an interactional phenomenon. In sum, although there seem to be two different viewpoints regarding face, these two viewpoints are not mutually exclusive. It would be more appropriate if face were understood in ELF contexts as having cognitive foundations and social constitution in interaction, and as belonging to individuals or collectives as well as to interpersonal relations (Spencer-Oatey 2007, p. 654).

12.6 Conclusion

This study performs an in-depth analysis of how an editor communicated with contributors in ELF email interactions. The study intended to uncover how the editor demonstrated her symbolic competence and facework during the editorial processes.

The findings revealed that the editor showed her symbolic competence (Kramsch 2011; Kramsch and Whiteside 2008) in negotiating with the contributor through subjectivity (positioning herself in different roles), performativity (using language to create alternative reality), historicity (referring to her own memories), and reframing (showing the ability to change the context). Taking this ecological perspective, one can see that in ELF email communication, meaning is relational, emergent, multiscalar and recursive, double-voiced, subjective, and historically contingent (Kramsch 2008).

In terms of face, the findings indicated that face can be multidimensional and emergent. Equally important, face can also be inherent in people's desires. Treating face as a conjointly co-constituted process and as relational and interactional, face interpretation as threatening, in stasis or supportive should be associated with previous and subsequent discourse (Arundale 1999, 2006, 2010). One's relationship as separateness or connectedness with others should also be determined by the earlier discourse to the present moment. Interpreting face as basic wants (Brown and Levinson 1987), helps us understand that face is not only a dialectical phenomenon but also individual considerations should be taken into account.

Finally, there is a suggestion from the findings that could shed light on future ELF research. While numerous ELF researchers are interested in how communication is achieved when ELF features occur (Cogo and Dewey 2006; Bjorkman 2008; Breiteneder 2009; Meierkord 2004; Ranta 2006) or what strategies ELF users employ (Cogo and Dewey 2006; Firth 1996; Walkinshaw and Kirkpatrick 2014) in speaking, this study takes it to the next level to elucidate how symbolic competence and facework are manifested in interactional and relational EFL email communication. Through understanding how ELF users demonstrate their symbolic competence through written discourse in emails, it is suggested that the concept of symbolic self (Kramsch 2011) should also be taken into consideration in ELF research because as the findings indicate, our discourses are subjective and historically grounded and the ability of maintain communication requires the ability frame or re-frame an event.

Appendix

Interview questions (Chinese)

1. 可以敘述一下跟這些投稿人互動的過程嗎?有沒有妳比較深刻的印象?
2. 在所有投稿人裡面, 妳覺得妳跟他們的關係如何?
3. 在所有投稿人裡面, 妳有覺得跟誰比較親近嗎?爲什麼?
4. 有覺得跟誰通 email 的時候是比較特殊或者關係改變的嗎?
5. 教學經驗對妳的 email 寫作有什麼影響嗎?

Interview questions (English)

1. Can you describe your interactions between you and the contributors? Are there any events that impressed you the most?
2. How do you feel about the relationship between you and the contributors?
3. Are there any contributors that you are closer with? Why?
4. Are there any special experiences in email communication with certain contributors? Is there a change of relationship between you and certain contributors?
5. Does your teaching experience affect your email writing?

References

Arundale, Robert B. 1999. An alternative model and ideology of communication for an alternative to politeness theory. *Pragmatics* 9(1): 119–153.

Arundale, Robert B. 2006. Face as relational and interactional: A communication framework for research on face, facework, and politeness. *Journal of Politeness Research* 2: 193–216.

Arundale, Robert B. 2010. Constituting face in conversation: Face, facework, and interactional achievement. *Journal of Pragmatics* 42: 2078–2015.

Biesenbach-Lucas, Sigrun. 2007. Students writing emails to faculty: An examination of e-politeness among native and non-native speakers of English. *Language Learning and Technology* 11(2): 59–81.

Biesenbach-Lucas, Sigrun, and Donald Weasenforth. 2002. Virtual office hours: Negotiation strategies in electronic conferencing. *Computer Assisted Language Learning* 15(2): 147–165.

Bjørge, Anne Kari. 2012. Expressing disagreement in ELF business negotiations: Theory and practice. *Applied Linguistics* 33(4): 406–427.

Bjorkman, Beyza. 2008. English as the lingua franca of engineering: The morphosyntax of academic speech events. *Nordic Journal of English Studies* 7(3): 103–122.

Bjorkman, Beyza. 2014. An analysis of polyadic English as a lingua franca (ELF) speech: A communicative strategies framework. *Journal of Pragmatics* 66: 122–138.

Bou-Franch, Patricia. 2011. Openings and closings in Spanish email conversations. *Journal of Pragmatics* 43: 1772–1785.

Braine, George. 2005. The challenge of academic publishing: A Hong Kong perspective. *TESOL Quarterly* 39(4): 707–716.

Breiteneder, Angelika. 2009. English as a lingua franca in Europe: An empirical perspective. *World Englishes* 28(2): 256–269.

Brown, Penelope, and Stephen C. Levinson. 1987. *Politeness: Some universals in language usage*. New York: Cambridge University Press.

Callahan, Laura. 2011. Workplace requests in Spanish and English: A case study of email communication between two supervisors and a subordinate. *Southwest Journal of Linguistics* 30(1): 27–56.

Cheung, Yin-Ling. 2010. First publication in referred English journals: Difficulties, coping strategies, and recommendations for student training. *System* 38: 134–141.

Cogo, Alessia, and Martin Dewey. 2006. Efficiency in ELF communication: From pragmatic motives to lexico-grammatical innovation. *Nordic Journal of English Studies* 5(2): 59–93.

Crystal, David. 2003. *English as a global language*, 2nd ed. Cambridge: Cambridge University Press.

Davies, Alan. 2004. The native speaker in applied linguistics. In *Handbook of applied linguistics*, ed. Alan Davies, and Catherine Elder, 431–449. Oxford: Blackweel.

Duff, Patricia. 2008. *Case study research in applied linguistics*. NY: Lawrence Erlbaum Associates.

Economidou-Kogetsidis, Maria. 2011. "Please answer me as soon as possible": Pragmatic failure in non-native speakers' e-mail requests to faculty. *Journal of Pragmatics* 43: 3193–3215.

Elder, Catherine, and Alan Davies. 2006. Assessing English as a lingua franca. *Annual Review of Applied Linguistics* 26: 282–301.

Erling, Elizabeth J., and Tom Bartlett. 2006. Making English their own: The use of ELF among students of English at the FUB. *Nordic Journal of English Studies* 5(2): 9–40.

Feak, Christine. 2009. Negotiating publication: Author responses to peer review of medical research articles in thoracic surgery. *REVISTA CANARIA DE ESTUDIOS INGLESES* 59: 17–34.

Firth, Alan. 1996. The discursive accomplishment of normality: On "lingua franca" English and conversation analysis. *Journal of Pragmatics* 26(2): 237–259.

Flowerdew, John. 1999. Writing for scholarly publication in English: The case of Hong Kong. *Journal of Second Language Writing* 8(2): 123–145.

Flowerdew, John. 2000. Discourse community, legitimate peripheral participation and the nonnative-English-speaking scholar. *TESOL Quarterly* 34(1): 127–150.

Flowerdew, John. 2008. Scholarly writers who use English as an additional language: What can Goffman's "stigma" tell us? *Journal of English for Academic Purposes* 7: 77–86.

Godsden, Hugh. 1995. Success in research article writing and revision: A socio-constructivist perspective. *English for Specific Purposes* 14(1): 37–57.

Godsden, Hugh. 2001. "Thank you for your critical comments and helpful suggestions": Compliance and conflict in authors' replies to referees' comments in peer reviews of scientific research papers. *Iberica* 3: 3–17.

Godsden, Hugh. 2003. "Why not give us the full story?": Functions of referees' comments in peer reviews of scientific research papers. *Journal of English for Academic Purposes* 2: 87–101.

Hallajian, Ali, and Maya Khemlani David. 2014. "Hello and good day to you dear Dr…" greeting and closings in supervisors-supervisees email exchanges. *Procedia-Social and Behavioral Sciences* 118: 85–93.

Hartford, Beverly S., and Kathleen Bardovi-Harlig. 1996. "At your earliest convenience:" A study of written student requests to faculty. In *Pragmatics and language learning,*ed. Lawrence. F. Bouton, 55–69, vol. 7. Urbana Champaign, IL: University of Illinois, Division of English as an International Language (DEIL).

Ingvarsdóttir, Hafdís, and Birna Arnbjörnsdóttir. 2013. ELF and academic writing: A perspective from the expanding circle. *Journal of English as a Lingua Franca* 2(1): 123–145.

Jenkins, Jennifer. 2000. *The phonology of English as an international language*. Oxford: Oxford University Press.

Kao, Shin-Mei, and Wen-Chun Wang. 2014. Lexical and organizational features in novice and experienced ELF presentations. *Journal of English as a Lingua Franca* 3(1): 49–79.

Kramsch, Claire. 2008. Ecological perspectives on foreign language education. *Language Teaching* 41(3): 389–408.

Kramsch, Claire. 2011. The symbolic dimensions of the interactional. *Language Teaching* 44(3): 354–367.

Kramsch, Claire, and Sune Vork Steffensen. 2008. Ecological perspectives on second language acquisition and socialization. In *Encyclopedia of language and education. language and socialization.*, ed. Patricia Duff and Nancy Hornberger, 17–28, vol. 8. New York: Springer.

Kramsch, Claire, and Anne Whiteside. 2008. Language ecology in multilingual settings: Towards a theory of symbolic competence. *Applied Linguistics* 29: 647–671.

Larsen-Freeman, Diane. 1997. Choas/complexity science and second language acquisition. *Applied Linguistics* 18(2): 141–165.

Leech, Geoffrey. 2014. *The Pragmatics of Politeness*. Oxford: Oxford University Press.

Li, Yongyan. 2007a. Shaping Chinese novice scientists' manuscripts for publication. *Journal of Second Language Writing* 16: 100–117.

Li, Yongyan. 2007b. Apprentice scholarly writing in a community of practice: An intraview of an NNES graduate student writing a research article. *TESOL Quarterly* 41(1): 55–79.

Meierkord, Christiane. 2004. Syntactic variation in interactions across international Englishes. *English World Wide* 25(1): 109–132.

Murphy, Margaret, and Mike Levy. 2006. Politeness in intercultural email communication: Australian and Korean perspectives. *Journal of Intercultural Communication,* 12. http://immi.se/intercultural/nr12/murphy.htm. Accessed 02 Aug 2014.

Osimk-Teasdale, Ruth. 2014. "I just wanted to give a partly answer": Capturing and exploring word class variation in ELF data. *Journal of English as a Lingua Franca* 3(1): 109–143.

Ranta, Elina. 2006. The attractive progressive. Why use the—ing form in English as a lingua franca? *Nordic Journal of English Studies* 5(2):95–116.

Scollon, Ron. 2008. *Analyzing public discourse: Discourse analysis in the making of public policy*. Abingdon: Routledge.

Seidlhofer, Barbara. 2001. Closing a conceptual gap: The case for a description of English as a lingua franca. *International Journal of Applied Linguistics* 11(2): 133–158.

Seidlhofer, Barbara. 2011. *Understanding English as a lingua franca*. Oxford: Oxford University Press.

Spencer-Oatey, Helen. 2007. Theories of identity and the analysis of face. *Journal of Pragmatics* 39:639–656.

Swales, John. 1996. Occluded genres in the academy: The case of the submission letter. In *Academic writing: Intercultural and textual issues*, ed. Eija Ventola, and Anna Mauranen, 45–58. Philadelphia: John Benjamins.

Swain, Merrill. 2006. Languaging, agency and collaboration in advanced second language proficiency. In *Advanced language learning: The contribution of Halliday and Vygotsky*, ed. Heidi Byrenes, 95–108. London: Continuum.

Uryu, Michiko, Sune V. Steffensen, and Claire Kramsch. 2014. The ecology of intercultural interaction: timescales, temporal ranges and identity dynamics. *Language Sciences* 41: 41–49.

Waldvogel, Joan. 2007. Greetings and closings in workplace email. *Journal of Commuter-Mediated Communication* 12: 456–477.

Walkinshaw, Ian, and Andy Kirkpatrick. 2014. Mutual face preservation among Asian speakers of English as a lingua franca. *Journal of English as a Lingua Franca* 3(2): 269–291.

Author Biography

Hsuan-Yu Tai (戴宣毓) is a PhD student at the Institute of Linguistics, National Chung Cheng University. He is also a part-time lecturer at the Department of Applied English, Tainan University of Technology. His research interests include applied linguistics, sociolinguistics, and second language writing.

Chapter 13
Top Secret: Hacking and Fraud Detection in Business Emails of a Taiwanese Company

Tzu-Wei Hsiang

Abstract A hacker's attempt to defraud a Taiwanese company was detected by an employee who noticed a difference in the email writing style used. Therefore, this study seeks to investigate the email writing styles used by the Taiwanese employee and the hacker, using Scollon and Scollon's (Intercultural communication 1995) intercultural communication model as a basis, comparing the hacker's emails with those of a company employee as they write to a customer located in Saudi Arabia. The three questions addressed are: (1) what email writing style does the Taiwanese employee use? (2) What email writing style does the hacker use? (3) What are the differences in style between the hacker and the Taiwanese employee? A total of 11 emails sent by the hacker and 20 emails sent by the Taiwanese employee are compared in this study. Use of the business emails was authorized by the manger of the Taiwanese company. It is found that the Taiwanese employee tends to use an inductive style, a strategy of involvement, and a peaceful tone when writing emails. Inductive means that beginning the email contains background information before getting to the main point of the email. The strategy of involvement means that the Taiwanese employee views supervisors and other employees as a whole team. Peaceful tone means that the employee wants to maintain and enhance the relationship with the customer. Conversely, the hacker's writing style is more deductive, uses the strategy of independence, and a challenging tone. Deductive means that the hacker tends to make the main point of the email in the beginning sentences. The strategy of independence means that the hacker refers only to him/herself when writing emails. The challenging tone is shown in the use of command patterns.

Keywords Business emails · Writing styles · Hacker · Fraud

T.-W. Hsiang (✉)
Institute of Linguistics, National Chung Cheng University, Minxiong, Taiwan
e-mail: vivian4586@gmail.com

Y. Chen et al. (eds.), *Email Discourse Among Chinese Using English as a Lingua Franca*, DOI 10.1007/978-981-287-888-5_13

13.1 Introduction

Many companies use email as their main communication tool. Therefore, the communication that takes place in the workplace has been a topic of extensive research in recent years. Furthermore, the appearance of email as the main medium for business communication has changed the way that individuals and companies work (Hewitt 2006; Evans 2012). Emails now play a very important role in the transmission of information and in dealing with everyday administrative work. This form of communication has largely replaced written memos, the telephone, and face-to-face interactions. The main advantage is that it can allow people to communicate speedily and transfer information easily between different time zones. This new medium of communication has new conventions that do not fully belong to either spoken or written varieties of language. Emails are multifunctional, and therefore, the language used should be different based on the particular purpose for which the correspondent wrote the email and on the relationship between senders and recipients (Lan and MacGregor 2010).

The current paper analyzes the email writing styles of two people, a hacker and an employee, as they write to a Saudi Arabian customer. The only paper we could identify that is specifically related to email and Middle Eastern countries is a study by Hallajian and David (2014), but the goals and methods of that paper are very different from the current paper. Hallajian and David (2014) examine an academic context, analyzing Iranian students' usage of opening, and closing markers when writing to a Malaysian university. This paper is related to a different Middle Eastern country, and examines a business context.

Very few academic papers have used business emails as the main data resource since business emails are related to company secrets. It is worth noting that the current paper uses authentic business emails as the data source, but each business email is a unique case, so generalization is difficult. Also this current paper is not only about analysis of business emails but also about email hacking and email fraud. It is very rare that a researcher has the chance to access this kind of email. Therefore, there are few if any papers or articles that analyze email hacking and fraud in a business setting.

Since this current paper is about email hacking and fraud, it is related to the field of forensic linguistics, which deals with the interaction between language and law (Wu 2002). Wu (2002) mentions that there are many forensic cases that relate to language itself. Forensic linguistics can be dealt with in various ways, from phonetics to semantics, even to pragmatics. For example, Shuy (1993) is a classic example of forensic linguistics. The background of Shuy's study is that a jet crashed and four passengers were killed. The insurance company of the jet developed the theory that the jet crashed because the engine of the plane failed, which caused toxic gas to leak into the cabin and impaired the pilots' judgement and actions, leading to the crash. After 5 years, the insurance company sued the engine manufacturer and the jet builder. Shuy was asked to listen to the tape recordings of the communication between the pilots and the ground-control centers, to determine whether the pilots' language showed any clues that might point to the effects of toxic gas. Shuy begins his analysis with the hypothesis that if the pilots were affected by toxic gas, their language would have some disturbances. Shuy analyzed the pilots' syntax, pronunciation, conversational cooperation, speech acts, and pauses to find out whether they had been affected or not. After his analysis, Shuy overturned his preliminary hypothesis that the pilots were affected by a toxic gas. The results show no meaningful change or difference from the beginning to the end of the flight. Therefore, it indicates that the pilots' language was not affected by toxic gas, but it was pilot error that caused the crash. Shuy's (1993) example shows that a person's language can reveal a lot of things, and can determine the judge's verdict.

Another classic example of forensic linguistics is that of Eagleson (1994), which describes a specific case study distinguishing whether a farewell letter was written by a husband or wife, based on spelling, grammatical morphology and syntax. Eagleson (1994) points out that when people write, they often leave clues to their own identity, so he wanted to identify clues in other known writing of the husband and the wife which could be matched with the farewell letter to identify who was the author of the farewell letter. After the comparison, the author of the farewell letter was shown to be the husband, since the husband's writing style has a high correlation with the farewell letter in spelling, grammatical morphology, syntax, and punctuation. Eagleson (1994) indicates that each person has a unique identity when they write. It is this unique identity that helps the police distinguishes the writer of the farewell letter. The language or writing style that people use or apply can reveal the difference. However, in forensic linguistics, each case is a unique case study. Shuy (1993) and Eagleson (1994) are both very different from the current study. They both look at detailed linguistic features, like syntax, grammatical morphology, pronunciation, or punctuation. Furthermore, their papers used tape recording or letters as their data, as opposed to the email data used the current study.

The previous paragraphs point to two main research gaps. First, business emails are not easy to access because they are associated with internal company secrets. That is why the majority of the literature related to email is about academic email. Furthermore, it is even more difficult to get business emails that contain hacker or fraud content. The second research gap is that in forensic linguistics, each case is unique, but there are very few papers or articles that analyze hacking and fraud business emails from the perspective of forensic linguistics. Based on these two research gaps, it is worth investigating hacking and fraud emails.

The theoretical framework of this study is mainly adapted from Scollon and Scollon (1995), using intercultural communication to analyze the emails. Meanwhile, the organization used by Shuy (1993) and Eagleson (1994) is adopted in this current study.

Scollon and Scollon (1995) propose that in human interaction, people have the need to be involved with other participants in order to show their interest. But sometimes, people also need to maintain some distance from other participants in order to express their respect of independence. These two aspects, involvement and independence produce an inherently paradoxical situation in all communication. The aspect of involvement is concerned with the person's right and need to be considered a normal, contributing, or supporting member of society (Scollon and Scollon 1995, p. 46). On other hand, according to the same study, the aspect of independence emphasizes the individuality of the participants. It focuses on their right to not be completely dominated by social values or groups. Scollon and Scollon (1995) also propose the notion of inductive and deductive patterning. The deductive pattern is widely favored by American and other western businessmen (Scollon and Scollon 1995, p. 87). The ideal of the deductive pattern is to get to the topic right away so that people know what they are talking about. Conversely, inductive patterns like to test the participants' potential acceptance of the topic before introducing it. In other words, the inductive pattern does not introduce the topic at the beginning. This pattern is more prevalent in Asian countries (Scollon and Scollon 1995).

The following research questions were chosen because the author wants to compare how the styles used by the Taiwanese employee and the hacker differ when writing emails:

1. What email writing style does the Taiwanese employee use?
2. What email writing style does the hacker use?
3. What are the differences in style between the hacker and the Taiwanese employee?

13.2 Methods

This study is about a hacking event affecting Company H, in which the hacker attempted email fraud in their account with Customer R. The backgrounds of the two companies have to be introduced briefly in order to clarify the situation. Company H is a Taiwan-based company that has been in the shipping and warehouse storage systems business for over 20 years. The customers are mainly in USA and Middle Eastern countries. The employees' English ability is viewed as very important since they have to use their second language, English, to communicate with the customers. The main communication between the company and the customers is conducted via email. Customer R is a leading company in Saudi Arabia, established in 1974. It has more than 30 years of experience in the Food Service Equipment industry.

The background of the email data also must be introduced in order to allow readers to understand the whole hacking and fraud event. An employee of Company H originally wrote an email to notify Customer R about a change in the method of payment, from Letter of Credit (L/C)[1] to Telegraphic Transfer (T/T).[2] However, a hacker hacks into Company H's email system and pretends to be the Company H employee. The hacker wants to change the bank account from Company H's bank account to the hacker's personal bank account. If the hacker were successful, Company H would lose 70,000 US dollars. Luckily, the hacker emails were discovered by another employee of Company H based on the different writing styles between the employee and the hacker. Therefore, this paper tries to investigate the different writing styles of these two people.

13.2.1 Data Collection

The current study is a case study. The background information of the emails and the companies were introduced in the previous section. About 45 emails were exchanged between the two companies, but only the hacker's emails are compared with the employee's emails. Customer R's email replies are not considered since this paper focuses on the difference between the hacker's and the company employee's writing styles. The data comprise 11 emails sent by the hacker and 20 emails sent by the company employee. The rest of the emails are not included as data since they were sent by the customer. The duration of the whole event was about 15–20 days. Use of the emails was authorized by the manager of the company, who is the author's relative, and all personal and corporate information is deleted.

13.2.2 Data Analysis

The emails are analyzed based on Scollon and Scollon's (1995) intercultural communication. The author first compared and noted the differences between the emails, then used this framework to explain the differences in writing styles. There must be some difference between the hacker and employee email usage because another employee was able to notice these discrepancies, leading the author to explore the nature of the differences.

[1]L/C (Letter of Credit) is a document from a bank guaranteeing that a seller will receive payment in full as long as certain delivery conditions have been met. In the event that the buyer is unable to make payment on the purchase, the bank will cover the outstanding amount. They are often used in international transactions to ensure that payment will be received where the buyer and seller may not know each other and are operating in different countries. This has become a very important aspect of international trade.

[2]T/T payment (Telegraphic Transfer) is used to refer to an electronic means of transferring funds overseas.

13.3 Results and Discussion

There are three parts in this section, corresponding to the three research questions. The first part provides an introduction of the writing style that the Taiwanese employee uses. The second part is about the writing style of the hacker. The third part is a comparison between the writing styles of the two people, the Taiwanese employee and the hacker.

13.3.1 The Taiwanese Employee's Writing Style

The following section and examples illustrate the writing styles that the Taiwanese employee tends to apply when writing to the customer. There are three aspects. The first is an inductive style. The employee likes to begin with background information and finally comes to the main point of the email. The second aspect involves the strategy of involvement. The employee views supervisors and other employees as a whole team. The third is that the employee uses a peaceful tone. The employee wants to maintain and strengthen the relationship between the company and the customer, therefore, she uses polite terms such as thank you, sorry to cause inconvenience, and looking forward to your help, to enhance the relationship.

13.3.1.1 Inductive Style

(1) The employee to the customer

Dear Mr. XXX,
Our bank remind us some problem is our certificate of L/C show nationality of vessel is name Liberia (Liberia is one of blacklist for United State bank) that will cause your payment might be frozen when you remit to us. <u>Would you please abandon this L/C and change by T/T payment</u>……..

(2) The employee to the customer
Dear Mr. XXX,
Thank you for your notice. Note that our company account is being audited at the moment so will not be used in receiving this payment. <u>I will send the bank details of our subsidiary company for T/T payment.</u>

(3) The employee to the customer
Dear Mr. XXX,
We had confirmed our acceptance to cancellation of LC to our bank and had advised our bank to send the cancellation message to your bank. <u>Please kindly help us to advise your bank to note the message.</u>

The underlined sentences are the main point of the email. Scollon and Scollon (1995) propose there are two basic patterns, deductive and inductive. The Taiwanese employee likes to use an inductive pattern, with the main point placed at the end. The reason why the Taiwanese employee uses an inductive pattern is because the power relation between the customer and the employee is quite different. The employee may think that the customer has more power than the employee. Also the employee thinks that because Company H is asking the customer to do them a favor, she should use an indirect method to inform the customer, beginning with the background information when writing the email. After providing the background information, the main purpose of email is stated. Using an inductive pattern is considered to be more polite than a deductive one in Chinese culture. That is why the employee likes to begin with the background information when writing emails. For example, the employee says "due to the Liberia is one of the blacklists of the United State bank." After the long introduction of the background information, the employee finally gets to the main point, changing the remitting process. Therefore, the employee uses the classic inductive way of writing the email. The turn exchange takes longer, but the Taiwanese employee considers it more polite to use the inductive pattern.

In short, the reason the Taiwanese employee uses the inductive pattern is because of the perceived difference in power and distance. First, she thinks that the customer is king because the customer can decide whether they want to do business with the company or not. Therefore, for the employee, the customer has more power. Second, the employee does not know the customer very well since they only use email to communicate. The employee does not know the customer's appearance or personality. She does not know whether the customer is a nice person or not. Therefore for the employee, the distance between the customer and the employee is very great, and the fast way is to use a more polite voice to write emails. For the employee, politeness means an inductive pattern. For these two reasons, the Taiwanese employee tends to use an inductive pattern.

13.3.1.2 Involvement

(4) The employee to the customer

Dear Mr. XXX,

Thank you for the reply. After checking with our bank, they told us that they have not received any message from your bank about the cancellation of L/C. Due to our bank requiring the telegram message which your bank has sent to check what happened regarding this situation, would you kindly help us to ask your bank to offer us this message?

The underlined sentences illustrate that the company employee uses "our" or "us" when writing emails to the customer. This indicates that, based on Scollon and Scollon (1995), she applies the strategy of involvement. She relates to other employees as a whole team. That is why she uses the word "our" instead of "I."

She treats this incident, the hacker invading, as concerning the whole company. She views this incident as a great deal. She understands that it is a huge event. The company will lose its benefit because of the fraud. She is very concerned about the company's income. She does not want the company to be damaged. Therefore, she uses "our" and "us" in order to show that the whole company, including supervisors and other employees, care about this event very much. Her email indicates that the whole company has the same feeling, wanting the money back.

13.3.1.3 Enhancement

(5) The employee to the customer

Dear Mr. XXX,

Thank you for your kindly reminds. We had finished the cancellation of this LC and paid the charge to our bank last week. Sorry to cause your inconvenience and looking forward your continue arrange about the T/T payment.

(6) The employee to the customer

Dear Mr. XXX,

Thank you for your kindly prompt help. After recheck, our bank have advised.....Sorry to cause your inconvenience and looking forward your continue arrange.

(7) The employee to the customer

Dear Mr. XXX,

Please see the attachment telegraphic message from our bank and kindly help us to advise your bank, thanks. Looking forward to your continue arrangement.

The underlined sentences demonstrate that the Taiwanese employee tends to use a very polite tone when writing the email. The employee wants to maintain and enhance the harmonious relationship with the customer. Therefore, the employee has to say "thank you for your kindly remind," "sorry to cause you inconvenience and looking forward…" or "looking forward to your continue arrangement" in order to strengthen and maintain the relations between the company and the customer. The employee wants the customer to feel that the company thanks them and cares deeply about what the customer does for them. That is why the employee uses "Thank you for your help" or "looking forward to your help." Also the employee wants the customer to have the feeling that the company does apologize about continually asking the customer for a favor. Therefore, the employee uses "sorry to cause your inconvenience" to express her sincere apology.

13.3.2 *The Hacker's Writing Style*

The following examples demonstrate the writing styles that the hacker tends to apply when writing to the customer. There are three aspects to the style that the hacker uses. The first is that the style is deductive. The hacker tends to point out the main point of the email in the beginning sentences. The second is using the strategy of independence. The hacker likes to use "I" when writing the emails. The third is that the hacker applies a challenging tone, using the command pattern. If the customer does not follow the hacker's directions, the relationship between the company and the customer is gone.

13.3.2.1 Deductive

(8) The hacker to the customer

Dear Mr. XXX,

With the following information you could make the T/T payment. The bank phone number is +852XXXXXXX. And IBAN number is the same as account number which is 81XXXXXXX. Bank code is XXX and swift code is XXXXXX.

The underlined sentences are the main point of the email. The hacker's style of writing emails is more like the deductive pattern of Scollon and Scollon (1995). The hacker does not care about the power relationship between the company and the customer. The hacker does not want to waste time explaining everything. The hacker just goes to the main point, providing the most important thing, the bank account. The reason the hacker likes to use a deductive pattern is because the most important thing for the hacker is money. The hacker does not care about or know the customer. Therefore, she/he does not want to be polite or feel sorry for the customer. She/he does not care if the relationship between the company and the customer gets worse or not. She/he just cares about money. That is why the hacker uses the deductive pattern when writing emails.

13.3.2.2 Independence

(9) The hacker to the customer

Dear Mr. XXX,

I have just been in contact with the bank as the payment hasn't been received yet. Please confirm from your bank to know what the issue with the payment. Also check if the payment can be revised to my boss's bank account if possible.

The underlined section indicates that the hacker tends to use a personal perspective. She/he likes to use "I" when writing emails to the customer. Based on Scollon and Scollon (1995), the hacker uses the strategy of independence. Using a personal perspective, such as "I" or "my," indicates that the hacker does not view other company employees as a whole team. The hacker does not see the company's benefit as his or her own benefit. She/he just cares whether the money is transmitted successfully into his/her account or not. She/he apparently does not think this fraud event is criminal. She/he directly and without any shame asks where "my" money is. Although the hacker mentions his or her boss's account in the email, this is because the hacker wants the customer to believe this event. The boss's bank account is surface usage in order to gain the customer's trust; indeed it is the hacker's bank account. However, if the hacker had said his or her own bank account, the customer would certainly notice that something was wrong since the money is normally transmitted into the company's official bank account rather than one of the employees' bank accounts. Therefore, the hacker might think that, for the customer, using the boss's bank account is less likely to cause suspicion than saying an individual's own bank account.

13.3.2.3 Challenge

(10) The hacker to the customer
Dear Mr. XXX,
See attached for the credit note. See below for the bank details for the payment.
Beneficiary Bank: Taipei XXX bank, XXXX Branch.
Bank Address: No. 92, Sec. XXX, XXXXXX Rd, Taipei, Taiwan, R.O.C
Account No: 32XX-XXXX-XXX3
Swift Code: TPXXXXXXX
For account name, you can fill either of the formats below;
Account name: PENG, XXX-XXX in favor of XXXXX LTD or
Account name: PENG, XXX-XXX/ XXXXX LTD.

(11) The hacker to the customer

Dear Mr. XXX,
See attached for the correction. Pay to our Hong Kong account with the detailed below:
Company name: XXXXX LTD.
Account number: 817XXXXXX
Beneficiary bank: HXXXX Hong Kong
Beneficiary bank address: 1 XXX Road central, Hong Kong
Beneficiary bank code: XXX
Swift code: XXXXXXXX
Send a copy of the bank payment slip when done.

The underlined sentences show that the hacker utilizes less polite forms when writing the email. The hacker says "send a copy when done," "pay to…" or just simply, directly and impolitely asks the customer to see the attachment file. This indicates that if the customer does not follow the directions, the harmonious relationship between the company and the customer will be impaired and damaged. The hacker's tone in the email is more like a demand. She/he does not show respect to

Table 13.1 A comparison of the two writing styles

The Taiwanese employee	The hacker
Inductive	Deductive
Involvement	Independence
Enhancement	Challenge

the customer; she/he thinks that the customer is his/her subordinate. The customer has to follow exactly what the hacker said. The relationship between the company and the customer, according to the usage in the hacker's emails, is not important, but rather worthless. Therefore, the hacker will not write to the customer in a polite or humble way, instead, the hacker uses a command style. For example, the hackers demand the customer to look at the attachment file or even send a copy of the payment slip to the company without using any polite words. If the customer fails those demands, the relationship between these two companies is gone.

13.3.3 A Comparison of the Two People's Writing Styles

A comparison between the writing styles of the employee and the hacker is outlined in the following paragraphs. The employee's writing style tends to use an inductive pattern, and the strategies of involvement and enhancement. For example, the employee likes to begin with the background at the beginning of the email and then follow with the main point of the email. This is the so-called inductive pattern. The employee also uses the strategy of involvement, such as "our" and "us," when writing the emails. The employee views the other employees as a whole team. At the same time, the employee also tries to maintain and strengthen the relationship between the company and the customer, a strategy of enhancement. Therefore, she might use terms like "thank you" and "looking forward your continue help" to express her feelings toward the customer.

In direct contrast, instead of using inductive patterns and the strategies of involvement and enhancement, the hacker uses deductive patterns and the strategies of independence and challenge when writing the emails. The hacker doesn't care about the company, the customer or their relationship; therefore, she/he does not want to spend time writing polite and humble emails. Table 13.1 summarizes the comparison of the two people's writing styles.

13.4 Conclusion

This paper has investigated a specific case study of business email hacking and fraud in a Taiwanese company. The research questions involved the different styles that the Taiwanese employee and the hacker used when writing emails. The former likes to use inductive patterns, involvement strategy, and enhancement; the latter tends to use deductive patterns, independent strategy, and challenge. The results indicate that people have different styles of writing emails. In this case, thanks to those differences, the hacker's emails were discovered.

Business emails are not like other kinds of emails; they are difficult for researchers to access and are quite unique. Therefore each business email is a specific case study and worth investigating. In this study, the situation was even more unique because it involved hacking and fraud. This is an important contribution to the literature since it describes a type of email that cannot readily be identified or accessed by researchers. For further research, it would be interesting to investigate other hackers' emails and try to make generalizations about hackers' writing styles.

References

Eagleson, Robert. 1994. Forensic analysis of personal written texts: A case study. In *Language and the Law*, ed. John Gibbons, 30–40. New York: Routledge.

Evans, Stephen. 2012. Designing email tasks for the business English classroom: Implications from a study of Hong Kong's Key industries. *English for Specific Purposes* 31: 202–212.

Hallajian, Ali, and Maya Khemlani David. 2014. "Hello and good day to you dear Dr…". Greetings and closings in supervisors-supervisees email exchanges. *Social and Behavioral Sciences* 118: 85–93.

Hewitt, Paul. 2006. Electronic mail and internal communication: A three-factor model. *Corporate Communication* 11: 78–92.

Lan, Li, and Lucy MacGregor. 2010. English in tiers in the workplace: A case study of email usage. In *Globalization, communication and the workplace*, ed. Forey Gail, and Jane Lockwood, 8–24. New York: Continuum International Publishing Group.

Scollon, Ron, and Suzanne Wong Scollon. 1995. *Intercultural communication*. Oxford: Blackwell Publisher Ltd.

Shuy, Roger W. 1993. Language evidence in distinguishing pilot error from product liability. *International Journal of the Sociology of Language* 100–101(1): 101–114.

Wu, Wei Ping. 2002. *Language and law: Research on linguistic issues in the legal field*. Shanghai: Shanghai Foreign Language Education Press. (吳偉平. 2002. 《語言與法律: 司法領域的語言學研究》 上海:上海外語教育出版社.).

Author Biography

Tzu-Wei Hsiang (向梓維) is a PhD student at the Institute of Linguistics, National Chung Cheng University. She is a part-time employee of a Taiwanese company. Her research interests include sociolinguistics, applied linguistics, and discourse analysis.

GPSR Compliance
The European Union's (EU) General Product Safety Regulation (GPSR) is a set of rules that requires consumer products to be safe and our obligations to ensure this.

If you have any concerns about our products, you can contact us on

ProductSafety@springernature.com

In case Publisher is established outside the EU, the EU authorized representative is:

Springer Nature Customer Service Center GmbH
Europaplatz 3
69115 Heidelberg, Germany

www.ingramcontent.com/pod-product-compliance
Lightning Source LLC
LaVergne TN
LVHW052253200926
848481LV00002B/357

9789811006760